The New Evangelization

The New Evangelization

Faith, People, Context and Practice

Edited by

Paul Grogan and Kirsteen Kim

Bloomsbury T&T Clark
An imprint of Bloomsbury Publishing Plc

B L O O M S B U R Y
LONDON • NEW DELHI • NEW YORK • SYDNEY

Bloomsbury T&T Clark
An imprint of Bloomsbury Publishing Plc

Imprint previously known as T&T Clark

50 Bedford Square   1385 Broadway
London   New York
WC1B 3DP   NY 10018
UK   USA

www.bloomsbury.com

BLOOMSBURY, T&T CLARK and the Diana logo are trademarks of
Bloomsbury Publishing Plc

First published 2015

© Paul Grogan and Kirsteen Kim, 2015

Paul Grogan and Kirsteen Kim have asserted their right under the Copyright,
Designs and Patents Act, 1988, to be identified as Editors of this work.

British Library Cataloguing-in-Publication Data
A catalogue record for this book is available from the British Library.

ISBN: HB: 978-0-567-65737-4
ePDF: 978-0-567-65739-8
ePub: 978-0-567-65738-1

Library of Congress Cataloging-in-Publication Data
The new evangelization: faith, people, context and practice/edited by Paul Grogan and
Kirsteen Kim.
pages cm
ISBN 978-0-567-65737-4 (hbk) –
ISBN 978-0-567-65738-1 (epub) –
ISBN 978-0-567-65739-8 (epdf) 1. Evangelistic work – Catholic Church.
2. Catholic Church – Doctrines. I. Grogan, Paul (Chaplain), editor.
BX2347.4.N49 2015
266'.2–dc23
2014035761

Typeset by Newgen Knowledge Works (P) Ltd., Chennai, India
Printed and bound in Great Britain

Contents

Foreword

The new evangelization is a challenge. In fact, it is one of the greatest challenges facing the contemporary Church in her witness to the Risen Christ, the Lord who by His Spirit guides her way through history until He will come again. Yet, the challenges facing those who seek to engage in the new evangelization are far from being confined to the sphere of the pastoral actualization of this most fundamental mission of the Church. Today, there exist numerous definitions of the expression 'new evangelization' with many significant differences among them, not least because of the many and varied cultural and ecclesial situations confronting the local Churches. However, already in 1974, Blessed Pope Paul VI had warned: 'Any partial and fragmentary definition which attempts to render the reality of evangelization in all its richness, complexity and dynamism does so only at the risk of impoverishing it and even of distorting it. It is impossible to grasp the concept of evangelization unless one tries to keep in view all its essential elements' (*Evangelii nuntiandi* 17).

The various contributors to *The New Evangelization: Faith, People, Context and Practice* have heeded Paul VI's warning by presenting a comprehensive analysis of many of the 'essential elements' of new evangelization. Each contributor sheds new light upon the significance of the expression 'new evangelization' itself and the reasons underlying the Church's call for this new approach by which the Gospel, delivered once and for all to the saints in Jesus Christ, is proclaimed with renewed enthusiasm, in contemporary language and with new methodologies capable of transmitting its deepest meaning. In chapter after chapter, the contributors seek to answer the most frequently asked questions and to address many of the more controversial issues pertaining to the mission of the new evangelization. Their profound responses not only are attentive to the spirit and teachings of the Second Vatican Council, but also engage in a realistic way with the present global context of cultural fragmentation and relativism.

One aspect to which the book is particularly attentive is the need to avoid the temptation to reduce the new evangelization to a kind of universal panacea predicated upon an insufficient or even false analysis of the historical, cultural and theological dynamics which constitute the background against which the Church is called to evangelize. If the new evangelization is to lie at the heart of the Church's mission in the coming decades, it must be understood in a way that is coherent with the command given to the Church by Jesus Christ to preach the Gospel, on the one hand, and how this command is to be realized in the situation of the world today, on the other. The new evangelization, therefore, indicates a renewed approach to Jesus's one and unchanging command to His disciples to bring the Gospel to all. It cannot be conceived as a complete breaking with the evangelical mission of the Church as it has been undertaken in the past. It is rather this same mission but in a key which is attentive to the new and often radically transformed ecclesial and cultural paradigms in which the Church is called to announce Jesus Christ, especially in those territories of ancient Christian tradition. The debate over the meaning of the expression 'new evangelization' will certainly continue, with some expressing reservations as to the reasonableness of the qualifying adjective. But the reality is that 'new' is not intended to qualify the content but rather to explicate further the condition and manner of its proclamation.

It is essential to recognize, nevertheless, that the Church does not evangelize because of the great challenge posed by secularization, but, first and foremost, because the Lord has commanded His Church to bring the Gospel to every person in all ages and places. Against this background, one of the most urgent tasks of the new evangelization is the construction of a project aimed at engendering or restoring in Christians a strong and enduring sense of ecclesial identity in the sense of belonging to the faith community which mediates the divine Revelation and makes possible a personal response to Jesus Christ through a faith that is at once personal and ecclesial. It is only through a strong personal sense of existential belonging to Christ through the Church that the Christian is able to fulfil his vocation in the world. Those who believe in His word are sent into the streets of the world to proclaim that the promise of salvation has become a reality. This proclamation, however, must necessarily entail a style of life which causes the disciples of the Lord to be recognized as distinct from those who do not follow Him.

The command of the Lord, 'Go therefore and make disciples of all nations' (*Mt* 28:19), is the very dream of Pope Francis, who in his Apostolic Exhortation *Evangelii gaudium* states: 'I dream of a "missionary option", that is, a missionary impulse capable of transforming everything, so that the Church's customs, ways of doing things, times and schedules, language and structures can be suitably channelled for the evangelization of today's world rather than for self-preservation' (no. 27). To respond to this command and, thus, to realize such a missionary dream require that the new evangelization begins from the credibility of our lives as believers and the conviction that grace acts and transforms to the point of converting the heart.

Rino Fisichella
President
Pontifical Council for the Promotion of the New Evangelization
00120 Vatican City State
November 24, 2014
Memorial of St. Andrea Dūng-Lạc and Companions, Martyrs

Acknowledgements

This book has its origins in the conference on 'Vatican II, 50 Years On: The New Evangelization' at Leeds Trinity University, UK, on 26–29 June 2012. We acknowledge with gratitude the close collaboration of Professor Freda Bridge, the first Vice-Chancellor of Leeds Trinity University, in organizing and hosting that event, and the support of Archbishop Arthur Roche, then the Bishop of Leeds and now the Secretary of the Congregation for Divine Worship and the Discipline of the Sacraments in Rome, who took a great personal interest in the project, and of Cardinal Vincent Nichols, Archbishop of Westminster, who kindly endorsed the conference. Professor Paul D. Murray, Director of the Centre for Catholic Studies, offered advice and practical support and the following bodies sponsored aspects of it: The Catenians, The Diocese of Leeds, EWTN and the Sisters of the Cross and Passion. We are grateful to Sister Anne Hammersley CP and Mgr John Wilson for contributing ideas, to Mrs Dominica Richmond who oversaw the liturgical celebrations and to those colleagues at Leeds Trinity who chaired sessions. We also wish to express our thanks to Kathy Stenton and Madeline Addinall in the vice-chancellor's office, the conference and events team, the marketing, communications, reprographics and media teams, the catering and the domestic services teams, the staff on reception and the student volunteers who helped with the smooth running of the event.

In preparing the publication, we are grateful to all the contributors for their ready assistance and particularly to Anna Turton and Miriam Cantwell at T&T Clark for their enthusiasm and professional help.

List of Contributors

Reverend Dr Richard K. Baawobr MAfr is Superior General, Missionaries of Africa.

Andrew Brookes OP is a practitioner of the new evangelization based at Blackfriars, Oxford, UK.

Professor Gavin D'Costa is Professor of Catholic Theology, University of Bristol, UK.

Fernando Cardinal Filoni is Prefect for the Congregation for the Evangelization of Peoples of the Holy See.

Francis Cardinal George OMI is Archbishop of Chicago, USA.

Dr John F. Gorski MM is Staff Missiologist/Theologian, National Office of the Pontifical Mission Societies in the United States (New York).

Monsignor Paul Grogan is Chaplain at Leeds Trinity University and Vocations Director for the Diocese of Leeds, UK.

Professor Kirsteen Kim PhD is Professor of Theology and World Christianity at Leeds Trinity University, UK.

Professor Dr Mathijs Lamberigts is Professor at the Faculty of Theology and Religious Studies and Coordinator of the Centre for the Study of the Second Vatican Council, Catholic University Leuven, Belgium.

Professor Ian Linden is Associate Professor in the Study of Religion at the School of Oriental and African Studies, London and Senior Adviser at the Tony Blair Faith Foundation.

Professor Dr Annemarie Mayer is Associate Professor at the Faculty of Theology and Religious Studies at the Catholic University Leuven, Belgium.

Reverend Deacon Stephen Morgan DPhil is Post-doctoral Research Associate in Theology at St Benet's Hall, University of Oxford, UK.

Professor Paul D. Murray is Professor of Systematic Theology and Dean and Director of the Centre for Catholic Studies, Department of Theology and Religion, Durham University, UK.

Professor Tracey Rowland is Dean of the John Paul II Institute in Melbourne, Australia and the Institute's Professor of Political Philosophy and Continental Theology.

Katharina Smith-Müller is Interreligious Adviser to the Catholic Bishops' Conference of England and Wales.

Dr Petroc Willey is Reader in the New Evangelisation at the School of the Annunciation, Buckfast Abbey, UK and Professor of Catechetics at Franciscan University, Steubenville, USA.

Dr Susan K. Wood SCL is Professor and Chair of the Department of Theology, Marquette University, USA.

1

Introduction

Kirsteen Kim

On 21 September 2010, Pope Benedict XVI established a new dicastery of the Roman Curia: the Pontifical Council for Promoting the New Evangelization. Evangelization is a biblical term that can be traced back to the proclamation of the angels at Jesus's birth and to Jesus's declared intention at the outset of his ministry to bring 'good news' or the gospel (*euangelion* in Greek). Through the apostles, the gospel was spread in all directions from Jerusalem in the first centuries to Africa, Asia and Europe. Half a millennium ago, the Americas also began to be evangelized and Western missions further expanded the regions of the world where Christ is known and followed. Today, there are Christian communities in virtually every nation and region. The promise that the disciples would witness to Jesus Christ 'in Jerusalem, in all Judaea and Samaria, and to the ends of earth' (Acts 1:8[1]) would seem to have been fulfilled. Evangelization might be said to be very nearly accomplished. Where it is not so the Congregation for the Evangelization of Peoples continues the mission *ad gentes* while, increasingly conscious of religious and cultural plurality, since the Second Vatican Council (1962–5) the Church has reached out to the world in dialogue. So why, 50 years after the Council, did the Catholic Church launch a programme of 'new evangelization' and what is meant by this term? The authors who debate these questions are leading academics, churchmen and practitioners who presented the first versions of these chapters at the conference on 'Vatican II, 50 Years On: The New Evangelization' organized and hosted by Leeds Trinity University, UK on 26–9 June 2012. Their answers both elucidate the meaning of the new evangelization and highlight the challenges involved in actualizing it in a way

---

[1] All biblical references are from the New Revised Standard Version.

which both honours the spirit and teaching of the Council and at the same time engages the changing global context and varied local situations.

Pope Benedict XVI and the Synod on the new evangelization

In the apostolic letter launching the council for the new evangelization, Pope Benedict reiterated that it is the duty of the Church to proclaim the gospel 'always and everywhere' after the example of Christ 'the first and supreme evangelizer' (*Ubicumque et semper* (US); 21 September 2010). However, he identified the 'abandonment of the faith', especially in societies and cultures which had seemed for many centuries to be 'permeated by the Gospel', as the primary challenge for evangelization today and justified the new Council because of the need for a further, deeper evangelization beyond the first one. Pointing out that mission is always shaped by its context, he called for 'a renewed missionary impulse' arising from 'a profound experience of God' (US prologue) 'to re-present the perennial truth of the Gospel of Christ', in those regions, where the process of secularization had led to an 'eclipse of the meaning of God'.[2] The new dicastery was mandated to address the problems of secularization in 'territories of Christian tradition' (US 2) and the press immediately branded the new evangelization as a plan to 're-evangelise the West'.[3] It was expected to pursue this especially by using modern forms of communication as instruments for the new evangelization and promoting the use of the *Catechism of the Catholic Church* (US 3). Many – clergy, religious and especially lay people – actively embraced the new evangelization as a much-needed initiative to share the heart of Christian faith in a clear, relevant and personal way in places where the original message had been forgotten or distorted.

Following this, the Thirteenth Ordinary General Assembly of the Synod of Bishops on 7–28 October 2012 was dedicated to the topic in order to 'trace new methods and means for transmitting the Good News' today (Preface).[4] The *Lineamenta* in preparation for the Synod amplified the context that demanded the new evangelization. This was described overwhelmingly as one of negative

---

[2] Vatican Information Service, 'Pope Creates a Dicastery for New Evangelization' (28 June 2010). Available at www.vis.va.

[3] For example, Nick Squires, 'Pope Launches Team to Re-evangelise the West', *The Telegraph* (29 June 2010).

[4] Synod of Bishops, *Lineamenta* (2 February 2011), Prologue.

cultural change (3, 6) resulting in fear of a loss of Christian identity and the foundations of faith (7).[5] The *Lineamenta* emphasized the duty to evangelize in obedience to the missionary mandate of Mark 16.15 and Matthew 28.20 (11, 18) and the primary model of the evangelist appeared to be the Apostle Paul who preached the Gospel with urgency and whether or not it was requested.[6] The new evangelization was described as the 'fundamental mission' of the Church (10) born out of personal encounter with Jesus Christ (11), grounded in the Tradition and manifested in the Church's life (12). It depended on faithful proclamation of the Word of God (13), renewed emphasis on catechesis and the catechumenate (14), the agency of local churches (15) and the ability of Christians to give an account of their faith (16).

The *Instrumentum laboris* for the Synod (19 June 2012) linked new evangelization to three other events considered significant in the life of the Church: the Year of Faith (2012–3), the twentieth anniversary of the publication of *The Catechism of the Catholic Church* and the opening of the Second Vatican Council. The common thread among these was identified as conversion, holiness and faith. Responding to issues raised by the bishops, the *Instrumentum* stressed the foundation of the new evangelization in the mission and mandate of Jesus Christ and its urgency (18–44), while additionally emphasizing the importance of the Church as the location of salvation (35–6) and the transformation of the parish as a vehicle of the new evangelization (80–4). Within the stress on catechesis and education (131–57), it further located the family as the 'model-place' for transmission of the faith (110–3) and the consecrated life as 'a dynamic source of energy' for it (114–7). The *Instrumentum* noted that secularization also has positive aspects (54) and that, somewhat paradoxically, alongside secularization, there was a 'return of a religious sense' and recognition of spiritual need, especially among the young (63). While this was welcomed, caution was expressed that some of this was 'naïve and emotional', leading to violence and fundamentalism (65), the exercise of emotional and psychological dominance over members and 'aggressive, proselytizing methods' (66). These criticisms were understood to be made particularly of many movements called 'Pentecostal'. Guided by Cardinal Donald Wuerl, Archbishop of Washington, USA, the Synod itself focused on secularized culture as the context of the new evangelization, proclamation of the good news as the core of it, the Church as

---

[5] It appeared to be drafted by Westerners. See in particular the reference to 'our culture' where 'discourse on God is so foreign' (*Lineamenta* 19; cf. 3).
[6] See the texts chosen to head each section of the *Lineamenta*.

its home and source, and parishes as its centres.[7] Its Message reflected on the proclamation of the Samaritan woman at the well (John 4) as the result of a personal encounter with Christ as paradigmatic for the new evangelization.[8]

However, the Propositions coming out of the Synod were much more wide-ranging than the preparatory documentation had suggested.[9] The discussion was broadened to set new evangelization in the context of the mission of Church as it originates in the sending activity of the Trinity and by the grace of the Holy Spirit who enables enthusiastic and courageous 'witness' (4). The Propositions related evangelization more positively to culture by encouraging inculturation of the faith (5) and a rounded anthropology (17). The Synod identified the new evangelization as just one form of evangelization and it insisted that 'each particular Church must have the freedom to evangelize according to her own traits and traditions' (7). It recognized secularization as a global challenge to the transmission of the faith (8) but also stressed the continued importance of the initial proclamation (9). In addition, it strengthened the connection of the new evangelization to other challenges such as globalization (13), conflict and violence (14) and violation of human rights (15) and religious freedom (16). Most noticeably, the propositions called strongly for serious commitment to life and justice as part of the new evangelization (19, 24, 25, 31–2, 56).

The outcomes of the Synod and the discussion around it raise a number of questions pertaining to the project of the new evangelization which recur in the varied contributions in this book. These may be grouped into four parts, into which we have arranged the chapters in this volume: First, how does the new evangelization relate to the teaching and spirit of the Second Vatican Council, in particular to its concern for religious freedom and its respect for other churches, cultures and religions? What is the biblical basis for new evangelization and the theological relationship between the new evangelization, evangelization in general and Christian mission? Second, how is the new evangelization understood within the post-conciliar context of the Church and mission as communion? What priority should it have within the world Church of which Europe forms an increasing minority and what is the role of the rest of the Church in it? Third, what is or are the context(s) of the new

---

[7]   Cf. Donald Wuerl, 'Relatio ante disceptationem' (Synod of Bishops; 8 October 2012); 'Relatio post disceptationem' (Synod of Bishops; 17 October 2012); cf. Donald Wuerl, *New Evangelization: Passing on the Catholic Faith Today* (Huntington, IN: Our Sunday Visitor, 2013).

[8]   Synod of Bishops, 'Message to the People of God' (26 October 2012).

[9]   Synod of Bishops, Final List of Propositions (27 October 2012).

evangelization? How should the resources of the Church be shared between the challenges of secularization, poverty and the need for social justice? How can evangelization be compatible with the imperative to interreligious dialogue, and what value do other cultures and religions have for it? Fourth, how should the new evangelization be practised? How vital is the 'transmission' of an essential content, mainly in words by preaching, catechesis and education? Are conversion and baptism the only proper responses to evangelization and what other responses might there be? In the focus on method and activity contributing to the new evangelization, what is the place of the encounter with Christ and with the other person, of spirituality and of community?

Examining the new evangelization

Opening Part I on the question of whether it represents continuity or discontinuity with the Second Vatican Council, Mathijs Lamberigts points out that the insights of the Council were gestating long before it and shows how some of the most vigorous debates at the Council were about the reform of the *Propaganda Fide* in view of the emergence of world religions and the need, already recognized, for the evangelization of Europe. Lamberigts asks whether it is possible to reconcile the evangelization promoted in *Ad gentes* with the dialogical approach of *Nostra aetate* and the religious freedom promoted by *Dignitatis humanae*. In view of the growing Christian and religious plurality in Europe, he concludes that it is necessary to consider 'which type of evangelization for which people?' and that, above all, the gospel must be preached in a way that is authentic and dialogical.

The first pope to use the term 'new evangelization' was John Paul II, while attending the nineteenth general assembly of the Latin American Bishops' Conference in 1983. John F. Gorski shares his knowledge of the Latin American context of the time, in which the term was already being used. He traces the development of the modern meaning of the term 'mission' from St Ignatius of Loyola in the sixteenth century to the Second Vatican Council which 'centred mission on the evangelization of peoples rather than the geographical expansion of the Church'. He then details the rediscovery of the term evangelization, which was being used by Protestants, from the Catholic catechetical renewal of the 1950s and 1960s to Paul VI's exhortation *Evangelii nuntiandi* (1975). In conclusion, Gorski shows how John Paul II's understanding of evangelization, as later expounded in *Redemptoris missio*, was shaped and sharpened by the Latin

American context. Tracey Rowland continues the story of the development of 'the new evangelization' by John Paul II and Benedict XVI. Both men, she claims, aimed to counter secularizing tendencies in the Church since the Council by re-centring the Church on Christ. Rowland shows how many of the emphases of the new evangelization as discussed at the Synod are rooted in the agenda of Joseph Ratzinger to present the person of Christ in both truth and love. She discusses a number of threats to new evangelization from this point of view: secularist interpretations of the conciliar document *Gaudium et spes*; reduction of the kingdom of God to a matter of values; conflation of the concept of evangelization with the practice of marketing and the (sorry) condition of Western culture.

In the second part, four more contributors look at the implications of the new evangelization for the Church and its mission. Susan K. Wood describes the Church as 'a people sent in mission', the sacrament and instrumental sign of the salvation and unity of Jesus Christ. In the United States as much as in Europe, she sees the need for the 'new evangelization' as described in *Redemptoris missio*. Referring throughout to the *Lineamenta* of the Synod, she first links the new evangelization with the call to conversion which, she points out, is a not only a doctrinal matter but also experiential, moral and ethical. Secondly she relates it to communion and the formation of communities of faith. Thirdly, she argues that the new evangelization should be complementary to the mission *ad gentes*. It calls for overcoming the Church's internal differences for a mission of engagement with wider culture and solidarity with the poor, of which Wood furnishes concrete examples. Francis George calls attention to Pope John XXIII's missionary vision of the Church as the 'catalyst' for human unity in the face of twentieth-century conflicts. He explains how, in order to make it a more effective instrument of mission in the world, and beginning with reform of the liturgy, the Council changed the Church's understanding of her governance structure from a juridical to a relational one. The ecclesiology of communion contributed to the breakdown of the distinction between mission and pastoral lands, recognized that all are already part of God's family even if not everybody yet realizes it and began a dialogue of faith and culture. George points out that, by making a distinction in *Redemptoris missio* between mission and evangelization, John Paul II reserved a special place for kerygmatic activity. Furthermore, whereas re-evangelization in the sense of restoring sinners to faith has always gone on, in the new evangelization it is whole cultures that are the focus of attention. He warns that the Church's communion, and therefore its mission, is weakened by politicized interpretations of the Council, fierce public opposition to the Church's moral teaching and militant atheism. Nevertheless, in his view, the anticipated springtime is being carried forward by the ongoing reform of the liturgy.

Paul D. Murray draws attention to the integral nature of evangelization and ecumenism in that disunity is 'a fundamental counter-sign to the world of the gospel of reconciliation that we proclaim'. He acknowledges debates about continuity and rupture that have raged in relation to the interpretation of Vatican II and sees Benedict XVI as one who sought to hold together both change and continuity. Murray then shows how the significant novelty of Vatican II's teaching on ecumenism coheres with this hermeneutic, including particularly the more recent development of Receptive Ecumenism. Although its agenda remained largely unfulfilled throughout the pontificate of Benedict XVI, he expects that Receptive Ecumenism will be at once more critical, and potentially more programmatic, for the current papacy of Francis. Ian Linden notes that, in its development as a global community, the Catholic Church has retained a distinctively Eurocentric character. Although at Vatican II the Church signalled its intention to be a global community, this was not yet realized, as shown by the fact that poverty was not the issue there that it was later recognized to be. Since then there has been a gradual 'global de-centring' of the Church, spearheaded by Latin America, towards a 'networked Church' especially in the context of the growing global interconnectedness since the 1990s. However, he believes that the counter-force of John Paul II's strong centralized leadership, together with rapid church growth in the developing world, has led to strong tensions across the world Church which present 'the dominant structural and theological challenge of the next decade'. In Linden's view, they were especially evident as Pope Benedict proposed the new evangelization in Europe while other parts of the Church simply got on with evangelization and compassionate service.

The third part of this book considers the new evangelization from two contextual perspectives: Africa and other religions. In the first case, Fernando Filoni dates the emergence of the use of the notion of 'new evangelization' to 1956 with the beginning of awareness of the decline in faith in older Christian societies, although was not until 1990 that John Paul II defined it in *Redemptoris missio* 33. Taking his cue from Pope Benedict's exhortation *Africae munus*, Filoni finds that new evangelization is also needed in Africa particularly because the first evangelization was mostly 'a form of religious colonization' which did not allow the gospel to 'take root in the cultural, social and economic ground' or fulfil the people's aspirations for freedom and justice. So he believes that the experience of the 'young churches' of Asia, Africa and Oceania on their way to ecclesial maturity has much to offer to the study of the new evangelization in Europe and America and he treats the African case particularly. Richard K. Baawobr takes Filoni's case study further. He first demonstrates how his society, the Missionaries of Africa, was renewed under the influence of Vatican II – juridically, vocationally, pastorally and educationally. Then he shows the impact of the Council on local churches in Africa through the organization of Small Christian Communities and increased lay participation, leading to a pervasive sense of the Church being 'the family of God'. As they gained ecclesial independence, Africans participated in mission locally and *ad gentes*; they translated and interpreted the Bible for their context, inculturated the liturgy, undertook justice and peace work and engaged in ecumenical and interreligious dialogue. Baawobr likens African experience to that of a little fish exploring the vast ocean with the Council for a compass and learning how she is part of a world Church and a human family.

With respect to the world religions, Gavin D'Costa uses Reniero Cantalamessa's periodization of evangelization in the Church to show that we are in a new moment in history. In this period, the secularized West now also includes many people from the world religions and the role of the laity is very central. D'Costa tackles head-on three objections to evangelization arising in this context: first, that it is no longer appropriate since the Church declared at the Council it is not necessary to belong to the Church in order to benefit from the salvation it offers; second, that evangelization which involves conversion is arrogant and mimics the worst aspects of colonialism; third, that mission to the Jews in particular is unacceptable both theologically and, in view of the Holocaust, psychologically. Having refuted these on the basis of his scrutiny of magisterial teaching and affirmed the continuing validity of evangelization, D'Costa concludes by pointing out that these post-conciliar objections are one additional reason for the new evangelization. Annemarie Mayer points out that other religions are increasingly present in the 'secularized' West that is being addressed by the new evangelization; in other words, faith and its abandonment cannot be separated. What is more the current context of plurality values religions, at least for personal reasons. Mayer reviews the stance of Vatican II regarding other religions and draws attention to its continuation in the Instruction *Dialogue and Proclamation* (1991) which, she argues, gives dialogue a new quality as 'a means of seeking after truth and of sharing it with others'. She concludes with some reflections on the kingdom as the central content of evangelization and on the new evangelization in a multi-religious context as a challenge to be a 'mission-shaped' Church.

The fourth and final part of this book is made up of examples of ways in which the new evangelization is being practised in the British context. Petroc Willey sees *The Catechism of the Catholic Church* as a 'ray of hope' in an otherwise 'inhospitable' landscape for evangelization. He explains why and how it is seen by the magisterium of the Church to be 'an irreplaceable point of reference' for the work of the new evangelization because it strengthens the 'lifelong apprenticeship' of all Christians to the faith, which necessarily includes responsibility to transmit faithfully the good news. It helps to maintain the catholicity of the Church – and therefore the communion within which the new evangelization takes place – and it fosters the spirituality which restores the 'ardour' of the new evangelization. Stephen Morgan studies the example of John Henry Newman because he believes Newman's real claim of faith and pastoral work is an inspiration for practising the new evangelization. He describes Newman's phrase *cor ad cor loquitur* as 'the paradigm of the new evangelization of those places where the struggle between the conviction of the heart and the scepticism of the mind . . . is a common experience'. To Newman, this meant that the medium of communication was deep friendship founded on dogmatic faith and combined with personal integrity. Such an example is sorely needed, Morgan concludes, in view of the extent of ignorance of doctrine and dissent from the Church's teaching. Andrew Brookes is convinced that call to conversion to Christ lies at the heart of evangelization, old or new. He draws on his practice and study of evangelization over many years to present an outline of a structured approach to the ministry, death and resurrection of Jesus, shaped with a view to inviting conversion and faith. Brookes sets his presentation of 'the truth about Jesus' within a framework of seven pastoral principles and formulates them with respect for both dogma and biblical criticism. He shows the need for such an approach in contemporary Britain and demonstrates that it is founded on the Church's teaching and is authentically Catholic. The final chapter in this section by Katharina Smith-Müller returns to the topic of interreligious dialogue and its relationship with proclamation of the gospel, drawing especially on the recent teaching document by the bishops of England and Wales, *Meeting God in Friend and Stranger* (2010). Smith-Müller gives concrete examples of initiatives in dialogue: shared pilgrimage, education about different faiths, inclusion of people of other faiths, shared social action and community development and peace walks. In doing so, she shows how interreligious dialogue can become intrinsic to the work of the Church, an integral part of evangelization as described in *Redemptoris missio* and a true reflection of the ministry of Christ.

Pope Francis and *Evangelii Gaudium*

After the inauguration of Francis as Pope and the promulgation in his first
year of the apostolic exhortation *Evangelii gaudium*, the new evangelization as
discussed at the Synod appears not as a definitive statement but as a further
milestone in the ongoing development of understanding of the Church's
mission.[10] The exhortation treated new evangelization as including ordinary
pastoral ministry, as well as re-evangelization and mission *ad gentes* (15).
Throughout, the first pope from outside Europe in 1,300 years drew attention
to the global nature of the Church and insisted that 'cultural diversity is not
a threat to Church unity' (117); on the contrary, he showed by his citations
the contributions made to magisterial teaching of bishops' conferences from
different continents. Pope Francis described evangelization as the 'missionary
impulse' which would focus the church outward rather than on its own
survival (27). He declared that it was integral to being Church: 'missionary
outreach' to all who do not know Christ, wherever they are, is '*paradigmatic
for all the Church's activity*' and, quoting his fellow Latin American bishops,
he called for a general move to a '*missionary* pastoral ministry' (15; italics
original). Throughout Pope Francis emphasized that 'realities are greater than
ideas' (233) and that evangelization should put the word into practice. He
envisaged 'a Church whose doors are open' (46) that 'goes forth with joy' (24)
and that is engaged with the world, even if that means it is 'bruised, hurting
and dirty' (49). While he affirmed preaching and instruction as essential
parts of evangelization, in his discernment of the context, he began not
with secularization but with economic injustice, oppression and exclusion
(52–75). Rather than the problems of the West, he drew attention to the harm
globalization from the West has done to other parts of the world (62), which he
contrasted with Jesus's teaching of the growth of the kingdom of God, with its
inclusion of the poor and insistence on peace and social dialogue. Nevertheless,
and even more surprisingly considering the criticism of secularized Europe in
preparation for the synod, Pope Francis was positive about the West as 'an
evangelized culture' (68); instead, he expressed concern about the weaknesses
of the popular culture of Catholic peoples which is prevalent in his own
continent (69).

---

[10] For a recent overview of the last century of the practice and theory of evangelization within the
Church's mission, see Stephen B. Bevans (ed.), *A Century of Catholic Mission*. Regnum Edinburgh
Centenary Series 15 (Oxford: Regnum, 2013).

Francis's intervention at such an early stage of his pontificate shows that the debate about the new evangelization is set to continue. The Pope construes the new evangelization as the renewed sharing of the good news and, as such, the very *raison d'être* of the Church that continues the mission of Jesus Christ. He offers an incarnational model of the Church's mission that stresses engagement with those beyond the Christian community. What is refreshingly new in *Evangelii gaudium* is its emphasis on the diversity and interconnectedness of the world Church and its dialogical approach to other traditions, which brings to the fore the question of who is evangelizing whom.

Part One

Vatican II and
the New Evangelization

2

Vatican II, Non-Christian Religions and the Challenges for (New) Evangelization Programmes

Mathijs Lamberigts

In some circles, it is *bon ton* to argue that Vatican II is the cause of the many crises Roman Catholicism is confronted with today. Quite a number of websites are pleading for a return to the pre-Vatican II period, some even with a very specific preference to the time of Pope Pius X and his anti-modernist actions. However, quite a number of recent publications, paying attention to the pre-Vatican II period, reveal that this period can be described as a long preparation of the Council,[1] a preparation in which movements such as the liturgical, biblical, patristic and the ecumenical movements played a considerable role, precisely because these movements, through discussions, debates, even disputes, got the opportunity to purify and deepen their insights.[2] The critics of Vatican II seem to forget that all documents of the Council received an overwhelming majority during the final votes; in other words, the Council fathers at the time agreed about the direction in which the *aggiornamento* should go. They did so after long and dense discussions. They were well aware of the tensions that existed between different groups. They knew that the texts were the result of compromises – the decisions of an ecumenical Council cannot be compared

---

[1] See Philippe Chenaux (ed.), *L'Eredità del Magistero di Pio XII* (Dibattito per il millennio 13; Rome: Lateran University Press, 2010).

[2] See Gilles Routhier, Philippe Roy and Karim Schelkens, *La théologie catholique entre intransigeance et renouveau. La réception des mouvements préconciliaires à Vatican II* (Bibliothèque de la Revue d'histoire ecclésiastique 95; Louvain-la-Neuve: Leuven, 2011); cf. also Étienne Fouilloux, 'Mouvements' théologico-spirituels et concile (1959–1962)', in Mathijs Lamberigts and Claude Soetens (eds), *A la veille du Concile Vatican II. Vota et réactions en Europe et dans le catholicisme oriental* (Instrumenta Theologica 9; Leuven: Peeters, 1992), pp. 185–99.

to that of a parliament – and that, just like in previous Councils, people would disagree about the correct interpretation of texts.[3] Be that as it may, most of the Council Fathers, when leaving Rome, were of the opinion that, with what was approved, they had given an appropriate answer to Pope John's appeal in favour of *aggiornamento*.[4] In passing, it should be said that when a pope is pleading for *aggiornamento*, it is clear that at least some things are going wrong. Vatican II published a series of texts, some of them with *ad intra* purposes, others with *ad extra* purposes. In this chapter, I would like to start with some general questions and some somewhat surprising findings.

Some questions

The questions run as follows: Is it possible to reconcile aims such as ecumenical dialogue and interreligious dialogue with the idea of evangelization so clearly emphasized in the document *Ad gentes*, 'Decree on the Missionary Activity of the Church'? What is the meaning of interreligious dialogue in a context where Christianity, just like for example Islam, is characterized by its firm belief in the unique and universal significance of its content for people all over the world?[5] How can the ideas expressed by Pope Emeritus Benedict about the evangelization of the once Christian but now secularized parts of the world be reconciled with the growing presence of other religions in these regions? How can the Gospel be preached in a multifaceted and pluralistic world? What is the meaning of ecumenical dialogue in light of the growing success of the Pentecostal Churches, for example in Latin America?[6] In Brazil, the Roman Catholic Church – at the time of the Council, Brazil was one of the most Catholic countries one could think of – lost about 25 per cent of the 'market', while other Christian denominations doubled their number of members. What does evangelizing mean in this context? The texts of the Gospel are the same, but while the Roman Catholic Church, according to Cardinal Hummes, risks becoming a fossil, other

---

[3] In this regard, Yves Congar, *Mon Journal du Concile* (presented and annotated by Eric Mahieu; Paris: Cerf, 2002) is revealing.
[4] On this topic, see Michael Bredeck, *Das Zweite Vatikanum als Konzil des Aggiornamento: zur hermeneutischen Grundlegung einer theologischen Konzilsinterpretation* (Paderborner theologische Studien 48; Paderborn: Schöningh, 2007).
[5] The impressive investment in education, nursing, social action, solidarity and the like have been the result of this conviction. But such claims can also result in negative consequences such as persecutions, crusades, suicide squads, theocratic regimes, only to mention a few.
[6] For the details, see José Oscar Beozzo, 'Die brasilianische Kirche nach dem Konzil. Zeichen der Zeit und aktuelle Herausforderung', in Peter Hünermann (ed.), *Das Zweite Vatikanische Konzil und die Zeichen der Zeit heute* (Freiburg-Basel-Vienna: Herder, 2006), pp. 451–73 (pp. 468–71).

Christian Churches are spectacularly growing, not only in this continent but also in Africa. Even if we are convinced that evangelization is an urgent need, the question will remain: which type of evangelization for which people?

More than 50 per cent of the world population is either Christian or Muslim. A bit less than 50 per cent of the world population belongs to other confessions or does not believe in a transcendent divine being. It is hard to believe that Christians (about one-third of the world population is described as Christian) are the only ones who are reasonable and right, the others being foolish and wrong. It is hard to believe that Christians, being the largest confessional group in the world, are foolish and wrong, the others being reasonable and right. Is it acceptable that Islamic constitutions are going to dominate people's religious and other views such that, for example, in Egypt, long-existing Coptic communities will be expected to live according to the norms of Islam? In such a context, the Jewish position is rather intriguing. As the prophet Micah said: 'For all peoples walk, each in the name of its god, but we will walk in the name of the Lord our God forever and ever' (Mic. 4.5). Still in the fourth-century AD, the Roman politician and intellectual, Symmachus (345–405) was of the opinion that the divine mystery was too rich and varied to be understood by any one religion, and many people today probably would agree with him. It goes without saying that such statements invite one to promote interreligious dialogue and they seemingly are of help for those who long for a better understanding and comprehension of the other, but it is not a simple matter to do so when one thinks, for example, of Christ's words: 'I am the way, the truth, and the life' (Jn 14.6): such a view – at least for those who believe it is right – should be promoted by all means, for God wants all to be saved (1 Tim. 2.4), but can become problematic in the context of respect for the human rights of all peoples.[7] Moreover, all religions have vivid memories of what religious and non-religious (ideological) domination can mean in concrete contexts. *Historia magistra vitae* (history is the teacher of life) but also *conscientia vitae* (history is the conscience of life), both for those who want to forgive and for those who want to take revenge. It goes without saying that this is true for all other nations, religions and the like and that it is true throughout their history. In this dossier, nobody can claim to be *sine macula et ruga* (without spot or wrinkle).

---

[7] That the secular theory of human rights can become a threat to the self-understanding of religious believers for relativizing the importance of their deeply held convictions can be considered as the other side of the coin; see David Hollenbach, 'Human Rights and Interreligious Dialogue: The Challenge to Mission in a Pluralistic World', *International Bulletin of Missionary Research* 6/3 (July 1982), pp. 98–101 (p. 100).

Some surprising findings

We all know that many of the congregations in the nineteenth century were founded with a view of doing missionary work. In this regard, one can think of the Scheutist Fathers, the White Fathers and the Oblates of Mary. Also orders such as the Jesuits, Dominicans, Franciscans and the like continued their missionary work that had started long before the French Revolution. Thousands of missionaries from Belgium, France, Germany, Ireland, Italy and the Netherlands, to mention only a few, left their home countries in order to spread the Gospel all over the world. While all these young men and women gave their best for the service of Christ and his Church, Europe gradually became a mission continent itself. In 1943, in the midst of World War II, two priests, Henri Godin and Yves Daniel, published their best seller: *France, pays de mission?*[8] Some years before, on 24 July 1941, the French bishops founded the *Mission de France*. Cardijn's *Jeunesse ouvrière chrétienne* (Young Christian Workers), which was intended to contribute to the Christian education and training of young people belonging to the working classes, had already found its way into many countries. The Catholic Church hierarchy, again,[9] became very well aware that it had lost ground among intellectuals and the working class, but, seemingly, the hierarchy did not know how to react properly, as became clear with regard to the priest-workers story,[10] a movement sanctioned not only in 1954, but also at the beginning of John XXIII's pontificate.[11]

While statistics made clear that many people in the southern hemisphere were attracted by the Christian faith, in Europe there was a growing awareness that Christianity was losing its relevance in the daily life of many. A considerable proportion of youngsters showed increased disinterest in Christianity and mission work. Growing ignorance about Christianity and its message was the result. Pope John's plea for *aggiornamento* was also influenced by this development. Vatican II tried to give an answer to this challenge, a challenge that had already started in the nineteenth century.

---

[8] Henri Godin and Yvan Daniel, *La France, pays de mission?* (Lyon: Cerf, 1943).
[9] The same awareness was already present at the end of the nineteenth century; in this regard, one might think of the founding of the *Aumôniers du Travail* in 1894 at Seraing near Liege (Belgium). This congregation indeed intended to reach out to the workers and the youth in industrialized regions.
[10] On this movement as such, see especially Émile Poulat, *Les prêtres ouvriers: naissance et fin* (Paris: Cerf, 1999).
[11] See Étienne Fouilloux, 'The Antepreparatory Phase: The Slow Emergence from Inertia (January, 1959–October 1962)', in Giuseppe Alberigo and Joseph A. Komonchak (eds), *History of Vatican II, Vol. I. Announcing and Preparing Vatican Council II: Toward a New Era in Catholicism* (Maryknoll, NY: Orbis Books, 1995), pp. 55–166 (p. 79 for further details).

The second surprise was that, given the fact that so many superiors general of mission congregations and bishops, having worked in the missions, were present at the Second Vatican Council, one could expect that a document on the missionary activity of the Church would be one of the easiest things to write at the Council. This was far from the case. The *vota* as submitted during the preparatory period made clear that quite a number of missionary bishops of Belgian and French origin pleaded in favour of an Africanization of Catholicism, while their English-speaking counterparts (quite often having an Irish background but also their native colleagues) held different opinions, opting for a more traditional line. In passing, studies on these *vota* have shown how sharp differences between countries, regions, members of different religious congregations and individual bishops could be, thus making clear that the often-heard suggestion that the Church before Vatican II was characterized by unity if not uniformity is simply a myth.[12] Even within the preparatory commission on missions, mostly constituted of members and consulters from Europe, with more than 50 per cent residing in Rome – a majority of the members belonging to the Curia – tensions existed between those who opted for a juridical approach and those who preferred a theological approach.[13] In any case, one cannot say that, even for bishops active in a region where Muslims had the majority, the relation with or conversion of them was really an important concern.[14] It is hard to imagine that these bishops in their daily activities were not confronted with adherents of other religious confessions. However, when thinking about the future Council, this matter was simply not a top priority for them.

An interlude: the *Vriendenkring*

The preparations with regard to the document *Ad gentes* are well studied. I simply mention the fact that the proposal of the decree as presented *in aula* on 6 November 1964, merely an introduction and 13 theses, was described as a text without a body: *ossa arida*. Paul VI was present at the general congregation that day and he hoped that the schema in principle might be approved. Yves Congar noted in his diary: 'He [the Pope] hopes that the schema will be approved in order to be perfected. (While, as I know, the missionary Superiors have sent

---

12 Fouilloux, 'The Antepreparatory Phase', pp. 129–31.
13 See Joseph A. Komonchak, 'The Struggle for the Council during the Preparation of Vatican II (1960–1962)', in Alberigo and Komonchak (eds), *History of Vatican II*, Vol. I, pp. 167–356 (pp. 192–96).
14 See José Oscar Beozzo, 'The External Climate', in Alberigo and Komonchak (eds), *History of Vatican II*, Vol. I, pp. 355–404 (pp. 388–92).

a letter demanding that the schema be rejected and replaced by another that they propose.)'[15] Henri de Lubac, in his *Carnets*, wrote: 'The pope seems to have advised accepting the schema, all the while saying that it will without doubt be "approved and perfected". . . . The pope is made to appear rather like a foreign dignitary making a state visit. That has rather distanced him from the council, conforming with a certain "Roman" ideology that wants the pope to appear always isolated, outside and above the episcopate.'[16] De Lubac is well aware of the drama: the pope is not well informed by his counsellors. Part of what Congar mentions can be reconstructed due to the conciliar papers of some superiors general, now available in the Leuven Center on the Study of Vatican II. It makes clear that the humiliation of a badly informed pope was unnecessary if people had been willing to listen to experts in the field. In the midst of the Second Vatican Council, a group of superiors general, most of them Dutch-speaking, and some bishops born in the Low Countries (Belgium and the Netherlands), were very unhappy with the developments concerning the document on the missions, developments that made clear that what should be considered as the essence of the Christian mission, preaching the Gospel, *de facto* and in concrete contexts had become a problem. Members of the so-called *Vriendenkring* (circle of friends) were the Capuchin Tarcisius van Valenberg, and the following superiors general: Léo Volker of the White Fathers, Henri Systermans of the Picpus Fathers, Henri Mondé of the Society of the Missions in Africa, Joseph van Kerckhoven of the Missionaries of the Sacred Heart, Cornélius Heiligers of the Montfortains and the procurator general of the Augustinians, Ad Van der Weyden. These superior generals and the bishops belonging to their congregations were of the opinion that the missionary efforts should be given the attention these deserved.[17]

In the *Vriendenkring*, people were well aware that even so-called Christian regions now should be characterized as de-Christianized, due to the many migrations so characteristic of post-World War II Western Europe. The superiors general complained about the arbitrariness of the *Propaganda Fide*, an institution that quite a number of African bishops wanted to do away with.[18] The members were well aware of the fact that in this 'new' period in history new forms of

---

[15] Congar, *Mon Journal du Concile*, p. 241 (my translation).
[16] Henri de Lubac, *Carnets du Concile*, Vol. I (introduced and annotated by Loïc Figoureux; Paris: Cerf, 2007), p. 275 (my translation).
[17] The archives reveal that all superiors general were very much in favour of working in the missions, but that they also struggled with the means to realize this.
[18] Cf. Report of the meeting of 21 February 1964 in the papers of Joseph van Kerckhoven, Centre for the Study of the Second Vatican Council, KU Leuven.

doing missionary work were needed, something which would be a challenge for the missionary congregations and their members who would have to start the dialogue with other world religions.[19] At the time these superiors general came together, there was even a rumour going around that no text about the missions would be presented at the council. Is it not strange that at a certain moment the suggestion was made not to speak about what can be considered as one of the essential tasks of the Church: mission? Already on 28 March 1964, the proposals of the superiors general were sent to the commission on the missions,[20] and there is good evidence that the commission very much benefited from the suggestions and ideas made. However, the essence of the critiques as made by the superiors general, among others with regard to the (for them unacceptable) reduction of the whole schema to a series of propositions, was not taken into account.[21] The proposal of the superiors general, very biblical in its content,[22] would be sent again to the secretary of the Council, Monsignor Felici. In the accompanying letter, dated 12 October 1964, the superiors general deplored, again, the reduction of the schema to a series of propositions about the Church's missionary activity.[23] It is still somewhat surprising to see that the advice of experts in that domain was not really taken into account. The result of such negligence is well known: the proposal was not approved in the way it was presented.

Due to the efforts of these committed people, the *Vriendenkring* effectively contributed to what became *Ad gentes*: even if one does not ask you to help, you still do it when and because you have the expertise. The contribution of the *Vriendenkring* was made possible because of its good contacts with Johannes Schütte, the general of the Divine Word Fathers and the spiritual father of *Ad gentes*. Due to a lack of space, I am not able to describe the efforts in detail, but what is of importance is all the time and energy invested in the preparation of a satisfying schema on the mission of the Church: the schema was promoted; missionary bishops were contacted.[24] Sincere collaboration and networking became key words.[25] In fact, it was something which was done by all, whether

---

[19] Cf. Reports of the meetings of 18 February and 19 March 1964 in the papers of Joseph van Kerckhoven, Centre for the Study of the Second Vatican Council, KU Leuven.

[20] A copy is included in the papers of Joseph van Kerckhoven, Centre for the Study of the Second Vatican Council, KU Leuven.

[21] Letter of Van Valenberg to the superiors general dated 12 May 1964 in the papers of Joseph van Kerckhoven, Centre for the Study of the Second Vatican Council, KU Leuven.

[22] *Acta Synodalia Sacrossancti Concilii Oecumenici Vaticani II*, III, 6, pp. 953–66.

[23] See letter of Van Valenberg dated 3 August 1964 in the papers of Joseph van Kerckhoven, Centre for the Study of the Second Vatican Council, KU Leuven.

[24] Letter of Van Valenberg to the members of the *Vriendenkring* dated 29 April 1965 in the papers of Joseph van Kerckhoven, Centre for the Study of the Second Vatican Council, KU Leuven.

[25] For the details, see the letters of van Valenberg of 20 February, 20 and 27 March 1965 in the papers of Joseph van Kerckhoven, Centre for the Study of the Second Vatican Council, KU Leuven.

they belonged to a minority or a majority.[26] It all happened under the radar, for the *Propaganda* did not like such 'conspiracies'[27] – an interesting aspect, resulting in the following questions: How must evangelization be done? Top down? Bottom up? In passing, it should be said that about 30 per cent of the fathers of the Council belonged to religious orders and congregations. In other words, these people were representing an important group. These people took initiatives, prepared *modi* and the like. Given that the conciliar regulations did not give the superiors general a fair chance to take the floor, most of their remarks will be found in the *Acta Synodalia* under the heading *Animadversiones scriptae*. That is, most of the council fathers did not know anything about them and, interesting as some remarks might have been, they were not heard during the general congregations. Instead the council fathers contacted leading figures such as Bernard Alfrink, Joseph Frings, Laureanus Rugambwa and Emil De Smedt.[28] In sum, these people were very committed, mindful of the Church's mission as described in *Ad gentes* 2: 'The pilgrim Church is missionary by her very nature, since it is from the mission of the Son and the mission of the Holy Spirit that she draws her origin, in accordance with the decree of God the Father.'

This story reveals at least three things: (1) The Catholic Church at the time had difficulties defining in an adequate way what mission should be. (2) The information as given to Paul VI was not correct or the president of the commission was not aware of what was experienced in concrete daily life situations. (3) The expertise available at that time was not optimally used.

Nostra Aetate

One of the most remarkable documents of the Second Vatican Council is, without any doubt, *Nostra aetate*. As explained elsewhere,[29] this document is

[26] With regard to the minority, see, for example, Philippe J. Roy, *Le Coetus internationalis patrum, un groupe d'opposants au sein du Concile Vatican II* (Université Laval, 2011; unpublished dissertation); cf. also the letters of Mgr D. Staffa to several superiors general and *periti*, as preserved in the Centre for the Study of the Second Vatican Council, KU Leuven.

[27] See the letter of Van Valenberg, 27 March 1965 in the Centre for the Study of the Second Vatican Council, KU Leuven.

[28] See the letters of Van Valenberg dated 29 April 1965; 18 June 1965 in the papers of Joseph van Kerckhoven, Centre for the Study of the Second Vatican Council, KU Leuven.

[29] For a survey of the genesis of this document, see Mathijs Lamberigts and Leo Declerck, 'Vatican II on the Jews: A Historical Survey', in Marianne Moyaert and Didier Pollefeyt (eds), *Never Revoked: Nostra Aetate as Ongoing Challenge for Jewish-Christian Dialogue* (Leuven/Grand Rapids, MI/ Cambridge: Peeters, 2010), pp. 13–56.

the result of a long and difficult process, and the subject of much controversy, even today. (It is one of the stumbling blocks in the dialogue between Rome and the followers of Monsignor Lefebvre; cf. also the recent consternation with regard to the Good Friday prayer for the Jews.) An initial proposal as prepared by the Secretariat for the Promotion of Christian Unity was ultimately not debated during the meeting of the central preparatory commission of June 1962 because of a concern not to intervene in the bitter discussions that were raging between the Jews and the Arabs.[30] Also during the council, it constantly remained a concern not to give the impression that the document had a political background. Several secret travels were made to the Middle East in order to convince the different Eastern Catholic Churches to support the text.[31] Many attempts were made to explain to the opponents of the text why such a text was needed. The broadening of the scope in 1964 resulted in new debates and disputes with regard to the theological value of what was believed by Hindus and Buddhists, debates which sometimes revealed the Christian gross ignorance (*ignorantia crassissima*) about these religions. Many were upset about what was said with regard to Islam and especially bishops from the Middle East had not forgotten that they had been the victims of many persecutions or as the Maronite Patriarch Meouchi (1894–1975) said: 'They [the Muslims]have persecuted the Christians for centuries and we are the sons of the martyrs. Their life is rather bestial and scandalous, despite the good example of the Christians . . . The animal man does not understand what belongs to the Spirit.'[32] The Coetus Internationalis Patrum, an organization in which Monsigor Marcel Lefebvre, at the time the superior general of the Spiritans, and Monsignor Carli of Segni played an important role, claimed, not without reason, that the text on the Jews should be considered as a rupture with the past. Despite all these critiques and oppositions, in the final text one can read:

> The Catholic Church rejects nothing that is true and holy in these religions. She
> regards with sincere reverence those ways of conduct and of life, those precepts
> and teachings which, though differing in many aspects from the ones she holds
> and sets forth, nonetheless often reflect a ray of that Truth which enlightens all
> men. Indeed, she proclaims, and ever must proclaim Christ 'the way, the truth,

---

[30] *Acta et Documenta Praeparatoria*, II, 4, pp. 22–3. Cf. also Komonchak, *The Struggle for the Council*, p. 271 (with additional literature).

[31] See Mathijs Lamberigts and Leo Declerck, 'Mgr E. J. De Smedt et le texte conciliaire sur la religion juive (Nostra Aetate, n 4)', *Ephemerides Theologicae Lovanienses* 85 (2009), pp. 341–84.

[32] '*Ils (the Muslims) ont persécuté les chrétiens pendant des siècles et nous sommes les fils des martyrs. Leur vie est plutôt animale et fait scandale, malgré le bon exemple des chrétiens . . . Homo animalis non intelligit quae Spiritus sunt*'. Archivio Segreto Vaticano (Rome), Concilium Vaticanum II, 1458.

and the life' (Jn 14:6), in whom men may find the fullness of religious life, in whom God has reconciled all things to Himself (*Nostra aetate* 2).

The text uses open categories such as 'true' and 'holy'.[33] These concepts invite Catholics to take seriously what is present in other religions, even when being different. The 'light' metaphor (a ray of that Truth which enlightens all men), clearly referring to John 1.9, well known in the patristic 'logos' theology – in previous versions, one could even find a quote from Irenaeus, *Adversus haereses* IV, 28, 2 – both recognizes the value of what is present in other religions and also the Church's task to proclaim and preach Christ, for Christ is the norm for dialogue, not the Church. In other words, the Gospel that must be preached urges all people, even Christians, to come to 'a religiously critical moment'.[34] The text as quoted suggests that a dialogue with all people of good will can enrich the Church itself, or as Siebenrock put it, it can result in receiving 'a new experience of the fullness of Christ'.[35] In the story of the *Vriendenkring*, the superiors general linked two elements: interreligious dialogue and new forms of mission. I do think that mission and dialogue, creed and encounter imply and evoke each other. It is what is suggested by the last part of paragraph 2: 'The Church, therefore, exhorts her sons, that through dialogue and collaboration with the followers of other religions, carried out with prudence and love and in witness to the Christian faith and life, they recognize, preserve and promote the good things, spiritual and moral, as well as the socio-cultural values found among these men.'

Nostra aetate starts with the following statement:

> In our time, when day by day mankind is being drawn closer together, and the ties between different peoples are becoming stronger, the Church examines more closely her relationship to non-Christian religions . . . One is the community of all peoples, one their origin, for God made the whole human race to live over the face of the earth. One also is their final goal, God. His providence, His manifestations of goodness, His saving design extend to all men, until that time when the elect will be united in the Holy City, the city ablaze with the glory of God, where the nations will walk in His light (*Nostra aetate* 1).

[33] For what follows, see the pertinent remarks of Roman A. Siebenrock, 'Theologischer Kommentar zur Erklärung über die Haltung der Kirche zu den nichtchristlichen Religionen Nostra aetate', in Peter Hünermann and Bernd Jochen Hilberath (eds), *Herders Theologischer Kommentar zum Zweiten Vatikanischen Konzil*, Vol. III (Freiburg-Basel-Vienna: Herder, 2005), pp. 657–58.
[34] 'ein religionskritisches Moment'. Siebenrock, 'Theologischer Kommentar zur Erklärung', p. 657.
[35] 'eine neue Erfahrung der Fülle Christi'. Siebenrock, 'Theologischer Kommentar zur Erklärung', p. 657.

In their belief in one God, creator of earth and of all that is on earth, Christians, Jews and Muslims have the same principles in common but, on the level of the details, they clearly differ. The Middle East, Nigeria, Brussels, London, India, Pakistan, North Ireland and the dramas happening everywhere both on macro- and micro-levels make clear that the (revealed) essence of faith in its concrete application to different world religions does not fit with daily life experiences. Against the background of 'universal' truth, people in concrete and thus contextual situations can easily get the idea that they are right in the (frightening) details and seem to forget that they have so many things in common with those they are attacking or by whom they are persecuted, perhaps eventually killed. Much of what we believe is based on what is revealed through historical figures such as Moses, Jesus and Muhammad. There is an enormous distance between faith claims as such and the way this faith will be lived out. It goes without saying that such aspects will complicate attempts to start a new evangelization process.

Religious liberty

Christianity once played a dominant if not dictatorial role. The *cuius regio, eius religio* adage, which required the ruled to adopt the religion of the ruler, is well known. In Leuven, buildings, names of streets and the like commemorate the difficult period such as English and Irish Catholics once had in England and Ireland. During the nineteenth century, the idea of religious liberty, finding its way in Protestant circles (such as during the re-installation of the Roman Catholic hierarchy in the Netherlands and England), was considered to be a heresy in encyclicals as promulgated by Popes Gregory XVI and Pius IX. In the beginning of the twentieth century, academic emancipation processes such as those of Loisy and Batiffol were blocked. Still in the 1950s, a promoter of the religious liberty idea, John Courtney Murray, was asked to stop publishing on this issue – an order he accepted.[36] The complex genesis of the document on religious liberty (*Dignitatis humanae*) is well studied by the Italian Silvia Scatena.[37]

---

[36] Cf. Dominique Gonnet, *La liberté religieuse à Vatican II. La contribution de John Courtney Murray* (Cogitatio Fidei) (Paris: Cerf, 1994); Gerald P. Fogarty, 'Vereinigte Staaten von Amerika', in Edwin Gatz (ed.), *Die britischen Inseln und Nordamerika* (Kirche und Katholizismus seit 1945, 4; Paderborn-Munich-Vienna-Zürich: Schöningh, 2002), pp. 89–143 (especially pp. 97–122).

[37] Silvia Scatena, *La fatica della libertà. L'elaborazione della dichiarazione «Dignitatis Humanae» sulla libertà religiosa del Vaticano II* (Testi e ricerche di scienze religiose. Nuova serie, 31; Bologna: Il Mulino, 2003).

The document on religious liberty was for the first time presented during the second session of the Council, on 19 November 1963. It was the first time the Roman Catholic Church had dealt with this topic in a congregation of bishops from all over the world. It was an historic moment. During this session, the text was not discussed. What is interesting is that at that time the text was chapter 5 of the schema on ecumenism – the idea of religious liberty was treated from an internal Christian perspective. Religious liberty was still considered to be a problem between Christians of different denominations.

During the third session (September 1964), the text on religious liberty became an independent declaration on religious freedom. The text was now more technical: a definition of what religious liberty is; the rights of religious communities were better defined; this was also the case for the bounds of external pressure. The document attempted to show how subjectivism and indifferentism in this matter could be avoided; indeed two aspects that were mentioned time and again by the opponents. In the introduction to the schema, the *relator*, Monsignor De Smedt, emphasized that the state cannot judge about truth questions *in religiosis*. The state, according to the text, did not and should not intervene in internal ecclesiastical matters, for it should be neutral.[38] In this matter, the role of the state should be limited to the definition of the lines within which people must be able to confess their faith in both public and private. A state does not have the right to promulgate anti-religious measures. It goes without saying that what is described here in rather general terms had enormous consequences. What about the Catholic idea that only the Catholic truth had the right to exist? What about the well-known thesis that non-Catholic errors could only be tolerated, but that they did not possess any rights? In these types of arguments, the ideal state was a Catholic state, a state in which its leaders had the duty to govern society according to Catholic norms, as defined by the magisterium. For those who supported this view, mostly belonging to the Italian and Spanish-language groups, it was evident that the Catholic Church was the only true Church, the only one that deserved to be supported by civil authority. Accepting religious liberty meant opening the door for liberalism and would result in the end of missionary work. Indeed, if all have the right to form their own ideas about truth in a similar way, why should people then still undertake the effort to convince others that their opinions offered a 'surplus'?

The advocates of the text were of the opinion that it did not make sense to claim religious rights for the Roman Catholic Church, while refusing them to

---

[38] *Acta Synodalia* III, 2, pp. 352–3.

others. The dignity of the human person is a value which applies to all human beings. Religious freedom was considered to be the only means by which one could confess one's own religious convictions in totalitarian contexts. It should be remembered that among the advocates of the idea were bishops in Communist countries, the bishops of the United States, the bishops of England, the bishops of West and Central Europe, to mention only a few. Most of these bishops knew very well what it meant to belong to a minority.

Other arguments in favour of the declaration run as follows: respect for religious liberty will contribute to a peaceful society among human beings with different confessions, in pluralistic contexts and the like. What was needed was a common platform to talk to and collaborate with other denominations and non-Christian religions or those with secular convictions. In this context, it should be said that the text strongly emphasized the duty to search for the truth: a freedom from external pressure did not mean that one had the right not to search for the truth. Religious freedom is a right and it is a duty. One has the right to err but on condition that one has earnestly searched for the truth.

The votes at the end of the Council made clear that the ideas of the second group were supported by most of the fathers. On 7 December 1965, *Dignitatis humanae*, 'Declaration on Religious Freedom' was passed as follows: 2,308 for; 70 against; 8 invalid.

Some concluding remarks

What to think about all this? First, neither 'the doctrine' nor 'the truth' are bearers of rights but the human person and his conscience (cf. *Dignitatis humanae* 1–2). Vatican II time and again emphasized the need to preach the gospel in an authentic way: in this regard, orthopraxis should be the key word. Christians have the same rights and duties as non-Christians. A time in which being a Catholic resulted in more privileges is, or should be, over (cf. the regulations in Spain in 1976; in Italy in 1984). In religious matters, states should be neutral. Papal documents such as *Evangelii nuntiandi* (1975) and *Centesimus annus* (1991), to mention only a few, made clear that the Roman Catholic Church is very much concerned with advocating the human rights of all.[39]

---

[39] Cf. Hermínio Rico, *John Paul II and the Legacy of Dignitatis Humanae* (Washington, DC: Georgetown University Press, 2002), p. 119.

Nostra aetate remains a manifesto for every authentic interreligious dialogue in freedom, both with other Christian denominations and with world religions. It will be a dialogue characterized by cultural and social interaction,[40] and thus become a multifaceted dialogue. It will be a challenging dialogue, based on respect and recognition of societal plurality. It belongs to the legacy of Vatican II to dialogue in respect: preaching the Gospel and the processes of evangelization must be done and promoted but within the contours described by the council fathers. True conversion will only happen in a situation of true freedom and respect.

But here there is another challenge: (interreligious) dialogue and the willingness to do it require a willingness to comprehend the essence of other (non-)religious convictions, without a guarantee that the others are willing to dialogue.[41] Willingness to dialogue is sometimes interpreted by the other parties as a sign of weakness. Indeed, the idea was mostly developed in Christian milieus, especially after World War II. The Auschwitz drama certainly was an important stimulus for a growing respect for other religions. But the end of World War II was also an acceleration point in the process of a decline for Christianity in Europe, including Catholicism.[42] The end of World War II was, for Europe, the definite end of its international dominance: de-colonization – for several countries in Africa the beginning of inner conflicts, wars and the like – de facto also meant a loss of economic power for the colonizing countries. In many of the former colonies, Christianity was regarded as being related to foreign economic and political powers. Christianity was, and is for example in Indian Hindu milieus, considered a foreign religion, a type of religious import.[43] Should interreligious dialogue be seen as a sign of weakness or a (unilateral) expression of deep respect for the other religious convictions?

However, the Vatican II view as sketched earlier found its implementation in many places. It remains true that Catholic minorities in several countries still do not enjoy such religious liberty and often are living under threats and in anxiety.[44] It remains true that even in countries where all the conditions are

---

[40] Cf. Guiseppe M. Siviero, 'La libertà religiosa dalla Dignitatis Humanae ai nostri giorni', in *Quaderni di Diritto Ecclesiale* 11 (1998), pp. 244–66 (p. 249).

[41] In this regard, see the helpful insights of David Hollenbach, 'Human Rights and Interreligious Dialogue', p. 98.

[42] The growth of Catholicism in the West some people refer to is partly the result of immigrations. It might be interesting to examine thoroughly the opportunities this new situation offers to local communities.

[43] Although such accusations are not always correct. Churches like the Syro-Malabar or the Syro-Malankara ones were present in India long before Hinduism was considered to be a religion.

[44] See especially Roland Minnerath, 'La déclaration Dignitatis Humanae à la fin du Concile Vatican II', in *Revue des sciences religieuses* 74 (2000), pp. 226–42.

present for a true dialogue in freedom, because of growing cultural relativism and pluralism and social fragmentation, religious disinterest is growing or, even worse, divisions within Christian communities are growing. In such a context there is a constant temptation to close the windows and look back to the past, an idealized past that never existed, for in that case it would still exist.

But it also remains true that time and again people are searching for meaning, for truth, for religious truth, a truth which is, for Christians, not a doctrine but a person, the one who is the way, the truth and life, the one we are waiting for. That is what we confess, that is what inspires our daily life and actions, that is why we must preach the Gospel, but we must do it in all humility and with respect for other religions.

3

From 'Mission' to 'Evangelization': The Latin American Origins of a Challenging Concept

John F. Gorski

On 30 June 2010, Pope Benedict XVI made a surprising announcement: he had decided to establish a new dicastery (department) in the Vatican Curia, a 'Pontifical Council for Promoting the New Evangelization'. On 21 September, he issued a *motu proprio* formalizing its existence and named the theologian Archbishop Salvatore Fisichella as its first president. It was surprising because Pope Benedict was on record as having called for the number of curial offices to be reduced rather than increased. Moreover, he had announced on 24 October 2010 at the conclusion of the Middle East Synod that 'The New Evangelization for the Transmission of the Christian Faith' would be the topic of the next worldwide Assembly of the Synod in 2012. What exactly is the 'new evangelization' that this new Vatican office is to promote? What are the origins of this concept? How did it develop? How does it affect the Catholic Church's worldwide missionary activity?

Ever since the risen Lord sent out his disciples to make disciples of all nations, the Catholic Church has engaged in what we now call 'missionary activity', the evangelization of those who do not yet know Christ so that local Churches could come to birth in their midst. But the way we speak of this activity has changed over the centuries. In fact for about 15 centuries, the word 'mission' was not used to refer to this activity. Also, the New Testament speaks of evangelizing or announcing the gospel, but the noun 'evangelization' began to be used by Catholics only about 50 years ago. In order to understand the term 'new evangelization', we have to understand first how the concept of 'mission' has evolved, for it was in the context of clarifying the meaning of mission that Pope

John Paul II officially introduced the concept of 'new evangelization' into the Catholic Church's vocabulary.

We can trace the development of the term mission, starting with the Second Vatican Council. When the Council centred mission on the evangelization of peoples rather than the geographical expansion of the Church, it brought about a transition from territorial to a situational idea of mission. How human groups relate to Christ in their concrete historical situations became more important than whether they lived in 'mission lands'. Paul VI gave great importance to evangelization as being the fundamental task of the Church, and the Latin American bishops' Puebla conference of 1979 called for a 'new evangelization' of human groups in new cultural situations. John Paul II made this a major concern in his teaching ministry. I will describe what I have witnessed in the past 40 years of accompanying Latin American bishops in their efforts to make the continent's Church truly 'missionary'. I realize that others may offer other perspectives. What is important is appreciating what the 'new evangelization' means and calls for. Understanding the origins of the concept may be of some help in fulfilling it.

The modern meaning of 'mission'[1]

In scholastic theology, 'mission' was used to speak of the Word and the Holy Spirit being sent by the Father – a focus apparently introduced in Vatican II's missionary decree, *Ad gentes* (AG 2–4) by Fr Yves Congar OP, but it did not refer to an activity of the Church. But the word 'mission' in its modern sense apparently goes back to St Ignatius of Loyola in the sixteenth century. By the fourth 'vow of the mission', certain Jesuits were sent to non-Christian lands (or to countries lost to Catholicism during the Protestant Reformation) as agents vested with the authority of the pope to propagate the Catholic faith. Those sent soon came to be called 'missionaries' and the places they were sent, 'missions'.

Historically, since the sixteenth century the concept of 'the missions' was closely associated with the practice of European (and later American) colonialism. The idea supposed that the 'established churches' of Western Europe had a duty to transplant their form of Christendom to the previously non-Christianized nations colonized by their countries. It implied the superiority of

[1] For a detailed overview of Catholic mission theology, see Stephen B. Bevans and Roger P. Schroeder, *Constants in Context: A Theology of Mission for Today* (Maryknoll, NY: Orbis Books, 2004).

the old Christendom and the inferiority of the peoples colonized. The religious mission was normally combined with the secular enterprise of 'civilizing' these peoples, in other words, transplanting Western cultural models. Thus the term 'mission' came to mean the complex of activities by which the Western ecclesiastical system was extended all over the world.

According to the jurisprudence in force when Catholic Christianity came to America and parts of Africa and Asia in the fifteenth and sixteenth centuries, the pope had direct authority over all peoples not yet embraced by Christendom, that is, subject to Christian authorities. It was assumed that he could delegate his powers to a secular power, as in the case of the *patronato* conceded to the kings of Spain and Portugal. When in the nineteenth century these empires were weakened and new colonial powers came to control what we often now call the 'Third World' (Africa, Asia, Latin America and the Pacific islands), the pope delegated his authority to the Congregation of Propaganda Fide (now called the 'Congregation for the Evangelization of Peoples'), which entrusted not-yet-Christianized territories to religious congregations or missionary institutes and delegated them to convert their inhabitants to Christianity and to 'plant the Church' there (as Apostolic Prefectures or Vicariates). Thus 'the missions' were generally identified with territories subject to the authority of Propaganda Fide.

In the first place, this way of seeing things supposed that human groups needed missionary activity simply because they lived in certain geographical areas. It likewise implied that people who lived in Europe and North America (and more recently, in countries like Australia) simply needed ordinary pastoral attention, teaching doctrine and administering the sacraments to those who already were Catholic.

Theologically also, this geographical and juridical concept of 'the missions' had some serious limitations. Conversion was often seen as the change of religion rather than an encounter with the living Christ and discipleship. The overt objective was really 'Christianization' rather than evangelization: the incorporation of more and more peoples into a socio-political and religious entity called 'Christendom'. The 'missions' were the responsibility of the 'missionaries'. It was not imagined that the entire Church is missionary by its nature or that all the faithful – bishops, priests, religious and laypeople – share in this missionary responsibility.

When the Latin American Church started to become actively missionary after the Council, the geographical and juridical criteria for defining mission were criticized as being seriously inadequate. For over 90 per cent of those in need of a primary evangelization (mostly Native American peoples and African Americans) did not live in the 'Propaganda territories' but in established dioceses. It was realized that people need missionary activity not because of they live in a certain type of ecclesiastical jurisdiction or territory but because they have not yet been evangelized in their cultural identity. The deficiencies of defining mission primarily by geography led to a 'situational' view of mission.

The Council dramatically transformed the understanding of mission, although many Catholics, including bishops and priests not updated in missiology, still think and speak in pre-conciliar way. The document 'on the missions' became the 'Decree on Missionary Activity' (*Ad gentes*). The change in terminology was not just a question of words but of concepts. The change was a costly process in the Council. The draft of that decree had to undergo more changes than any other document of the Council, but it was finally accepted with greater unanimity than any other.

Ad gentes in the first place affirmed that the entire Church of her very nature is missionary. In other words, mission is not just a concern of religious congregations, missionary institutes or 'professional missionaries'. The juridical perspective viewed mission as an exercise of authority to submit nations to the true religion. The Council's decree rather based the mission of the Church on the Father's loving initiative in sending his Son and the Holy Spirit to communicate divine life to humanity.

One of the most significant contributions of *Ad gentes* was the following. Although the decree sometimes continues to employ the phrase 'the missions' in the traditional sense, it introduces a new, more dynamic concept: 'missionary activity'. It is based on the conviction that the evangelizing mission of the Church is one, but it is differentiated in its exercise given the condition of the ones for whom it is directed, the different types of human groups evangelized. Thus, *Ad gentes* 6 distinguishes *missionary activity*, directed to the evangelization of those peoples or groups who do not yet know Christ and among which no mature local Church exists, from *pastoral activity*, directed to the ongoing evangelization of those who are already Catholic. This distinction was one of the Council's 'best kept secrets' until its emphatic reiteration by John Paul II in the encyclical *Redemptoris missio* 33. Of course, for those who do not know this encyclical, it is still a secret. We shall get back to this distinction later. But first we'll take a look at developments during the pontificate of Paul VI, in which the concept of 'evangelization' acquired a new breadth and depth of meaning and a new importance.

Catholic theology rediscovers evangelization

The New Testament frequently uses the noun 'gospel' and the verb 'evangelize' [or 'announce the Gospel']. In the eighteenth century, when some Protestants started to recognize the importance of mission activity (during the two centuries after Luther and Calvin, Protestant churches did not send missionaries), they coined the nouns 'evangelization' and 'evangelism'. Until 1955, this word is scarcely found in Catholic theological literature; since it was a 'Protestant term', it was simply avoided. It was rediscovered in the Catholic catechetical renewal of the 1950s and 60s which stressed that the teaching of the faith should have a 'kerygmatic' dynamic, one that emphasized the 'good news' of the gospel. At that time, evangelization was distinguished from catechesis. Evangelization was considered as the first proclamation of the good news, and catechesis, the progressive formation in the faith of those who were already evangelized. In Asia, some missionaries and missiologists even spoke of a process of 'pre-evangelization', an announcing of how non-Christians are prepared for the explicit Gospel message. Thus the word 'evangelization' was ready to be used in the Second Vatican Council 40 years ago. In the documents of the Council the words 'evangelization' and 'evangelize' are used most frequently in *Ad gentes*, and normally in the sense of a first announcing of the gospel to those who do not yet know Christ.

Ten years after the Council, in late 1974, Pope Paul VI convoked an Assembly of the Synod of Bishops to consider the different dimensions of 'Evangelization in Today's World'. The pope assumed and organized the input of the Synod and communicated it to the whole Church in his apostolic exhortation *Evangelii nuntiandi* (8 December 1975). In it, he stressed that evangelization is the specific and fundamental task of the Church. The Church exists to evangelize, to announce the gospel. Evangelization is above all – and can never omit – the explicit announcing of the gospel, making known the person and message of Jesus Christ. But evangelization is more; it is a complex, rich and dynamic reality that cannot be fully understood unless all of its elements are taken into account. Paul VI makes a point of not reducing evangelization to mission activity, the first announcing of Christ to those who do not yet know him. While bringing the gospel to every sector of the human race is of great importance, Paul also insists on its penetration into every level and aspect of human life, particularly in the evangelization of culture and of cultures. This implies a transformation of scales of values, patterns of behaviour, structures of relationships and ways of thinking. Evangelization is a process that starts with a witness of life and word that leads to an announcing of the gospel and which invites the person evangelized to conversion and incorporation into an ecclesial community and sacramental life. The end result is that the one evangelized himself/herself becomes an evangelizer of others. The pope emphasizes the responsibility of the local churches – of bishops, priests, religious and laity – in evangelization (something that was hardly taken for granted), but strangely does not speak specifically of life-long missionaries or missionary institutes.

Unfortunately, *Evangelii nuntiandi* does not give a clear definition of 'evangelization'. *Evangelii nuntiandi* describes the multiple and rich elements involved in evangelization, the process involved, its effects and those responsible for it, but it does not define the term. I personally like the definition proposed in the *Instrumentum laboris* prepared in 1973 for the Synod of Bishops on 'Evangelization in the Modern World' (1974): 'Evangelization is the totality of those activities by which people are brought to participate in the mystery of Christ.'[2] I like this definition because it reminds us that the objective of evangelization is a personal encounter with the person of Christ, and a participation in his paschal mystery. Personal encounter with Christ implies discipleship, and discipleship implies belonging to that community of disciples which is the Church. I see this (more than the salvation of individual souls) as the objective of all evangelization and of missionary activity in particular. The Church is necessary in salvation because the historical participation in God's saving plan is of utmost importance. God wants this participation to be fully human: realized with awareness, freedom, responsibility and heartfelt joy, not alone, but with others in society and culture.

Since *Evangelii nuntiandi*, the word 'evangelization' has become quite popular. Catholics began to speak a lot of evangelization and called just about everything they did evangelization, even if it did not make bring people to participate in the mystery of Christ. Some missionaries and missiologists focused more on the 'elements' of evangelization and on the 'methods' used for doing it rather than on its theological foundations. While 'evangelization' was the thing to do, a crisis arose regarding the need and urgency of missionary activity. Some considered it useful for promoting the well-being of poor and oppressed peoples overseas and mutual toleration of religions and cultures, but not necessary for the salvation of persons. But if not 'necessary for salvation', how could mission be urgent? The Catholic Bishops of the United States recognized this problem in

---

[2] 'Vox "evangelizationis" significat igitur complexum omnium activitatum quibus homines ad participandum mysterium Christi adducuntur'; cited in Giovanni Caprile, *Il Sinodo dei Vescovi, III Asamblea Generale (1974)* (Roma: Edizioni Civiltà Cattólica, 1975), p. 920.

1986 and produced the Pastoral Letter: *To the Ends of the Earth.*[3] In 1990, Pope John Paul II recognized the global scope of this crisis and wrote the challenging encyclical *Redemptoris missio*, 'On the Permanent Validity of the Church's Missionary Mandate'. In the following paragraphs, I shall highlight only a few of his thoughts; those that help us understand what makes missionary activity specific and distinctive.

John Paul II gave new energy to the conciliar concept of 'missionary activity' in its specific sense, and he did this in various ways. As the Council did in *Ad gentes* 6, the pope affirms that the Church has one evangelizing mission, but that the exercise of this is differentiated due to the different situations in which human groups find themselves. It was in this context that called for a 'new evangelization' and gave it a rather clear meaning.

Basic to John Paul II's missiology is his emphasis on the importance of distinguishing missionary activity, oriented towards those who are beyond the visible limits of the Church, from ordinary pastoral attention to those who already find themselves in the Church. To this mission activity in its proper sense he gave the name 'mission *ad gentes*', a new term popularized in Latin American missionary circles since the Third General Conference of CELAM, the Latin American Council of Catholic Bishops celebrated in Puebla, Mexico in 1979, but not yet widely used elsewhere. Here are his words as found in *Redemptoris missio* 33:

> First, there is the situation which the Church's missionary activity addresses: peoples, groups, and socio-cultural contexts in which Christ and his Gospel are not known, or which lack Christian communities sufficiently mature to be able to incarnate the faith in their own environment and proclaim it to other groups. This is mission *ad gentes* in the proper sense of the term.
>
> Secondly, there are Christian communities with adequate and solid ecclesial structures. They are fervent in their faith and in Christian living. They bear witness to the Gospel in their surroundings and have a sense of commitment to the universal mission. In these communities the Church carries out her pastoral activity and pastoral care.

In the years prior to *Redemptoris missio*, only certain missionary groups and missiologists underscored this distinction between mission and pastoral activity. Even after *Redemptoris missio* this distinction is still unknown to or ignored by many church leaders, theologians and even many missioners who still direct

---

[3] United States Conference of Catholic Bishops, *To the Ends of the Earth: A Pastoral Statement on World Mission* (Washington, DC: USCCB, 1986).

their efforts mainly to general pastoral care, the attention given to the faithful who frequent their parishes. They give so much attention to local and immediate pastoral problems, that the challenge of missionary activity in its specific sense is often ignored or postponed.

New evangelization

When John Paul II issued *Redemptoris missio* in 1990, 25 years had elapsed since the Council's mission decree *Ad gentes*. In that quarter-century, the socio-cultural and religious conditions affecting the world's peoples kept on changing, as did the Church's awareness of how these affected her evangelizing mission. The distinction between human groups that needed missionary activity and groups that needed ordinary pastoral attention was valid but no longer sufficient. It is true that there still were entire peoples which did *not yet* know Christ, whose ancestral cultures were not affected by the gospel, and that there were other groups that were evangelized and constituted as Christian communities. But there were also considerable groups that were *no longer Christians*, for whom Jesus Christ, his Gospel and his Church were of minimal or no importance. It was to these groups that John Paul pointed to in the next paragraph of *Redemptoris missio* 33:

> Thirdly, there is an intermediate situation, particularly in countries with ancient Christian roots, and occasionally in the younger Churches as well, where entire groups of the baptized have lost a living sense of the faith, or even no longer consider themselves members of the Church, and live a life far removed from Christ and his Gospel. In this case what is needed is a 'new evangelization' or a 're-evangelization'.

In the decade or so after the Puebla conference, John Paul urged a 'new evangelization' particularly in the context of the Church's preparation for two events: the fifth centenary of the Gospel's arrival in America (1492–1992) and the beginning of a new millennium (2000–1). In the first case, the message was directed to Latin America and in the second, to a progressively secularized Europe. In the first case, the accent was on an evangelization that was 'new in its ardour, in its methods and in its expression'. In the second case, its stress was on a 're-evangelization' of people who were baptized but who have grown indifferent to religion. As Pope Benedict XVI observed in the *Motu Propio* (*Ubicumque et semper*), John Paul II 'made this urgent task a central point in his wide-reaching

Magisterial teaching' and 'systematically explored [it] in depth on numerous occasions'.

As far as I can understand the ways things developed, it was John Paul's involvement in the Latin American Bishops' Conference in Puebla, Mexico in 1979, shortly after his election that sharpened his focus on evangelization and gave him the words with which to speak of it. The term 'new evangelization' had appeared in Latin American documents at least since 1968. In the final 'Message' (6) of their Second General Conference (that of Medellín), the Latin American Bishops committed themselves to 'foster a new evangelization'.[4] This was a 'one-liner'. The idea was there, but it was still rather vague in its substance. I found other uses of the term 'new evangelization' in 1969 and 70 in the context of the indigenous apostolate in Latin America. Correspondence with missiologists in Africa and Asia makes me believe that it was not used in other continents. It does not appear in Paul VI's *Evangelii nuntiandi* (1975). I believe that it was the Latin American Church's use of the term, particularly in the Puebla Document, that directly influenced John Paul.

The Puebla Document (numbers 365–7) urges the Church to concentrate on three types of 'situations most in need of evangelization' (the penultimate draft called them 'missionary situations').[5] First are the 'permanent situations', the indigenous peoples and African American populations which are yet to be evangelized in their cultural identity. Second are the 'new situations that call for a New Evangelization' (spelled with capital letters in the original text), human groups affected by recent socio-cultural changes, such as migration, urbanization and secularization. Finally are 'particularly difficult situations', groups whose urgent need of evangelization is often postponed: university students and other young people, military, business and labour leaders as well as the world of social communications (this item came from the pre-Puebla input of Bishop Juan Gerardi of Guatemala, martyred in 1998). I believe that the paragraph of the Puebla Document that concretely shaped John Paul's thinking was number 366 that identified 'new situations that require a New Evangelization'. The pope certainly knew that page of the document quite well, because in *Redemptoris missio* (64) he praised as exemplary the commitment of the Latin American Bishops to missionary activity beyond their frontiers, as formulated in number 368.

---

[4] The final document can be read at on the CELAM website at http://www.celam.org/conferencia_medellin.php.

[5] The final document can be read at on the CELAM website at http://www.celam.org/conferencia_puebla.php.

Puebla number 366 was not the result of a 'spontaneous generation' during the course of the conference. It had its own pre-history in the creative thinking of Bishop Roger Aubry CSsR (1923–2010), the one charged with drafting the text of Puebla's sub-chapter on 'The Criteria for Evangelization and its Universal Dimension'. Aubry, the Vicar Apostolic of Reyes in Bolivia's Amazon area, north of La Paz, was President of the Mission Department of CELAM from late 1974 to early 1979. Since its inception in 1966, this department had been committed to the specific evangelization of the continent's indigenous peoples and the need to go beyond inadequate territorial criteria for determining what is 'mission' in the specific sense. Central to the Department's vision was the concept of 'missionary situations' among human groups barely evangelized in their cultural identity. Aubry brought this line of thought to a new level and developed the concept of 'new missionary situations'.

Aubry, perhaps more than anyone else, contributed to shaping a Latin American theology of mission with its own accents and to the missionary commitment of the continent's episcopate. His profoundly biblical theology, formed by his mentor François Xavier Durrwell, was centred on the paschal mystery and further shaped by the Council's *Ad gentes*. His reading of that decree confirmed his conviction, born from his understanding of the paschal mystery, that the Church is missionary by her very nature. He reiterated the importance given in *Ad gentes* 6 to the distinction between missionary activity and ordinary pastoral activity. In the sixth paragraph of that number, these words caught his attention: 'Moreover, the groups among which the Church dwells are often radically changed, for one reason or other, so that an entirely new set of circumstances may arise. Then the Church must deliberate whether these conditions might again call for her missionary activity'. Here the Council affirmed that changed conditions, even among previously evangelized human groups, may call for new missionary activity in the specific sense. Aubry was invited to address Latin America's National Directors of the Pontifical Mission Societies in Sao Paulo in January 1976. In that talk, describing 'Where is mission?' he called attention to this text, ignored by most other commentators on *Ad gentes*. This was the origin of the concept of 'new missionary situations' that would enter into the reflections of the CELAM Mission Department in the years before Puebla. It would become the substance of Puebla number 366, which affirmed that new missionary situations called for a 'new evangelization'. I believe that this is the text that gave John Paul II the language with which to speak of the need for a specifically original evangelization of those affected by changing socio-cultural situations. Incidentally, it was probably Bishop Aubry who coined the term '*ad gentes* mission' and introduced it into the Puebla document (368) to speak of the universal dimension of missionary activity in the specific sense.

The cultural identity of those who are served by missionary activity is implicit in the Council. John Paul II makes it explicit (RM 34). The pontiff calls attention not only to traditional cultures but also to new socio-cultural situations. He speaks of three 'spheres of mission': territorial, social and cultural (RM 37). What is interesting is that he considers these challenges not only to evangelization in general, but also to mission *ad gentes* in its proper sense. For John Paul, missionary activity can no longer be limited to the first announcement of the Gospel to peoples *not yet evangelized* in and from their cultural identity. This *territorial sphere* of missionary activity is still extensive. It encompasses two-thirds of humanity or more than 4 billion people, mainly, but not exclusively, in Africa and Asia. The pope admits that this situation also exists in traditionally Christian regions, like Latin America (consider the urgent missionary situation of so many indigenous peoples and Afro-American and Asian American populations, perhaps one-third of the continent's inhabitants). Whereas the territorial sphere is perduring, related to people with centuries-old religions and cultures there are new situations, one 'social' and the other 'cultural'. The distinction I see is this. The 'social sphere' refers to new ways of living together or of structuring relationships among human groups. The 'cultural sphere' refers to new value systems and new ways of thinking. The first non-geographical sphere pertains to new *social* worlds and realities. It is the situation of those human groups involved in the phenomena of urbanization and migration, and particularly the new cultures of the poor, the marginalized and of youth. John Paul even dares to affirm that big cities should be 'the privileged places' of *ad gentes* mission today. The third sphere of *ad gentes* mission and the second non-territorial sphere are the *cultural areas or modern 'Areopagi'*, towards which the Church's missionary activity should be directed. A modern 'Areopagus' (a public meeting place) is the world of social communication, which shapes and diffuses new modern and post-modern cultural models. Another 'Areopagus' of the modern world is constituted by the phenomena of generalized awareness (John XXIII and the Constitution *Gaudium et spes* called them 'signs of the times') regarding human rights, promotion of women and children, integrity of creation and the culture of politics, economics and scientific investigation.

In the teaching of John Paul II, all of these human situations or 'spheres of mission', whether historic-geographical or socio-cultural, demand *ad gentes* missionary activity. The traditional territorial sphere refers broadly to *traditional cultures*, the peoples of Africa and Asia and the culturally non-Western populations of America, perhaps somewhat 'Christianized' historically, but hardly evangelized. The new, non-geographical spheres, the social and cultural spheres, refer to *new cultures* or new cultural situations. All of these require the attention and response of the missionary Church.

I believe that it is in an effort to urge new forms of missionary activity towards those distanced from the Church because of new socio-cultural and religious situations, that Pope John Paul II uses two original ways of speaking: the 'new evangelization' of *Redemptoris missio* 33 and the 'new spheres' of mission or 'modern Areopagi' in number 37. While *ad gentes* mission is directed to those who are 'not yet evangelized' in their traditional culture or new cultural situation, there is another situation, that of those who are 'no longer Christians', for whom a 'new evangelization' is necessary. These are entire groups of baptized people in the countries of ancient Christendom for whom Jesus is not really important, who maintain their distance from the Church and have lost the living sense of Christian faith.

Does this new evangelization of the de-Christianized qualify as missionary activity *in its specific sense*? It certainly does not fit into the category of ordinary pastoral activity to the faithful who belong to mature ecclesial communities and who are already committed to universal mission. Missionary activity in the specific sense is an evangelization of human groups among whom Christ and his Gospel are not known and who do not belong to the visible Church. Some of these groups are 'not yet Christians'. Others are 'no longer Christians'. Because of this, many of us Latin American missiologists are convinced that the 'new evangelization' of Pope John Paul II is a form of missionary activity in the specific sense.

If the 'new evangelization' is a dimension of *ad gentes* missionary activity, why is it necessary or opportune to create a new department in the Roman Curia dedicated to this problematic? After all, we know that the Congregation for the Evangelization of Peoples, traditionally known as Propaganda Fide, already exists, and has existed for almost 500 years. Here, I offer some very personal opinions. I have no way of knowing whether they correspond to the thought of Pope Emeritus Benedict. As a former National Director of the Pontifical Mission Societies in Bolivia (1985–9) and as Past President of the International Association of Catholic Missiologists (2000–4), I have had a limited experience of dealing with that missionary dicastery. Obviously my observations are rather superficial, generalized and subject to nuancing or correction.

On the one hand, what I have observed is that Propaganda Fide has existed principally to supervise the ecclesiastical organization and operations of the so-called mission territories. Its scope of action is vast, embracing two-thirds of humanity. It extends to dozens of Apostolic Vicariates and Prefectures in certain geographical areas (such as Latin America and the Middle East) as well as over a thousand missionary jurisdictions elevated to the category of dioceses and archdioceses in Africa, Asia and Oceania. The nature of its task seems to be mostly juridical (e.g. the naming of bishops in these jurisdictions) and economic (the financing of the operations of the Church in these areas). The Congregation has inherited an inevitable historical and structural burden. I believe it would be unrealistic to expect that it re-orientate itself to attend to the challenges presented by the multitude of 'new missionary situations' that are not territorial but rather social and cultural.

On the other hand, I have been able to observe that the new departments of the Holy See created principally after Vatican II, the Pontifical Councils are more agile and better equipped to attend to the challenges in their particular field of apostolate. I have had direct operative relations with the Pontifical Councils for Promoting Christian Unity and for Interreligious Dialogue and indirect or occasional contacts with the Councils for the Laity, Cultures and Justice and Peace. I have observed that the 'staff people' in these Councils are chosen for their academic preparation and competency in the specialization of the department.

I believe that Pope Benedict, concerned about the multiple 'new missionary situations' that call for a 'new evangelization', considered it opportune to create a new Pontifical Council charged with responding to this challenge. Archbishop Fisichella and the staff people were chosen for their competency in the field of evangelization. We know that Benedict XVI, like his predecessor, John Paul II, showed in his teaching ministry a particular concern for the re-evangelization of de-Christianized human groups in Europe. But should the call for a 'new evangelization' be limited to that continent? Is a new department of the Vatican to be created for the needs of one continent? At present, over 60 per cent of the world's Catholics live in Latin America, Africa and Asia. In these continents the challenges presented by Pentecostalism, the encounter with new and traditional cultures and the dialogue with other religions are greater challenges than de-Christianization. John Paul II obviously was not thinking of limiting his concern for the 'new evangelization' to the continent of Europe. In the 1980s, he was calling for a 'new evangelization' in Latin America. After giving a specific definition to the term in *Redemptoris missio* 33, he insisted that 'new evangelization' be one of the three guiding themes of the IV General Conference of the Latin American

Episcopate (Santo Domingo, 1992). Obviously, he did not have the intention of limiting it to Europe or to the phenomenon of de-Christianization.

I have tried to show in these pages my belief that the idea of the 'new evangelization' had its origins in Latin American missiological reflection, and that the use of the term in Puebla in 1979 was a decisive influence on the thinking of John Paul II. I have been a witness of the process in which all of this happened. I hope that these observations and reflections may be of some use to some of my sisters and brothers in Church as the new Pontifical Council to Promote the New Evangelization is being set up. Surely, this reality will have some resonance or repercussion in the life of local Churches and Episcopal Conferences.

4

Christ, Culture and the New Evangelization

Tracey Rowland

In the year 381 AD, St Gregory of Nazianzus, who was a veteran of the Council of Constantinople, wrote: 'To tell the truth, I am convinced that every assembly of bishops is to be avoided, for I have never experienced a happy ending to any council; not even the abolition of abuses . . . but only ambition or wrangling about what was taking place.'[1] St Gregory's friend, St Basil the Great, held a similar judgement. He spoke of the 'shocking disorder and confusion' generated by Church Councils. In the nineteenth century, Blessed John Henry Newman concluded that Councils had 'generally two characteristics – a great deal of violence and intrigue on the part of the actors in them, and a great resistance to their definitions on the part of portions of Christendom'.[2] Closer to home, in our own time, the British historian Philip Trower has described the conflict over different interpretations of the Second Vatican Council as nothing less than a 'theological star wars', played out over the heads of the faithful.[3] This chapter focuses not so much on the fallout from the star wars as on the Christocentric reading which flows through the magisterial works of John Paul II and Benedict XVI.

The Christocentric accent of the Second Vatican Council

In a reflection on the Second Vatican Council, written in 1975 in what were the final years of the papacy of Paul VI, Professor Joseph Ratzinger concluded that

[1] Cited by Joseph Ratzinger, *Principles of Catholic Theology* (San Francisco: Ignatius, 1987), p. 368.
[2] Cited in Ian Ker, 'Newman, the Councils and Vatican II', *Communio: International Catholic Review* 28 (Winter, 2001), pp. 708–28 (p. 714).
[3] Philip Trower, *Turmoil and Truth: The Historical Roots of the Modern Crisis in the Catholic Church* (San Francisco: Ignatius, 2003), p. 32.

when viewed by those who live through them or at least close to their time, nearly all Councils seem to have destroyed equilibrium and created a crisis.[4] However, he was equally certain that when viewed from the distance of centuries, things tend to look rather more positive. In a preface to the *Theological Highlights of Vatican II*, published in 1966, Ratzinger was already trying to transcend the divisions between what he termed the clichés of progressive and conservative interpretations of the Council. He described his reflections as an attempt to 'delineate the inner aspects, the spiritual profile of the Council'.[5] He went on to say that the idea of 'renewal' had a twofold intention – 'its point of reference is contemporary man in his reality and in his world, taken as it is. But the measure of its renewal is Christ, as scripture witnesses Him'.[6] Recalling Paul VI's Opening Address to the second session of the Council, Ratzinger acknowledged that 'while the accents can be variously placed', what most impressed him was 'how Christ-centric it was'.[7]

Ratzinger's emphasis on the Christocentric accent was also shared by John Paul II. At the 1985 Synod of Bishops, called to reflect upon the Council's reception, Christocentrism emerged as one of the key Conciliar motifs. In particular, reference was made to paragraph 22 of *Gaudium et spes*, 'The Pastoral Constitution on the Church in the Modern World':

> The Truth is that only in the mystery of the incarnate Word does the mystery of man take on light. For Adam, the first man, was a figure of Him who was to come, namely Christ the Lord. Christ, the final Adam, by the revelation of the mystery of the Father, and His Love, fully reveals man to man himself and makes his supreme calling clear.

As the English theologian Paul McPartlan has noted, this particular paragraph appears to have been taken word for word from Henri de Lubac's book *Catholicisme*, first published in 1947. The central point of the paragraph is that the human person only understands his or her identity to the extent that she or he is open to a relationship with Christ. Christology is deemed necessary for any adequate anthropology. Christ is the eschatological Adam to whom the first Adam already pointed, the true image of God who transforms man once more into a likeness of God. By emphasizing this paragraph, John Paul II and Cardinal Ratzinger, as he was, effectively undercut any secularizing potential of

---

[4] Ratzinger, *Principles of Catholic Theology*, p. 369.
[5] Ratzinger, *Theological Highlights of Vatican II* (New York: Paulist Press, 1966), p. 2.
[6] Ibid.
[7] Ibid., p. 40.

the document which was notorious for being loosely drafted. If Christology is a necessary component of any adequate anthropology, then secular humanism is always inadequate. This was Henri de Lubac's thesis in *The Drama of Atheistic Humanism*. According to this reading, the point of *Gaudium et spes* was not to accommodate Catholicism to the culture of modernity, but to affirm certain aspirations of so-called modern man, such as the longing for human freedom and self-fulfilment, and to argue that only a Christocentric anthropology has any hope of realizing these legitimate aspirations. The Christocentric accent, which Ratzinger had detected in the address of Paul VI to the second session of the Council, and which he had praised in his commentary of 1966, finally started to overtake an earlier, self-secularizing accommodation to modernity interpretation during the papacy of John Paul II (1978–2005).

Notwithstanding Paul VI's own Christocentric accent, the accommodation to modernity interpretation dominated during his pontificate. One of the buzz-words in vogue at the time of the Council was *aggiornamento*, or renewal. John XXIII had spoken of the need for theological and ecclesial renewal and he had noted that while the beliefs of the Church do not change the language in which they are expressed is not so immutable. As a consequence, the word *aggiornamento*, literally renewal, was often interpreted as a pastoral call to 'correlate' the teachings and the practices of the faith to the avant-garde elements in Western culture of the 1960s and 70s. The notion of correlate quickly mutated into the notion of 'accommodate'. This interpretation of *Gaudium et spes* was widely fostered in the theological publications of Edward Schillebeeckx OP and others associated with the *Concilium* journal. At a recent symposium on the 'Enduring Relevance of Edward Schillebeeckx for Contemporary Theology', Professors Lieven Boeve and Ben Vedder noted that the implication of Schillebeeckx's theology is that 'Tradition is not unchanging; it constantly relates to the spirit of the times.'[8]

Whatever one makes of Schillebeeck's view of tradition, and arguably it is not one that Benedict XVI shared, it is a fact that in the 1960s and 70s the mountain of publications critical of various dimensions of the culture of modernity to which Schillebeeckx and his followers were busily trying to correlate the faith, with devastating pastoral consequences in Belgium and Holland, and wherever else the strategy was implemented, had yet to be written. Ecclesial leaders had decided to embrace modernity just as it was beginning to be subjected to a powerful critique by the non-Catholic intellectual elite. Paradoxically, it was in

---

[8] Lieven Boeve and Ben Vedder, 'In Memoriam Edward Schillebeeckx, OP (1914–2009)', in Lieven Boeve, Frederiek Depoortere and Stephan van Erp (eds), *Edward Schillebeeckx and Contemporary Theology* (London: T&T Clark, 2010), p. x.

trying desperately hard to be 'modern' that the Church in the final decades of the
twentieth century made itself look very much behind the times. In this context,
the Canadian philosopher Kenneth Schmitz observed that in the 1960s Catholic
intellectuals did not think about the culture of modernity, since this was not
part of their conceptual framework. All they had was the category 'modern
philosophy'.[9] In other words, they were dealing with a complex sociological
phenomenon they did not fully comprehend because they were only working
across the philosophical dimension, not the multifaceted and inter-linking
dimensions which require a more interdisciplinary analysis. While there were
some exceptional scholars who had a broader perspective, such as Romano
Guardini at the University of Munich and Hans Urs von Balthasar in Switzerland,
neither of whom attended the Council, Schmitz's sociological generalization is
insightful. The historian John O'Malley was later to write: 'At the time of the
Council we did not think to ask from it any consistent theoretical foundation for
aggiornamento, because most of us were not aware of the importance of having
one.'[10] The Protestant theologian Karl Barth was onto the problem as early as
1966 when in an interview with Pope Paul VI he asked the question: What does
aggiornamento mean? Accommodation to what?[11]

The answer given by John Paul II to such a question was, in effect, 'we don't
want to accommodate to anything, we want to re-center on Christ.' The Rector
of Mundelein seminary in Chicago, Fr Robert Barron, has expressed this idea
as, 'philosophy, ethics and cultural forms do not position him [Christ], rather he
positions them. To understand that reversal is to grasp the nettle of the Christian
thing.'[12] The same idea can be found in the document 'Faith and Inculturation'
of the International Theological Commission, published in the watershed year
of 1989:

> In the 'last times' inaugurated at Pentecost, the risen Christ, Alpha and Omega,
> enters into the history of peoples: from that moment, the sense of history and
> thus of culture is unsealed and the Holy Spirit reveals it by actualising and
> communicating it to all. The Church is the sacrament of this revelation and its
> communication. It recenters every culture into which Christ is received, placing
> it in the axis of the world which is coming and restores the union broken by the

---

[9]   Kenneth L. Schmitz, 'Postmodernism and the Catholic Tradition', *American Catholic Philosophical Quarterly* LXXIII/2 (1999), pp. 223–53 (p. 235).
[10] John O'Malley, *Tradition and Transition: Historical Perspectives on Vatican II* (Wilmington, DE: M. Glazier, 1989), p. 45.
[11] Karl Barth, *Ad Limina Apostolorum* (Edinburgh: St. Andrews Press, 1969), p. 20.
[12] Robert Barron, *The Priority of Christ: Toward a Post-Liberal Catholicism* (Grand Rapids, MI: Brazos Press, 2007), p. 341.

prince of this world. Culture is thus eschatologically situated; it tends toward its completion in Christ, but it cannot be saved except by associating itself with the repudiation of evil.[13]

John Paul II described the two alternative cultures, based on the two alternative axes – the axis of the Risen Christ and the axis of the Prince of this world – as a civilization of love and a culture of death. The culture of death is one whose foundational principles resist being centred on Christ and the world which is to come. Its hallmarks are that it treats human life as a commodity or mere biological product; it acknowledges no absolute truth, goodness or beauty and in the absence of such absolutes power becomes the only legitimate political currency. These hallmarks have been well catalogued in the encyclicals of the post-Conciliar pontiffs. However, more positively, on the topic of the civilization of love, which is the objective of the new evangelization, there are key insights to be found in the Trinitarian encyclicals of John Paul II. The encyclicals *Redemptor hominis* (1979), *Dives in misericordia* (1980) and *Dominum et vivificantem* (1986) each addressed the issue of the human person's relationship with one of the Persons of the Holy Trinity. Taken as a trilogy, they testify to the dramatic seriousness with which John Paul II took the notion of Christocentrism. In *Redemptor hominis* (10.1), John Paul II wrote: 'The man who wishes to understand himself thoroughly . . . must draw near to Christ. He must, so to speak, enter into him with all his own self, he must appropriate and assimilate the whole of the reality of the Incarnation and Redemption in order to find himself.' For those uncertain what 'assimilating the whole of the reality of the Incarnation' might mean, in *Dominum et vivificantem* (50), John Paul II added:

> The Incarnation of God the Son signifies the taking up into the unity with God not only of human nature, but in this human nature, in a sense, of everything that is 'flesh': the whole of humanity, the entire visible and material world. The Incarnation then, also has a cosmic significance, a cosmic dimension. The 'first-born of all creation', becoming incarnate in the individual humanity of Christ, unites himself in some way with the entire reality of man, which is 'flesh' – and in this reality with all 'flesh', with the whole of creation.

With reference to the need to 'assimilate the whole reality of redemption' in *Dives in misericordia* (7.4), John Paul II concluded:

> The Cross . . . upon which Christ conducts his final dialogue with the Father, emerges from the very heart of the love that man, created in the image and

---

[13] International Theological Commission, 'Faith and Inculturation', *Origins* 18/47 (1989), pp. 800–7.

likeness of God, has been given as a gift, according to God's paternal plan. God, as Christ has revealed him, does not merely remain closely linked with the world as the Creator and the ultimate source of existence. He is also father: he is linked to man, whom he called to existence in the visible world, by a bond still more intimate than that of creation. It is love which not only creates the good but also grants participation in the very life of God: Father, Son and Holy Spirit.

These are just three of the many paragraphs that could be selected from the works of John Paul II which touch upon the theme of deification, the notion that the human person has been made in the image of God to grow into the likeness of Christ.

In his book *Divine Likeness: Toward a Trinitarian Anthropology of the Family*, Cardinal Ouellet linked this Trinitarian anthropology to the sacramental theology of marriage. He argued that we need to 'understand the . . . exchange of love between man and woman within the horizon of the *imago Dei*, as the couple's participation in the exchange of "gifts" between the divine Persons'.[14] Ouellet has also described marriage as a 'supernatural work of art, which shines in the midst of society as a real symbol of the Church indissolubly united to Christ'.[15]

These themes of deification and the nuptial mystery are subsequently amplified through the encyclicals and apostolic exhortations of Benedict XVI, though where the early encyclicals of the papacy of John Paul II focused on the human person's relationship with a particular Person of the Holy Trinity, the encyclicals of the papacy of Benedict XVI have made their way through the theological virtues. There has been one on love and one on hope and the anticipated third encyclical on faith was drafted by Benedict but promulgated as the first encyclical of the pontificate of Francis. The theological virtues of faith, hope and love each work on the faculties of the soul, the intellect, the memory and the will, to assist the person's spiritual growth, thereby deepening the level of intimacy with God. Without the work of the theological virtues, no intimacy with God would be possible.

The relationship of love and reason

Another and related central theme in the pontificate of Benedict was the notion that love and reason are the 'twin pillars of all reality'. In his *Introduction*

[14] Marc Ouellet, *Divine Likeness: Toward a Trinitarian Anthropology of the Family* (Grand Rapids, MI: Wm B. Eerdmans, 2006), p. 100.
[15] Ibid., p. 99.

to Christianity, first published in 1968, and subsequently translated into 17 languages, Ratzinger wrote that, with the arrival of Christianity, purely philosophical thinking was transcended on two fundamental points: whereas the philosophical God is essentially self-centred, thought simply contemplating itself; the God of faith is basically defined by relationship and whereas for the philosophical god, thought is divine, for Christianity, love is divine.[16] He further argued that the fact that the Christian God is personal is at the same time an option for the primacy of the particular over the universal, and of freedom as against the primacy of some cosmic necessity. The *Logos* of St. John's prologue completely transcends the *logos* of the Stoics since a 'world created and willed on the risk of freedom and love is no longer mathematics'.[17] This theme can also be found in Cardinal Ratzinger's 1999 millennium address to the scholars of the Sorbonne. In this speech, he concluded that one of the most important Patristic insights is the notion that 'within the ordering of religion to a rational view of reality, the primacy of the *Logos* and the primacy of love were revealed to be one and the same'.[18] Love and reason are therefore 'the twin pillars of all reality'.[19]

Commenting on Pope Benedict's interest in the integration of the cognitive and affective dimensions of the human person, Pablo Blanco Sarto published the following helpful summary in the *Anglican Theological Review*:

> Ratzinger offers a description of the Christian faith in personalist terms: that is to say, he focuses on the effect of faith on the existence and moral condition of the believer, just as the *Weltanschauung* of existentialism sustains the philosophy of dialogue in which Ratzinger was formed. We have to take into account the personal character of every act of faith: it is an action of understanding that we find through a meeting and a personal relationship and, in this way, an act that involves the human person completely: [the]intelligence, [the] feelings and [the] will.[20]

The relationship between the affective and the cognitive dimensions of the human person was also a central theme in the works of Romano Guardini

---

[16] Joseph Ratzinger, *Introduction to Christianity* (San Francisco: Ignatius, 1990), pp. 147–8.

[17] Ibid., p. 160.

[18] Joseph Ratzinger, '2000 Years after What?' address at the Sorbonne, Paris, November 27, 1999; quotation in text taken from translation of Maria Klepecka based on the Polish translation published in *Christianitas* 3/4 (2000), pp. 11–23.

[19] Joseph Ratzinger, *Truth and Tolerance: Christian Belief and World Religions* (San Francisco: Ignatius, 2003), p. 183. For a penetrating analysis of the relationship between love and reason in the theology of St Thomas Aquinas and the theology of Hans Urs von Balthasar, see David C. Schindler, 'Towards a Non-Possessive Concept of Knowledge: On the Relation between Reason and Love in Aquinas and Balthasar', *Modern Theology* 22/4 (October 2006), pp. 577–607.

[20] Pablo Blanco Sarto, 'Logos and Dia-Logos: Faith, Reason (and Love) According to Joseph Ratzinger', *Anglican Theological Review* 92/3 (2010), pp. 499–509 (p. 506).

(1885–1965), who was mentioned earlier as one of those Catholic scholars influential in the Conciliar era who had thought about the components of what we now call the culture of Modernity. Guardini was one of the young Ratzinger's intellectual heroes. Ratzinger was later to write, 'we were taught by Guardini that the essence of Christianity is not an idea, not a system of thought, not a plan of action. The essence of Christianity is a Person: Jesus Christ himself.'[21] This idea becomes the foundation stone of the encyclical *Deus caritas est*. In various homilies and speeches, Benedict XVI sent a message that Dominican *Veritas* and Franciscan *Caritas et amor* are equally important and that spiritual pathologies arise when one or the other becomes eclipsed in personal and ecclesial life.

The area in which this has been a huge problem is religious education. Before the Second Vatican Council, there was a focus on the cognitive dimension but there was often a poor integration of dogmatic theology and spirituality. After the Council, the pendulum swung in the opposite direction. The content became rather shallow, hard areas were glossed over and controversial issues were often left out altogether. Religious Education became sitting around in a circle talking about one's most intimate spiritual experiences. Apart from its lack of a cognitive dimension and thus its propensity to bore the brighter students towards atheism, it was a huge invasion of personal privacy. As has so often been the case in ecclesial history, religious education needs to find a middle path between two extremes. On the one hand, there is the danger of returning to an overly rationalist propositional model, where students are asked merely to master a body of knowledge – to see Christianity as merely an intellectual framework. As Henri de Lubac warned in the 1940s, there is a danger of deluding ourselves into believing that we have tamed the *mystery* of God, and that we have said all there is to be said by means of correct propositions. On the other hand, an overly affective approach leaves students vulnerable to thinking that God is like an elephant, some people get hold of his ears, others his tail, others his trunk and so on. In other words, there is the danger of having students leave Catholic schools without any sense of what is or is not Catholic belief. Students who leave the Catholic education system knowing little more than that Christ was kind to the socially marginalized will not be even nominally Catholic for long.

It would appear that the middle path through these dangers has been indicated due to the extraordinary work of Sofia Cavalletti and her Catechesis

---

[21] Joseph Ratzinger, 'Guardini on Christ in our Century', *Crisis Magazine* (June 1996), pp. 11–5 (p. 15).

of the Good Shepherd. Through the use of concrete materials, children as young as 3 years of age can be enchanted by the wonder of God and inducted. Their induction into the life of the Church is achieved by simple, concrete presentations of the sacraments, the liturgy and the Scriptures, all conducted within the framework of authentic Christian teaching. The doctrinal propositions serve as boundary markers indicating the way rather than as substitutes for the mystery itself. Much of the challenge involved in the renewal of Religious Education involves freeing teachers themselves from one or other of these deeply rooted extreme approaches.[22]

Hindrances to a Christocentric new evangelization

In addition to fostering a form of catechesis which engages both the intellectual and affective dimensions of the person, catechists need to be attentive to some of the hindrances to a Christocentric new evangelization. These hindrances might be classified under the umbrella of 'self-secularizing ideas and practices'.

Secularist interpretations of the conciliar document *Gaudium et spes*

A first class of hindrances might be classified as secularist interpretations of the Conciliar document *Gaudium et spes*, particularly of paragraph 36, which states:

> If by the autonomy of earthly affairs we mean that created things and societies themselves enjoy their own laws and values which must gradually be deciphered, put to use, and regulated by men, then it is entirely right to demand that autonomy. Such is not merely required by modern men, but harmonizes also with the will of the Creator. For by the very circumstances of their having been created, all things are endowed with their own stability, truth, goodness, proper laws and order.

This paragraph, or at least the bit about all things being 'endowed with their own stability, truth, goodness, proper laws and order' is a paraphrase of

---

[22] See, for example: Sofia Cavalletti, *The Religious Potential of the Child: Experiencing Scripture and Liturgy with Young Children* (Chicago: Liturgy Training Publications, 1992); Sofia Cavalletti, *History's Golden Thread: The History of Salvation* (Chicago: Liturgy Training Publications, 1999); Sofia Cavalletti and Patricia Coulter, *Ways to Nurture the Relationship with God* (Chicago: Liturgy Training Publications, 2010).

Question 85 of the *Summa Theologica* of St Thomas Aquinas and Book VI: 12 of St Augustine's *De Trinitate*. It is perfectly capable of a non-self-secularizing interpretation. However the use of the word 'autonomy' has given rise to a variety of interpretations, most broadly the idea that God and the supernatural realm is one thing and the world and so-called secular realm is another and that the latter exists in a state of total independence from the former. In theological parlance, a relationship of total independence is said to be an 'extrinsic' relationship. There have been many populariest interpretations of this paragraph which view the relationship as extrinsic.

Cardinal Angelo Scola of Milan has recently complained of precisely this problem. He has lamented that there is a 'latent ambiguity' around the interpretation of the principle of the 'autonomy of earthly affairs' mentioned in paragraph 36 of *Gaudium et spes*. With reference to some of the interpretations of this paragraph, Scola suggested that it might be right to ask 'if the Catholic world, called to address the great contemporary anthropological and ethical challenges, has not been co-responsible, whether by naivety, delay or lack of attention, for the current [secularist] state of things'.[23] According to Scola, paragraph 36 is an acknowledgement that there is a realm of life which is the responsibility of the laity (cf. *Apostolicam actuositatem*, 7). In other words, it is a paragraph drafted to send a message to the world that the Catholic Church is not in favour of theocracy. It is not, however, authority for the proposition that there might be aspects of life which have no intrinsic relationship to the Creator.

A concrete illustration of the ambiguity fostered by the use of the word 'autonomy' may be found in the following paragraph from Robert A. Krieg's work, *Catholic Theologians in Nazi Germany*, which is in many ways a very interesting and well-researched book. Speaking of two different species of Catholics, Krieg concluded:

> On the one hand, insofar as they stand in the theological orientation of Pope Pius XI and Catholic Action, they are intent on transforming secular society into a Christian one, dedicated to Christ the King. On the other hand, to the degree that they are inspired by the Second Vatican Council, they are guided by a respect for the 'rightful autonomy' of human affairs and a commitment to what Pope Paul VI identified as 'the progress of peoples', anchored in a pledge to defend human rights.[24]

[23] Angela Scola, 'El Peligro de una Falsa "Autonomia"', *Humanitas: Revista de Antropologica y Cultura Christianas* 66 (Autumn 2012), pp. 296–301 (p. 299).
[24] Robert A. Krieg, *Catholic Theologians in Nazi Germany* (London: Continuum, 2004), p. 175.

The problem with the idea expressed here is that there is a false dichotomy – the choice offered is between a Christian society and one 'committed to "the progress of peoples", anchored in a pledge to defend human rights'. The whole point of John Paul II's interpretation of the Council is that the progress of peoples runs on a Christocentric trajectory. Removing Christ from the project, and in particular, trying to foster an account of human rights which is not based on the theological anthropology outlined in John Paul II's various encyclicals, is a recipe for secularism. Nonetheless, Krieg's dichotomy is a good illustration of the split that has occurred within the Catholic community in the post-Conciliar era. It is often characterized as a division between those interested in social justice issues and those interested in the sacrality of life issues, and between those focused on the world and those focused on heaven. If one scans the encyclicals of John Paul II and Benedict XVI, it is clear that they regarded this kind of bifurcation as pathological. Benedict XVI summarized the problem in his encyclical *Caritas in veritate* (2009) when he said that 'a humanism that excludes God is an inhuman humanism' (78).

This is a very theologically complex area which requires, among other things, an understanding of what John Paul II meant when he spoke of Christ uniting himself with the whole of creation. To understand the meaning of autonomy one needs to understand, for example, that God is in all things – not as part of their essence, or as an accident, but as an agent is present to that upon which it works.[25] Joseph Ratzinger addressed the issue obliquely in his work *The End of Time*:

> The *exitus*, or better, the free creative act of God, does in fact aim at *reditus*, but this does not mean that created being is revoked. Rather, it means that the coming into its own of the creature as an autonomous creature answers back in freedom to the love of God, accepts its creation as a command to love, so that a dialogue of love begins – that entirely new unity that only love can create. In it the being of the other is not absorbed, not annulled, but rather becomes wholly what it is precisely in giving itself.[26]

To return to Cardinal Scola, in an essay on the Christocentrism of John Paul II, he concluded with the rather chilling observation that 'only Christians can make the antichrist possible since the anti-Christ is possible only if he maintains a

---

[25] Thomas Aquinas, *Summa Theologiae: A Guide and Commentary* (Brian Davies (ed. and trans.); Oxford: Oxford University Press, 2014), p. Q.1.

[26] Joseph Ratzinger, *The End of Time* (Mahwah, NJ: Paulist Press, 2004), pp. 20–1.

Christianity without Christ as the point of reference.'[27] A similar conclusion has been reached by the Anglican theologian Oliver O'Donovan. O'Donovan argues that the possibilities open to contemporary societies and people with a history and memory of the Gospel proclamation do not include naïve malevolence, but only a formation that is demonic to the extent that it is not redeemed and redemptive. For O'Donovan, the 'redemptive reality within history becomes the occasion for a disclosure of the historical possibilities of evil, an evil shaped in imitation and replication of the redemptive good.'[28]

Reduction of the kingdom of God to the values of the kingdom

This leads to a second problematic or self-secularizing practice, described by Ratzinger in the following terms:

> . . . a Christianity and a theology that reduce[s] the core of Jesus ['s] message, the 'kingdom of God' to the 'values of the kingdom' while identifying these values with the main watchwords of political moralism, and proclaiming them, at the same time, to be the synthesis of all religions – all the while forgetting about God, despite the fact that it is precisely he who is the subject and the cause of the kingdom of God . . . does not open the way to regeneration, it actually blocks it.[29]

As early as 1963, Hans Urs von Balthasar was onto this problem. He argued that:

> The Gospel and the Church are plundered like a fruit tree, but the fruits, once separated from the tree, go rotten and are no longer fruitful. The 'ideas' of Christ cannot be separated from Him, and so they are of no use to the world unless they are fought for by Christians who believe in Christ, or at least by men who are inwardly, though unconsciously, open to Him and governed by Him. Radiance is only possible when the radiant centre is active and alive. There can be no shining from stars long dead.[30]

---

[27] Angela Scola, '"Claim" of Christ, "Claim" of the World: On the Trinitarian Encyclicals of John Paul II', *Communio* 18 (Fall 1991), pp. 322–31 (p. 331).

[28] Oliver O'Donovan, *The Desire of the Nations: Rediscovering the Roots of Political Theology* (Cambridge: Cambridge University Press, 1996), p. 251.

[29] Joseph Ratzinger, 'Europe in the Crisis of Cultures', *Communio: International Catholic Review* 32 (2005), pp. 345–56 (pp. 346–7).

[30] Hans Urs von Balthasar, *Das Ganze in Fragment, Aspekte de Geschichtestheologie* (Einsiedeln, 1963) as quoted in John Saward, 'Chesterton and Balthasar: The Likeness is Greater', *Chesterton Review* XXII/3 (August 1996), p. 314.

Von Balthasar also quoted the somewhat more robust statement of the French writer Georges Bernanos, to the effect that every time the Church sends out some idea wrapped up in politically correct language, like 'little red riding hood with her pigtails and basket she gets raped at the next corner by some slogan in uniform'.[31]

This practice of muting the Christocentric button is a popular notion in Catholic institutions such as schools and hospitals where people are fearful of offending the non-Catholic users. According to this mentality, Christ is not to be mentioned for fear of upsetting Buddhists or Muslims or anyone who pays homage to a different deity. Only the fruits of a Christian culture can be affirmed, not Christ himself. The whole of Benedict XVI's encyclical *Caritas in veritate* (2009) can be read as a strong criticism of this mentality. The American Protestant theologian, Stanley Hauerwas, is similarly critical of practices of this kind. He argues that 'postmodernism is the outworking of mistakes in Christian theology correlative to the attempt to make Christianity "true" apart from faithful witness.' In other words, post-modernity would not have arisen but for people trying to market Christianity without Christ. Hauerwas concludes that:

> Modernity, drawing on the metaphysics of a transcendent god, was the attempt to be historical without Christ. Postmodernity, facing the agony of living in history with no end, is the denial of history. In the wake of such a denial, the only remaining comfort is the shopping mall, which gives us the illusion of creating histories through choice, thus hiding from us the reality that none of us can avoid having our lives determined by money. Money, in modernity, is the institutionalization of the univocity of being that Scotus thought necessary to ensure the unmediated knowledge of God.[32]

Conflation of the concept of evangelization with the practice of marketing

A third problematic and self-secularizing practice is to conflate the concept of evangelization with the practice of marketing. If one approaches evangelization as a marketing campaign, complete with strategic plans, motivational posters and key performance indicators, it is likely to fail because the work of the grace cannot be subjected to the laws of supply and demand and other market forces.

---

[31] Hans Urs von Balthasar, *Bernanos: An Ecclesial Existence* (San Francisco: Ignatius, 1996), p. 43.
[32] Stanley Hauerwas, 'The Christian Difference or Surviving Postmodernism', in Graham Ward (ed.), *The Blackwell Companion to Postmodern Theology* (Oxford: Blackwell, 2007), pp. 144–62 (p. 149).

God is not a commodity. There needs to be a personal encounter with Christ which is something that cannot be artificially manufactured or conjured. The following statements in the works of Joseph Ratzinger underscore this point:

> Saints, in fact reformed the Church in depth, not by working up plans for new structures, but by reforming themselves. What the Church needs in order to respond to the needs of man in every age is holiness, not management.[33]

> The saints were all people of imagination, not functionaries of apparatuses.[34]

> I have said very often that I think we have too much bureaucracy. Therefore, it will be necessary in any case to simplify things. Everything should not take place by way of committees; there must even also be the personal encounter.[35]

> St. Paul was effective, not because of brilliant rhetoric and sophisticated strategies, but rather because he exerted himself and left himself vulnerable in the service of the Gospel.[36]

In summary, one cannot approach the work of evangelization using the strategies of corporate management because the work of evangelization is rather more personal in nature. To use Max Weber's terminology, there is a difference between charismatic authority which is personal and bureaucratic authority which is impersonal. Weber noted that the position of Catholic religious is a perfect example of charismatic authority. In other words, the authority does not arise from holding particular qualifications or having attended professional development sessions. It arises from a reputation for wisdom and holiness, for making good prudential judgements.

Since the post 1960s crisis in religious vocations, many lay people now find themselves undertaking works which were once undertaken by religious. While this is not a problem in itself, what is becoming a problem is how to retain a Catholic ethos in an institution where those in positions of responsibility have little or no scope for the exercise of their prudential judgement, or for being Christ-like, because almost every action they perform is regulated by policies and protocols. They answer not to God or the mother superior or their bishop but to boards of management which are usually stacked with lawyers and accountants whose major concern is to save money and protect the Church from law suits,

---

[33] Joseph Ratzinger with Vittorio Messori, *The Ratzinger Report: An Exclusive Interview on the State of the Church* (Salvator Attanasio and Graham Harrison (trans.); San Francisco: Ignatius Press, 1985), p. 53.

[34] Ibid., p. 67.

[35] Joseph Ratzinger, *Salt of the Earth: The Church at the End of the Millennium* (San Francisco: Ignatius, 1996), p. 266.

[36] Joseph Ratzinger, *Images of Hope* (San Francisco: Ignatius, 2006), p. 26.

not to take risks in the service of the Gospel. This is not to argue that there is no place for policy and protocols, or for advice from lawyers and accountants, but it is to draw attention to a problem addressed by Alasdair MacIntyre in many of his earlier writings: that modern corporate practices are set up precisely to protect individuals from having to exercise their prudential judgement or behave in a personal way. This gives rise to innumerable practical day-to-day problems for Church agencies. The structural forms of organizations do have an impact upon the possibilities for the work of evangelization and this is a contemporary pastoral problem which needs urgent interdisciplinary attention.

The condition of Western culture

Moving from self-secularizing practices to a summary pathology report on the condition of Western culture, David Bentley Hart, the author of *Atheist Delusions*, has argued that 'with the withdrawal of Christian culture, all the glories of the ancient world that it baptized and redeemed have perished with it in the general cataclysm.'[37] In other words, atheists do not sift through the debris and separate what they perceive to be the Christian junk from the classical Greek treasure. Everything that has ever been associated with Christian culture is tainted and rejected. Bentley Hart concludes that 'the only futures open to post-Christian culture are conscious nihilism with its inevitable devotion to death or the narcotic banality of the Last Man.'[38] Here the concept of a 'Last Man' is taken from Friedrich Nietzsche and refers to the type of person Australians call 'bogans', people with very limited cultural horizons who are mostly interested in transient satisfactions, people who live from one football game to the next, people who really have no principles for self-transcendence.

Bentley Hart's thesis is also consistent with the conclusion of Alexander Boot, author of the highly acclaimed book *How the West Was Lost*, although Boot adds the argument that the nihilist and the Last Man exist in a symbiotic relationship. Boot uses the label 'Modman nihilist' (i.e. a modern philosopher of nihilist disposition) to refer to the sophisticated academic type of nihilist and the label 'Modman Philistine' to refer to the type Nietzsche called the Last Man. Boot believes that Modman Nihilist and Modman Philistine are involved in a

---

[37] David Bentley Hart, 'God or Nothingness', in Carl E. Braaten and Christopher R. Seitz (eds), *I Am the Lord Your God: Christian Reflections on the Ten Commandments* (Grand Rapids, MI: Eerdmans, 2005), pp. 55–77 (p. 69).
[38] Ibid., pp. 71–2.

culture war against Catholic 'Westman' because, even though their two worlds rarely collide, and even though they are not consciously working together, their success is due to their combined social impact. The existence of one validates the behaviour and mind-set of the other. If Boot is right in this sociological analysis, it means that Christians need to be as worried by the Philistine Last Man as they are of the professional academic nihilist. Together they create a kind of anti-culture in which there are no standards, no gradations of excellence in any sphere of human activity outside of economic performance. Catholic youth need access to a high Catholic culture which is sufficiently attractive to compete with the nihilist and Philistine alternatives. In this context it is important to understand that the Nietzschean criticism of Christianity was not primarily that it was not *rational*, but that it was not *erotic*. The charge was that it promotes a boring bourgeois conformity that only appeals to people without talent. For young people to be attracted to the Christian option, that option has to appear as the more exciting, more erotic (in the sense of passionately idealistic), alternative.

At the root of the Philistine outlook is a rejection of the proposition that some modes of being and self-expression are actually superior to others. In some Western countries where liberation theology has been popular, those who seek to promote a high Catholic culture, or what Benedict XVI called 'the humanism of the Incarnation', are often criticized for their bourgeois, or worse, elitist attitudes. Their defence of beauty is construed as a symptom of having received an upper class education, something of which they should be ashamed should this be true. From the point of view of John Paul II or Benedict XVI, however, beauty is a transcendental property of being, and it deserves to be defended no less than truth and goodness. In a paper delivered at the Sacred Heart University in Milan in 1977, 1 year before his election to the papacy, Cardinal Wojtyła wrote that 'the ultimate danger of the new European culture is that a culture without clear values and well-defined forms can very easily become a consumer good.'[39] This, in a nutshell, is one of the problems with Modman Philistine.

Parallel criticisms of contemporary consumer junk-culture can also be found in the works of many non-Catholic authors, including the British writer Roger Scruton. Scruton has argued that to possess a culture is not only to possess a body of knowledge or expertise; it is not simply to have accumulated facts, references and theories. It is to possess a sensibility, a response, a way of seeing things, which is in some way redemptive. Thus culture is not a mere matter of

---

[39] Karol Wojtyła, *Person and Community: Selected Essays* (Theresa Sandok (trans.); New York: Peter Lang, 1993), p. 274, n. 15.

academic knowledge but of a mode of participation in various social practices. More specifically, Scruton argues that the high culture of Europe was built on the liturgical practices of the Church, and as a consequence, 'the art of European culture bears witness to the communion of the European peoples either by honouring or defiling the thought of God's incarnation.'[40] For Scruton, it is the belief in the Incarnation which holds Western culture together and neither the Euro nor Disneyland nor the hybrid Euro-Disney are adequate substitutes.

Conclusion

This chapter began with the young Professor Ratzinger's observation that while Church Councils seem to have a great propensity to create chaos for the generations who live through them, for the generations who come after them they can be seen in retrospect to have been a necessary corrective and a moment in history when seeds are sown for a harvest that is reaped at a later time. It may well be that for the generations that lie in the future Vatican II will be remembered as the Council that finally brought to a close the trauma of the Reformation through its profound Christocentrism, as the Council that brought to an end a whole series of unhelpful dualisms which had crept into the theological establishment after the Council of Trent, as the Council that emphasized that Christ himself is the revelation of the Father to humanity and through such an emphasis fostered a renewal of the Patristic insight that the meaning of life is found in the quest for deification, that is, an ever-deepening participation in the life of the Trinity. And it will no doubt be the case that Vatican II will be remembered as the Council that brought to an end the presentation of the Church's teaching about marriage in the language of contract law and Stoic philosophy, and in its place fostered a sacramental theology rooted in the nuptial mystery teachings of Pope John Paul II. In short-hand terms, it will be remembered as the Council that killed Jansenism. Finally, Vatican II will no doubt be remembered as the Council that fostered the *Communio* ecclesiology and thereby contributed significantly to a deeper understanding of the different and mutually supporting missions in the life of the Church, both clerical and lay.

It may also be the case that in the libraries of the great universities there will be collections of documents about things that happened in the 1960s and there will be books with titles like '1968 and all that', and someone will write

---

[40] Roger Scruton, *The Philosopher on Dover Beach* (Manchester: Carcanet, 1990), p. 123.

a thesis on the topic of whether there is any historical basis for the claim that in 1977 a priest said Mass in the swimming pool at the University of Sydney because he was trying to be 'relevant' to youth, or whether this is an urban myth. As Ratzinger wrote in his *Principles of Catholic Theology*:

> Whether or not the Council becomes a positive force in the history of the Church depends only indirectly on texts and organizations, the crucial question is whether there are individuals – saints – who, by their personal willingness, which cannot be forced, are ready to effect something new and living. The ultimate decision about the historical significance of Vatican Council II depends on whether or not there are individuals prepared to experience in themselves the drama of the separation of the wheat from the cockle and thus to give to the whole a singleness of meaning that it cannot gain from words alone.[41]

---

[41] Ratzinger, *Principles of Catholic Theology*, p. 377.

Part Two

The Church of
the New Evangelization

5

The Church: A People Sent in Mission

Susan K. Wood

What is new about the 'new evangelization'? While this topic hit headline Catholic news with the publication of the *Lineamenta* entitled 'The New Evangelization for the Transmission of the Christian Faith' (2011) in preparation for the XIII Ordinary General Assembly of the Synod of Bishops from 7 to 28 October 2012, this same document notes that this relatively new expression was introduced by Pope John Paul II during his apostolic visit to Poland in 1979.[1] It figured prominently in Pope John Paul II's encyclical *Redemptoris missio* (1990), which described it as addressing countries with ancient Christian roots, and occasionally younger churches as well, 'where entire groups of the baptized have lost a living sense of the faith, or even no longer consider themselves members of the Church, and live a life far removed from Christ and his Gospel'. *Redemptoris missio* stated that what is needed in this case is a 'new evangelization' or a 're-evangelization' (RM 33). Pope Francis issued his Apostolic Exhortation on evangelization, *Evangelii gaudium* on 24 November 2014.

This effort of new evangelization is addressed to primarily lukewarm Christians, former Christians or secular societies that were once Christian. Missionary activity proper, namely the mission *ad gentes*, by contrast, is directed towards '"peoples or groups who do not yet believe in Christ", "who are far from Christ", in whom the Church "has not yet taken root" and whose culture has not yet been influenced by the Gospel'. In other words,

---

[1] Other documents from the magisterium on evangelization include Vatican II, *Ad Gentes* (1965); Paul VI, *Evangelii Nuntiandi* (1975); John Paul II, *Redemptoris Missio* (1990); John Paul II, *Ecclesia in America* (1999); Congregation of the Doctrine of the Faith, *Dominus Iesus* (2000); Congregation for the Doctrine of the Faith, Doctrinal Note 'On Some Aspects of Evangelization' (2007); Francis, *Evangelii Gaudium* (2013).

'it is addressed to groups and settings which are non-Christian because the preaching of the Gospel and the presence of the Church are either absent or insufficient' (RM 34). *Redemptoris missio* cautions that there are no clear boundaries between the new evangelization, pastoral care of the faithful and missionary activity, and notes that there is a real and growing interdependence among these various saving activities of the Church. Even though *Redemptoris missio* makes it very clear that the new evangelization does not replace the more traditional missionary and evangelizing activities of the church, generally we can say that the new evangelization is directed *ad intra* to the members or former members or formerly Christian societies, while what we have known as the *missio ad gentes*, mission to the peoples, has been directed *ad extra*. *Redemptoris missio* says that each of these activities should be a credible sign and a stimulus for the other (RM 34).

Obviously, the need for such an effort is great. Pope Benedict XVI's concern for a secularized Europe was well known. In the United States, the second largest Christian group after Catholics comprises former Catholics. The *Lineamenta* describe the new evangelization as a spiritual activity 'capable of recapturing in our times the courage and forcefulness of the first Christians and the first missionaries' (5). The motivation of the effort of the new evangelization is to re-Christianize society and, yes, even the members of the Church. The reason for the need of this effort includes the usual human weaknesses and infidelities, consumerist culture, individualism, a spirit of relativism and just plain weariness. The new evangelization is issued as a call to conversion and a re-vitalization of Christian life.

The document from the Congregation for the Doctrine of the Faith, Doctrinal Note 'On Some Aspects of Evangelization' (2007), notes 'a growing confusion which leads many to leave the missionary command of the Lord unheard and ineffective' (cf. Mt. 28.19). The congregation cites the concern that missionary activities limit conscience and religious freedom and that 'some maintain that Christ should not be proclaimed to those who do not know him, nor should joining the Church be promoted, since it would also be possible to be saved without explicit knowledge of Christ and without formal incorporation in the Church' (3).

Evangelization is inseparable from mission, so in effect, the new evangelization, being focused *ad intra*, is a missionary effort directed at the lukewarm within the Church itself and at those people and societies who were once Christian. In the first part of this chapter, I link the new evangelization with the call to conversion. The second part relates the new evangelization to communion and community. The third part argues that the new evangelization needs to encompass mission *ad extra*, for the revival of Christianity has to be a revival of its missionary impetus. It cannot be turned in upon itself, but always needs to be turned outwards to the world. It argues that the new evangelization could be enriched by an emphasis on engagement and dialogue with secular culture. The new evangelization as comprising both *ad intra* and *ad extra* relationships can be summarized as a call to conversion, communion and solidarity, the themes of Pope John Paul II's apostolic exhortation, *Ecclesia in America* (1999).

Throughout, it will be evident that the 'new evangelization' is not particularly new insofar as a number of theological initiatives in addition to more practical efforts attempted to address the relevance of faith within a growing secular culture in the twentieth century. I argue that the new evangelization requires bold new initiatives, even if they risk failure, rather than a retreat to an ecclesiastical culture of the past that may appear to have embodied a robust Catholic culture, if faith is to speak to people of our time.

Called to conversion

The conversion required by the new evangelization is a retrieval of the capacity 'to listen and understand the words of the Gospel as a living and life-giving message' (*Lineamenta* 6).[2] How is this to be achieved? In the words of Paul, words that introduce chapter one of the *Lineamenta*, '. . . how are they to believe in him of whom they have never heard and how are they to hear without a preacher?' (Rom. 10.14). The Gospel must be proclaimed in way that transforms those who listen. This, of course, means not just transmitting information about the faith, but eliciting faith. According to Louis Marie-Chauvet's analysis of the Liturgy of the Word, the texts read in the liturgy belong to a canon accepted by the community, thereby indicating an authority of the texts acknowledged by the community. The ongoing reception of this canon officially received in the Church occurs as the assembly recognizes them as an exemplar of its own identity. The proclamation of these texts, as opposed to other non-canonical texts, gives the community its identity since the texts proclaim a past experience of the people of God as the living word of God for the community today. It is not

---

[2] Synod of Bishops, *Lineamenta*, 'The New Evangelization for the Transmission of the Christian Faith' (2011) in preparation for the XIII Ordinary General Assembly of the Synod of Bishops from 7 to 28 October 2012.

a past word – merely a historical word – but a living word for the community's life in the world in our time.[3]

This is where preaching differs from biblical exegesis. The first elicits faith; the second explains what the text meant when it was written or interprets it theologically. The ordained minister guarantees both the apostolicity of what is read and assures that these texts function as an exemplar of the community's identity. As a member of the assembly, he stands within the assembly and testifies that this text reflects the present life and faith of the community. Thus the four constitutive elements of the Liturgy of the Word are: (1) texts of past events accepted as authoritative; (2) texts proclaimed as living today; (3) their reception by a community recognizing its own identity in them and (4) ordained ministry that guarantees their apostolicity and exemplarity.[4] The word proclaimed becomes the autobiography of the community of faith. In order for this process to achieve the result of eliciting faith, the person who proclaims and preaches the word must be a person of deep faith, for the word preached is always an embodied word.

The temptation is often to reduce the message and revelation of Jesus to knowledge, but knowledge of itself does not save or liberate. Conversion occurs when God in Jesus Christ draws near to us and our lives are transformed in the encounter. Not only doctrine, but also the experiential, the moral and ethical dimensions of life, and justice are the matter of evangelization. Evangelization must touch people's lives where they live. The Protestant theologian Wolfhart Pannenberg once said that a church shrivels up and dies if it no longer sheds light on people's lives.[5]

Called to communion

Conversion calls us to relationship, both with God and then with God's people. This turning to God occurs so that we can discover again the love and fervour that may have been lost. Like the wife of Hosea, we need to allow ourselves to be lured into the wilderness so we can hear the tender words of God who removes the names of the Baals from our mouths, who renews covenant with us and who binds himself to us in faithfulness. In this conversion, God says 'You are my

---

[3] Louis-Marie Chauvet, *Symbol and Sacrament* (Collegeville, MN: Liturgical Press, 1995).
[4] Ibid., p. 210.
[5] Quoted in Louis McNeil, 'Evangelization', in *The New Dictionary of Theology* (Wilmington, DE: Michael Glazier, 1987), pp. 357–60 (p. 359).

people' and we say 'You are our God' (Hos. 2.14–23). We do not just hear this word addressed to us in the deepest recesses of our hearts; we also hear it in the word of God in proclamation within a faith community. As the *Lineamenta* says, 'The transmission of the faith is never an individual, isolated undertaking, but a communal, ecclesial event' (2).

Hearing the word of God as described in the call to conversion presupposes a faith already active with a community that can resonate with and recognize the faith that is proclaimed. The new evangelization cannot just be about individuals, but must also form communities of faith. Even though each of us is saved personally, the second chapter of *Lumen gentium* (Vatican II's 'Dogmatic Constitution on the Church'; LG) says that God has, however, willed to make women and men holy and to save them, not as individuals without any bond between them, but rather to make them into a people who might acknowledge him and serve him in holiness (LG 9). The task and gift of becoming holy is also the formation of a community; it is not an individualistic endeavour.

Faith communities require that people know each other, worship in common and share in the many activities in parish life. A community involves face-to-face relationships, mutual sharing of life's joys and sorrows and the exercise of shared responsibility for its common life. Most Catholics encounter the Church in their local parish or not at all. While not usurping the role of the pastor, a vibrant parish is a ministerial community, with the members contributing their charisms, under the discernment and ordering of the pastor, to their common life. A vibrant parish is engaged in *diakonia*, *martyria* and *leitourgia* – service to those in need, witness to the faith through catechesis, baptismal preparation classes, marriage preparation, evangelization and, not least, worship through well-prepared and prayerfully conducted liturgies incorporating preaching which has the power to move the hearts of the faithful.

A city parish in Louisville, Kentucky, on the verge of closure and rather moribund on account of the loss of residential neighbourhoods in the area, is now well-known for its experience of revitalization. This was accomplished through three strategies. The parish determined that it would have excellent preaching, excellent liturgical music, and that for its parish missional outreach it would be a hospital for all the disenfranchised people in the church – the divorced and remarried, the gays and lesbians and so forth. This was a three-pronged effort inclusive of word, sacrament and mission. A nearby Protestant theological centre now takes people there to see this parish as an example of congregational revitalization. This endeavour shows how worship and missional outreach mutually enrich each other.

Frankly, in the United States at least, the shortage of priests, which leads to the clustering of parishes and the closing of inner city parishes, militates against faith community formation. We need to find new models to keep faith communities alive in the absence of a resident pastor so we do not end up with anonymous communities where parishioners receive the religious ministrations of the ordained, but are not actively engaged in the faith community. Catholics have tended to have a priest-centred model of parishes. When the priest leaves, the parish closes. Although the ministerial priesthood differs essentially and not only in degree from the common priesthood of the faithful (LG 10), the church precedes any ministerial service to the church, ministry arises from the Church for the Church and the sacrament of Orders reflects the order of the church.[6] While it is imperative that these communities remain Eucharistic, it is as imperative that they be communities of faith, not just a collection of individuals.

The Rite of Christian Initiation of Adults (RCIA) is a process in many parishes that fosters individual conversion, growth and faith; at the same time, it initiates new members into a faith community. Within a theology of initiation, the parish is the contextualized and particular place of Christian formation. The Universal Church comes to event in a particular place, in particular circumstances, in a particular culture and with a particular community. The parish evangelizes, forms, initiates and nurtures new Christians. The RCIA marks a number of stages within a process of initiation that encompasses the entire life of the parish community. The initiation of adults is the responsibility of all the baptized,[7] not only through their active participation as sponsors and catechists, but also through the witness of their lives. As a baptismal community, the parish is a formation community in Christian living. The weakest link in the implementation of the RCIA, however, has been the period of mystagogia, the period after the reception of the sacraments of initiation when the new members are instructed in the meaning of that which they have received and deepen their new life. This is a point at which the new evangelization needs to be implemented.

Admittedly, other social and cultural factors beyond the issues of ordained ministry militate against the formation of faith communities such as the loss of ethnic neighbourhoods, the dispersion of extended families and the

---

[6] Susan K. Wood (ed.), 'Presbyteral Identity within Parish Identity', *Ordering the Baptismal Priesthood* (Collegeville, MN: Liturgical Press, 2003), pp. 175–94 (p. 177).
[7] International Commission on English in the Liturgy (ICEL), *Rite of Christian Initiation of Adults* (ICEL, 1985), p. 9.

individualistic secular culture of the twenty-first century. Even though the parish is the primary place of Christian formation, many other forms of intentional faith communities, prayer groups and communities of Christian service also embody the evangelical mission of the church and do not require ordained leadership.

Called to solidarity

The new evangelization would be short-circuited if these efforts were limited *ad intra* and the church retreated to a comfort zone in isolation from the rest of culture. The new evangelization calls us to engage in dialogue with the sectors of economy, scientific and technological research, and social communication because they, too, require evangelization (*Lineamenta* 6). The *Lineamenta* assert

> a new evangelization is synonymous with mission, requiring the capacity to set out anew, go beyond boundaries and broaden horizons. The new evangelization is the opposite of self-sufficiency, a withdrawal into oneself, a *status quo* mentality and an idea that pastoral programmes are simply to proceed as they did in the past. Today, a 'business as usual' attitude can no longer be the case. Some local Churches, already engaged in renewal, reconfirm the fact that now is the time for the Church to call upon every Christian community to evaluate their pastoral practice on the basis of the missionary character of their programmes and activities. (10)

Thus the *Lineamenta*'s vision for the new evangelization is bold rather than reactive and looks to the future rather than to the past.

Nevertheless, a tension or dialectic unmistakably stretches between the church's active role as proclaimer and its reflective role as hearer and disciple (2), between the initial mission *ad gentes* and the new evangelization *ad intra* of those people who have already heard Christ proclaimed (5), between renewed spiritual efforts in the life of faith within the local churches and the conviction that the continent of Europe must not simply appeal to its former Christian heritage, but decide about its future in conformity with the person and message of Jesus Christ (5), between reading and interpreting new situations in human history (6) and retrieving an explicit Catholic culture we once knew. Perhaps these reflect the same tensions and dialectics as the efforts towards *aggiornamento* and *ressourcement*, updating and retrieval of the sources, at Vatican II.

The new evangelization must not be co-opted by the church's own culture wars: the Rahnerians versus the von Baltharians, the laity versus the clergy, the sisters versus the bishops, those who prefer the Tridentine Mass and those who regularly worship with Paul VI's *novus odo Missae,* or contextual theology versus Neo-Scholasticism. Frankly, many of these are often false dichotomies, and those who try to drive a wedge between the polarities frequently seriously misrepresent one pole or the other.

Talk of a smaller, leaner, more committed church sometimes gives the impression of a rigorist church more in line with the Donatists than with Augustine's vision of the church as a hospital for sinners or the description of the church attributed to the novelist James Joyce, 'Here comes everybody.' In this life, as the evangelist Matthew tells us, the tares and the wheat grow together until the harvest (Mt. 13.24–30). While the new evangelization wants to fertilize the wheat, it must not yank out the tares.

A nostalgia for a church of the 1940s and 50s, especially when accompanied by the ecclesiastical dress of that period, the liturgy of that period and a preference for a neo-Scholastic theology to the exclusion of all other methodologies, does not witness to the evangelization of culture as it exists in the twenty-first century or represent the inculturation of the Gospel necessary for that task. Family life, social communication, the migration of peoples with the resulting increased heterogeneity, scientific and technological advancements, political realignments, the women's movement, the growing political and religious fundamentalisms and so on, all of these witness to a profoundly altered world than the world before the Vietnam War, the fall of the Berlin wall, the wars in Iraq and Afghanistan; before the economic need for two-income families or before our current crises of ordained ministry, both in terms of the worldwide sex abuse crisis and in terms of the shortage of ordained ministers. We cannot simply look to a romanticized past to address and evangelize the world of today.

The temptation exists to find a scapegoat for the current crisis of faith, crises in the church and crisis of Christian culture. A concern surfaces that some theologies have given the impression that because grace is ubiquitous, there is no need for the church or sacraments, and that because non-Christians can be saved apart from explicit faith, there is no need for evangelization or missionary efforts. Theologians of the 1940s and 50s such as Karl Rahner and Henri de Lubac, whom the neo-Scholastics criticized in the 1950s for compromising the gratuity of grace and who then later became important figures behind the scenes at Vatican II as *periti,* are once again the objects of a restorationist movement retrieving neo-Scholasticism.[8] Here I am careful to say 'neo-Scholasticism', not 'Scholasticism', for de Lubac argued for a retrieval of what he considered to be an authentic reading of Thomas Aquinas. While the academic discussion on de Lubac's *Surnaturel* has remained cordial and mutually respectful with its recognition of the ambiguities within the writing of the Angelic doctor, there have been some pretty flagrant mis-representations of the work of Karl Rahner.[9]

Ironically, both Rahner and de Lubac, in their own cultures, and utilizing very different theological methods, were attempting to show how the human being is innately oriented to God. This is essentially the same position as the fundamental catechism question those of us raised in the pre-Vatican II era memorized from the catechism: 'Why did God make you? God made me to know him, to love him, and to serve him in this world and to be happy with him forever in heaven.' Rahner did this through his theology of the supernatural existential, which he clearly identified as itself a gift of grace, while de Lubac approached the topic via a fresh reading of Thomas Aquinas.

De Lubac really carved out a mediating position in the culture of his time. The context within which he wrote was Catholicism in France from the 1930s to the early 1950s. France was the arena of a bitter struggle between supporters of the Third Republic, who were anti-clerical and secular, and traditional Catholics, who were politically monarchist and ecclesially ultramontanist. The movement *Action française*, condemned by Pius XI in 1926, was led by the agnostic Charles Maurras (1868–1952), who supported a restored monarchy and opposed anti-clericalism and republicanism. De Lubac and those with him associated with the '*nouvelle théologie*' addressed a spiritual and theological crisis in a cultural context, similar to what the new evangelization is addressing, where religious faith and the Church were in danger of becoming irrelevant in an increasingly secular Europe.

The movement identified as the '*nouvelle théologie*', aimed to renew theology by a return to its biblical and patristic sources. Jean Daniélou outlined the general orientation of this movement and noted the gulf that had opened up between

---

[8] For just a few examples of the literature, see Lawrence Feingold, *The Natural Desire to See God According to St. Thomas Aquinas and His Interpreters* (Ave Maria, FL: Sapientia Press of Ave Maria University, 2010); Steven A. Long, *Natura Pura: On the Recovery of Nature in the Doctrine of Grace* (New York: Fordham University Press, 2010). For a response, see Edward T. Oakes, S. J., 'The *Surnaturel* Controversy: A Survey and a Response', *Nova et Vetera*, English Edition, 9/3 (2011), pp. 625–56.

[9] Here I would list Richard Schenk, OP, '*Officium Signa Temporum Perscrutandi*: New Encounters of Gospel and Culture in the Context of the New Evangelization', in Steven Boguslawski, OP and Robert Fastiggi (eds), *Called to Holiness and Communion: Vatican II on the Church* (Scranton, PA: University of Scranton Press, 2009), pp. 69–105.

theology and the pressing concerns of the day.[10] He surveyed a progressive rupture between exegesis and systematic theology, with each discipline developing according to its own method with a consequent aridity within systematic theology. The 'new' orientation aimed at a reunification of theology, including a return to Scripture, a retrieval of the Fathers and a liturgical revival. The patristic contributions that Daniélou wished to retrieve included a notion of history, which he described as foreign to Thomism; the social dimension of the salvation of humanity, emphasized in the subtitle of de Lubac's work *Catholicism, 'The Social Aspects of Dogma'* and, finally, a more existential theology, which had the capacity of engendering faith. This, essentially, was the theological arm of an evangelizing movement in France.

Another initiative during the same time period and in the same country was the worker priest spawned by Fr Jacques Loew, who started working on the docks in Marseille in 1941. Pius XII somewhat reluctantly approved the worker priest movement in 1945. Karol Wojtyla, the future John Paul II, along with a fellow Polish priest, visited the priest workers in Belgium and France in 1947 and wrote an article on them for the *Tygdnik Powszechny*, a Polish Roman Catholic weekly magazine.[11] The workers were recalled, however, in 1953, although they were allowed to return to their industrial workplaces in 1963. A similar initiative was begun in England in the 1960s.

This type of evangelization is continued in a similar manner by the Little Brothers of Jesus, an outgrowth of the work of Charles de Foucault, who was killed in 1914 without having recruited any members of a community during his lifetime. The brothers work a full day in the mines, on the docks and in various similar places of labour, live in communities of two or three and have the Blessed Sacrament in their simple dwellings. There is also a community of sisters who do the same. Some would say that the priest worker movement failed. Not all efforts of evangelization will be successful, but this movement was an attempt at bringing Christian witness to a segment of culture that would not have otherwise encountered the Gospel. It is an example of the new evangelization, long before the title, directed *ad extra*.

Yet another similar movement is the Catholic Worker Movement, founded in 1933 in the United States during the Great Depression by Dorothy Day. Dorothy Day was known for her deep devotion to the Eucharist and her radical commitment to social justice and the poor. The movement is known best for its houses of hospitality and its newspaper, the *Catholic Worker*. Catholic workers

---

[10] Jean Daniélou, *Les orientations présentes de la pensée religieuse*, Études 249 (1946), pp. 5–21.
[11] John Cornwell, *The Pope in Winter* (New York: Viking, 2004), p. 33.

are volunteers who live a simple lifestyle in community and are known for their service to the poor, their pacifism and their commitment to social justice. Most are rooted in the Gospel and the Catholic faith, although some of the houses identify themselves as interfaith. Each house is independent, and there is no 'Catholic Worker headquarters'. The website in 2012 reported approximately 213 catholic worker communities, most of them in the United States with about 20 internationally.

The worker priest movement, the Little Brothers and Sisters of Jesus and the Catholic Worker movement are all three examples of radical Christian living among the poor for witness to those who may not have contact with Christianity through more traditional avenues. The primary purpose of each of these new and bold initiatives is witness by way of lifestyle and an accompaniment of the poor and non-believers. Admittedly, the worker priest movement and the Catholic Worker movement are not without their critics, usually because of their political alignments. The point here is that the new evangelization calls us to equally bold initiatives, some of which may fail. Without such attempts, however, the church will remain isolated from those who would not otherwise hear the Gospel.

To move from France and the United States to Germany, two well-known German Catholic theologians, Karl Rahner and Walter Kasper, have framed their theology to respond to a secular culture. Kasper introduced his monumental *The God of Jesus Christ* with 60 pages of natural theology rather than with revelation, since natural theology does not depend upon faith or revelation for its argument for the intelligibility and rationality of belief in God.[12] Similarly, Rahner began with his anthropocentric turn, giving an account of the human being as 'hearer of the Word' and as 'spirit in the world' in order to argue for the human grace-given capability to receive God's gift of God's self to us in uncreated grace. Both theologians were addressing secular culture in the light of faith and trying to make sense of that faith in a contemporary context marked by pluralism of all kinds. Today Karl Rahner is sometimes explicitly or implicitly blamed for contributing to the idea that since grace is ubiquitous in the world, there is no need for the church or sacraments,[13] but this risks reducing the church and sacraments to an instrumentalist function.

This criticism also fails to recognize that theology, as also evangelization, mediates between the Gospel, as understood and lived in the context of church

---

[12] Walter Kasper, *The God of Jesus Christ* (new edition; New York: T&T Clark International–Continuum, 2012), pp. 65–115.

[13] See, for example, Congregation for the Doctrine of the Faith, 'Doctrinal Note on Some Aspects of Evangelization' (3 December 2007), p. 3. Rahner was trying to give a theological account of what has been affirmed in the dogmatic tradition of the church, namely, that non-Christians can be saved apart from baptism by blood or water. See LG 16.

life and doctrine, and the given culture to which and in which that Gospel is preached. This mediation, however, goes both ways. In addition to communicating and mediating the meaning of the Gospel to a particular cultural context, the constitutive meaning of the faith of the community is itself constantly open to development, change and refinement through its encounter with culture.[14] The evangelizer must also be evangelized. This is none other than the capacity of faith to grow and be purified. The only language accessible to the expression of faith in a form intelligible to the human community is culturally given.

The role of the Church

The ubiquitous presence of grace in the world does require an account of the role of the church, but this can be done without denying the universal presence of that grace. The meaning and necessity of the church and the sacraments lies within *Lumen gentium*'s vision of the church as 'a sacrament or instrumental sign of intimate union with God and of the unity of all humanity' (LG 1); Christians have an obligation to be visible signs of that communion. To be this sign and instrument of communion is also the mission of the church. The church's mission is also to make implicit faith explicit, to articulate the Trinitarian form of salvation, to be that community of salvation.

This does not mean that everyone need be a formal member of the church. In *Redemptoris missio*, John Paul II says,

> Universality of salvation does not mean that it is given only to those who believe explicitly in Christ and join the Church. If salvation is meant for all, it must be offered concretely to all . . . The salvation of Christ is available to them through a grace which, though relating them mysteriously with the Church, does not bring them into it formally but enlightens them in a way adapted to their state of spirit and life situation. (10)

The document issued by the Congregation of the Doctrine of the Faith, *Dominus Iesus*, 'On the Unicity and Salvific Universality of Jesus Christ and the Church' (DI; 2000), interprets the possibility of salvation for non-Christians in relation to Christ and the church:

> For those who are not formally and visibly members of the Church, 'salvation in Christ is accessible by virtue of a grace which, while having a mysterious

---

[14]   Robert Doran, *What is Systematic Theology?* (Toronto: University of Toronto Press, 2005), p. 203.

relationship to the Church, does not make them formally part of the church, but enlightens them in a way which is accommodated to their spiritual and material situation. This grace comes from Christ; it is the result of his sacrifice and is communicated by the Holy Spirit'; it has a relationship with the Church, which 'according to the plan of the Father, has her origin in the mission of the Son and the Holy Spirit'. (DI 20)

The precise manner in which the non-Christian is related to Christ and the church remains mysterious. However, any position that would consider the church as one way of salvation alongside those constituted by the other religions, seen as complementary or substantially equivalent to the church, even if converging with the church towards the eschatological kingdom of God, is expressly rejected in the document (DI 20). At the same time, the document acknowledges, 'the various religious traditions contain and offer religious elements which come from God, and which are part of what "the Spirit brings about in human hearts and in the history of peoples, in cultures, and religions"' (DI 21).

As the preface to *Gaudium et spes*, the Pastoral Constitution of the Church in the Modern World (GS), notes there is nothing truly human that does not affect the disciples of Christ. 'Their community is composed of people united in Christ who are directed by the Holy Spirit in their pilgrimage toward the Father's kingdom and who have received the message of salvation to be communicated to everyone. For this reason it feels itself closely linked to the human race and its history' (GS 1). The church works to achieve that 'universal community of sisters and brothers which is the response to humanity's calling' (GS 1).

Thus the document *Dominus Iesus*' insistence on the unicity and salvific universality of Jesus Christ and the Church is on target. Just because not all belong formally to the church and grace is accessible beyond the visible boundaries of the church does not mean that the church has lost its role in God's plan for salvation for its role is to be the sacrament and instrumental sign of that unity.

A people sent in mission

The church does not have a mission; it is missionary by its very nature since 'it draws its origin from the mission of the Son and the mission of the Holy Spirit, in accordance with the plan of God the Father' (*Ad gentes* 2). In its evangelizing mission, while the church proclaims a gospel offering a salvation that is both transcendent and eschatological, this gospel must also penetrate societies and cultures, and influence political and social orders. As a sign to the nations, the church's mission is to represent and proclaim the love of God and to give testimony to hope. It accomplishes this through its preaching of the Gospel, its celebration of the Eucharist and its commitment to social and political transformation. In these activities, the church is both the sacrament and servant of the kingdom of God.

Clearly, Pope Francis sees a goal of evangelization as promoting a relationship with Jesus Christ that is transformative not only personally, but also culturally. The Gospel must 'have a real impact on God's faithful people and the concrete needs of the present time' (*Evangelii gaudium* 95). Evangelization is primarily missional in character and entails offering others 'an explicit witness to the saving love of the Lord, who despite our imperfections offers us his closeness' (121). Francis makes a plea for spirit-filled evangelizers. What is needed is a spirituality that can engage hearts. Avoiding a temptation for a privatized and individualistic spirituality, a profound contemplative encounter with the love of Jesus impels us to engage in mission and evangelization.

The people of God – inclusive of lay, clergy and religious – are called to this mission of witness and proclamation that the world may be transformed into the reign of God and that the human community may be formed into the universal community of brothers and sisters with Christ, sons and daughters of God the Father through the power of the Holy Spirit.

6

The Ecclesiology of Communion: From Jurisdiction to Relationship

Francis George

The topic of new evangelization and its relationship to the ecclesiology of the Second Vatican Council, which describes the Church as agent of mission and the Church as communion, is of great importance to everyone who is part of the Catholic Church today. However, before we discuss that it is necessary to have a collective understanding of the relationship between evangelization and of mission.

Evangelization and mission

On the one hand, before the Council, the way in which mission was understood was in the light of the territorial division between lands where Christ is not known, where the Church is not established, and, on the other hand, lands of pastoral governance, where the Church is fully established and calls upon her people to take care of her life and ministries and then sends some of these people to foreign or 'mission' lands.

Missions were basically foreign missions. This difference was encoded in the Church's law. There was the Roman Congregation Propaganda Fidei with its own application of canon law, and then there were the pastoral lands under the ordinary governance of the rest of the Roman dicasteries, with the universal code being normative for governance. The local Churches were not called local Churches in mission lands. They were vicariates apostolic, not dioceses, and they were headed by an ordained bishop who was called a Vicar Apostolic, that is, his authority came directly from the Pope in order to govern those lands which were designated as territories of religious orders who received a 'mandatum'. The mandate from the Holy See was given through Propaganda Fidei to different orders. My own order had Northern Canada with its eight vicariates and a lot of other places as well. The Holy Cross Fathers, for another example, had Bangladesh. (It is Bangladesh now, it was East Pakistan before that and it was part of India when the Holy Cross Order was given responsibility for evangelizing it.) The religious order brought in other pastoral workers, especially religious women. There were not so many lay people involved in mission at the time. The goal was, of course, to establish a local Church and begin to receive vocations to religious orders of women and of men from the local people and to build up a local presbyterate.

The receiving of missionaries in foreign lands from more established Churches in pastoral lands meant that the established Churches were called to be generous not only in taking care of their own needs but also to share many of their resources with people who had not yet been introduced to their Saviour and where the Church was not well established. That was largely the sense of mission before the Second Vatican Council. The ecclesiology of communion altered that sense. Propaganda Fidei still exists as the Congregation for the Evangelization of Peoples but, as was heard last night, the sense of mission became universalized in the Council, so that the division between pastoral lands and mission territories (pagan lands, if you like) was no longer clear. The pastoral lands were found to be mission territories. There were, and are, people within Europe and North America and South America who had not yet been introduced to Christ. When the basic distinction between pastoral lands and mission territories broke down, the mandatum was eliminated and most vicariates apostolic became local Churches. The Vicar Apostolic became the bishop of a new local Church, and Propaganda Fidei helped him by offering resources for Churches that still did not have sufficient resources of their own. The mission then was from local Church to local Church. Sensitivity to decolonization after the World War II meant that the missionaries were not to come without an invitation. They are invited by a local Church and they serve under the terms of a contract between a local bishop and the missionary congregation, not under a mandatum from the Holy See. This new practice reflects the ecclesiology of ecclesial communion that describes the unity of the universal Church as a communion of local or particular Churches. The understanding of mission, therefore, is now less territorial than it was before the Council. In practice there are still problems of 'mission', because many Churches are not self-sufficient; what we have learned in making contracts is that no Church is self-sufficient, everyone gives and everyone receives. We all give and receive different gifts, but everyone is needy and everyone is rich in some way and that is what communion is about: relationships based on the sharing of gifts.

There was also a sense of mission before the Council which was sometimes associated with secondary evangelization. Primary evangelization was in pagan lands, mission territories. One preached who Christ is, converted people, established the Church. But there was something in pastoral lands called a parish mission which was re-evangelization, perhaps not new evangelization but secondary evangelization in missiological theory. My own order came into existence as a group of diocesan priests who worked to re-establish the Church in Southern France when Napoleon fell in 1815. They used parish missions – parochial missions – as their method of evangelizing. Under Napoleon, the Church could worship, the Churches were opened and the clergy licensed. They could not, however, preach to young people outside of the Church. They could not have youth groups nor attend to groups with special needs, like prisoners. The restoration of religious freedom in post-revolutionary France meant that the Church was free to reach beyond parochial structures and to preach missions to all in public places other than the Church buildings.

What happened in secondary evangelization? It did not mean introducing people to Jesus Christ. They had a sense of who he was. The message, rather, was moral. The kerygma had been proclaimed, the people had been catechized in some fashion, but moral injunctions were necessary to bring sinners who were believers back to the way of Christ. The goal of the parish missions was to bring people to make a good confession and put in place the help necessary to live a good life from day to day, avoiding adultery and drunkenness and personal corruption. Assuming that all the structures were in place, that the catechesis was complete, the people still needed to be reminded that religion is a serious business and that they should abandon a sinful way of life. After the Council, however, it was recognized that even in so-called pastoral lands the people need not just moral instruction; they also need to be introduced to Christ for the first time. Now, the goal of evangelizing has again been refocused with a call to a new evangelization.

Why do we need a new evangelization beyond primary evangelization and re-evangelization? Because it is not just individuals who have now slipped from the grasp of Christ, it is whole cultures. Although not exclusively so, the primary goal of the new evangelization is to attend to the new forms of secularization that close off the world from God. Cultures that once were Christian have now been secularized. Societies associate 'freedom' with control of their own destiny rather than with surrender to God.

The world is more united than it was when the Council was called, but the unity is based on a false claim to an autonomy that is not consistent with acknowledging God as creator and redeemer. There is a need for a new evangelization because people who used to know who Christ is have forgotten him or, in fact, deliberately rejected him. The new evangelization was proclaimed first by Pope John Paul II, who was a cultural and philosophical anthropologist. He was sensitive to the way culture carried faith, and he used the phrase 'evangelization of culture', which is behind the new evangelization, particularly when we are talking about secularized cultures. The Church is to be the agent of both personal conversion and transforming society in the light of the Gospel.

Before speaking of the Church as agent of evangelization, let us go back to the purpose of calling the Council. It was a missionary purpose. John XXIII, in explaining the Council in *Humanae salutis*, published on December 25, 1961, set out the primary reasons for convoking the Council. It was a document written, if you recall, in the shadow of the gathering Cuban missile crisis. In that crisis, the Pope was helpful in negotiating between President Kennedy and Chairman Khrushchev, but the world came to the very brink of an exchange of nuclear weapons. Pope John had also been a chaplain in the Italian army in the World War I and saw Catholics killing Catholics in the name of their nation states. He had lived through the consequences of the Russian revolution, when classes killed other classes in the name of social justice. He had lived through the Nazi experiment, where whole races were condemned to serfdom if they were Slavic and to extermination if they were Jewish; and he was aware of the racism endemic in all societies in some way. He was concerned that the world, at war with itself, was going to destroy itself. He was concerned about *pacem in terris* (peace in the world) and he knew that the world, divided among its peoples, needed an agent to tell the human race that it is a human family, to tell various individuals that are separated by class, by nations, by injustices of various kinds, that they are a family in God. The Church therefore has to enter into conversation, into dialogue, with everyone in order to find the similarities among faiths and peoples and then build on them, building relationships even outside the visible Church for the sake of friendship among peoples. We have brought to the fore ministries for justice, ministries for peace, ministries for charity, inserting those missionary concerns right into the sacramental life of our ministries as they were lived before the Council. John XXIII's vision of the Church as the catalyst for human unity was his purpose in calling the Council.

In fact, the very first definition of the Church in *Lumen gentium* ('Dogmatic Constitution on the Church') is not 'people of God' or 'temple of the Spirit' or 'the body of Christ'. It is 'the sacrament of the unity of the human race' – the efficacious sign of the unity of the human race. This is not a definition of Church that we think about often enough. The ecclesiology of communion, which is a network of relationships based on the sharing of gifts from Christ, is designed to be a catalyst or a leaven for the solidarity of the human race. Ecclesial communion and human solidarity are partners in mission as the Church finds her way in a new relationship to the world that Christ died to save. We needed a new relationship. The Church was in danger of becoming a museum; the Council was called to change the world, and to change the Church enough to be effective in changing the world, so that we could all live in God's peace. Although Pope John said the Council was to be pastoral, called to make the world's peoples more united, inevitably, through its shifting of the focus of mission, there was also doctrinal development.

The Church as agent of evangelization

Having reflected on the context of mission, I would like to speak about how the Council changed the Church in her understanding of her governance structure in order to make her a more effective instrument of mission in the world. We will talk also about the worship of God, which is the primary action of the Church in the world because it creates the right relationship to God that is necessary in order to have a right relationship to one another. The Council first attended to worship rather than to the world or even to a concern for the Church, as such, because it is worship that determines our relationships, and right relationships are the basis for biblical justice.

I will talk also about the Church's internal communion, using primarily the encyclical of Paul VI, *Ecclesiam suam* (1964) that was written during the Council. It is a masterful summary of the dialogic methodology of the Council, which set the stage for her dialogue with the world in its various components. Finally, we will talk about the promised springtime, what happened and what did not happen. How do we read the signs of the times of the last 50 years, strengthen our new sense of ecclesial self-consciousness and clarify the missionary challenges that we have to meet if the Council is to redeem its own promise?

Pope Benedict XVI has explained the doctrinal developments from the Council by appealing to continuity of principle in changing circumstances.

Circumstances create challenges to principles; in different circumstances, one sees something in the principle or in a doctrine that was not seen before. Missionaries are used to this new development when they go into a place with their understanding of the faith, which is always coloured by their own culture. There is no abstract faith without cultural expression. Greco-Roman culture has remained normative in some basic formulations of the faith, as was the Jewish culture before it. But as the faith encounters 'new' peoples, the indigenous peoples of the then new world some 500 years ago, for example, the principles have to be re-interpreted, organically developed. Reform means there has been a change, not just a reiteration of the same thing again and again. In a changing world, principles themselves sometimes take on a different cast as well.

Pope Benedict explained this as the 'hermeneutic of reform'. There is development of doctrine in the Second Vatican Council because of a changed understanding of the Church's pastoral life and her mission. It was a reform Council, which means some things changed. What changed, first of all, was our awareness of the Church and her mission in the world today. The Council taught nothing that contradicted what Christ had said or she herself had lived in other ages, but the continuity has to be carefully worked out, because what we are to do will depend in fact upon an interpretation of teaching designed to protect and advance the Church's mission today. How has communion ecclesiology affected not only the Church's sense of mission but also her understanding of governance?

The first self-conscious reflections on the nature of the Church were juridical. The earliest councils were about relations within the Trinity, the relationship of Christ to all humanity as Saviour, the natures of Christ himself. Those doctrinal Councils were succeeded by the reform councils in the middle ages, because the Church herself was touched with corruption in mores and government and needed to call herself back to a more evangelical way of life. After 2,000 years, the Church herself became the subject of an ecumenical Council. The Church's unity had been taken for granted when she was the unifying principle of Christendom. When that unity was broken by the Reformation and the development of nation states, the first responses were juridical, not directly doctrinal.

One could easily argue that the Reformation was rooted in the scandal of the Church's pastors and the faithful not living in conformity to what they were professing as they proclaimed the Gospel. But schism in the Church predated the Reformation and was always answered in juridical terms by the medieval jurists. James of Viterbo, for example, a noted late medieval canonist in the early years of the fourteenth century, wrote the first canonical treatise in ecclesiology. The great ecclesiologist after the Council of Trent, in the aftermath of the Protestant reform, was Saint Robert Bellarmine (1542–1621). He built on the work of the late medieval jurists who studied ecclesiastical structures of governance in relation to the various civil societies in which the Church lived. Bellarmine worked out of that received juridical framework for understanding the Church as a visible society, because the reformers were saying the structures of the Church are adventitious: the external structures do not matter. The Church is only the work of internal grace. It does not matter, therefore, what form the governance of the Church takes because, since the Church is invisible, her structures are not essential to her life. It is true, of course, that invisible grace is the very lifeblood of the Church, but the apostolic structures of the Church are a matter of faith. Cardinal Bellarmine's solution was to define the Church as a perfect society like the nation states, which were quite extensive in their reach and control. The Church's members are not morally perfect any more than the state's citizens are morally perfect; but both church and state are institutionally perfect in the legal sense that both have everything needed to do their work in order to accomplish their mission. The Church has all the gifts necessary to fulfil her salvific mission from Christ, just as the state has everything that it needs in order to fulfil its purpose in society.

Saint Robert Bellarmine explained, in a more theological framework, how the Church possesses all that is necessary for her mission because her gifts are rooted in Christ's will for his Church. He defined Church authority and its juridical limits and gave these a basis in Scripture and Tradition; he clarified the rights and duties of different classes of Church members. The Church was, in a sense, almost examined from the outside, as if by an observer. The analogy for the Church's self-understanding was the Kingdom of France or the Republic of Venice. That controlling metaphor meant that Church governance was still legitimated by jurisdiction, by the legal power to act. This left the Church in the modern age for 400 years as one party to the dilemma of competing jurisdictions. How does one separate the domain of the Church from the claims of the new nation states after the Treaty of Westphalia in 1648? Both church and state are perfect societies; both are complete; both have their rights and each makes both religious and secular claims. How does one separate the domains of competence and, more than that, how can church and state peacefully and respectfully cooperate? The Catholic Church was never a Department of State in any country, but it was very closely united to the civil government in various countries. Theories of the proper subordination of state to Church and of the

Church's liberty of action in the secular sphere were elaborated over a period of several hundred years. The Church needed an ecclesiology that established her freedom in the world for the sake of her mission that transcends the world. She also needed to explain how civil society was properly autonomous without being totalitarian.

Before the Second Vatican Council, Pope Pius XII had already begun to draw on the thought of German theologians who, in the nineteenth century, moved beyond the juridical framework of the perfect society based upon jurisdiction towards an ecclesiology based upon the biblical metaphors that describe the Church in the New Testament. The Church is related to Christ and to the Holy Spirit as herself a mystery of faith and, in 1943, Pope Pius XII wrote on the Church as the Mystical Body of Christ, defining the Church's nature from the sources of her life from within rather than from her external juridical organization. Pius XII wrote to combat the false notion that there are two different churches: an interior or spiritual Church of all who believe in Christ and an external, visibly structured Church, which can be analysed without reference to her nature as a mystery of faith. He overcame ecclesial dualism by identifying the Mystical Body of Christ with the societies and structures of the Roman Catholic Church, with no overlap. The famous '*subsistit in*' of *Lumen gentium* says the same in the context of communion ecclesiology.

The Council recognized the existence of gifts from Christ outside of visible Catholic communion, particularly in the sacrament of common Baptism. These elements of ecclesial reality outside of the visible structure of the Catholic Church relate people to the Church in a way that makes salvation available. These are called '*vestigiae ecclesiae*' (vestiges of the Church) found outside of visible Catholic communion. These elements of the Church outside of her pastoral and visible unity serve to include all Christians, in a certain limited sense, in her membership in such a way that it is possible to dialogue with them as brothers and sisters, to see something in them that is also in us, to see them as friends and as fellow believers.

This is the conviction also found in the mission document of the Council, *Ad gentes*. The '*semina verbi*' (the seeds of the Word; 11) are to be discovered in natural religions and in non-Christian religions so that, again, missionaries can dialogue with peoples of other faiths or of no faith at all, because seeds of the Word who created the world are present among all peoples. God created the world and the world therefore is good, even in its now fallen and wounded state. The cosmos speaks of God to those who are listening. Our discerning everywhere 'vestiges of the Church' and 'seeds of the Word' enables the Second Vatican

Council to say that all are already part of God's family, even if not everybody yet realizes it. Catholics should therefore be the ones to initiate dialogue. This imperative presupposes that the Church is free to do so everywhere in the world. Freedom of religion is the necessary condition for mission.

The Council finessed the political dimensions of how the Church should be in the world by sidestepping the relationship between Church and State and emphasizing instead the relationship between faith and culture. The most provocative and original sections of the Constitution on the Church in the Modern World, *Gaudium et spes* are in the second chapter, on culture. While not yet as biblically grounded as it must be, the Council's discussion of culture, or second nature, made of culture a theological term, like first nature and grace. The Church's parameters shifted from the tension between two perfect societies to the relationship between two normative systems: faith and culture, both of which tell us what to think and how to act and what is true and valuable and what is not. We are who we are because of our culture far more profoundly than because we are citizens of a particular nation state. Both faith and culture are normative for those who are believers. Both are systems complete in themselves and both tell us what is important, what to think, how to act. If the Church is to be in the world as a leaven, then she must engage cultures as such. Just as the legalistic approach to understanding the Church is inadequate to her full internal reality as a mystery of faith, so also her external relations with the world through the institution of the state, while obviously still of great importance, become secondary. The relationship between the Church and the world is defined first of all by dialogue between faith and the cultures of the world.

The Council Fathers were concerned about the conditions for authentic dialogue between the universal faith and a particular culture in order to properly situate the Church in the world in a new age. The Council therefore spoke to the freedom of the Church to fulfil her mission publicly and to the personal freedom of conscience that is a natural right. The Council's document on religious liberty, *Dignitatis humanae*, depended partially on the prior work of John Courtney Murray, S. J. His ground-breaking articles in *Theological Studies* in the United States in the 1950s remained, however, largely an institutional analysis.[1] In countries where the state claims vast jurisdiction over its citizens' lives, Father

---

[1] John Courtney Murray, S. J., 'The Church and Totalitarian Democracy', *Theological Studies* 14 (December 1952), pp. 525–63; 'Leo XIII on Church and State: The General Structure of the Controversy', *Theological Studies* 14 (March 1953), pp. 1–30; 'Leo XIII: Separation of Church and State', *Theological Studies* 14 (June 1953), pp. 145–314; 'Leo XIII: Two Concepts of Government', *Theological Studies* 14 (December 1953): 551–67; 'Leo XIII: Two Concepts of Government: Government and the Order of Culture', *Theological Studies* 15 (March 1954), pp. 1–33.

Murray argued, a legally defined relationship between the Church and the state is necessary because the Church could not otherwise be free. But in the case of a state with limited government, and the best example of that kind of restriction placed on the state in constitutional law has been the First Amendment to the US Constitution, the state is contained within its own limited domain and therefore leaves free every other domain of human activity, without unnecessary regulation. The United States does not have a government ministry of religion, nor of culture, as European states sometimes have. These are none of the state's business, supposedly. Our constitutional guarantees were thought to give the Church greater freedom of action for her mission.

The document on religious liberty in the modern world, however, starts not from institutional considerations but from anthropology. *Dignitatis humanae*, the Council's 'Declaration on Religious Freedom' is based more on French personalism than it is upon American constitutional theory. It describes who we are as free people, men and women made in God's image and likeness and therefore necessarily exercising our religious duties to God and expressing our religious faith publicly in society. The state must respect and permit that freedom. The dignity of each human person is therefore the foundation of *Dignitatis humanae*, and the document explains how that dignity is given to every human person because of his or her relationship to God, not to the state. *Dignitatis humanae* also speaks of freedom of conscience, but it talks about freedom of conscience *vis-à-vis* the state, not *vis-à-vis* the Church. Freedom of conscience means a person has the right and the obligation to act according to his or her conscience, but conscience is a practical principle in Catholic moral teaching. Freedom of conscience does not mean that one has the right in the Church to interpret personally or to deny what God has revealed in Christ. Freedom of conscience is often understood as a function of the sovereign self in an individualistic society. It then means that individuals have a right to deny what is declared by the Church as authentically revealed. Every individual would then be a Church of one; but Jesus did not come and die on the cross and rise from the dead so that each one could believe whatever he liked and do whatever he wanted. Obviously, the Church is communal. Freedom of conscience is understood within the community of faith differently from the way it is understood within the civil community. It must be, as a principle of both belief and action, respected totally in the civil community; within the community of faith, it must be respected as a principle of action, but not as a principle of belief. Faith is a response to what has been revealed by God. Its contents are assented to as a whole, or else it is not faith in God who reveals himself. Saint Thomas Aquinas explained that, if one believes every article of the creed but one, he or she does not believe any of the articles because 'faith' would be reduced to an 'assent' to an individual's personal value system. In the realm of faith, an individual's intelligence cannot be the criterion of what God had revealed, as if God's words were not trustworthy without our verification.

The Council's teaching on the relationship between culture and world and on the freedom of religion and conscience do build on what was taught before, but the Council truly shifts the tradition so that there is a reinterpretation and a new emphasis rather than a simple reiteration of the teaching. There is authentic development; there is reform. Reform means the principle remains but it is now worked out in different ways because circumstances have changed and new insights have come to shape the Church's living tradition. That is sometimes hard to grasp, particularly in a pragmatic society where we judge by conclusions: we taught this and now we teach that. If the continuity is not grasped, then there is a contradiction between what was said before and what was said after.

Besides the shift in perspective from church/state to faith/culture in defining the Church's relation to the world, another example of 'reform' would be the case of usury, which was redefined when the meaning of money changed from being simply a substitute for a commodity in systems based on barter to being itself a commodity in a commercialist system and then a capitalist system. The nature of money changed because of changed circumstances, but the principle remained the same: concern for social justice between peoples who are dependent upon one another for the common good. If circumstances change the whole system of commercial exchange, then, one must work to establish more explicitly the doctrinal or moral principles that remain stable.

Mission and the theology of communion

If there has been development in the Church's understanding of her relationship to worldly governance, so also has the Church clarified her sense of her own governance. In the theology of communion, the Church is a network of relationships founded upon the exchange of gifts from Christ. First of all, the gift of God's life – divine life – in the form of sanctifying grace brings us into intimate relationship with God. The Church is always a mystery, because she brings us into an invisible participation in the life of the relationships of the Blessed Trinity. Then the visible gifts of Christ are shared in ecclesial communion, particularly the proclamation of the Gospel, the celebration of the seven sacraments of the apostolic churches and the structures of apostolic governance.

A gift is a commodity with a person attached. If one refuses a gift, then a person, the giver, is rejected. If your Grandma knits socks for you and gives them to you for Christmas and you say, 'Grandma, I don't want your socks', you have not only refused the gift, you have rejected your grandmother and broken the relationship. Visible ecclesial communion is a network of relationships based upon sharing the gifts of Christ. How is Church governance understood as a gift from Christ in the framework of communion ecclesiology? Communion among bishops is called collegiality, and a major theological challenge after the Council has been to situate correctly the relationships among collegiality, primacy and apostolicity. These relationships continue to be discussed, often within ecumenical dialogue. But the Council also developed the Church's understanding of the sacrament of Holy Orders as the sacrament of governance based upon Christ's love for his Church.

Before the Council, the sense of priestly identity had been largely influenced by Sulpician spirituality, which is built on the mystery of the Incarnation. The ordained priest was seen as another Christ. This is, of course, quite true; but it is true of every baptized person. The specific dimension of the mystery of Christ that is made visible in Holy Orders is not Christ's relationship to his Father but rather Christ's relationship to the Church – his headship. In a theology that is grounded in relationships, the new relationship to God given in Baptism is filiation; we become God's sons and daughters in Christ, the eternal Son. A little child is brought into Church for Baptism as a creature of God. It is wonderful to be made in God's image and likeness, but there is more. The child leaves the Church as a son or a daughter of God, which is the relationship that brings one into salvation. It is eternal. It cannot be taken away. You cannot 'unbaptize' people any more than you can 'unbirth' them. In Holy Orders, the new relationship given to the ordained priest is that of Christ's own relation to his Church. What is given to the priest by reason of ordination is not the sanctifying grace that comes with baptism, but the sacramental grace that permits him to participate in and make visible Christ's governance of his people. That is not a relationship necessary for a priest's personal salvation, like the relation given in the gift of Baptism, but it is necessary for the authentic and apostolic governance of Christ's Church.

How is this development a reform? St Thomas Aquinas's theology of Holy Orders defined the priest primarily as the one who celebrates the Eucharist and consecrates the bread and wine that become the Body and Blood of Christ. His presbyteral reality was almost subsumed, in people's minds, into Eucharistic piety and the power to consecrate. There was, consequently, a long-standing theological discussion about whether or not episcopacy was simply ordained priesthood plus jurisdiction. Bishops were consecrated, not ordained. The Council settled the question of the sacramental nature of the episcopate by teaching that the bishop was first of all a pastor. Because of the reception of Holy Orders, bishops have apostolic authority directly from Jesus Christ to govern the Church. Their ministry does not depend upon their being granted jurisdiction, even from the Holy See. Before the Council, when bishops went to Rome for their *ad limina* visits, they received what were called quinquennial faculties. These were faculties given by the pope, so the bishops could govern legitimately. That does not happen any longer. Every bishop, by reason of his inclusion in the apostolic college with and under the successor of Peter, shares directly in the authority that Christ gave to his apostles to govern Christ's people; he has to do that, of course, in communion with and under Peter, in relationship to all other bishops. He cannot break these relationships and go his own way and still be governing as Christ wants him to govern.

The Fathers of the Council placed the priestly power to confect the Eucharist in the context of pastoral authority over the Body of Christ. It was a pastoral council. Bishops and priests can make present and give to people the sacramental Body of Christ because they have pastoral authority over the people as the Mystical Body of Christ. Priests always have a title. The idea of priesthood as a prerogative – that I can consecrate the Eucharist without a Church – is a false idea of priesthood. You have to have a title, and you are ordained for a diocese which is a local Church, not for a parish. A parish is a Eucharistic community, but it is not a local Church. The local Church is the diocese, which is the primary nexus for this network of relationships, according to the ecclesiology of the Second Vatican Council. As Catholics celebrate the Eucharist, they recognize three pastors, each related to the other: the pastor of the Eucharistic community we call a parish, who is celebrating the Eucharist, and two other pastors named in the celebration of the Eucharist: the local bishop and the universal pastor, the pope. When all three work together, communion is safe and the relationships are assured. When they start to separate, we have the danger of schism. The ordained priesthood and episcopacy constitute what is the sacrament of good governance of the Church. The gift of ordained priesthood is given so that Christ's people will be governed in Christ's name in a visible way, so you know whom you have to go to and where you should gather when you want to be governed by Jesus Christ.

That is an important point in discerning vocations. A prospective seminarian must be asked: Can you govern? Can you be a father? Can you be a husband? Are you at home with the responsibilities of adult men? If that is not the case, no matter how devotional a man might be, no matter how smart he is, no matter how holy he is, he is not called to ordained priesthood in the Church. Holy Orders is clearly, in the Second Vatican Council's teaching, the way in which Christ visibly governs his people through those who participate in his headship sacramentally. The Reformers taught that Christ is head of the Church, of course, but they abolished the sacrament of Holy Orders. Christ's headship is invisible, and what is visible in the Church is only ministry, not a relationship with headship. Ministry is a function dependent on expertise and not on a relationship given by Christ. Governance of the Church then becomes truly adventitious and is very often in the hands of a lay vestry or of a king. Those who are called to ministry in Protestantism desire to preach the Word of God as a grace-filled call but, in the Catholic perspective, lay ministers can proclaim the Gospel and do other ecclesial service. We have lay ecclesial ministers. They are called to ecclesial services that are based sacramentally on Baptism, and Baptism is not a call to governance. Governance in an Apostolic Church is one of the gifts of Christ that we share as Catholics with the other Apostolic Churches, the Orthodox and the Oriental Churches. There was a genuine development in Conciliar teaching of our understanding of the theology of orders *vis-à-vis* the governance of the Church.

These reflections on the Church and her governance impact the understanding of mission. Since the Church, the agent of mission, is a communion, a set of relationships based on sharing Christ's gifts to his people, the purpose of mission is to enlarge the network of people who share Christ's gifts. Christ wants everybody to share all his gifts, and that is the purpose of mission. Some people have some of the gifts. We have all the gifts, we believe, in Catholic communion, even when we do not use them very well. We can always learn from others who might use them better. The goal is that the whole world understands who its Saviour is and come to love him in his Church before he comes in glory. That is the purpose of the Church: to universalize the sharing of all the gifts Christ wants his people to enjoy.

Pope John Paul II said 20 years after the writing of the Dogmatic Constitution on the Church, *Lumen gentium*,

> The universal Church is presented as a communion of Churches and indirectly
> therefore as a communion of nations. Each of these brings its own 'gifts' to the

whole, just as do single human generations and epochs, particular scientific and social gains, and the stages of civilization which are gradually attained. In particular, by reason of that characteristic of universality which adorns and distinguishes her, the Church knows that she must harmonize those 'gifts' in a higher unity, in order that they may contribute to the progressive acclimation of Christ's one single kingdom.[2]

In the multi-cultural parishes that we have almost everywhere now, cultural differences must not remain obstacles that create walls but rather become gifts to be shared. If they are offered in such a way that people say: 'Oh, this is another way to be Catholic and therefore we are one', the communion is strengthened. A Church building is itself a gift to newcomers who did not build it. It is not ours; it is theirs as well, because we are to share everything as a gift, including our differences.

On other occasions, speaking in more philosophical terms, Pope John Paul II described ecclesial communion as 'a relationship of reciprocal inclusion'.[3] Everybody gives and everybody receives. The bond of Catholic communion means the Church is herself everywhere. She is extensively Catholic. It means, more importantly, that the qualitative foundation for this extensive catholicity is love shared – the communion of persons formed by mutual self-giving in Christ, who gave himself up to death for our sake. This is intensive catholicity, and it gives the Church her proper personality as a school of love, a communion of love. This self-conscious sharing is expressed within the Church in our common profession of faith and in works of charity; it is expressed externally in dialogue with those who do not share this faith. In dialogue, the Church helps all people to discover the dignity of each person, and she helps to unite all in a communion of loving concern which, even apart from an explicit faith, strengthens human solidarity and fosters the unity of the human race. What Professor Tracey Rowland implies in this volume about truth and love being not only the foundations of the Church but also the only arms – the only means that the Church uses in order to proclaim who Christ is – is basic to a proper understanding of missionary work. Truth and love can take a long time to work themselves out, but we must be content with truth and love because they are the only tools the Gospel gives us.

The relationships constituting the communion of the Catholic Church are therefore multiple and diverse – ontological, visible, invisible. Those relations

---

[2] John Paul II, Address to the Roman Curia (21 December 1984), p. 3.
[3] Ibid., p. 5.

based on common sharing reinforce equality in ecclesial communion. Those relations, on the other hand, that are based on particular missions or charisms tend to accentuate differences in ecclesial communion. Thus, the calling to ordained priesthood or episcopacy, or the founding of a religious order, the creation of new particular Churches, the development of movements for the Church's social action, can all seem to diminish communion by separating groups of believers, unless the differentiation of these groups is articulated relationally to the whole and seen as a gift for everyone, even if you are not yourself an ordained priest or a married person or a member of *Comunione e Liberazione*. A major, although invisible, source of inequality in ecclesial relationships is the different degrees of love in the hearts of believers. Love, however, cannot threaten communion. I say that because in modern, liberal societies equality is the great value. There is equality in the Church, but equality is a juridical relationship that is constitutionally protected in many ways. Love is the internal source of our unity, and love is unequal. I once got in trouble for saying that God loves the Blessed Virgin Mary more than he loves Francis George. I think that is, however, pretty obvious. The Church thinks so too. Does that mean that we are somehow unequal? No. We are all given the gifts we have; we are all called by Christ. In the end, it is all gift and therefore it is all love. In a family, even in God's family, all relationships are not equal.

The promise of springtime for the Church in mission

What can be said about the anticipated springtime of the Church? The Council was called 50 years ago with the hope for a new springtime for the faith. The popes since the Council tried to implement the Council according to their particular gifts. Paul VI reformed the curia and instituted the Roman Synod of Bishops, which is a permanent entity outside of the curial structure. It is an exercise of collegiality outside an ecumenical Council and enables us as bishops to strengthen our pastoral and teaching ministry through participating in a governance structure greater than the perspective of our own particular Churches or our conferences. Paul VI explained the theology of communion in his first encyclical, *Ecclesiam suam* (6 August 1964). Anticipating the ecclesiology of the Council and contributing to it, he tried to make his own governance exemplary of it.

Pope John Paul II connected the theology of communion with the Church's mission in both theoretical and practical fashion. He retained and developed thinking on mission so it was not completely captured by evangelization, as it almost was after Pope Paul VI's *Evangelii nuntiandi* (1975). Pope John Paul II wrote *Redemptoris missio* (1990) to show that evangelization is the primary dimension of mission, of course, but there are elements of the missionary vocation which are not evangelization in the strict kerygmatic sense. John Paul II implemented the Council by preaching to the whole world who Christ is. He strengthened the organic unity of believers gathered into ecclesial communion, no matter what divisions or historical animosities there might be among peoples. As a bishop in Poland, he strengthened the unity between the Polish and German peoples. He strengthened inter-faith relations to safeguard peace among nations, and he coined the phrase 'the evangelization of culture' which entered into the programme for the new evangelization.

Pope Benedict XVI restored and strengthened our ecclesial consciousness by emphasizing the central place of worship in spirit and in truth. He recapitulated the Church's entire tradition in homilies and encyclicals. The Council's work was clarified as development in the sense of reform: continuity of principle but in changing circumstances. He showed how the Council itself, if properly understood, should not be a source of division in a Church which is supposed to use its internal unity in order to bring the world to the peace of Christ.

Fifty years after the Council, two questions need to be asked: What weakens ecclesial self-consciousness and therefore the mission of the Church, and what strengthens it? What weakens it, first of all, is a political interpretation of the Council in terms of liberal and conservative ideologies. The division between liberals and conservatives is a modern division rooted in the creation of the secular nation state that situates people *vis-à-vis* authority, not *vis-à-vis* truth. The words 'liberal' and 'conservative' do not appear in the Gospel; truth and falsehood do. Liberals tend to be critical of authority, for good reason often, and conservatives tend to safeguard it, often for good reason too; we work out our political life by compromises between the two camps. The Church, however, is concerned about what is true and what is false; these are the Gospel terms. If the analysis of Church polity remains at the level of secular politics, the Church as a repository of faith is lost. The Council was not directly concerned with the exercise of authority in the Church, although it did change our sense of how it was exercised in the sacrament of Holy Orders. The Council was concerned with the way in which the truths revealed by God could be made more readily available to the contemporary world, by changing the Church enough to make her a better dialogue partner with everyone in the world. The liberal/conservative politicization of the Church betrays the work of the Holy Spirit by dividing the Church internally and paralyzing her mission to the world.

Secondly, what weakens the force of the self-consciousness that should be ours as members of the Catholic Church is the often fierce public opposition to the Church's moral teaching. I remember reading when I was in secondary school that the Church's relationship to Protestant faith communities is complicated by our doctrinal differences but, in moral teaching, we are all agreed. That is certainly not true any longer. Religious and political opposition to the faith is now based on the Church's teaching on moral issues, primarily her defence of life, no matter its frailty, and her teaching on the gift of human sexuality. In a post-Freudian culture, personal identity and freedom are so bound up with sexuality that a broader vision of the nature and destiny of man, as incorporated in the documents of Vatican II, cannot be heard. When personal freedom is reduced to sexual freedom, the Church's moral teaching becomes an object of disdain and even, at times, of hatred. It is dismissed and then actively opposed.

Dialogue with the world imposes therefore a constant search for ways to express the faith more effectively in shaping cultural development. Since much of our moral theology, particularly what is taught about the protection of human life and the nature of the gift of human sexuality, is derived from the natural moral law, a comment that Pope Benedict XVI made when he spoke to the Bundestag on a trip to Germany needs to be further explored. Arguing against legal positivism, Pope Benedict spoke about the natural moral law less as an analysis of the natural finality of a human action, as it is in Saint Thomas, than as a moral theory that expresses a human ecology.[4] In other words, if I understood him correctly, he was saying that the natural moral law can be expressed not only in terms of the natural ends of particular actions but also in terms of relationships and their strengthening or their being broken. This notion might insert moral theology more clearly into the theology of communion.

Thirdly, what hinders people's taking to heart and bringing to mind the Council's sense of ecclesiality is a militant atheism. Ten years ago we did not have atheist clubs in high schools in the United States. We do now. Militant atheism today is not based on communism but rather on an aggressive secularism. Forgetting God means that we forget who we are. The political interpretation of the Council, the growing opposition to the Church by reason of her moral teachings, the appearance of a militant atheism, all militate against our having an

---

[4] Benedict XVI, Address to the *Bundestag* (22 September 2011).

easy comprehension of ourselves as part of the network of ecclesial relationships that the Council called communion.

Fifty years ago, the human race was at war with itself and threatened to destroy itself, and the Church called for unity. Today the world is more united. We are still at war with ourselves, in part, but there is ecological consciousness, a sense of the globe that is now part of our imagination; that is a marvellous advance in the uniting of peoples. Social communication is also widespread. There is cultural unity unlike anything we have seen before. That is why secularism – as the Western cultures are more secularized and are the vehicle for universal culture – is everywhere. It is in parts of African cultures, parts of the South American cultures, parts of Asian cultures. The challenge of a new evangelization is universal, wherever religion is driven out of public life. The problem with reducing religion to a private enterprise is that it becomes a hobby and is no longer a matter of life and death. Related to this cultural phenomenon is a kind of easy universalism that assumes everyone will be saved, no matter what anyone does. Why then go on mission if we are all going to be saved anyway? That driving force behind Augustine, behind Francis Xavier, which arguably might have been too narrow, is gone and, therefore, a primary motivation for mission is not there.

Motivation from generosity remains – sharing the gifts of Christ – but salvation does not depend upon it. The Council taught that people can be saved without explicitly being visibly gathered into Catholic communion, even though it is objectively more difficult. This world, while not divided quite so much, is now in danger of being closed in on itself, giving birth to a new totalitarianism justified by the search for control. That is what secularism, in the pejorative sense, means, as opposed to a healthy secularity.

What happened then to the anticipated springtime? What strikes me as a pastor is that there is an enormous generosity of spirit, greater than I have seen in a long time, among Catholics. It is more and more evident and it is more and more universal. 'Inclusivity' is a secular term, but it can be used to mean 'catholic'. While 'inclusivity' can carry evangelically ambiguous meanings, its frequent use means that it is nearly impossible to live now with a narrowly restricted consciousness. When I was growing up, people lived in their family, their parish and their neighbourhood, often without being aware of or concerned about people at the other side of the globe or even on the other side of my own city. No one can live that way now. We live with a global consciousness and there is, I believe, in many people a great generosity of spirit. We can see it when people are asked to help in Haiti after an earthquake or to aid the Philippines after a flood.

There is an enormous outpouring of generosity, and not only among Catholics. Generosity of spirit means that there is a new universalism afoot, and that is something I think of as a sign of what the Council wanted to accomplish. Where there is generosity of spirit, God is at work. God is love, and when personal generosity expands to self-sacrifice, God's grace is transforming the world.

Finally, the promise of springtime is carried on by the ongoing reform of the liturgy which was central to Pope Benedict's magisterium and at the heart of his ministry, the right worship of God. The somewhat uneven efforts at liturgical renewal, sometimes staying at the surface of practice or the history of rites, are now being re-examined. Revisiting *Sacrosanctum concilium* will carry forward the life of the Church as a communion with God himself through the power of the Holy Spirit. Worship is also eschatological: uniting us to God through the promise of a heavenly kingdom helps us to realize that there can be here only a springtime, and never a full-blown summer.

The Church's mission is lived in the tension between hope and promised fulfilment. The Council's results can be more visibly seen by those whose faith enables them to discern the signs of the times and to translate that vision into pastoral strategies that make the Church effectively a unifying leaven in the world.

7

Ecumenism, Evangelization and Conflicting Narratives of Vatican II: Reading *Unitatis Redintegratio* with His Holiness Benedict XVI Roman Pontiff Emeritus

Paul D. Murray

Actions speak louder than words: as in our personal lives so also in our institutional ecclesial existence, the first way in which we proclaim and witness to the Gospel is in the quality of our living and relating. Here the uncomfortable truth is that for as long as the Christian churches are structurally and sacramentally divided then we are presenting a fundamental counter-sign to the world of the gospel of reconciliation that we proclaim. Ecumenism and evangelization are thus correctly viewed as necessary correlates rather than as competing concerns. Accordingly, this chapter takes Vatican II's teaching on ecumenism as a lens through which to engage the wider issue of the appropriate hermeneutic for interpreting the Council's significance as an event in Catholic tradition.

As is evident in various other chapters within this volume, one of the live issues pertaining to the continuing reception of the Second Vatican Council concerns the question as to how we are properly to understand it as an event in Catholic self-understanding and self-definition relative to all that went before. To use the language that became both current and hotly contested during the papacy of His Holiness Benedict XVI, the issue concerns the extent to which we can speak appropriately of the continuity of Catholic tradition through the teaching of the Council, or whether we are faced here with discontinuity and radical fresh departure. The heated debate that surrounded this question

during the previous papacy – yet now, at least for the time-being, largely
dropped from view – was frequently marked by seemingly diametrically
opposed positions, each passionately advocated. Indeed, not only are there
competing narratives of Vatican II and its significance, but there are also, as
Massimo Faggioli's recent work, *Vatican II: The Battle for Meaning*, makes
clear, differing accounts and analyses of how these competing narratives are
themselves to be understood.[1]

This basic issue of continuity or discontinuity in Catholic tradition through
Vatican II comes to particular focus in relation to the Council's teaching on
ecumenism, for here we are faced, at very least, with a clear example of contrast
with pre-conciliar teaching: not necessarily discontinuity but certainly contrast.
To address this issue, first, attention is given to the way in which the standard
recounting of what is going on in the divergent readings of Vatican II – wherein
continuity and change are placed in binary opposition – is potentially unsettled
by Pope Benedict's dual emphasis on both 'reform' *and* 'continuity'.[2] Second,
the Council's teaching on ecumenism will be presented as exemplifying this
dual emphasis on reform and continuity. Here the argument, in essence, is
that far from the Council's articulation of a distinctively Catholic theology and
practice of ecumenism being in tension with the Council's understanding –
continuous with previous Catholic tradition – of the catholicity of the
Church, this ecumenical teaching is correctly to be seen *both* as flowing from
a recovered sense of what such catholicity authentically means *and* as itself
serving the full flourishing of this catholicity. In the light of this, the third
section of this chapter focuses on the close relationship that exists between
this ecumenical teaching and the wider movement in ecumenical theology
and practice that has recently become known as 'Receptive Ecumenism'. In
turn, by way of further indication of the robustness of this development and
the authenticity of its application of Vatican II's ecumenical teaching, the final
section focuses on the further significant resonance that pertains between
the instincts and key principles of Receptive Ecumenism and the longer-term
thinking in this regard of Joseph Ratzinger as a private theologian yet primary
shaper of the pontifical teaching of Pope Benedict XVI. The conclusion is that
just as Vatican II is authentically *both* Catholic *and* ecumenical so also must
contemporary Catholicism become.

---

[1] See Massimo Faggioli, *Vatican II: The Battle for Meaning* (Mahwah, NJ: Paulist Press, 2012).
[2] See Pope Benedict XVI, 'A Proper Hermeneutic for the Second Vatican Council', in Matthew L. Lamb
and Matthew Levering (eds), *Vatican II: Renewal within Tradition* (New York: Oxford University
Press, 2008), pp. ix–xv.

The conflicting narratives of Vatican II and Pope Benedict XVI's hermeneutic of reform within the continuity of the tradition

One relatively standard way of telling the story of modern Catholicism that has shaped much post-conciliar catechesis and theological history is to draw a sharp contrast between Catholic teaching and practice before and after Vatican II and to emphasize the freshness and greater appropriateness of the latter relative to the former. Although such categories are of limited value, let us follow convention and refer to this as the 'progressivist' appropriation of the Council. For present purposes, this progressivist rendition of the story of modern Catholicism can be viewed as coming to its most refined and sustained expression in the monumental five volume *History of Vatican II* of which Giuseppe Alberigo of Bologna was the coordinating editor, the first volume of which appeared in English in 1995.[3]

When, then, in his January 2005 address to the Roman Curia, Pope Benedict XVI cautioned against a hermeneutic of Vatican II premised upon discontinuity with prior tradition as the organizing category and emphasized instead the need to interpret the Vatican II documents in continuity with prior Catholic tradition,[4] he was widely interpreted in various quarters, both positively and negatively, as directing his fire explicitly and primarily against Alberigo's 'Bologna School' and as wanting, more generally, to reign in and qualify the degree of freshness introduced into Catholic tradition by Vatican II.[5] Apparently in keeping with this agenda were a series of practical initiatives during Benedict XVI's papacy also directed at emphasizing the continuity of pre-conciliar and post-conciliar Catholicism: the liberalization of permission to celebrate the pre-1962 rite; new translations for the ordinary form of the Eucharistic rite that sought to recapture something of the dignity and formality of the Latin originals, regarded as having been insufficiently preserved in earlier vernacular translations; together with a string of statements from the Congregation for the Doctrine of the Faith (CDF) both during his papacy and in near-recent years under his prefecture, clarifying various aspects of post-conciliar ecclesial self-understanding. As a consequence,

---

[3] See Giuseppe Alberigo and Joseph A. Komonchak (eds), *History of Vatican II*, vols 1–5 (Leuven and New York: Peeters & Orbis, 1995–2006).

[4] See Pope Benedict XVI, 'A Proper Hermeneutic for the Second Vatican Council', in particular: 'renewal in the continuity of the one subject–Church', p. x.

[5] See Nicholas Lash, *Theology for Pilgrims* (Notre Dame, IN: University of Notre Dame Press, 2008), pp. 253–84. For a very different assessment of the value of a hermeneutic of 'continuity' over one of 'discontinuity' in relation to the texts of Vatican II, see Agostino Marchetto, *The Second Vatican Ecumenical Council: A Counterpoint for the History of the Council* (Kenneth D. Whitehead (trans.); Scranton: University of Scranton Press, 2010 [2005]).

the hermeneutic of continuity apparently espoused by Pope Benedict and in the air from at least the time of the 1985 Extraordinary Synod of Bishops held to mark the twentieth anniversary of the close of the Council,[6] over which as Cardinal Prefect of the CDF he would have had significant influence, was similarly assumed to be a deliberate counter-point to the changes in Catholicism that had been introduced in the name of the Council.

More recently, however, helpful fresh perspective has been given to this question of the precise hermeneutic of Vatican II that was being advocated by Pope Benedict by viewing his primary interlocutors as being not – or at least, not first and foremost – the progressivist agenda of Alberigo and his Bologna School colleagues but, rather, the Lefebvrist denunciation of Vatican II as being in radical discontinuity with Catholic tradition and, hence, as requiring to be rejected as improperly Catholic. This is a line of interpretation that has been pressed most convincingly by the French-Canadian theologian Gilles Routhier.[7] On the basis of a close analysis of the correspondence between the CDF under the then Cardinal Ratzinger and the Society of St Pius X, Routhier persuasively argues that Pope Benedict's primary aim in speaking of a hermeneutic of continuity is not in order to counter the Bologna School's emphasis on the freshness of Vatican II but rather to refute the charge of radical discontinuity posed by the Lefebvrists and so maintain the abiding significance of Vatican II as authentically Catholic.

Furthermore, Routhier, as also Komonchak, notably draws attention to the fact that Benedict never spoke simply of a straightforward continuity between Vatican II and broader Catholic tradition but, rather, in terms of *reform within the continuity of the tradition*: in a manner, that is, that properly seeks to hold both the fact of change and the dynamic integrity of Catholic identity together.[8] In this regard, we need remind ourselves that it is a basic assumption in the Catholic worldview that we should take the history of the Church in its entirety as being of significance and not just privileged moments within it. While there

---

[6] There we find the same principle articulated concerning the need to interpret the Council's teachings 'in continuity with the great tradition of the Church'. Synod of Bishops, *The Church, in the Word of God Celebrates the Mysteries of Christ for the Salvation of the World. The Final Report of the 1985 Extraordinary Synod* I.5.

[7] See Gilles Routhier, 'The Hermeneutic of Reform as a Task for Theology', *Irish Theological Quarterly* 77/3 (2012), pp. 219–43; see also Joseph A. Komonchak, 'Novelty in Continuity', *The Tablet* (31 January 2009), pp. 5–6.

[8] For example, in the aforementioned 2005 address, we find phrases such as: 'renewal in the continuity of the one subject-Church', Pope Benedict XVI, 'A Proper Hermeneutic for the Second Vatican Council', p. x; also 'It is precisely in this combination of continuity and discontinuity at different levels that the very nature of true reform consists' and 'In this process of innovation in continuity . . .' (p. xiii).

are always shortcomings – sometimes profound and intense – the conviction is that the Spirit has not abandoned the Church. Consequently, the authentic Catholic approach to tradition is not to value only a subset, rendering other aspects redundant, even fundamentally mistaken. Rather, an authentic Catholic approach to tradition is always to ask, with due historical sensitivity, after what the Spirit was doing in a given age and how, with deep continuity with what went before, that is appropriately to be taken forwards in potentially radically changed circumstances. As Joseph Ratzinger himself expressed it:

> There is no 'pre-' or 'post-' conciliar Church: there is but one, unique Church that walks the path toward the Lord, ever deepening and ever better understanding the treasure of faith that he himself has entrusted to her. There are no leaps in this history, there are no fractures, and there is no break in continuity. In no wise did the Council intend to introduce a temporal dichotomy in the Church.[9]

Vatican II as both Catholic and ecumenical

As already alluded to, this more general question concerning the appropriate hermeneutic for Vatican II comes to particularly sharp focus in relation to the Council's teaching on ecumenism, for here we are presented with a clear case of contrast with pre-conciliar Catholic teaching; one that has been celebrated by friend and foe alike as an instance of definite novelty. Nicholas Lash comments that for those who have grown up since the Council, it is difficult 'to appreciate how profoundly different, for better and for worse, is the *sensibility* of Catholicism today from that of the pre-conciliar Church'.[10] Nowhere is this more the case than in relation to Catholic teaching and practice of ecumenism.[11] Where for the progressivist this contrast is emblematic of the achievement of the Council, for the arch-traditionalist it goes to the core of the Council's incautious compromising of authentic Catholic tradition.

---

[9] Joseph Cardinal Ratzinger with Vittorio Messori, *The Ratzinger Report: An Exclusive Interview on the State of the Church* (Salvator Attanasio and Graham Harrison (trans.); San Francisco: Ignatius Press, 1985), p. 35. On the need for a more sophisticated and constructive reading of post-Tridentine theology and Catholic tradition than progressivist bracketing of it characteristically allows, see Christopher Ruddy, 'Ressourcement and the *Enduring* Legacy of Post-Tridentine Theology', in Gabriel Flynn and Paul D. Murray (eds), *Ressourcement: A Movement for Renewal in Twentieth-Century Catholic Theology* (Oxford: Oxford University Press, 2012), pp. 185–201.

[10] See Nicholas Lash (ed.), 'What Happened at Vatican II', in *Theology for Pilgrims*, pp. 240–8 (p. 243).

[11] For further on what follows, see Paul D. Murray, 'Roman Catholicism and Ecumenism', in Lewis Ayres and Medi-Ann Volpe (eds), *The Oxford Companion to Catholicism* (Oxford: Oxford University Press, forthcoming in 2015).

The question is, then, raised as to how this novelty in the Council's ecumenical teaching coheres with Benedict XVI's hermeneutic of *reform within the continuity of the tradition*? Is it to be properly understood as being situated within some deep continuities in Catholic self-understanding, in such manner as accords with the relatively strenuous demands of this hermeneutic? If so, then while this would not itself be to take a stand on whether this is the sole appropriate hermeneutic for interpreting the Council in all its parts (a discussion that lies well beyond the confines of this chapter), it would be to demonstrate that this particular, disputed, aspect of the Council's teaching needs no softening in order to be judged as valid when measured against this highly influential and relatively cautious way of interpreting the Council. By doing so, it would confidently enable us properly to understand the Council as being at once *both* Catholic *and* ecumenical. With that, it would also give pause to consider that Benedict XVI's hermeneutic of *reform within the continuity of the tradition* is not necessarily as reactionary as some have assumed – an intended instrument for seeking to close-down the creativity of the Council – but a means of seeking to situate it in accurate perspective and so enable it to do its properly reforming work in the life of the Church. Let us first remind ourselves of the prevailing situation prior to the Council.

In the face of the rise of the modern ecumenical movement among the Protestant traditions and, ultimately, Orthodoxy also, the 1917 Code of Canon Law had forbidden Catholics from even participating in meetings with other Christians (c. 1325), let alone from sharing in their rituals (*communicatio in sacris*; c. 1258).[12] The formal Roman mind-set was that the one true Church of Christ is to be straightforwardly and exclusively identified with the Catholic Church and that, as such, association with other Christians is to be rejected as a false 'irenicism' that would suggest a false equivalence between Catholicism and the other traditions. The only way forward, it was believed, was that of unidirectional return to Rome.[13] This deeply held conviction came to clearest expression in Pope Pius XI's 1928 encyclical *Mortalium animos*, 'On Fostering Religious Union', where we find: 'There is only one way in which the unity of Christians may be fostered and that is by promoting the return to the one true

---

[12] For English translation, see Edward N. Peters, *The 1917 Pio-Benedictine Code of Canon Law* (San Francisco, CA: Ignatius Press, 2001).

[13] It needs noting that at unofficial levels there were more positive Catholic openings to ecumenism and remarkable pioneers, such as Paul Courturier and Yves Congar. For further, see Paul D. Murray, 'Roman Catholicism and Ecumenism'; also 'Expanding Catholicity through Ecumenicity in the Work of Yves Congar: *Ressourcement*, Receptive Ecumenism, and Catholic Reform', in Flynn and Murray (eds), *Ressourcement*, pp. 457–81.

Church of Christ of those who are separated from it; for from that one true Church they have in the past unhappily fallen away'.[14] The same basic strict identity between the Church of Christ and the Catholic Church is to be found clearly in Pope Pius XII's 1943 encyclical *Mystici corporis christi* and again subsequently in his 1950 encyclical *Humani generis*.[15]

The contrast both of tone and content with what we find in the Vatican II documents is clear to view. The two key documents here are *Lumen gentium*, 'The Dogmatic Constitution on the Church' (LG), and *Unitatis redintegratio*, 'The Decree on Ecumenism' (UR). For present purposes, it will be most effective to provide an ordered synthetic summary of some of the key distinctive emphases to be found in these documents. First, relinquishing the previous attitude of one-sided fault, the Catholic Church's complicity in the historic breaks of the sixteenth century is acknowledged (UR 3). Far more significant than this, however, is the transparent acknowledgement that 'some and even very many of the significant elements and endowments which together go to build up and give life to the Church itself, can exist outside the visible boundaries of the Catholic Church'.[16] Indeed, 'To the extent that these elements are found in other Christian communities, the one Church of Christ is effectively present in them' (UR 3). On this basis, Pope John Paul II would later underline this in his remarkable 1995 encyclical on ecumenism, *Ut unum sint* (UUS), by drawing the implication that these 'elements of sanctification and truth' present in the other traditions constitute an 'objective basis' for a 'communion, albeit imperfect, which exists between (them) and the Catholic Church' (UUS 11). Moreover, these ecclesial elements are viewed as significant not just for the status of the other churches and communities in their own right and, hence, for their relationship *vis-à-vis* the Catholic Church but also – and at a number of levels – for the interior life of the Catholic Church itself: This is first so in that while 'every fullness of the means of salvation' (UR 3) is present in the Roman Catholic Church, 'the divisions among Christians prevent the church from realizing in practice the fullness of catholicity (*plenitude catholicitatis*) proper to her' and from expressing 'in actual life her full catholicity in all her bearings' (UR 4).

---

[14] Pius XI, *Mortalium Animos*, 'Encyclical Letter on Fostering Religious Union' (6 January 1928).

[15] See Pius XII, *Mystici Corporis Christi*, 'On the Mystical Body of Christ' (29 June 1943); Pius XII, *Humani Generis*, 'Concerning Some False Opinions Threatening to Undermine the Foundations of Catholic Doctrine' (12 August 1950).

[16] UR 3; also 'many elements of sanctification and truth are found outside of its visible confines' LG 8 and 'It follows that the separated churches and communities as such, though we believe them to be deficient in some respects, have been by no means deprived of significance and importance in the mystery of salvation' UR 3.

More significant, however, even than this recognition as to the negative impact of the divisions on diminishing the catholicity of the Catholic Church is the considerably bolder recognition that some of these ecclesial elements may on occasion have come to fuller flower in one or other of the other traditions than they have been able to do within Catholicism. In UR 4, we find: 'anything wrought by the grace of the Holy Spirit in the hearts of our separated brethren can be a help to our own edification. Whatever is truly Christian is never contrary to what genuinely belongs to the faith; indeed, it can always bring a deeper realization of the mystery of Christ and the Church'(UR 4).[17] In the context of reflecting specifically on relations with the Eastern churches, UR 17 notes: 'It is hardly surprising, then, if from time to time one tradition has come nearer to a full appreciation of some aspects of a mystery of revelation than the other, or has expressed it to better advantage.' Pope John Paul II again explicitly drew the implication in UUS 14 by referring to other Christian communities as places 'where certain features of the Christian mystery have at times been more effectively emphasized'.[18]

It is all of this that lies behind the ecumenical imperative of *Unitatis redintegratio* and the emphasis that is placed both there and in *Lumen gentium* on Catholicism's own need to learn, to be renewed, purified and even reformed.[19] Communion with the Bishop of Rome is still unashamedly viewed here as an essential aspect of the unity of the Church but the implication is that this would not be communion with the Bishop of Rome as currently structured within Catholicism. As such, this is not ecumenical engagement conceived as any one-sided 'return to Rome' in its current dispensation but as a call to growth on both sides and mutual journeying to a new relationship. In accordance with this, in UR 4 we find the remarkable acknowledgement: 'their [Catholics] primary duty is to make a careful and honest appraisal of whatever needs to be done or renewed in the Catholic household itself.' We are here in a different thought-frame entirely, it would seem, to that with which *Mortalium animos* was working: far from a strict and exclusive identity being assumed between the Church of Christ and the Catholic Church, there is something, at least, of the Church of Christ outside of the Catholic Church and something,

---

[17] More generally: 'Catholics must gladly acknowledge and esteem the truly Christian endowments from our common heritage which are to be found among our separated brethren . . .' (UR 4).

[18] Also UUS 48 where he speaks of the Catholic Church discovering 'what God is bringing about in the members of other churches and ecclesial communities'.

[19] For example, UR 6 speaks of ecumenism as a 'renewal' (*renovatio*) and a 'continual reformation' (*perennis reformatio*) and, similarly, LG 8 speaks of the church as being in a state of '*semper purificanda*', of always being purified.

indeed, from which Catholicism itself has to receive; it is not just the Protestant and Orthodox traditions which have a journey to travel but also Catholicism.

Returning, then, in the light of this clear contrast between pre- and post-conciliar ecumenical teaching to the governing concern of this chapter: what does it mean to read and appropriate *Unitatis redintegratio* in the light of Benedict XVI's proposed hermeneutic of *reform within the continuity of the tradition*? Does this hermeneutic represent, as some have feared, a potential side-lining and repositioning of the remarkable ecumenical openings just outlined? Does it place fidelity to Catholic tradition and ecumenical commitment, Catholicity and ecumenicity, in necessary tension and opposition? Does it leave Vatican II's ecumenical teaching as an apparent aberration, in some ways not fully and properly Catholic? Or alternatively, might his hermeneutic precisely help us understand Vatican II as properly *both* Catholic *and* ecumenical? Indeed, Vatican II as being fully Catholic precisely by being properly ecumenical and properly ecumenical precisely by being fully Catholic?

Within the terms of Benedict XVI's general hermeneutic and the specific readings of Vatican II it promoted, a key question comes down to the way in which the Council's teaching on ecumenism coheres with and has implications for the way in which the notorious *subsistit in* ('subsists in') clause of *Lumen gentium* 8 should properly be read. How, that is, is the clear and unique direct equivalence between the Church of Christ and the Catholic Church that is to be found in pre-conciliar teaching, as earlier noted, to be squared with Vatican II's equally clear recognition of there being elements of the Church of Christ in the other traditions?

'Elements' appears to suggest a partial presence, at least, of the Church of Christ in these other traditions. Again, it also seems significant that when in LG 8 the fathers of the Council turned to speak specifically of the relationship between the one Church of Christ and the Catholic Church – having spent the first seven sections of the document talking of the Church of Christ within the purview of salvation history without any specific reference to the Catholic Church – they opted, after considerable debate and consideration of alternatives, not to say straightforwardly that 'this Church of Christ *is* (*est*) the Catholic Church' but that 'this Church of Christ *subsists in* (*subsistit in*) the Catholic Church' (LG 8).[20] This, likewise, seems to suggest a non-exclusive relationship, at least of some

---

[20] For something of the to and fro of debate that has raged in this regard, see Francis A. Sullivan, S. J., 'The Meaning of *Subsistit In* as Explained by the Congregation for the Doctrine of the Faith', *Theological Studies* 69 (2008), pp. 116–24; 'A Response to Karl Becker, S. J., on the Meaning of *Subsistit In*', *Theological Studies* 67 (2006), pp. 395–409.

kind: as to quite how it does or does not reinterpret this relationship, however, has been a matter of fierce debate.

At one end of the spectrum, Leonardo Boff and others – variously appealing to what they believe best befits the line of travel, or 'spirit', of the Council's teaching and interpreting '*subsistit*' as 'exists in' or 'is present in', as distinct from the strict and exclusive equivalence of 'is' – find here an opening to an ecclesiological pluralism wherein the Church of Christ can be regarded as subsisting equivalently in many different traditions, one of which is the Roman Catholic Church.[21] If this is the case, then we would indeed be faced with a clear case of significant discontinuity with pre-conciliar teaching of the sort that arch-traditionalists denounce and arch-progressivists celebrate. While this would not in itself directly render Vatican II's ecumenical teaching illegitimate, it would, to say the least, lead those many whose frame of reference and criteria of legitimacy is shaped by Benedict XVI's hermeneutic of *reform within the continuity of the tradition* to be significantly lukewarm in its regard.

For such reasons, a huge amount of labour has been invested in trawling through the various drafts of what ultimately became *Lumen gentium*, together with the transcripts of relevant meetings, and the diaries of the participants in order to seek to establish the intent that lay behind the eventual adoption of *subsistit* rather than *est*. But in relation at least to this relativizing and non-exclusive reading of *subsists* as 'is present/exists in', we do not need to resort to such measures in order to raise significant questions about its cogency. If the Council texts are viewed as a coherent whole, then taken at face value we can see that they simply do not support such a reading.

Sure, LG and UR each give clear statement – in distinction to pre-conciliar tradition – to there being key elements of the Church of Christ in the other traditions and in ways significant for the Catholic Church itself but something essential pertaining to the unity of the Church is still regarded as missing from these traditions that is uniquely to be found within the Catholic Church alone. As UR 3 puts it: 'our separated brethren, whether considered as individuals or as communities and churches, are not blessed with that unity which Jesus Christ wished to bestow on all those who through Him were born again into one body', whereas, 'We believe that this unity subsists in the Catholic Church as something she can never lose' UR 4.

---

[21] See Leonardo Boff, *Church: Charism and Power. Liberation Theology and the Institutional Church* (John W. Diercksmeier (trans.); New York and London: Crossroad & SCM Press, 1985 [1981]).

The implication is that while the *subsistit in* of LG 8 might allow, with real freshness, for the presence of something of the one Church of Christ in the other traditions from which Catholicism itself needs to learn and receive, all that is essential to this one Church of Christ – including, most particularly, the unity that properly pertains to it – is nevertheless to be regarded as being uniquely, as distinct from perfectly, present in the Catholic Church alone. This might be to express the claim for a unique relationship between the Church of Christ and the Catholic Church far more creatively, constructively and subtly than we find in *Mortalium animos* or *Mystici corporis* but it is, nevertheless, still to express such a claim. As Lawrence Welsh and Guy Mansini put it in a recent critical survey:

> The Church . . . as founded by Christ subsists in the Catholic Church, but the Catholic Church does not exhaust, as it were, absolutely all ecclesial reality; no, elements of the Church and sometimes even churches exist outside her. There is ecclesial being outside the one and unique Church. But there is no subsistence of the one and *unique* Church founded by Christ except singularly, uniquely. And that is in the Catholic Church.[22]

In turn and if required, one might supplement the surface-level textual reading outlined here by drawing upon the more disputed terrain of Council historiography. For one reading at least of the history of the introduction of *subsistit* into conciliar discussion also favours the notion that it maintains a unique claim relative to the other traditions. Drawing on the influential, if contested, work of Alexandra von Teuffenbach, Avery Cardinal Dulles, S. J. challenges the common assumption that *subsistit* was intentionally and directly introduced as an alternative to the less ambiguous *est* with the aim of softening and loosening the unqualified claim for equivalence between the Church of Christ and the Catholic Church that the latter implies. The argument is that when *est* was found wanting on grounds of unqualified equivalence it was first replaced not by *subsistit* but by '*adest in*', or 'is present in' – the very phrase that the more ecclesiological relativist readings wish to find in *subsistit* – which was in turn rejected precisely on account of these relativistic implications. Consequently, when on 25 November 1963 the Theological Commission replaced *adest* with *subsistit* – as recommended by Sebastian Tromp, S. J. who had favoured *est* and was a 'stout defender of the position

[22] Lawrence J. Welch and Guy Mansini, OSB, '*Lumen Gentium* No. 8, and *Subsistit in*, Again', *New Blackfriars* 90/1029 (2009), pp. 602–17 (p. 613).

of *Mystici corporis*' – they are properly to be understood as wanting to say something stronger than *adest* and which maintains something of a uniqueness of relationship, albeit in significantly revised form. Dulles concludes:

> It is regrettable that the commentaries generally give the impression that *subsistit in* was a replacement for *est* and was introduced to provide for the ecclesial reality of other Christian communities. In point of fact, it was introduced as a replacement for '*adest in*' in order to safeguard the full presence of the Church of Christ in the Catholic communion.[23]

All of this in turn provides the background to the then Joseph Ratzinger's conceptually driven – drawing on the use of subsistence in Christological and Trinitiarian discourse – analogous interpretation of *subsistit* as maintaining *both* a uniqueness of relationship between the Church of Christ and the Catholic Church *and* ecclesial existence beyond the Catholic Church. From 2002, for example, we find:

> With the term *subsistit*, the Council was trying to express the particular quality of the Catholic Church and the fact that this quality cannot be multiplied: the Church exists as an active agent within historical reality. The distinction between *subsistit* and *est* does, however, imply the drama of the schism of the Church: although the Church is only one, and does really exist, there is being that is derived from the being of the Church, an ecclesiastical entity, even outside the one Church.[24]

The point of all of this for present purposes is not to claim that the disputed interpretation of this key clause in LG is now settled. Rather, it is to claim that far from Benedict XVI's hermeneutic of *reform within the continuity of the tradition* requiring the rejection, downplaying or side-lining of Vatican II teaching on ecumenism and Catholic engagement with the other Christian traditions, it is fully commensurate with it. Far from the Council's teaching on the catholicity of the Catholic Church being in tension with its teaching on ecumenicity, the full flourishing of the former requires the latter. Indeed, ecumenicity is in service of the Church becoming more catholic not less catholic.

---

[23] Avery Cardinal Dulles, 'Nature, Mission, and Structure of the Church', in Matthew L. Lamb and Matthew Levering (eds), *Vatican II*, pp. 25–36, p. 28, drawing on Alexandra von Teuffenbach, *Die Bedeutung des subsistit in (LG 8): Zum Selbstverständnis der katholischen Kirche* (Munich: Herbert Utz, 2002), especially pp. 363–92.

[24] Joseph Cardinal Ratzinger, 'The Ecclesiology of the Constitution *Lumen Gentium*', in Stephan Otto Horn and Vinzenz Pfnür (eds), *Pilgrim Fellowship of Faith: The Church as Communion* (Henry Taylor (trans.); San Francisco: Ignatius, 2005 [2002]), pp. 123–52 (pp. 147–8).

In recent years and drawing on key developments in ecumenical theology throughout the twentieth century and into the twenty-first century, Receptive Ecumenism has been articulated as an intentionally clear, even radical, outworking of the implications of Vatican II's Catholic ecumenical vision that is appropriate for the particular ecumenical climate in which we find ourselves and the challenges now presenting. Having in the first two sections of this chapter established the coherence that exists between Vatican II's ecumenical teaching and Benedict XVI's influential fundamental hermeneutical principle, the final two sections treat more briefly of the basic vision and intent at work in Receptive Ecumenism and the significant resonance that exists independently between that and some key writings of Joseph Ratzinger on ecumenism.

Receptive ecumenism as vehicle for Vatican II's ecumenical vision

Essential to the Catholic ecumenical vocation as articulated in the Vatican II texts is the core conviction that the absolutely non-negotiable goal is to work for and walk towards the full structural and sacramental communion – as distinct from uniformity – of the Christian traditions. In this perspective, the classical 'Life and Work' concern for ecumenical encounter, shared prayer and mission is both essential and insufficient. It is the basic oxygen and lifeblood of ecumenism, without which nothing else is possible; and is, as such, both the essential first-phase and abiding sustaining context of all ecumenical progress. Equally, no amount of this will in itself solve the ecumenical problem, which in its essence is to do with the broken sign-value we give to the world.

In Catholic ecumenical understanding, for the repair of this broken sign-value we need not just to be able to relate to each other across our differences but to travel to a place wherein these differences either are overcome or cease to be causes of structural and sacramental division between us. Herein we confront a problem: there is a tried and tested family of second-phase ecumenical strategies that have, until recently, proven very powerful in the context of the classical bilateral and multi-lateral dialogues, enabling many perceived historic communion-dividing differences either to be overcome or to be relativized; but these same strategies no longer appear capable of yielding their fruits, at least in the context of very mature dialogues such as the Anglican-Roman Catholic International Commission (ARCIC).

In the period following the Council, right through the second major phase of ARCIC's activity (ARCIC II), this key second-phase ecumenism did remarkable work in showing one supposed historic area of division after another either not to be a real point of difference or not to warrant a breach in communion. A complex cocktail of strategies was variously deployed to facilitate this: ranging from clarifying misunderstandings, through drawing upon fresh scholarship and understanding as appropriate and recognizing that the richness of Christian truth allows for diversity of expression and emphasis, through to being able to imagine an ideal future agreed understanding and practice to which each would be able to subscribe. These strategies, which have given such remarkable service in the context of the classical dialogues, still have great potential in the context of the younger dialogues wherein there can still be many false perceptions and assumptions to overcome. In the context of the more mature dialogues, however, it is becoming increasingly difficult to see what further work they can achieve, at least for the foreseeable future. Herein lies the problem – the apparent road-block on the formal ecumenical way – causing much talk of our being in an ecumenical winter or ecumenical cul-de-sac. The felt contrast with the energy and over-optimism flowing from the entry of Catholicism into the ecumenical movement after Vatican II is intense.

The point is that while the classical bilateral strategies are well-suited to resolving relatively 'soft-wood' issues based on misperceptions (e.g. concerning respective Eucharistic doctrine) and the erroneous assumption that the coherence of doctrinal truth requires uniformity of expression and emphasis (e.g. concerning the doctrine of justification), they are less well-suited to the more 'hard-wood' matters of substantive and significant differences between the traditions that now confront us: concerning, for example, the quite different understandings of the appropriate relationship between the universal and the local in Catholicism and Anglicanism; or the quite different procedures and structures of ecclesial decision-making; or differing discernments, at the formal level at least, of the legitimacy of ordaining women to the presbyterate. In such cases, no amount of merely clarifying respective positions will lead to substantive harmony and coherence, howsoever differentiated, as we are dealing with substantive differences. What is required, rather, is a strategy that explicitly, honestly and patiently exposes each to the challenge of the other and that calls each not simply to an expanded understanding of the other but to self-criticism and potential change in the face of the other.

It is, perhaps, held within the mysterious providence of God that during the same period as the churches collectively have been rubbing-up against these limitations in such phase-two problem-solving ecumenism and have been beginning to hear the call to 'go deeper' into the way of real ecumenical conversion, they have each also been coming to a more sober and realistic understanding of their own respective limitations and internal difficulties in various regards and their related inability to solve such matters from within their own existing resources alone. In this regard, the Christian traditions are like hamsters running around their wheels: confined by their own existing prevailing logics, which simply get reinforced the more energetically they are pushed at and which are in need of the intervention of fresh energy, fresh initiative, fresh resource from outside if closed routines and dysfunctional habits are really to be opened to renewal.

In this way, Receptive Ecumenism brings to the foreground the dispositions of self-critical hospitality, humble learning and ongoing conversion that have always been quietly essential to good ecumenical work and offers them as an explicit strategy for contemporary ecumenical engagement and progress. By doing so, it seeks to provide *both* a constructive way of walking forwards in this new phase of ecumenical endeavour in which the second-phase strategies are no longer, for the time being, seemingly capable of yielding further fruit *and* a much needed instrument for internal ecclesial renewal through transformative ecumenical learning. It is, perhaps, worth emphasizing that this is not a matter of romantic, dewy-eyed idealism but of felt need and enlightened self-interested pragmatism: the point is that it is our own interest to seek and to solve the problems we, respectively, have and receptive ecumenical learning provides a powerful resource for doing this.

With this, far from Receptive Ecumenism implying any lowest common-denominator dilution or diminishment in the respective identities of the traditions, it works towards their enrichment and expansion. In the case, for example, of Catholicism, it is not a matter of making the Catholic Church less Catholic but 'more fully, more richly Catholic and, hence, more fully, more richly the Church of Christ; more clearly "the sacrament of intimate union with God and of the unity of all mankind"'.[25] The conviction, as UR 6 puts it, is that 'Every renewal of the Church . . . essentially consists in an increase of fidelity to her own calling.'

---

[25] Paul D. Murray (ed.), 'Receptive Ecumenism and Catholic Learning: Establishing the Agenda', in *Receptive Ecumenism and the Call to Catholic Learning: Exploring a Way for Contemporary Ecumenism* (Oxford: Oxford University Press, 2008), pp. 5–25 (p. 18), citing LG 1.

Viewed in these ways, in essence Receptive Ecumenism is nothing new: simply, as William James would put it, 'a new name for some old ways of thinking'.[26] It pulls out one of the constituent cords that have always helped form the ecumenical rope, or the ecumenical plait, and gives particular focus to it in order to allow it now to do its work in a more intense way. At its heart is the conviction that further substantial progress is indeed possible on the way towards full structural and sacramental unity but only if a fundamental, counter-instinctual move is made away from traditions asking, 'What do the others need to learn about us if we are to make any progress towards agreement?' to asking instead 'What do *we* need to learn from our others if *we* are to make any progress towards addressing *our own* practical and theological problems?'

This required receptive ecclesial learning is envisaged as operating not only in relation to such things as hymnody, spirituality and devotional practices but as extending to methods of evangelization and to doctrinal and ecclesial self-understanding and, even more so, respective structural and organizational-cultural realities. Here the conviction is that further substantive ecumenical progress will happen as a felicitous by-product of a more immediate and practically rooted concern for a somewhat self-interested yet genuinely transformative ecumenical learning from each other through which each comes to recognize themselves in the other, the other in themselves and each together in the communion of the Trinity, 'united but not absorbed'.[27] And again as in personal conversion so also in ecumenical conversion, the related conviction is that God is good, taking us where we are in our respective needs and using these as the means to move us forwards under the draw of grace. But the question is in turn raised: if Receptive Ecumenism supposedly represents an articulation of Vatican II's Catholic ecumenical vision, developed for a context in which the second-phase strategies of classical bilateral and multilateral ecumenism no longer seem able to function as effective vehicles for pursuing the formal ecumenical goal, how does this cohere with Joseph Cardinal Ratzinger's and Benedict XVI's understanding of the contemporary ecumenical task?

---

[26] This is the sub-title that James gave to his hugely influential 1907 published lectures on pragmatism, see William James, *Pragmatism* (1907). Frederick H. Burkhardt, Fredson Bowers and Ignas K. Skrupskelis (eds), *The Works of William James*, Vol. I (Cambridge, MA: Harvard University Press, 1975).

[27] The evocative phrase 'united not absorbed' derives from the Malines Conversations convened by Cardinal Mercier from 1921 to 1925 between Church of England theologians and ecclesiastics and an informal group of Catholic counterparts and specifically from the work of the leading Catholic contributor, Dom Lambert Beauduin (1873–1960), founder of the ecumenical monastery of Chevetogne in 1925. For the text of Beauduin's paper, read by Cardinal Mercier in his own name at the fourth Malines conversation, see Lord Halifax (ed.), *The Conversations at Malines, 1921–1925: Original Documents* (London: Philip Allan, 1930), pp. 241–61.

Receptive ecumenical resonance with the writings of Joseph Cardinal Ratzinger and Pope Benedict XVI

Space does not permit here for an exhaustive synthetic treatment of all of the relevant ecumenical writings of Joseph Ratzinger as a private theologian, Cardinal Ratzinger as Prefect of the CDF and Pope Benedict XVI as Roman Pontiff.[28]

For present purposes, attention will largely focus on two writings of Joseph Ratzinger issued as a private theologian during his time as Prefect of the CDF and indicating the direction of travel of his own thinking on relevant matters: one a lengthy open 'letter' to the editor of the *Tübinger Theologische Quartalschrift* in 1986 and the other an essay 'On the Ecumenical Situation' first published in 1995. As will become apparent, the resonance, in part at least, between what is to be found here and what has come to quite independent articulation in Receptive Ecumenism is quite remarkable.

In his 1986 letter, Ratzinger starts out by acknowledging the significant contrast between the energy and apparent pace of achievement that marked ecumenical engagement in the years following Vatican II and what many have experienced as an immensely disappointing subsequent slow-down, at least at the formal level.[29] Similarly in the 1995 essay, for all the promise and hopes raised by this remarkable ecumenical opening, the goal of restored communion has not been reached.[30] To some extent, however, he views this contrast as reflecting a misperception: the apparent rapid pace of immediate post-conciliar ecumenical progress was in fact the coming to fruit of developments that had long been gestating and maturing, building on much patient work in the decades previous. As such, what has been experienced as a 'great disappointment' (p. 136) was in fact inevitable and 'foreseeable' (p. 135):

> The speed with which so much that was new and hitherto unexpected suddenly became possible seemed to give ground for hope of a rapid and complete end

---

[28] Indeed, a question properly arises as to whether it would even be appropriate to offer such a synthetic account. Here it is simply worth noting that while there are differences of tone and emphasis – for example, the bleak pessimism about the state of contemporary Western culture that marked much of Joseph Ratzinger's writings and which was also pronounced in the writings of the CDF under his prefecture is less pronounced in his pontifical writings – all of the key theological emphases of his pontifical teaching can, unsurprisingly, already be found in his earlier prolific writings.

[29] Translated and republished as Joseph Ratzinger (ed.), 'The Progress of Ecumenism', in *Church, Ecumenism and Politics: New Essays in Ecclesiology* (Slough and New York: St Paul & Crossroad, 1988 [1987]), pp. 135–42 (p. 135; also pp. 136 and 138).

[30] Joseph Ratzinger, 'On the Ecumenical Situation', in Stephan Otto Horn and Vinzenz Pfnür (eds), *Pilgrim Fellowship of Faith*, pp. 253–69 (p. 253), originally printed in Jean-Louis Leuba (ed.), *Perspectives actuelles sur l'œcuménisme* (Louvain-le-Neuve: Artel, 1995), pp. 231–44.

to the division. But when everything that had become possible in this way was translated into official forms a kind of standstill had necessarily to occur.[31]

Far from suggesting the need to redefine the ecumenical goal and to aim for something less ambitious than a path towards full communion, this disappointing of false expectations regarding the likely pace of further progress requires a steadfast orientation towards this goal, a recalibration of anticipated ecumenical timescales and a corresponding emphasis on the need for patient labour and real change within each of the traditions as distinct from the mere reconciliation through sophisticated negotiation of existing frameworks as they currently exist. In each of these parts, the consonance with key emphases in Receptive Ecumenism is striking.

As Ratzinger writes, a 'first' essential strand of ecumenical endeavour 'will and must continue to consist of us trying to find complete unity; to think up models of unity; to try to investigate obstacles to unity'.[32] But this will only flow from real conversion to Christ under grace rather than mere 'diplomatic skill and the ability to compromise of those conducting the negotiations'.[33] For this reason, real ecumenism must always consist 'not just in learned debates but above all in prayer and penance'.[34]

With this, we need to recognize that the timescale is not in our hands – 'we know neither the day nor the hour'[35] – and we cannot concoct, produce or force its realization – 'nor are we able to determine, when and how unity will come into existence . . . we do not create unity'.[36] Equally, however, we cannot resign ourselves either to apathy or to quietism: 'we should not sit around twiddling our thumbs'.[37] While leaving 'to God what is his business alone', we need also 'to discover what then in all seriousness are our tasks'.[38] Indeed – and again in eloquent harmony with Receptive Ecumenism – 'Ecumenism is really nothing other than living at present in an eschatological light, in the light of Christ who is coming again. It thus also signifies that we recognize the provisional nature of our activity, which we ourselves cannot finish'.[39] The question this in turn prompts is what this suggests about the appropriate mode of committed ecumenical action

---

[31] Ratzinger, 'The Progress of Ecumenism', p. 135; also p. 138.
[32] 'The Progress of Ecumenism', p. 140; also 'On the Ecumenical Situation', p. 266.
[33] 'The Progress of Ecumenism', p. 137.
[34] 'The Progress of Ecumenism', p. 140; also p. 138; 'On the Ecumenical Situation', pp. 256–8.
[35] Ratzinger, 'The Progress of Ecumenism', p. 140.
[36] 'The Progress of Ecumenism', p. 140; also 'On the Ecumenical Situation', p. 265.
[37] 'The Progress of Ecumenism', p. 140.
[38] Ibid., p. 142; also p. 265.
[39] 'On the Ecumenical Situation', p. 269.

for as long as we live short of the realization of our proper goal. How should we appropriately both live in anticipation of this goal and bear witness to it in a manner that combines 'activity and patience'?[40]

To respond to this, he makes a constructive move, in his own terms, which analogously also goes to the heart of Receptive Ecumenism. Referring appreciatively to Oscar Cullmann's introduction of the language of 'unity through diversity' into the discussion, he reflects on how, while schism is itself 'evil', there can nevertheless be something important, even providential, at issue in each of the diverse expressions of Christian life and truth that are at issue in situations of schism.[41] He then proceeds, most remarkably, to draw the implication from this in terms that could have been taken directly from the writings on Receptive Ecumenism:

> Following the path indicated by Cullman we should therefore first try to find unity through diversity. That means to accept what is fruitful in these divisions, to take the poison out of it and to receive precisely the positive element from this diversity – naturally in the hope that finally the division will cease to be a division at all and is merely a polarity without opposition.[42]

And as to what this actually means in practice: 'Here it would therefore be a question of continually learning afresh from the other as other while respecting his or her otherness. As people who are divided we can also be one.'[43] Again, 'Faith must be a matter of constant education for loving, for reverence before someone else's belief.'[44] This even needs to take priority over insistently seeking to teach the other.[45]

In conclusion and as consequence, while Ratzinger believes that ecumenical dialogue and theological engagement should certainly continue, he thinks – again as in Receptive Ecumenism – that they should be less focused on problem-solving within a given time-frame. As he puts it: 'I would say that theological dialogues, as a search for unity of belief, should certainly continue. But the actual meetings should be carried on in a much more relaxed way, less oriented toward success, in a more "humble" way, with more serenity and patience.'[46]

---

[40] 'The Progress of Ecumenism', p. 142.

[41] Ratzinger, 'The Progress of Ecumenism', p. 138, with reference to Oscar Cullmann, *Einheit durch Vielfalt: Grundlegung und Beitrag zur Diskussion über die Möglichkeiten ihrer Verwirklichung* (Tübingen: J. C. B. Mohr, 1986); and again on p. 139.

[42] 'The Progress of Ecumenism', p. 139; also 'On the Ecumenical Situation', p. 258.

[43] 'The Progress of Ecumenism', p. 140.

[44] 'On the Ecumenical Situation', p. 267.

[45] For example, 'Catholics should not try to pressurize Protestants into recognising the papacy and their understanding of the apostolic succession . . .' 'The Progress of Ecumenism', p. 141.

[46] 'On the Ecumenical Situation', p. 266.

Taken together these analyses of the contemporary ecumenical dilemma offered by Joseph Ratzinger while Cardinal Prefect of the CDF and his related prescient ideas about how best to respond with integrity in constructive mode are all highly suggestive. As has been indicated repeatedly throughout, they resonate strongly with the independently pursued analysis and strategic proposals of Receptive Ecumenism. In one sense, this might not be surprising given that they each stem from the common stock of Vatican II's Catholic ecumenical vision and it certainly further strengthens the claim of Receptive Ecumenism to be situated within a sound mainstream reading of UR and LG.

In turn, however, if there is distinction between Receptive Ecumenism and Joseph Ratzinger's ecumenical thinking here, it perhaps relates to the fact that while Cardinal Ratzinger, in his fascinating 1986 letter, clearly identified the need to take the real otherness of the ecumenical other seriously and to ask as to what might be learned from this, he did not develop this into an explicit strategy for receptive ecclesial renewal or practical programme of transformative ecumenical engagement in the way that Receptive Ecumenism seeks to do. Nor did he take the step of recognizing that the logic of this need for transformative receptive attentiveness places responsibility on Catholicism not simply to highlight the need for it at a theoretical level but to take the initiative – even unilaterally so if needs be – in modelling it. By contrast, throughout his prefecture of the CDF and his subsequent pontificate, these ponderings, these musings, remained just that, interesting ponderings and musings, rather than explicitly promoted and enacted practical principles. They may have been in composition but their time for performance was not yet.

Conclusion

Starting out by acknowledging the significant debates that have raged in relation to the interpretation of Vatican II, this chapter considered Benedict XVI's hermeneutic of *reform within the continuity of the tradition* and read this constructively as seeking to hold together both change and continuity in Catholic tradition, identity and self-understanding. The second section engaged the significant novelty of Vatican II's teaching on ecumenism and showed how this can be shown to cohere with this hermeneutic and, specifically if needs be, with Joseph Ratzinger's/Benedict XVI's interpretation of the *subsistit* phrase of *Lumen gentium* 8. In turn, the third section engaged Receptive Ecumenism as a self-conscious development of this Catholic ecumenical vision of Vatican II, explicitly fitted for the specific challenges of the contemporary ecumenical context: not a 'second-best' downsizing and accommodation of the ecumenical hope to a situation in which the goal of full structural and sacramental communion now appears to elude us but the golden highway now opens to us; a demanding but effective means of walking towards that goal by the only means possible – that is, by transformative and real learning from each other so that each can recognize themselves in the other, the other in themselves and each together in the communion of the Trinity, 'united but not absorbed'. The fourth section then complemented this by noting the significant and, perhaps, surprising resonance that exists with some of Cardinal Ratzinger's analogous analysis of the contemporary ecumenical scene and the needs and opportunities it poses but also drew to a close by noting that this was an agenda which in practice remained unfulfilled throughout the pontificate of Pope Benedict XVI.

This last point can be pressed further, in a manner at once more critical and potentially more programmatic for the current papacy of His Holiness Pope Francis. Throughout the two previous papacies the recognition alluded to earlier, of the Catholic Church – as with all the other traditions, each in their own ways – having significant internal, and not simply external, challenges on its hands that must be addressed, had been routinely institutionally suppressed, with emphasis placed instead on the church's external challenges and the need for internal discipline and unity if they are to be met. The election of Pope Francis and his words and initiatives have, by contrast, removed the taint of disloyalty from the recognition that the time has come for us in the Catholic Church to put our own house in order *ad intra* if we are to speak and witness with any credibility *ad extra*. That this time of Catholic conversion might be also pursued via the way of Receptive Ecumenism begins eloquently to be suggested by Pope Francis's own words on the ecumenical endeavour, such as in the context of his Wednesday morning exhortation during the 2014 Octave of Prayer for Christian Unity, where we find:

> It is good to acknowledge the grace with which God blesses us and, even more so, to find in other Christians something of which we are in need, something that we can receive as a gift from our brothers and our sisters. The Canadian group that prepared the prayers for this Week of Prayer has not invited the communities to think about what they can give their Christian neighbours, but has exhorted them to meet to understand what all can receive from time to time from the others. This requires something more. It requires much prayer,

humility, reflection and constant conversion. Let us go forward on this path, praying for the unity of Christians, so that this scandal may cease and be no longer with us.[47]

If Benedict XVI helps us to read *Unitatis redintegratio* aright, it is to be urgently hoped that Pope Francis will now help us to live it aright for the tri-fold sake of the health of Catholicism, the furthering of the ecumenical journey and the quality of our witness to the world and proclaiming of the gospel in act and structure.

---

[47] Pope Francis, General Audience (22 January 2014).

8

Global Catholicism: Evangelization and a Networked Church

Ian Linden[1]

What has the growing interconnectedness of the world meant for the Church and how has the Church reacted to it? What impact did the Second Vatican Council have on this process? What are its implications for evangelization? Oddly, these questions are rarely asked or directly answered.

Globalization and the Church

Contemporary accounts of this global interconnectedness vary greatly. Perspective alters the picture. But few would deny that the development of a single global market, created by countless economic transactions in cyberspace, and in real time, is both a unique and a significant feature. Economic globalization is a self-generating *process* driven by market forces, subject to the *policies* of a number of different key agencies and the decisions of remarkably few players. None of this seems directly relevant to changes within the Church. Although the Church may, and does, have important things to say about desirable and undesirable forms of economic activity.

The proximate cause of the growth of this global market is a dramatic communications revolution, redolent of the development of an information economy and a networked society throughout the industrialized world, reaching increasingly into the global South. The pre-condition for this change is the unique human ability to inhabit and manipulate a shared symbolic universe, a capacity open to a concept of sacramentality, but now digitalized and directed

[1] This chapter is a new version of a chapter originally published in Ian Linden's book *Global Catholicism: Toward a Networked Church: Revised and Updated Second Edition* by Ian Linden, © Ian Linden, used with kind permission by Hurst Publishers, UK.

to financial gain. What is taking place *might* be expected to reduce the world's diversity of human languages and the particularity of its cultures to a drab homogeneity, hitting the rewind button on the biblical story of the Tower of Babel.[2] This does not appear to be happening even if some languages are dying out. But it has obvious relevance to the future of the Church and its impact on the world. Indeed, it has hastened the birth of a more networked Church.

The shift to an information economy may herald the beginning of a new epoch in human history on the model of the changes induced by the move from agricultural to industrial production. It is certainly a distinctive new phase, driven by technology and transnational expansion with its quest for profit, marked off from several previous periods of globalization. Former epoch changes, notably from agricultural to urbanized industrial societies – which had a massive impact on the Church – have taken place at different rates in different regions of the world. The growth of information economies may herald greater transformation.

Each epoch had a profound impact on the nature of production. But each change of epoch also had an impact on states' projection of power and on the nature of human sociability and experience. So contemporary globalization is characterized by significant cultural as well as economic changes, taking place in a global patchwork of different economic formations. The Church as a global institution and a major provider of what Pope John Paul II called 'life's interpretative keys', the prism through which we see and understand the world, is inevitably affected.[3]

Economics is about how people make a living so many anthropologists place economic change as a sub-set of cultural change. Catholicism has something to say about both and, notably, about justice, equity and charity. Setting economics apart from its social and cultural framework can obscure profound causal relations and interactions. Worse, it creates a zone of human activity and study, self-defined by hard-line economists as ethics-free. In the context of globalization, culture and ethics both make up key dimensions of the technological and wealth-generating – profit-motivated – transformations that have been underway since the invention of the micro-chip in 1971. Both deeply concern the Church.[4]

---

[2] Manuel Castells, *The Rise of the Network Society* (2nd edition; Malden, MA: Blackwell, 2000), p. 101. It has, of course, done nothing of the sort, though several cultures struggle for hegemony.

[3] Ian Linden, *A New Map of the World* (London: Darton, Longman & Todd, 2004) attempts a critique of Castells's thesis that such an epoch change as occurred from agricultural to industrial society has now occurred with the growth of an information economy and network society.

[4] Brad S. Gregory, *The Unintended Reformation. How Religious Revolutions Secularized Society* (Cambridge, MA: Harvard University Press, 2012), pp. 295–6 provides a fascinating historical

The global economic crisis, beginning in Europe in 2008, is the consequence of a metastatic growth of the financial services sector within the global market, facilitated by the micro-chip, de-humanized by automated computer programmes and driven by cycles of capital accumulation. In cultural terms, this has been accompanied by the ideology of *economism*: economic growth seen as the supreme value of the modern state, driving out principles of equity, co-operation and trust at best to be sequestered in a marginal, image-oriented, add-on activity described as 'corporate social responsibility', at worst as – imagined – individual rational choice as the arbiter of the Common Good. The financial market has been configured as an otiose High God beyond human control, unpredictable and punitive.[5]

Globalization and evangelization

So, in what sense is it meaningful to talk about a Church, made up of 1.3 billion members, involved in, or interacting with, 'globalization'? Despite its size and scope, it is uncommon to factor in the Roman Catholic Church when describing the main features of today's interconnectedness, or reflecting on the vagaries of global markets. True, the Catholic Church as an agency, beneficiary or victim of globalization features only as a minor player in relation to the epoch-making changes that have been sketched earlier. But not a negligible player if its previous history, its impact on values, economic ethics, human rights, human development and our social imagination are considered.

It is unlikely that contemporary changes of the magnitude described earlier could fail to evoke *some* elements of a new consciousness in the Church about its global presence, some new ways of conceptualizing and talking about its mode of action, its deepest identity, what might be meant by evangelization in a changing world, the vision, values and virtues it needs to be promoting. But for a Church that, since the time of its foundation, relies heavily for its legitimacy on the principle of historical continuity, and on monarchical forms of authority, modernity and innovation are not alluring flags of convenience. The natural inclination today is to look back: to the radical thinking of the Church Fathers on poverty, to the Franciscans on usury, to the Salamanca Dominicans on

---

meta-narrative of how economics became detached from any account of human living – and its consequences.

[5] Robert Harris, *The Fear Index* (London: Hutchinson, 2011) is a fine literary reflection on these themes in the form of a high tension thriller about an out-of-control computer programme.

natural rights, to affirm wittingly or unwittingly a European rather than a global consciousness. What officially is projected into the public domain about today's Catholicism is predominantly ritual and tradition.

Then, what *are* the future implications of an epoch change of this potential magnitude for the Church? At the most mundane level, the Church as an international institution exists in a connected world featuring numerous other supra-national organizations – some intergovernmental and some non-governmental. From 1971 to 1993, the global tally of transnational corporations rose from 7,000 to 37,000. If the Church is to be more than another big corporation, competing for a spiritual market share, if it is to fulfil its mandate as light of the world, it needs to be present in a unique way in mass media, in cyberspace, on the internet, as well as in parishes, in nation-states and in international fora.

The multidimensional and culturally multi-vocal nature of Christian presence and engagement in the twenty-first century still awaits adequate theological elaboration and institutional expression. This is a necessary pre-condition for finding the right measures for the pursuit of a new evangelization today.

Because of the heavy weighting given to tradition, continuity and the supra-national nature of the authority vested in the Petrine Office, explanations of how the Catholic Church is reacting to contemporary globalization, and its impact on Church life, demand historical treatment. The Church post-Vatican II entered a new period but it did so in a way determined by events and with internal dynamics generated at least as far back as the French Revolution. The debate about whether the Second Vatican Council represented continuity or change in the Church reflects the fault-lines in contemporary ecclesiology far more than disagreements based on conflicting historical evidence.

Changes in the nature of political power, from Roman emperors to kings and princes, from alliances of throne and altar to revolutionary committees and liberal democratic parliaments, have signalled tactical shifts moving the Church and its ecclesiology from one track to another. This has involved not only a shift in the way ecclesiastical power is projected. It resulted in, and was accompanied by, lasting changes in theological focus and emphasis, and even, to some extent, in the manner in which members of the Church experienced the reality of Church life through changing political contexts.

Central to understanding this complex story is the role of the supranational and – at least in pretension – the *global* papacy, and reactions to its claims and to the projection of its power. When Louis XIV called a general assembly of the French clergy in 1682, he declared what he hoped would be a final division of powers: 'the Pope has only received from God a spiritual power. Kings and princes are not subject in temporal matters to any ecclesiastical authority.'[6] From the United States of John Locke to the presidential campaign of John F. Kennedy, Catholics remained suspect, guilty until proven otherwise of not giving wholehearted allegiance to the national sovereignty. Dorothy Day, kneeling when the American anthem was played, represented both Church as counter-culture and Church as threat. The Catholic Church, like any contemporary transnational corporation, was seen in the 1960s – not unreasonably – as a potential political force, or at least a force not fully under the control of the state. And until the later half of the nineteenth century, this force exerted not merely soft power, getting the state to want what the Church wanted, laws enacted favourable to the Church's mission and favourable to its ethical framework. It also exerted some significant – though proxy – military capacity.

One solution to this perceived challenge by the Church to national sovereignty was to cut out the Pope as intermediary in bestowal of legitimacy on monarchs and governments. The king could present himself as anointed by God and receiving authority directly, or via local bishops – more easily under the king's control. Bishop Bossuet's defence of the Gallican clergy who accepted this position in France, his precarious stance caught between Louis XIV and the Pope, would probably find sympathy with the bishops of the Patriotic Church of China today. Bossuet's clever compromises, and the abrogation of the Pope's former claims, provided a way forward for clergy and bishops, at least so long as Kings were moderately and publicly pious. The old formula *cuius regio, eius religio* – agreed at the Peace of Augsburg in 1555, which required the ruled to adopt the religion of the ruler – did not require kings to be saintly for it to work. But after the French Revolution, with its rationalism and anti-clericalism, and in the nineteenth century sea of revolutions, the attraction of 'ultramontanism' (a reference to Rome 'beyond the mountains') sprang from a need for papal authority. The local Church was acutely aware of its vulnerability. Rome appeared as the only, if symbolic, port in a storm.[7]

---

[6] Émile Perreau-Saussine, 'French Catholic Political Thought from the Deconfessionalism of the State to the Recognition of Religious Freedom', in Ira Katznelson and Gareth Stedman Jones (eds), *Religion and the Political Imagination* (Cambridge: Cambridge University Press, 2010), pp. 150–70 (p. 15).

[7] In the context of revolutionary upheaval Bossuet's Gallican dispensation that allowed, in his own kingdom, a king to trump the Pope's authority, now manifestly did not work for the French Church. The papacy appeared to the French hierarchy again as the only bulwark against tyranny. The Savoyard philosopher, Joseph de Maistre, after 1789 famously rallied much of the French Church in his championing of Rome's authority.

Papal infallibility declared by the first Vatican Council in its constitution, *Pastor aeternus*,[8] reinforced the spiritual power of the papacy – its soft power. At the same time, as a necessary balancing concession, Rome finally conceded temporal power. Under the impact of liberalism and nationalism in Europe, the Vatican had already lost its capacity to marshal hard power alliances. The Church of Constantine was, at least theoretically, relegated to history. The days of the confessional state were numbered. From 1929, the Church would henceforth seek protection of its rights and privileges primarily through negotiated concordats. The Vatican concordat with Italy provided the Holy See as a legal entity with the useful protection of a sovereign state, the Vatican City. The role of its nuncios and apostolic delegates to other countries, its presence at the United Nations and in its constituent bodies, were an important expression of its future globalization.

Globalization with an ultramontane papacy

The Church's globalization through an ultramontane (or Rome-oriented) papacy that could make use of a notional sovereign state in the twentieth century and its antipathy to popular sovereignty and nascent democracy have complex causes. Because of the Vatican's location in Italy, and because of a deliberate concentration of power in the Pope and in a Curial bureaucracy, Catholicism's subsequent development as a global community has retained a distinctive Eurocentric character.

The Church around the world found a way forward politically with Christian Democracy as a means for Catholics to achieve the *restoration* of the social order. Only later came a call for a *new* social and economic order, characterized by development, justice and peace, a world that is more fully human, and the need for human liberation. But a ready accommodation with dictatorships by the Catholic Right seeking to crush Communism was the other dimension of a thoroughly politicized Catholicism.

The second Vatican Council, 1962–5, brought together bishops and archbishops from every continent, patriarchs from ancient Middle Eastern Churches in communion with Rome, heads of mission societies and, as guests, representatives from other Churches and a handful of women observers

---

[8] *Pastor Aeternus*, Dogmatic Constitution on the Church of Christ (1870), in Josef Neuner and Jacques Dupuis (eds), *The Christian Faith* (revised edition; London: Collins, 1982).

who were not permitted to participate in debates. It represented few of their preoccupations adequately. As an essentially European Council, at least as far as who was influential, largely European concerns prevailed and emerged in Council documents. The dominant voices, and the major contributors to its documents, in order of importance and in terms of determining outcomes, were French, Italian, German and Dutch, alongside Italian curial officials, and some effective American interventions.

Only in the preparation of the document that finally emerged as *Nostra aetate*, on other faiths – and because of its origins as a statement on Judaism – did the contribution of the Middle Eastern bishops prove decisive. On religious freedom, the US theologians made a major contribution. They also influenced *Gaudium et spes* ('Pastoral Constitution on the Church in the Modern World') through key amendments. Beyond these documents, and apart from the 'Decree on the Church's Missionary Activity' (*Ad gentes*), of its very nature *explicitly* global in scope, bishops from other nations sometimes starred, sometimes captivated the bishops in the aula, but played only a small determinative role.[9]

By the eve of the second Vatican Council, the Catholic Church had become a self-consciously global community: African babies featured as emotive beneficiaries of European charitable giving, missionary clergy were financially supported by Catholics in the developed world and prayers were regularly said for the persecuted Church behind the Iron Curtain, whether in China, Eastern Europe or the Soviet Union, by Catholics around the world. American Catholics were proud of, and looked to, Asia and Latin America as heroic fields of missionary endeavour. But structurally the Catholic Church was an Italian/European-led, and dominated, international organization. At the time, the influential theologian, Karl Rahner expressed this ambiguity by speaking of the Catholic Church as being on the verge of *becoming* a global Church. Yet, as far as control of its leading structures was concerned, this was more than half a century away from realization. The size of the Catholic community in Latin America, for example, and the extraordinary success of Catholic religious orders there, has still not been reflected in the number of leadership roles in the Vatican. The disproportionate European weighting in the council, compared to the fast-growing Churches of the developing world, is still manifest in the Vatican today, though somewhat diminished.

⁹   Giuseppe Alberigo and Joseph A. Komonchak, *History of Vatican II*, Vols I–V (Maryknoll, NY: Orbis, 1995–2006).

The second Vatican Council, when it was not addressing the core issue of the nature of the Church itself, spoke mainly to the spiritual and ecclesiastical mind-set and problems of bishops from the richer developed world. For a variety of reasons, it failed to give a clear theological priority to the plight of those suffering from persistent poverty, the 'little ones', the 'Jesus agenda'. The theological agenda and pressures on the Church in the developed world preoccupied the assembled Fathers most: matters of authority in the Church, Latin in the liturgy, ecumenism, the challenge of Judaism and other faiths. Were more than perhaps 1 per cent of the global Catholic community worried whether human beings had a 'natural desire for the supernatural', were they expressing confusion about the nature of revelation or fears about rationalism, relativism and modern biblical exegesis? It seems unlikely. Only in *Gaudium et spes* would the world see the Church indisputably trying to come to terms with contemporary ideas and life, with 'modernity', with the hopes and fears of the world, and then only as work in progress. This is not to diminish the council's extraordinary importance but merely to set it in historical context.

The Second Vatican Council: towards a networked Church

Notwithstanding today's fractious debate about continuity and change, the Council was not a moment of 'radical discontinuity'. But this does not mean that the majority of the bishops had no sense of it being a turning point. Bishops felt themselves part of a global movement with a new sense of collegiality. It was taken as a great and irrevocable event by council participants and by Catholics around the world, a spiritual awakening breathing new life into the Church. Significant changes in theological emphases emerged to justify this impression.

Due to pioneering theological work that had preceded the Council, notably for example, from Jacques Maritain, Yves Congar, Marie-Dominique Chenu and Karl Rahner, the Council conceded transformation of the temporal sphere to the laity. Constructing Christendom, an idea that now mutated into building 'the Kingdom of God', transforming the economic, social and political spheres, was acknowledged as the work of lay people. With the whole Church they shared, in the opening lines of *Gaudium et spes*, 'the joys and hopes, the grief and anguish of the people of our time, especially of those who are poor or afflicted', and not as alien observers but as co-workers in the world's transformation. By the 1971

Synod of Bishops, this task was being described as a constitutive dimension of the preaching of the gospel, at the very heart of the Church's mission.[10]

Yet, the clear account of a lay/clerical division of responsibilities among Christians had the side effect of perpetuating a division between a hierarchy, endowed with spiritual power and institutional authority, and a laity, whose job description included the acquisition of temporal power, the duty to transform the world by action for justice and peace but under the authority of the hierarchy. It perversely gave succour to an enduring, if threatened, clericalism. Bishops, priests, religious and laity together made up 'the People of God', but soon the term drifted through popular usage into meaning 'the laity' alone. This left bishops, priests and religious, in that order, projected as exclusive bearers of the title 'the Church'.

In theory, a division of roles demanded the withdrawal of clergy from the political sphere, a theme taken up strongly by Paul VI and John Paul II. In practice, this was neither applied rigorously nor impartially, least of all in the case of Christian Democracy in Italy and *Solidarnosc* in Poland. Clerical support, sometimes involvement, in both these political movements was given far more than a benign blind eye, though Pope John Paul II, unlike Paul VI, had no stake in the future of Christian Democracy. Liberation theology in Latin America was afforded the opposite, and subject to the closest scrutiny and public criticism.

At the level of Pope and Vatican, the separation of spheres inferred a distinction between sacred and secular judgement, the former necessarily general and applying for all time to all contexts, the latter contextual, concrete, specific and lay. This acted as a persistent limitation on wholehearted clerical support for structural change and social justice that went beyond giving succour to the victims of injustice. If the action could be deemed political, the biblical injunction to 'read the signs of the times' was not to be taken as determining action for the whole Church. Nuncios worked diplomatically behind the scenes on specific human rights abuses, Catholics in ecumenical bodies challenged governments openly, but there was only very limited co-ordination between different levels of the Church. The people of God marched against injustice in divided columns easily ambushed by the extreme Right.

That poverty was the 'dog that didn't bark' at the council was in some ways a reflection of these divisions. The absence of in-depth spiritual reflection on

---

[10] Joseph Gremillion (ed.), *The Gospel of Justice and Peace: Catholic Social Teaching since Pope John* (Maryknoll, NY: Orbis Books, 1976), pp. 513–29 contains the document known as 'Justice in the World'.

global poverty in the council texts left a theological need crying out to be filled. The Latin American Church which was most concerned with the plight of the poor, now suffering under dictatorships and military oligarchies, immediately assumed the task. The spirituality of what soon became known as 'the Church of the Poor' created a continent-wide and, later, a global agenda for a 'new humanity', the birth of a global Church from below joined in common cause with like-minded bishops.

What made the socio-economic and political context of Latin America special for the Church was that, by the 1950s, and only to some degree in response to the threat, or pull, of Marxist ideology, a critical mass of bishops, priests and sisters was already engaged in pro-poor projects at a parish or diocesan level. They were poised to create a new, Gospel-based vision of evangelization.[11] A variety of lay organizations responding to poverty around the world, notably Catholic development agencies in Europe and North America, emerged and expanded in the 1960s. It was not long before they were absorbing and reflecting core aspects of this new vision.

During the early years of his papacy, Paul VI gave priority to this concern for the poor, addressing the theme of global justice in his encyclical *Populorum progressio*, a document that still has a contemporary ring almost half a century later, so Latin American initiatives were not initially seen as threatening. But the warm, popular reception of liberation theology in, for example, Brazil, Peru and Central America, and its interpellation of a Church of the poor, evoked a strong backlash. Under powerful pressures, an increasingly anxious pope began to retreat. A concerted counter-attack gained momentum, involving the Roman Curia – that had not been reformed as most bishops had hoped – in alliance with conservative Church leaders in Latin America. This was reinforced by the shadowy efforts of the CIA. Poised between honesty, speaking truth to power, and hope, seeking redistribution of power to the poor, a vital movement for the spiritual health of the Church was vulnerable.

The persecution of Christians applying Catholic social teaching to the circumstances of Latin America, analysing and acting on their local circumstances, a task recommended in papal encyclicals of the day, is well documented.[12] What is not always appreciated is that the elaboration and dissemination of liberation theology was part of a global de-centring of the Catholic Church. The process

---

[11] Ian Linden, *Global Catholicism: Diversity and Change since Vatican II* (2nd edition; New York: Columbia University Press, 2009), pp. 111–7.
[12] Ibid., pp. 91–153.

was also underway in Asia, and to a much lesser degree in Africa. The famous call from the father of liberation theology, Gustavo Gutiérrez, to 'drink from our own wells' was backed up by the new synods of bishops.[13] Drawn from around the world, set in motion by Paul VI who accepted that work for social justice was constitutive of true evangelization, the gathered bishops endorsed the idea that this demanded analysis of the causes of injustice.

This process of de-centring, spearheaded by Latin America, heralded an important development in the globalization of the Church. Within the global body, Rome spoke definitively – *Roma locuta est* – with messages passed down to local Churches as to the ends of empire. But now other centres were developing. The most notable nodes in these developing networks were the continent-wide Latin American and Asian bishops' conferences. These had emerged in the 1950s and created important secretariats, clearing houses for pastoral methodologies and funds to support them, and in consequence secondary power centres. The Asian Churches soon came to rival the European and American laity with a strong professional middle-class who were respectful towards, but far from subservient, Rome. Those participating in the new Catholic organizations and confronting problems not found in Italy or Europe encountered like-minded and articulate co-workers. Together they discussed and forged ways of working involving a dialectic between biblical study and pastoral action, each with social and liturgical dimensions. Pastoral institutes with a justice and peace or human rights mandate formed subsidiary nodes that encouraged ecumenical collaboration. From Cuernavaca to Rio del Plata, Uruguay to Nicaragua, radical theologians from different denominations moved easily from seminaries into such centres. Via these networks and those of the religious orders, contextual theology entered the bloodstream of the global Church influencing activists as far afield as South Africa, South Korea and the Philippines where comparable political regimes prevailed. Contextual theology soon found fertile soil and spread through the World Council of Churches.

The development of this embryonic networked Church was a natural consequence of the working out of the major Vatican II constitutions, particularly that on the Church, *Lumen gentium*. The ecclesiology of this seminal document offered a sophisticated collegial vision that set hierarchy and laity in the context of a community of communities, or better, a communion of the *people of God*. Yet the high theology of the council never quite touched base with the reality that it was bringing to birth. Pope Paul VI, under pressure from a curia that

---

[13] Gustavo Gutiérrez, *We Drink from Our Own Wells* (Maryknoll, NY: Orbis Books, 1984).

never conceded defeat, clung to a version of the papacy defined as supremacy rather than primacy.

The then Father Joseph Ratzinger, an influential German theologian, shared and contributed to the council vision. It re-balanced the lop-sided picture of the Church that the hastily ended first Vatican Council had bequeathed. Bishops were returned to their rightful place alongside the pope who, as the bearer of the Petrine Office, was *primus inter pares* in the global college of bishops. Each part of the people of God had its role and significance, not so much in the pre-war formula of different functions in the *body of Christ*, but as bearers of different Pauline gifts distributed throughout the people of God, making up a pilgrim nation, in the service of the world and for the building of the Kingdom.[14]

The conjuncture of these different developments with their institutional, cultural, biblically motivated and theological elements was the precondition for realizing a truly global Church. It was a Church in which a degree of what would now be called multiculturalism was both inevitable and theologically mandated. Although, the clerical Church enforced rigid seminary discipline, and where it could, a uniform liturgical culture – or at least tried to do so, the laity were necessarily rooted, *inculturated* in diverse cultures and not easily subject to this discipline.[15] The pressures against too much diversity grew. They were reinforced by Pope Benedict's missiology, an understanding of the defining qualities of Christian mission that claimed Hellenist thought as providential. By 2007, the bishops of Southern Africa were pushing back on the previous incorporation of African religious practices and rites in the Christian life cycle and worship.[16] The Asian bishops were less easily swayed.

Throughout this period, the Church of Eastern Europe and the Communist world understandably looked to Rome, just as the embattled Church had done after the French Revolution, and for much the same reasons. Just as the early Church in Eastern Europe and Western Asia was repelled by the barbarian cultures in which they lived, so the Church under Communism looked to the promise of a new Christian culture. Communism was a threatening and ideological enemy, a clear and present danger. With liberal democracy, some degree of accommodation could be achieved. Communism was far worse than

---

[14] Austin Flannery (ed.), *The Basic Sixteen Documents: Vatican Council II* (Dublin: Dominican Publications/Costello Publishing Co., 1996), pp. 1–95.

[15] Nicholas M. Creary, *Domesticating a Religious Import: The Jesuits and the Inculturation of the Catholic Church in Zimbabwe, 1879–1980* (New York: Fordham University Press, 2011), p. 234. This book contains an excellent chapter on the *Kurova Guva* controversy.

[16] Ibid., pp. 148–53.

that: it was *the* enemy, for Rome after John XXIII died, beyond any possible accommodation.

Under the pressures of the Cold War, the global Church almost split along geopolitical lines. Catholics in Moscow, for example, with access to only limited information, saw Cardinal Paulo Arns of Sao Paolo in Brazil as a crypto-Communist. In reality, he was the inspired – some would say saintly – architect of a coherent pastoral strategy that honoured a preferential option for the poor in Latin America's greatest megacity. A Polish Pope, John Paul II, appeared not to understand why the allegations of the Latin American conservatives, that liberation theology was Communist infiltration of the Church, should not be taken at face value. Rome could seem very different from an Eastern European tower block than from a Latin American *barrio* – though in both contexts some local bishops found Vatican interventions, at times, misguided, irritating and unhelpful.

Controlling a networked Church

The spread of Latin American liberation theology through a de-centred networked Church did not commend to Rome any loosening of central control. It promoted the opposite: the conclusion that official globalization of the Church should only take place on an ultramontane pattern of information flows between centre and periphery. The Vatican and its curia, at times, looked for all the world like a living proof of Weber's theory of bureaucracy: power sustained through a mastery of information flows, through secrecy and arcane structures, and controlled by a tight-knit elite cadre of officials.

The election of John Paul II to the papacy in 1978, bringing with him a compelling and alternative experience of Catholicism under Communism – and National Socialism – did little to promote a positive attitude towards the secular nor towards accommodation with secular societies. To survive, he believed, the Church had to be a united, alternative society, a counter-culture. John Paul II's strong leadership provided a powerful counter-force to the growth of a networked model of global Catholicism. The new Pope tirelessly visited local Churches modelling at the periphery the symbolic power of the centre, and highlighted with theatrical charisma the authority of the papacy. Liberation theology was attacked because of its Marxist sociology, and absorbed into a centrally proclaimed and carefully circumscribed 'preferential option for the poor'. His manifest concern for the poor moderated the strictures of the Sacred

Congregation of the Doctrine of the Faith but anyone obviously tainted with radical or 'relativist' ideas stood little chance of elevation to higher office. A few approved movements thrived, some, such as the badly flawed Legionaries of Christ, reflecting badly on the Pope's judgement or awareness of the man leading the organization.[17]

The ability to work effectively with a wide register of cultures and idioms towards a common goal is the touchstone of successful globalized institutions. The Catholic Church's ambiguity towards *inculturation*, the incarnation of Christian living in a particular culture, people making their own the gospel message, has continued to characterize the post-Vatican II period. On the one hand, there has been the acknowledged need to root new Churches in their own soil after missionary success – and in the context of successful Independence movements. And there was a manifest respect for ancient cultures based on a doctrine of the Holy Spirit:

> For thousands of years you have lived in this land and fashioned a culture that endures to this day. And during all this time, the Spirit of God has been with you. Your 'dreaming', which influences your lives so strongly that, no matter what happens, you remain forever the people of your culture, is your way of touching the mystery of God's Spirit in you and in creation . . . Jesus calls you to accept his words and his values into your own culture. To develop in this way will make you more than ever truly Aboriginal.

This is Pope John Paul II speaking in Alice Springs, Australia.[18] In the encyclical *Redemptoris missio* (1990), he expressed his thinking in more general terms in the idiom of his strong doctrine of the Holy Spirit: 'The Spirit's presence and activity affect not only individuals but also society and history, peoples, cultures and religions.'[19] Yet, on the other hand, from the Chinese rites controversy in the early seventeenth century to Cardinal Joseph Ratzinger's warnings to the Theological Advisory Commission of the Federation of Asian Bishops Conferences in the 1990s, the application of such a rich theology of the Holy

---

[17] The founder of the Legionaries of Christ, Father Marcial Maciel, a clever sex abuser, maintained a friendship with Pope John Paul II who apparently dismissed all allegations against him. The movement was brought under papal control by Pope Benedict XVI in 2010 when longstanding allegations against Maciel were finally dealt with.
[18] John Paul II Address to the Aborigines and Torres Strait Islanders in Blatherskite Park, Alice Springs (29 November 1986), pp. 2, 12.
[19] See Jacques Dupuis, *Toward a Christian Theology of Religious Pluralism* (Maryknoll, NY: Orbis Books, 1997), pp. 220–3 where he takes this further and concludes that 'the fruits of the Spirit of God in the religious tradition of peoples testifies to God's saving and revealing action among them and through their history'.

Spirit to the lives of Christians in the developing world has been circumscribed by Rome. 'Its experience of the other religions has led the Church in Asia to [a] positive appreciation of their role in the divine economy of salvation', the Asian theologians declared, moving only a tiny step further than Pope John Paul II but a step too far for the Congregation of the Doctrine of the Faith (CDF) in Rome.[20]

By the 1990s, the once promising synods of bishops, in contrast to the comparative freedoms of their early creative days, were tightly and, sometimes, humiliatingly checked. Formally under full papal authority, their degree of freedom and importance depended on each Pope's attitude to collegiality. The globally networked programmes of *Caritas Internationalis*, with a budget of $5 billion and a staff of 1 million around the world – the once democratically structured international development arm of the Church located in Rome with a lay secretary-general – were closely monitored, frequently interfered with, and then brought under the control of a clerical dicastery, Cor Unum. In the hothouse of clerical Rome, matters not tightly under curial direction smacked of culpable inattention, or, at least, the potential loss of central control.[21] Whether in inclusive language in the English translation of the Mass, seminary education or exploratory theological writings, Rome practised an obsessive micro-management.

To what degree this reflected Cardinal Ratzinger's style of leadership, *his* policies being implemented after he took over as cardinal prefect of the Vatican's increasingly powerful theological monitoring/censorship body the CDF, is a matter of speculation. They were policies that, in the main, dovetailed with Pope John Paul II's concern for discipline and a united front against Communism. Cardinal Ratzinger's fear of conciliar reform running out of control informed the attitudes of the CDF. As an Augustinian with no illusions about human nature, he always had reservations about where the council's optimistic Christian humanism would take the Church. Cardinal Ratzinger believed that nothing less than the eternal truths of the faith were the responsibility of his doctrinal congregation. His duty was to be a safe pair of hands.

---

[20] Ibid., p. 220. Dupuis's work as a Jesuit was in India. He was a theological adviser to the Indian Bishops and in this sense an 'Asian' theologian. He was investigated by the CDF for much the same views as expressed here on religious pluralism.

[21] Dr Leslie-Anne Knight was barred from standing for re-election as general-secretary of Caritas Internationalis in 2011 by the Vatican. She had been under pressure from Cor Unum from whom she had allegedly shown un-diplomatic levels of independence alongside making justice and development – as a constitutive dimension of evangelization – central to policy. See Duncan MacClaren, 'Reining in Caritas', *The Tablet* (12 May 2012), pp. 8–9.

By the time Cardinal Ratzinger was elected Pope Benedict XVI, millennium celebrations had given way to a new chaotic decade. Globalization had created a two-speed Church with Rome's centripetal demands curtailing pluralist and centrifugal forces unleashed by the council. Lay people who experienced the council as permission to be equal partners in the mission of the Church had long since felt as if this permission were being revoked. Clerical structures had begun to be inherently unstable after the late 1960s as vocations nose-dived in the developed world – while remaining broadly sustained in the developing world. By the beginning of the new millennium already depleted Catholic congregations were melting away from Mass attendance in Europe, sometimes precipitously as in Ireland, in the wake of child abuse scandals. The future of the Church now lay, even more obviously, in the global South with its non-Western cultures, and its religious idiom of burgeoning Pentecostalism and non-Christian religions.

Tensions became more acute as Pope Benedict XVI promoted an idea of the Church's mission that seemed to present a European worldview as inextricably and essentially linked to the gospel message – and thus to Christian culture and Church culture – not simply by the historical accident of a Hellenised Palestine, but by divine dispensation. In Sunday homilies, the specificity of an Aramaic historical Jesus had long been in danger of being lost behind a *Logos* of Greek philosophy. In the 1970s, a ground-breaking book by the South African Dominican theologian, Albert Nolan, *Jesus before Christianity*, told the story of a Jesus situated in the complex socio-economic and political world of his time.[22] The book rooted the council's Christian humanism historically. Because of its historical focus, the Church did not feature and so it appealed openly to, and gently challenged, secular audiences. The book was a runaway success. It narrowly missed censure. Meanwhile African and Asian theologians and laity, in growing numbers, were spontaneously inculturating their faith with scant regard for Greek thought, and sometimes creating hybrid forms of Catholicism.

The Pope presented his missiology with subtlety but it was easily read as a fundamental binary opposition: either a Christian culture in which Faith and Reason – equated with Greek philosophical categories and the Augustinian tradition – come together in a final emancipation of humanity, or an inexorable drift into moral relativism so that things fell apart. It showed an understandable intellectual rigour after his experience of Germany's drift into Nazi Rule, and

---

[22] Albert Nolan, *Jesus before Christianity* (3rd edition; Maryknoll, NY: Orbis Books, 2001).

the betrayal of the German Christians. But it was unpalatable to many African and Asian Christians. And yet, the spectre of spreading Pentecostalism, globally successful, with its negligible concern for the rich history of Christian thought, and limited interest in reasoned theological reflection, seemed to provide a contemporary lesson in what might await if the Pope took his hand off the tiller.

The Church in China suggests an important exception to these trends. It has been providing the Pope with an unexpected ally. The Christian revival in twenty-first century China is a prodigious event, even if clearly linked in part to rapid social and economic change. One of several reasons is an underlying Confucian culture, or at least a family-based culture that finds resonance in Thomas Aquinas's vision of an organic society. Aristotle is alive and well in the philosophy syllabi of some Chinese university departments. Both Christian and Confucian ethics provide the principal social cement and framework of meaning for a society stressed to breaking point by mass labour migration. They provide an insurance against the imminent danger of society fragmenting under the impact of fast-tracked manufacturing industry, rapid urbanization and the marketization of the economy. In the face of a Communist Party with a necessarily ambiguous relationship to resurgent religion, even a significant part of the Patriotic Church now looks to Rome for legitimacy.

Globalization from below

The dynamics of global Catholicism today still retain the residual polarities of its ultramontane versus Gallican antecedents. Relations between Rome and national hierarchies can be a stand-off, punctuated by overbearing intrusions from Rome, as for example in matters liturgical and educational, the clumsy attack on Women Religious in the United States, or the initial head-in-sands reaction to the cover-up of sex abuse scandals. The inability to confront and defeat clericalism, the dominance of a priestly elite put on a pedestal by the laity – though not for much longer – the failure to implement more than fragments of the vision of the Second Vatican Council, has had dire consequences. It indirectly allowed the moral decay that allowed clerical child abuse to continue unchecked. It led directly to a form of globalization at times both culturally blinkered and dysfunctional.

The other side of this coin is the development of a networked Church. The global networks of lay people, clergy and religious orders in a pilgrim Church retain the potential to be a second transformative tier of Catholics. They cannot be effectively reined in by Rome, only cut loose. Asian, African and Latin American missionaries now undertake 'reverse mission' to Europe and around the world, bringing with them their own cultural experience. Inside this global Church are the smaller networks of the big religious societies and orders, such as the Jesuits and Dominicans, tightly co-ordinated and global in scope. To miss this dimension of globalization in the Church is to miss the cutting edge of contemporary Catholicism.

Reaction to human trafficking, a major scourge of today's globalization, offers a small but remarkable example of the networked Church at work. Sisters in Africa, Asia, Western and Eastern Europe have become closely networked, combining to combat the trade and to provide pastoral care for its victims. Women trapped into prostitution by deceptive job offers and enticing travel are cared for by women religious, both before and after repatriation to their home countries. Their international connections rival those of the gangs that carry out the trade.[23]

Yet formal bodies in Rome representing women religious globally have minimal contact with the Pope and power centres in the Vatican. They form, through no fault of their own, an alternative Church, often seen as threatening because female, and not easily fitted into male authority structures, nor wishing to be co-opted and controlled by bishops. The October 2009 African Synod declared that the 'Church has the duty to contribute to the recognition and liberation of women, following the example of Christ's own esteem for them.' Many interventions at the synod implied that this applied in the life of the Church itself. Pope Benedict recognized in *Africae munus*, his 2011 authoritative version of the Synod's deliberations, that, if the development of African women did not take place, neither would the development of Africa but, unlike the proceedings of the actual synod, there was no suggestion that this applied also to the development of the African and global Church. Future generations will look back on this stubborn patriarchy with amazement and reproach, onto a vision of a Church trapped in the past confronting a secularized world trapped in the present.[24]

---

[23] Roman Catholics Sisters lobby at the United Nations on sexual trafficking and formed an international network in Europe, RENATE, with links to Sisters in Africa, Latin America and Asia through their individual religious congregations. The links with Nigeria have been the most impressive in practical outcomes.

[24] On Africa and *Africae Munus* see the Jesuit, Peter Henriot's perceptive comments in *The Tablet* (3 December 2011), p. 2.

Networks dedicated to working for human rights and justice and peace, a direct product of Paul VI's initial implementation of the Council's vision, also illustrate characteristic information flows independent of Rome. The Pontifical Council for Justice and Peace does not aim to control local justice and peace commissions and, to a great extent, works independently of them on global themes despite limited resources. Under the leadership of its Ghanaian Cardinal, Peter Turkson, it complements their work and can enhance it. It has, though, to bear in mind the, sometimes, different interests and emphases of the more powerful Vatican Secretariat of State.

This second-tier global Church is characterized by fast information flows recording a wide range of human rights violations and injustices, with an ecumenical outreach that was an early goal of the Pontifical Council for Justice and Peace. It is linked to Catholic international development agencies, pastoral institutes and comparable secular organizations and is not afraid to name names when it comes to injustice and human rights violations. If financial support is any measure, the Catholic international development agencies, such as Catholic Relief Services in the United States and the agencies organized in Europe in the CIDSE grouping, are spectacularly well supported by laity, and are awarded government funds due to the quality of their work. Much of the laity identify with them as the globalized compassionate service that they wish to see undertaken by their Church. They are under the formal control of their bishops' conferences, and usually blessed by a supportive bishop willing to ward off criticism from the minority and often lay-led Catholic Right.

Other lay movements, *Communio e Liberazione*, *Focolare*, the *Saint Egidio* community and *Opus Dei*, for example, form different kinds of networks, impressive in other ways. They have to varying degrees internationalized their memberships while retaining good relationships with Rome and local hierarchies, some even creating their own seminaries. They cut across geographical structures of parish and diocese. The latter are, of course, geographical entities yet not necessarily without global outreach; parish twinning and exchange visits between different parts of the world are frequent today. The values, vision and pastoral emphases of these different sub-communities vary considerably and cater for a range of forms of lay participation in the life of the Church. Put together, this wide spectrum of interconnectedness illustrates the complex dynamics of an emergent networked Church.

The *vie associative* of this Catholic 'civil society' represents a strong counter-force to a globalization characterized by carefully controlled flows to and from the symbolic centre of Rome. Lay movements do not, it should be emphasized, consciously contest the centrality of Rome. Some movements may positively – even aggressively – promote Vatican messages. In addition, *ad limina* visits by bishops to the Vatican for debriefing, papal visits to different countries, World Youth Days, beatifications, great conclaves and election of popes in Rome, the role of papal nuncios and Curial directives, all reinforce and reflect this centrist model.

Catholics, attracted to a living symbol of their global community, are drawn to Rome in the hope of seeing the Pope, and to St. Peter's Basilica, where they can visit the tombs of former Popes. Some 4.2 million visited the Holy See in 2006. They travel, in the words of the defiant Catholic hymn, *God Bless our Pope*, to be 'full in the panting heart of Rome', to immerse themselves in an unique experience of the symbolic continuity of their tradition, and to re-experience their belonging.[25] This is not in motivation too different from the Muslim *hajj* to Mecca and the vast crowds who prayerfully circumambulate the *kaaba* – as standard an image of Islam as are pilgrims in St Peter's Square for Catholicism.

There are other corresponding stereotyped media images of the Church: the Swiss guards, pope-mobiles, altar boys swinging thuribles, huge phalanxes of men in clerical garb processing to the altar, the ascetic priest distributing communion, the distant figure on the Vatican balcony arms raised in blessing. But the other globalized Church experienced daily, less visible and rarely depicted in the news, is of a polycentric Church that dares not speak its name. You do not cross the Tiber to reach it. It has ancient antecedents: pilgrimages to historic shrines, Lourdes, Fatima, Medjugorje, Walsingham, some of them mediaeval in origin such as Santiago de Compostela. Some of these centres have never been approved by Rome. On Friday and Saturday, 11–12 December 2009, a total of 6.1 million pilgrims are said to have visited the Basilica of Our Lady of Guadaloupe on a hill at Tepeyac, Mexico, on their annual pilgrimage.[26] The site dates from the sixteenth century. The number of pilgrims to Tepeyac are exceptional. Annual pilgrimage is not. The Holy Land itself has a strong Catholic presence in Jerusalem which, because of its ancient Arab Christian heritage, might also be described as semi-detached from Rome. For Catholics, pilgrimage retains its deep religious allure as formal religious observance declines.

---

[25] Drawn from the 1615 Scottish Psalter. 'Full in the panting heart of Rome, Beneath the apostle's crowning dome, From pilgrims' lips that kiss the ground, Breathes in all only one sound, God Bless our Pope, the Great the Good'.

[26] Zenit, '6.1 Million Pilgrims Visit Guadalupe Shrine' (14 December 2009), www.zenit.org. The claim is that the numbers rose from 6 million the year before – but the figures seem incredible.

The overwhelming magnitude of the problems facing the world in the twenty-first century, the environmental challenges of diminishing carbon-based energy resources, falling water tables, global warming, the persistence of chronic poverty and disease in Africa and South Asia, predatory political elites and terrorism, a defective global financial architecture and regulatory capacity, is daunting. There is surely a place for a return to a dialogue of joint responsibility like SODEPAX, the Joint Committee on Society, Development, and Peace formed by Paul VI's newly created Justice and Peace Commission and the WCC's Commission on the Churches' Participation in Development in Geneva in April 1968. Born out of the hope generated by the Second Vatican Council and the congruence of concerns about poverty and human development, it seemed the beginning of a new dialogue informed by a new spirit of common ecumenical endeavour. It generated national and regional networks and continued until 1980 when it ran out of steam, finance and support and was downgraded to a joint working group. It had developed its own freewheeling identity that ultimately suited neither of its constituent bodies.[27]

Ecumenical progress in confronting some common problems, such as establishing a shared ethics of evangelization, *has* occurred. The World Evangelical Alliance joined with leaders of other faiths, the Pontifical Council for Inter-religious Dialogue and its partner WCC body, to inaugurate an important series of discussions about proselytism and conversion in Lariano, Italy, in May 2006.[28] The principle that evangelism must always, and in all senses, be non-coercive is widely accepted. Yet this has made little impact on governments and multilateral bodies who often see faith-inspired development work as a cloak for proselytism.

Today the town of Assisi remains a centre for interfaith dialogue and work for peace. Pope Benedict re-focused the twenty-fifth anniversary of Pope John Paul II's Assisi event in October 2011. His theme was pilgrimage and collaboration for the Common Good in a time of economic crisis. In some ways, this downgraded the lofty ideal of the meeting envisioned by Pope John Paul II: the centrality of prayer in each tradition, and the value of this prayer irrespective of its origin. In other ways, for example, the participation of secular thinkers brought by the Pontifical Council for Culture, and in its core theme, it elevated the meeting to

---

[27] Nicholas Lossky, José Miguez Bonino, John Pobee, Tom F. Stransky, Geoffrey Wainwright and Pauline Webb (eds), *Dictionary of the Ecumenical Movement* (2nd edition; Geneva: World Council of Churches Publications, 2002), pp. 1055–6.
[28] These resulted in a joint document: *Christian Witness in a Multi-Religious World: Recommendations for Conduct* (2011).

a serious engagement with the hopes and fears of the world in the twenty-first century.

At a local level, ecumenical collaboration in areas of common concern such as immigration, inner city poverty and deprivation, drugs and gang crime has been growing in the last decade. Christians of all denominations in Europe can be found working together to support immigrants and asylum seekers and in a range of charitable activities, building bridges that Church leaders can cross. In parts of the developing world, this Christian response to refugees is routine and barely worthy of comment. People of other faiths are now being drawn into these collaborative projects.

Official statements dealing with the overlapping problems of the twenty-first century have appeared in a variety of forms, from papal speeches and allocutions to encyclicals. Pope Benedict's *Caritas in veritate* (2009) is a notable example. But, perhaps because they seek to get beyond symptoms to the roots of the problem – and the Church in the fullest sense of the word can be *radical* in its thinking – these have been at high levels of generality, with some loss of engagement, and loss of insights about structural injustice compared to the decades after the council.

Broad-brush advocacy for a global body to regulate the global market and financial system appears as a persistent Catholic theme. Middle-level axioms and recommendations, such as support for a Tobin tax on financial transactions from the Pontifical Council for Justice and Peace, remain in short supply, and clearly do not always carry the full support of other influential parts of the Vatican. Catholic Social Teaching points to personal ethical conduct and in the past to structures – of sin – thus deepening the debate beyond superficial remedies. And there it stays. Since Rome prescribes middle axioms and specific scientific procedures in bio-ethics, why should it feel disqualified from doing the same in other spheres related to the protection of the human person in society?

The Millennium Development Goals (MDGs), set and agreed by the world's governments at the turn of the century, are both promises by the rich to the poor and middle-level prescriptions with timeframes set by governments. The different faiths have begun to join together in pressing governments to do more and in promoting practical measures to achieve the MDGs. The Vatican has sometimes spoken out in favour of action at a government's request, notably on Third World debt and in support of aid. But, with little time before the deadline is reached for their achievement in 2015, the Roman Catholic Church and the member Churches of the WCC need to ask themselves if their different responses to globalization, and their hopes for a globalized Christian community, are any longer adequate to fulfil the simple demands of justice. The idea that global challenges of the magnitude of the MDGs can be won with current levels of co-ordination and co-operation between faiths is simply implausible. Progress has stalled at the level of theological convergence towards organic unity between Churches. This has made collaboration in tackling the massive problems of the twenty-first century that much more difficult. Relationships with other faiths present additional problems. But there is now a pressing need to join with them in working for the global common good.

Coming to agreement about what the common good means in practice is no simple matter. Muslim claims for a distinctive charter of Islamic rights, and Asian exceptionalism, cannot simply be ignored. Arguably an overlapping cross-cultural consensus around the imperative to acknowledge a core of human rights, applicable in contemporary situations where people and communities are *in extremis*, is immediately achievable. Retaining agreement around the full spectrum of the rights in the UN Universal Declaration, sometimes challenged about their universality, may be more difficult in a polycentric world dominated by Asian and Islamic cultures and states.[29]

In this context, the words of Aloysius Pieris, an Indian Jesuit theologian, some three decades ago, are particularly relevant today: 'The irruption of the Third World is also the irruption of the non-Christian world. The vast majority of God's poor perceive their ultimate concern and symbolise their struggle for liberation in the idiom of non-Christian religions and culture.'[30] To make all things new, to model the good news of the gospel, innovative ways of working together, and with other faiths, have become not an option but a necessity.

Catholicism in the information age

The Second Vatican Council was experienced by Catholics as a great event in the life of the Church, an opportunity for bringing the Christian message afresh into a rapidly changing world. The laity came of age. Externally, a new openness to

---

[29] See Charles Taylor, 'Conditions of an Unforced Consensus on Human Rights', in Joanne R. Bauer and Daniel A. Bell (eds), *The East Asian Challenge for Human Rights* (Cambridge: Cambridge University Press, 1999), pp. 124–44, which uses John Rawls's phrase from his *Political Liberalism* (New York: Columbia University Press, 1993); Sebastiano Maffettone, 'Global Justice: Between Leviathan and Cosmopolis', *Global Policy* 3/4 (November 2012), pp. 443–54.

[30] Aloysius Pieris, 'The Place of Non-Christian Religious and Cultures in the Evolution of Third World Theology', in Virginia Fabella and Sergio Torres (eds), *Irruption of the Third World: Challenges to Theology* (Maryknoll, NY: Orbis Books, 1983), pp. 113–39.

other faiths and to the quest for Christian unity was proclaimed. The Church's missionary life was given greater depth and clarity, a rich, holistic understanding of evangelization developed: 'the grace and vocation proper to the Church, her deepest identity' (Paul VI, *Evangelii nuntiandi* 14). Religious liberty, informed conscience and human rights were extolled. In the Church's inner life, the use of the vernacular rather than Latin enabled the celebration of the Eucharist to become more participatory and focus attention on the true mystery of the Eucharist. In the Church's organizational structure, the council re-balanced the locus of authority in the Petrine office with a vision of the bishops' global collegiality with the Pope. The debate about the Church's response to 'modernity' was formally opened. Dialogue was a recurrent theme. Many Catholics felt excitement and had shared perhaps unrealistic expectations.

But the same Catholics experienced the period after 1975 no less as a disappointment, a golden opportunity for renewal squandered. The laity encountered back-tracking, presented as prudence rather than fear of change. Roadblocks constantly appeared on the path of reform. The sense of a new common endeavour and community between bishops, religious, priests and laity began to evaporate. The Church went into the information age divided, some like an Irish wolfhound, curling up in a ball, looking wistfully inwards and backwards. The division cut into all parts of the Church. Splits over strategy appeared in bishops' conferences caught between lay leaders and clergy wanting to implement the council and Rome putting on the brakes. A tiny, but noisy, vigilante force grew up after the council informing to higher authority on those not sharing ultraconservative positions for supposed excesses inspired by Vatican II. A small group of concerned laity continue today to denounce – the official term is delate – their parish priests, sometimes bishops, to Rome for acting faithfully in the spirit of the Council.

Another part of the Church simply got on with a new wave of evangelization and compassionate service. Its global scope in development, health and education in particular, was, and is, prodigious. When it came to the key neuralgic issue in this compassionate service, they were not diverted. None was more neuralgic than artificial contraception condemned in 1968 by Paul VI in his famous encyclical *Humanae vitae*. Condom-use continues to be denounced from on high and their distribution and use goes on surreptitiously from below. Each side knew that the other side knew that they knew. But the truth sadly did not set anyone free. So ambiguity prevailed and continues even in the face of the HIV/AIDS pandemic and the danger of undermining government campaigns to reduce the spread of the disease.

The child-abuse scandals and their attempted cover-ups added a new dimension: a widespread collapse in trust and authority. The consequences have been dire in Catholic countries such as Ireland and Austria, deeply damaging in others. The revelation of the involvement of Church personnel in Spain in the kidnap and sale of babies for adoption has added to a widespread indictment of the Church. The magnitude of this erosion of trust may not yet have been fully assimilated by the Vatican, nor by a surprisingly large number of bishops. The principal cause of the mishandling of this scandal, the retention of clericalism, a dominant feature of Catholic culture and a consequence of the Council's momentum stalling is sustained and enforced from the centre, as is the undervaluing of women's leadership and their role in evangelization.

Even on the fiftieth anniversary of the council's opening, the sense of lost opportunities did not seem to have registered in Rome. English-speaking Catholics around the world are slowly coming to terms with a new Vatican-imposed translation of the Mass. The international group of bishops commissioned to produce the translation, who had laboured over it for years, were simply overruled by Rome. The Vatican's main purpose in rejecting significant parts of the bishops' text seems to have been to make the liturgy as un-vernacular and Latinate as possible – without actually using Latin. It was symptomatic of a wider turning back of the clock. The final translation was the product of a pre-collegial, pre-networked Church, and, of course, had the corresponding supporters. Many more were, and remain, simply confused by the conflictive messages emanating from those in authority.

Yet in the 50 years after the Council, Catholicism engaged with the titanic forces of the twentieth century, contested Communism and uncontested nationalism, even if at great cost. In some cases, it provided the core content for a cultural nationalism that resisted and finally emerged triumphant from oppression and autocratic, Communist regimes. In its critical engagement with nationalism Catholicism has been successful, it could be argued, far more successful than Islam. The tables may be turned in a regionally differentiated world dominated by a global economy. Catholic social teaching informed the original vision of the founding fathers of the European Union, though it remains to be seen if this multinational vision will prevail. It informs Catholic critiques of bad governance and bad international relations around the world. The Catholic Church may become a significant feature in a powerful Chinese global presence in the future.

The Church today provides health, education but, above all, hope to the developing world, offering a critique of the corrosive corruption of venal political elites and proposing a politics of the Common Good. It is a force for peace in good times and bad and a significant player in the struggle for human rights and social justice at all levels. Rome has persevered in its condemnation of capital punishment and in the promotion of nuclear disarmament, often despite contrary views from bishops' conferences. In its theology of grace the Church has insights for the reform of contemporary global capitalism, now so obviously in crisis.[31]

In short, the Catholic Church is a Church of sinners, and therefore welcoming as a home for those who identify themselves with such a religious word and all that goes with it. Few would deny that. But it is also a Church of saints who can make the ordinary extraordinary and point to the transcendent. This reality as a global community, a sacrament of humanity, a school for the purification of desire, despite and because of all that human frailty and wickedness can throw at it, will not change. It represents the profoundest continuity that links the pre-conciliar Church to the post-conciliar Church of today.

The Catholic Church is, without doubt, entering a threatening new phase of globalization, marked by overlapping crises, both internal and external. It is unclear if under these circumstances Catholicism can steer a course between an enforced Eurocentric uniformity, labouring under the weight of historical precedent, and the healthy diversity of a networked Church, faithful to the Gospel and thus able to enlighten the world. This will be the dominant structural and theological challenge of the next decade. It will certainly define what global Catholicism looks like, and acts like, in coming years.

---

[31] Kathryn Tanner, *The Economy of Grace* (Minneapolis, MN: Fortress Press, 2005).

Part Three

The New Evangelization in Context

9

The Growth of the Young Churches: From the First Evangelization to a Complex Ecclesial Maturity

Fernando Filoni

The theme entrusted to me regards the contribution that the Christian experience of the young Churches can offer to the study of the new evangelization. However, this should not be done in a one-way direction because of human mobility, media interaction and, above all, the exchange of experiences that link the ancient Christianities, the European and the American, to those of Asia, Africa and Oceania. This exchange can only take place in an ecclesiological framework of communion[1] and, at the same time, of gifts received and given between the Churches. It is in this spirit that I present my contribution regarding the growth of the young Churches in the context that goes from the first evangelization to a more complex ecclesial maturity.

The notion of evangelization

Before getting to the heart of our discourse, I would like to try to clarify our subject: evangelization today. In the Catholic world, on the one hand, the notion of 'evangelization', generally used in the biblical world to describe the first

---

[1] Many are the texts that recall and develop this thesis. The first is the Final Report of the Extraordinary Synod of 1985, II, C, 1: 'The Ecclesiology of Communion is the Central and Fundamental Idea of the Council's Documents' (*Ecclesia sub Verbo Dei mysteria Christi celebrans pro salute mundi*). This indication is confirmed in *Christifideles Laici* 19 and in *Novo millennio ineunte* 43 that speaks of the Church as home and school of communion. Among the texts that make reference to it, we can mention, first of all, Walter Kasper, *Il futuro dalla forza dello Spirito. Sinodo straordinario dei vescovi 1985 – Documenti e commento* (Brescia: Queriniana, 1986 [1985]); Jean Rigal, *L'ecclesiologie de communion. Son evolution historique et ses fondements* (Paris: Cerf, 1997).

proclamation, emerges for the first time – barring errors – in 1956.[2] Presenting it as a 'significant' theme of the pastoral theology of that time, Pierre André Liégé links it to the birth of a living awareness of the emergence of missionary situations also in traditionally Christian societies; in practice, the need for evangelization would come from the awareness of the fall-off of the faith in older Christian societies. Two articles in *Gregorianum* by Domenico Grasso[3] go back to 1960–1. After reviewing the various meanings used for the term, he concludes that it would be expedient to reserve it for missionary preaching, namely, for the first proclamation of Christ to those who do not know him and which, in Scriptures, is the *kerygma*.

In the conciliar documents, the term 'evangelization' recurs 31 times.[4] On the other hand, there are two conciliar documents which deal with the missionary character of the Church: in brief, the Constitution on the Church, *Lumen gentium* (1964), and in a systematic way the 'Decree on the Church's Missionary Activity', *Ad gentes* (1965). However, the Council did not use the term evangelization in the sense of 'new evangelization'. In fact, this terminology was not known and terms such as 'witness' were used (i.e. what Christians had to give to the other baptized and non-baptized persons), 'exemplariness' (attributed to Christians with regard to others) and 'pastoral commitment' (attributed to the clergy, to men/women religious, to committed laypersons). In his study *Evangelizzazione: Senso di un termine* (*Evangelization: Meaning of a Term*),[5] Domenico Grasso individuated three different meanings: the first is that of missionary preaching and finds its criterion in the word and life of Christ; the second is broader and includes the entire ministry of the Word – not only the first proclamation – in all its different areas;[6] while the third embraces the Church's entire ministry

---

[2] Pierre-André Liégé, 'Évangélisation', in *Catholicisme* IV (Paris: Letouzey and Ané, 1956), pp. 756–64.

[3] Domenico Grasso, 'Il kerygma e la predicazione', *Gregorianum* 41 (1960), pp. 424–50; 'Evangelizzazione, Catechesi, Omelia', *Gregorianum* 42 (1961), pp. 242–67. After the Council on this theme he would write 'La predicazione missionaria', in Johannes Schütte (ed.), *Il destino delle missioni. Il successo o il fallimento delle missioni dipende dal loro radicale ripensamento* (Roma and Brescia: Herder & Morcelliana, 1969), pp. 215–30; *L'annuncio della salvezza. Teologia della predicazione* (Napoli: M. D'Auria, 1966).

[4] The term appears 21 times in *Ad Gentes*, 4 in *Apostolicam Actuositatem*, 3 in *Presbyterorum Ordinis* and once each in *Lumen Gentium*, *Christus Dominus* and *Gaudium et Spes*.

[5] Domenico Grasso, 'Evangelizzazione. Senso di un termine', in Mariasusai Dhavamony (ed.), *Evangelisation* (Roma: Università Gregoriana Editrice, 1975), pp. 21–47.

[6] *Lumen Gentium* 35 explains the prophetic nature of the apostolate of the laity and indicates the 'evangelization or proclamation of Christ, by word and the testimony of life [. . .] in the ordinary circumstances of the world'. In *Presbyterorum ordinis* 5 it is linked to the Eucharist, 'the source and the summit of all preaching of the Gospel', whereas in number 19 it is related to 'methods of evangelization and the apostolate'. *Gaudium et spes* 44 insists on a relationship with culture teaching that 'this kind of adaptation and preaching of the revealed Word must ever be the law of all evangelization'. It would above all be the decree *Ad Gentes* that used the term: number 20 would link

and includes the relationship between the proclamation of the Gospel and the sacraments, ecclesial ministries, witness and apostolate. 'In this last sense anyone who promotes, organizes and collaborates in the Church's action for the spread of the Gospel among peoples who still do not know it is carrying out evangelization.'[7]

It is against this background that the notion of 'new evangelization' develops. Although there is no complete history of the term and at times the terms 'second evangelization',[8] 'self-evangelization' and 're-evangelization' appear, it can be said that it appears for the first time in the 'Message to the Peoples of Latin America', signed in Medellín on 6 September 1968 by the bishops of that continent who sought 'to encourage a new and intensive evangelization and catechesis, which may reach the elite and the masses obtaining a lucid and committed faith'.[9] Later (1973), in a trilogy of works on the 'second evangelization', J. Grand'Maison linked this to the problems of secularization and the need to renew pastoral care.[10] Finally, Cardinal Stefan Wyszynski used the term to call for a strong ecclesial commitment. He did this on 21 September 1978 in Fulda, Germany, where he asked the German bishops for a strong ecclesial commitment to the Christian rebirth of Europe. Instead the first time it was used by a pope was in the homily that John Paul II gave at Mogila on 9 June 1979, during his first visit to Poland: 'On the threshold of the third millennium, in these new times, these new conditions of life, the Gospel is again being proclaimed. A *new evangelization* has begun, as if it were a new proclamation, even if in reality it is the same as ever. The cross stands high over the revolving world.'[11] A few days later, on 20 June 1979, in the concelebration with the European bishops, John Paul II spoke instead about 'self-evangelization': 'There exists therefore for Europe the problem that was defined in *Evangelii nuntiandi* as "self-evangelization". The Church must always evangelize herself. Catholic

---

this commitment to diverse tasks and ministries, while 38–41 would speak of the 'evangelization of the world', the 'evangelization of the nations' and the 'evangelization of non-Christians'. In short, 'since the whole Church is missionary, and the work of evangelization the fundamental task of the people of God, this sacred Synod invites all to undertake a profound interior renewal so that being vitally conscious of their responsibility for the spread of the Gospel they might play their part in missionary work among the nations' (AG 35).

[7] Grasso, 'Evangelizzazione. Senso di un termine', pp. 29–30.
[8] Jacques Grand'Maison, *La seconde évangelisation*. I: *Les témoins*. II: *Outils d'apport*. II/1: *Outils majeurs*. II/2: *Les témoins* (Montréal: Fides, 1973).
[9] Piersandro Vanzan (ed.), *Enchiridion. Documenti della Chiesa Latinoamericana* (Bologna: EMI, 1995), p. 266.
[10] Grand'Maison, *La seconde évangelisation*.
[11] He could have been inspired by the words of Cardinal Wiszynski spoken at Fulda in 1978.

and Christian Europe needs this evangelization.' Beyond the terms, the theological framework of understanding probably goes back to Paul VI's apostolic exhortation *Evangelii nuntiandi* 13–5 where it is asserted that the Church must continuously evangelize herself, because only an evangelized Church can be evangelizing. It is a short step from this 'self-evangelization' to the 'new evangelization'.

But the classic form would be that of the discourse given at the Nineteenth Ordinary Assembly of CELAM in Port-au-Prince on 9 March 1983. Recalling the date of the fifth centenary of the evangelization of America, John Paul would say that 'the commemoration of five hundred years of evangelization will have its full significance if it is your commitment as bishops, together with your priests and your faithful; certainly not a commitment to re-evangelization but rather to a new evangelization. New in its ardour, in its methods and in its expressions.'[12] A detailed and precise explanation of the term would be presented in the opening discourse for the Fourth General Conference of the Latin American Bishops given by John Paul II in Santo Domingo on 12 October 1992: 'The new evangelization must therefore provide a complete, ready and lively response that makes the Catholic faith stronger, in its fundamental truths, in its individual, family and social dimensions.'[13] It would later be the text of John Paul II's 1990 encyclical, *Redemptoris missio* 33 that would impose it.[14] As we can note, until that moment, the language was neither precise nor uniform but moved in the framework of a reflection on the life of the Church and a missionary response to the secularized world. The new evangelization is for the whole Church, present on all the continents, even on those where Christianity is a small minority as in Asia. 'In my Apostolic Letter *Tertio millennio adveniente*', says Blessed John Paul II,

> I set out a programme for the Church to welcome the Third Millennium of Christianity, a programme centered on the challenges of the new evangelization. An important feature of that plan was the holding of continental Synods so that Bishops could address the question of evangelization according to the particular situation and needs of each continent. This series of Synods [is] linked by the common theme of the new evangelization (*Ecclesia in Asia* 2).

---

[12] John Paul II, Speech to the XIX Assembly of CELAM, Port au Prince (9 March 1983), p. 3.
[13] John Paul II, Inaugural Address, The Fourth General Conference of the Latin American Bishops, Santo Domingo, 12 October 1992; my translation.
[14] Already the introduction of the encyclical points out that 'missionary activity renews the Church, revitalizes faith and Christian identity, and offers fresh enthusiasm and new incentive' (*Redemptoris Missio* 2). But the passage that imposes this category is *Redemptoris Missio* 33.

In practice, the missiological theses of a now worldwide mission intersect there with the more practical ones of pastoral attention to the life of the Christian communities. Clearly indicated as fundamental causes for a new era of proclamation of the Gospel are: (1) the fact that a great part of the human family does not know Christ yet and (2) the Church and the world are facing new challenges (*Ecclesia in Asia* 29). The new evangelization arose from attention to history and its challenges. From this viewpoint, *Redemptoris missio* 37 takes on particular importance: this text analyses precisely the challenges to the faith from its human context, first from the viewpoint of the territorial areas, then from the new social worlds or phenomena and, finally, from the cultural areas or modern areopaguses. Here the provocations emerge that come up from the cities and their peripheries, from the rural world and its problems, from the future and migrations, from scientific research and international relations, from culture and the media. It is difficult to specify whether these themes are pastoral 'care', missionary 'activity' or 'new' evangelization because – as *Redemptoris missio* 34 recalls – the boundaries between these categories 'are not clearly definable, and it is unthinkable to create barriers between them or to put them into watertight compartments'.

What we can say is that these analyses involve an obvious use of the human sciences in addition to a serious reflection on the relation between these problems and the Gospel. Against the backdrop of the mission's attention to the historic circumstances of its exercise, the new evangelization is the Church's response to a history where the loss of faith or its privatization is a characteristic of profoundly secularized societies. In explaining the proclamation to a de-Christianized world, *Evangelii nuntiandi* 52 indicates three types of peoples who need the Gospel: (1) innumerable people who have been baptized but who live outside the Christian life; (2) simple people who have a certain faith but an imperfect knowledge of its foundations; and (3) intellectuals who feel the need for a Gospel that is different from the one they received as children. Some indications follow different categories of people which seem useful to me to mention here: non-believers, those who do not practise, and the masses of wandering and exhausted people, sheep without a shepherd, as Jesus described them (cf. 55–7).

Here I would like to refer to the teaching of Benedict XVI in his post-synodal apostolic exhortation *Africae munus* (2011) where he draws our attention to two aspects, one particularly related to Africa, when he says: 'If this effort [to evangelize] is to be more effective, the *missio ad gentes* must keep pace with the new evangelization' (*Africae munus* 165). In Africa too – he emphasized – situations demand a new presentation of the Gospel. A second aspect relates, instead, to every continent:

> The new evangelization needs to integrate the intellectual dimension of the faith into the living experience of the encounter with Jesus Christ present and at work in the ecclesial community. Being Christian is born not of an ethical decision or a lofty ideal, but an encounter with an event, a person, which gives life a new horizon and a decisive direction. Catechesis must therefore integrate its theoretical dimension, which deals with concepts to be learned by heart, and its practical dimension, which is experienced at the liturgical, spiritual, ecclesial, cultural and charitable levels, in order that the seed of God's word, once fallen on fertile ground, can sink deep roots and grow to maturity.

This is why, in the following paragraph Benedict XVI speaks of the need to employ new methods of evangelization but also points out that 'no medium can or should replace personal contact, verbal proclamation, and the witness of an authentic Christian life' (*Africae munus* 166).

The new evangelization in mission Churches: methods

But what can be said about the new evangelization on the other continents where Christians are sometimes an insignificant minority and for this reason discriminated against and persecuted? Entering into the theme that has been proposed to me, first of all I wish to describe the physiognomy of these Churches, their way of living the Gospel in the complex situations in which they find themselves. Born from missionary activity, the young Churches are increasingly acquiring their own physiognomy: they have their own hierarchy, they are rich in vocations and religious institutions; they are establishing their own structures and pastoral services. If at one time it was considered that the *plantatio* of a Church was complete when it had its own local hierarchy, today we know that the maturity of a Church is linked to witness to the Gospel in its concrete conditions of life. In their commitment, the young Churches undoubtedly manifest a surprising vivacity in living the Gospel and a great ability to adjust to the conditions in which they live; certainly there are limits and defects that depend both on insufficient discernment of their culture and on the adoption of patterns of life characteristic of secularized societies. The concern for life that distinguishes them cannot hide an increase in alcoholism, drug addiction and violence; unfortunately, the importance of the family goes side by side with the minority situation of women; the organization of civil life is not always respectful of freedom and democracy. Within the framework of a profound transformation, the awareness of the colonial past, the difficult reality of the present and the uncertainty about a positive future often lead to an identity crisis. Therefore, it is necessary for them to go through a process of re-evangelization 'to first remake the Christian fabric of the ecclesial community itself'.[15] The young Churches must not only face the emerging challenges but also evangelize the Christian communities that are weakened also because of an incomplete evangelization. We know that some recently founded Churches manifest a critical attitude regarding the evangelization carried out by foreign men and women missionaries because they imported a church based on the model, if not the photocopy of the church of origin, or for their poor sensitivity towards the cultural, religious dimension of the human groups to be evangelized, or for the use of enormous economic resources to build structures (schools, hospitals–clinics, seminaries, bishops, residences, pastoral centres) far removed from the economic possibilities and artistic sensibility of the autochthonous human groups, or for dependence on the Western churches for human and economic resources, or for the slight attention to inter-cultural and inter-religious dialogue, or, finally, the insufficient or even distorted formation of the clergy and consecrated life. To this can be added, as we said earlier, the vast problems of planetary changes: secularism, religious indifference, moral relativism, hedonism and consumerism which penetrate the societies of the emerging countries and erode their traditional moral and religious values.

In view of these observations, I would like to start from Paul VI's remark which we find in *Evangelii nuntiandi*: 'What matters is to evangelize man's culture and cultures (not in a purely decorative way, as it were, by applying a thin veneer, but in a vital way, in depth and right to their very roots), in the wide and rich sense which these terms have in *Gaudium et spes*, always taking the person as one's starting-point and always coming back to the relationships of people among themselves and with God' (EN 20).

In order to give a concrete meaning to the so-called new evangelization, we must have recourse to the process of inculturation. The crisis of Christianity in the West, and not only Christianity but also other religions too, consists essentially in the difficulty of making the religious message communicable, up-to-date, significant, comprehensive and understandable in the changing

---

[15] Benedict XVI, *Ubicumque et Semper*, Apostolic Letter issued Motu Proprio 'Establishing the Pontifical Council for Promoting the New Evangelization' (21 September 2010).

cultures. In *Centesimus annus*, Pope John Paul II warned: 'All human activity takes place within a culture and interacts with culture' (*Centesimus annus* 51). If the Gospel does not penetrate a man or woman's nature, he or she will not believe with all their humanity. Faith must become culture and it does so to the extent that it becomes the foundation of one's being, thinking and acting. A faith that does not become culture is a faith that is not fully accepted, entirely thought-out and faithfully lived. For this, the process of inculturation is an urgent priority, a condition for a real evangelization first of the non-Christians but, at the same time, for the Christians who have to re-appropriate the faith in order to live and transmit it. In the West, in view of the human being's declared inability to know the truth, a re-inculturation of the Gospel, faith and the Church is urgent. The multiplication of rites, a more refined pastoral care, an emphasis on a greater and more effective professionalism and organization will not build up the communities that have lost the sense of the sacred and hope in the future. While it is true that our times must record an apostasy from God and our churches are subject to weakness, it is also true that what is needed is to put a new evangelization into effect where the important reference term is an evangelization that must become new in its methods, enthusiasm and methodology. This is also required for the young Churches.

In the Apostolic Exhortations of the different continents, inculturation almost constitutes the explanation and foundation of the new evangelization. It is a debt, and not only a duty, which the Church has contracted with Latin America because the first evangelization, except for some cases of heroic missionaries, was mostly a form of religious colonization. The same is true for Africa and Asia. Faith did not become culture: in brief, it did not become the substance and structure of personal and social life. Many times, it was grafted on incomplete and impoverished anthropologies. This process cannot be skipped with impunity because, in a certain sense, it is identified with the evangelization process itself. As Paul VI wrote:

> For the Church it is a question not only of preaching the Gospel in ever wider geographic areas or to ever greater numbers of people, but also of affecting and as it were upsetting, through the power of the Gospel, mankind's criteria of judgment, determining values, points of interest, lines of thought, sources of inspiration and models of life, which are in contrast with the Word of God and the plan of salvation (EN 19).

With all their limits, the young churches, however, are communities that are growing. Some aspects of their way of understanding and living life are particularly important as far as evangelization is concerned. The growth of these Churches and their vitality is linked not so much to some pastoral initiatives as to an understanding of life different to that of the West, more sensitive to the search for full meaning and ways of whole and sound life. From a historical viewpoint, until the 1990s some Asian theologians had tried to develop a form of gnosis by adapting to the faith elements of philosophy from the major religious expressions, such as Buddhism and Hinduism, but in my view it did not really come to much.[16] Perception was sought in the profound relationship that binds the Asian world to a large extent but this lacked the meaning of a real and authentic evangelization.[17] Striving to achieve a synthesis between cultures and the proclamation of the Gospel has in truth always revealed disagreements and difficulties, especially because of the diversity of the Western model[18] and the perception of the weakness of Western Christian life itself.[19] The importance of the East lies in the fact that it focuses a lot of attention on what the West is lacking.

These themes are not irrelevant for the new evangelization. Certainly, without a renewal of its culture and a dialogue with other ways of life, the West will hardly undertake a new evangelization. As Helmut Gollwitzer has so clearly demonstrated, separation from the orthodox world of the East and the Islamization of the North African Churches ended up by transforming the Church of Christ into a white people's Church with dramatic consequences for the other peoples with whom Christians would come into contact at a time of great explorations.[20] Today, this means we need to re-examine the Church's place in world history and the role that the Gospel of Christ must again have in all humanity.

In brief, the new evangelization will not be accomplished or, at least, will not produce the fruits we believe it can give unless – together with the proclamation of and witness to the Gospel – it also recognizes a new different truly human culture. This cultural commitment today rests above all on believers. In this task,

---

[16] Michael Amaladoss, *Making All Things New: Mission in Dialogue* (Maryknoll, NY: Orbis Books, 1990); Aloysius Pieris, *An Asian Theology of Liberation* (Maryknoll, NY: Orbis Books, 1988).

[17] In some cases, it was a form of monistic pantheism; see Francis X. D'Sa, *Dio l'Uno e Trino e l'Uno-Tutto. Introduzione all'incontro tra cristianesimo e induismo* (Brescia: Queriniana, 1996 [1987]).

[18] The most severe form of this criticism is expressed by Grace Davie, *Europe – The Exceptional Case: Parameters of Faith in the Modern World* (London: Darton Longman & Todd, 2002).

[19] By presenting Christian life as the result of a complex synthesis between the contemplative, sacramental and active dimensions, Aloysius Pieris comes to the conclusion that Christian life today is marked by profound divisions: the liturgy does not any longer generate a spirituality nor does it not give life to a social and historical commitment. Pieris, *An Asian Theology of Liberation*.

[20] Helmut Gollwitzer, 'Why Black Theology', in Gayraud S. Wilmore and James H. Cone (eds), *Black Theology: A Documentary History, 1966–1979* (Maryknoll, NY: Orbis Books, 1979), pp. 152–73 (p. 154).

Catholics will only play a part if they unite 'faith the friend of the intelligence', on which Benedict XVI insisted several times,[21] to the 'spiritual wisdom' of life which is characteristic of the Eastern world and, with them, of the Eastern Churches. Therefore, a new evangelization as inculturated evangelization is needed: an evangelization that strives to make the Gospel take root in the cultural, social and economic ground of human groups in order to re-express its message and respond to their needs by fulfilling their aspirations and establishing the kingdom of freedom and justice. This means making the Gospel announcement understandable, significant, integral and liberating for every human group in its cultural and religious identity. It also implies in-depth study and knowledge both of Christ's message and the existential situations of peoples. It implies acceptance of the diversity of anthropological models, creativity, human and cultural sensitivity, and respect for the various ways in which man organizes his life models.

The new evangelization: the contribution of the young Churches

With the Second Vatican Council, the mission came out from the ancient confines that had been imposed on it by canon law and that reserved responsibility for it to the sole pontifical authority, in order to raise the awareness of the entire Catholic episcopate. A decisive shift in emphasis was brought about in favour of the local Church's importance but, at the same time, the Council attributed a universal dimension to the pastoral responsibility of the bishops as components of the episcopal college that succeeds the apostolic college in the mission entrusted to it by Christ. The bishop must see in his particular Church the image of the universal Church because the one and only Catholic Church is constituted in and by the local Churches. It is always a local

---

[21] Joseph Ratzinger's thought on the relationship between faith and reason was first expressed in the public confrontation between himself and Jürgen Habermas on 19 January 2004 in Münich on 'The pre-political moral foundations of the free state'. See Jürgen Habermas and Joseph Ratzinger, *The Dialectics of Secularization. On Reason and Religion*, Brian McNeil, C. R. V. (trans.); San Francisco: Ignatius Press, 2006). After he became Pope with the name Benedict XVI, the theme returned in the famous Regensburg discourse of 12 September 2006, in the discourse which he should have given at the Sapienza University of Rome on 17 January 2008 and in the one given at the Collège des Bernardins in Paris on 12 September 2008. After the Regensburg discourse, Habermas would go back to his confrontation with him in a long article: 'Ein Bewusstsein von dem, was fehlt. Über Glauben und Wissen und den Defaitismus der modernen Vernunft', *Neue Zürcher Zeitung*, 10 February 2007.

Church, a concrete, historic community of disciples that prays, announces, interprets and, in the light of its Lord, illuminates and is inserted into the course of humanity's history in order to be in the midst of all peoples. In the local Church, the universal Church makes its home among the people, just as in Christ's humanity God made his tent among us. Speaking of new evangelization from the point of view of mission means asking how and how much young Churches, engaged in a profound dialogue with their world, can give an example, methods and content to all Christians. The background, outlined previously, recalls how the growth of young Churches requires both a re-examination and a re-adjustment of relationship between Churches as well as an understanding of the cultural task connected to this.

In a world that is changing, it should be said that most of these young Churches – where there are also forms of traditionalism – have chosen a form of spiritual renewal able to accompany the growth of these societies. In fact, Churches have had an important role in the defence of human rights, in social action and in building a democratic infrastructure and today they have an important role with regard to awareness of culture in people's lives.

The contribution of these young Churches to this new evangelization needs to start above all from what already forms their lives. Their work of evangelization is done through (a) the catechumenate and the work of catechists; (b) an extensive charitable commitment, developed through schools, universities, hospitals and dispensaries; (c) the promotion of base communities; (d) attention to popular religious forms and (e) the organization of missionary outposts entrusted to catechists and visited by missionaries. Particular emphasis should be given to the Scriptures, now commonly used, and to the liturgy, accompanied by songs, dances and processions inspired by local religiosity. Obviously, this methodology also includes basic questions such as the value of traditional religions, the relationship between tradition and modernity, the significance and characteristics of the local culture, the development of local Churches and of regional Churches.

Now I would like to focus briefly on Africa. This continent has become in these past years a land of economic occupation because of its potentialities in terms of very desirable raw resources, infrastructural development and lands to be used for intense production in view of possible natural and international crises in the field of food production. To tell the truth, after colonialism Africa went through a long season of economic neglect and little political attention, but certainly not ecclesiological attention, at least on the Catholic side. The Congregation for the Evangelization of Peoples and the international Catholic organizations poured enormous investments into education, health and social accomplishments to the direct benefit of often marginalized and forgotten populations. At the same time, it educated in its own Roman Colleges hundreds upon hundreds of priests, women religious and catechists, without counting the many laypersons and ecclesiastics who benefited from scholarships and from updating courses also for bishops and professors.

The question in its complexity was brought out in an international Congress organized in Rome by the Pontifical Urbaniana University, 14–6 May 2012, with the theme: 'Listening to Africa: Its Context, Its Expectations, Its Potential'. As was noted there, on the ecclesiological level there is often a temptation to believe that Africa is a copy of Christianity conceived in a purely Western image. As a matter of fact, the Rector Alberto Trevisiol explained that 'the testimonies of theology and African philosophy show us that Africa is not a photocopy of the West and must not be one.' The Congress was meant to be a first response to the apostolic exhortation *Africae munus*, a document that is put in continuity with the other apostolic exhortation *Ecclesia in Africa* (1995) of John Paul II. Here I would like to quote the opening words from *Africae munus* where Benedict XVI writes:

> Africa's commitment to the Lord Jesus Christ is a precious treasure which I entrust at the beginning of this third millennium to the bishops, priests, permanent deacons, consecrated persons, catechists and lay faithful of that beloved continent and its neighbouring islands. Through this mission, Africa is led to explore its Christian vocation more deeply; it is called, in the name of Jesus, to live reconciliation between individuals and communities and to promote peace and justice in truth for all (*Africae munus* 1).

I would ask that attention be paid to this document. We from the Congregation for the Evangelization of Peoples have asked all the African Bishops to study it carefully, both together and individually, because it is the fruit of the Church herself in Africa and constitutes an outline for her to follow from the standpoint of both evangelization and social and political promotion. *Africae munus* also points out the ills and the possibilities of getting out of them. It is not by chance that it uses appealing and meaningful terminology. For example, it talks about 'work areas' as places in which the human, political, social and ecclesial fabric is built or rebuilt and it makes clear reference to reconciliation because of the many ills that afflict this continent, and especially to the fractures of a tribal kind, religious antagonism, structural deficiencies, the crisis of justice, the violations of human rights and in particular of peace. Wars and violence still afflict a population that is often exhausted and decimated. But if Africa suffers because of these ills, it also has within itself the ability and potential that should not be underestimated. The Pope lists several of these: I mention, for example, the family, living together, the wisdom of the elders, the energies of the young people, the tribal traditions, the propensity for participation and consent as methods of work and development.

Evangelization and inculturation

A few notes on evangelization and inculturation: Ever since the concept of inculturation – I am referring to the second half of the 1970s – put faith and culture at the centre of its reflection, much use was made of the references to the Second Vatican Council that spoke about 'adaptations' (*Ad gentes* 22; *Sacrosanctum concilium* 37–40; *Gaudium et spes* 44), a term that was not readily accepted in the missionary world and often generated misunderstandings. 'Incarnation' was also spoken about but this has a fuller theological value. To tell the truth, the substratum in which the terminology was moving was slippery because there was not always a correct evaluation between faith and culture in reference to the local and ancestral traditions. The proclamation of the Gospel was really marginalized when it was 'unheard' or made 'ineffective', according to the expression of the Congregation for the Doctrine of the Faith which felt obliged in 2007 to issue a Doctrinal Note 'On Some Aspects of Evangelization'. It pointed out the attitude whereby 'some maintain that Christ should not be proclaimed to those who do not know him, nor should joining the Church be promoted, since it would also be possible to be saved without explicit knowledge of Christ and without formal incorporation in the Church' (3). So the Vatican Dicastery shifted the axis of the question by not centring it on 'relationships' but bringing it back to the 'primary motive of evangelization', which is the 'love of Christ for the eternal salvation of all' (8).

By focusing the missionary work and the evangelization on Christ, it is clear that the effort to inculturate the Christian message cannot be limited to ritual or behavioural aspects but it must remain open to the expression of that symbolic field that interacts in different ways with life, without forgetting any longer the heart and the end of evangelization. In practice, there is great listening to culture and local religiosity because, as an old proverb says, 'a person who knows others is intelligent but a person who knows himself is wise.' It is what *Redemptoris missio* taught when, referring to the conciliar teaching on the Spirit, it recalls his action 'in the heart of every person, through the "seeds of the Word", to be found in human initiatives – including religious ones – and in mankind's efforts to attain truth, goodness and God himself' (28).

Looking back, we should also recall the debates that have accompanied the choice and assessment of missionary methods. We should begin with the formula of the three autonomies or of the *three-self* of Henry Venn (1796–1873), an Anglican pastor and secretary of the Church Missionary Society; his thesis of the three autonomies – self-governing, self-propagating and self-supporting – was criticized also from the point of view of cultural sensitivity absent here and from that of *self*, which is indicative of an absolute autonomy rather than a clear responsibility. Then we should remember the text of the Anglican Roland Allen (1868–1947) on Paul's and our own missionary methods.[22] His invitation to trust converts more was anticipated in the Catholic world by the schema *super missionibus apostolicis* of Vatican I.[23] Presented to the fathers on 26 July 1870 after the majority of them had already left Rome, the text was never discussed in the Assembly but the substance of its thought would later be reiterated by *Maximum illud* (1919).

The new evangelization: a model

The new evangelization involves an ecclesiological and pastoral revolution. It can accept a humble and merciful path but it must give it a sense of witness to a passionate encounter already experienced; it can become hospitality open to everyone, accompanying everyone on their journey. The model is Jesus, sitting down at table, in his surprising hospitality. While hospitality and eating together were at that time subject to severe regulations of 'purity' as a way to the encounter with God, Jesus opens hospitality to the physical and spiritual reintegration of everyone, in particular of sinners. The hidden and ineffable God is thus the God of love and forgiveness. However, we cannot fail to take these forms of ecclesial experience to heart which emphasize direct person-to-person communication, following a way that can be traced back to Christ and the apostles and that is confirmed in *Evangelii nuntiandi*, which recalls how,

> side by side with the collective proclamation of the Gospel, the other form of transmission, the person-to-person one, remains valid and important. [. . .] It

---

[22] Roland Allen, *Missionary Methods: St. Paul's or Ours?* (Cambridge: Lutterworth Press, 2006 [1912]).
[23] See on this subject, Klaus Schatz, 'Die Missionen auf dem I Vatikanum' (The Missions in the First Vatican Council), *Theologie und Philosophie* 63 (1988), pp. 342–69.

must not happen that the pressing need to proclaim the Good News to the multitudes should cause us to forget this form of proclamation whereby an individual's personal conscience is reached and touched by an entirely unique world that he receives from someone else. (46)

Similar forms are proposed in *Redemptoris missio*, chapter 5, 'The Paths of Mission'.

In fact, the new evangelization is mostly a real evangelization which tries to satisfy people's needs for spiritual and evangelical renewal. In the effort to enter people's souls, these forms seem at times to develop proclamation and its importance as hope for the poor and the marginalized rather than its content. Appreciation of the power of proclamation is an important discovery but we should never forget that Christ is and remains the centre of this commitment. This must be reasserted because the search for 'experience' of the power of the kerygmatic proclamation often intercepts the emotional aspect of the person. Insisting, for example, on a kerygmatic crisis of the head, the heart and the hands, namely, on a change in the way of thinking, loving and behaving is important, but it is necessary to integrate this proclamation with careful growth in the profession of the faith, in its celebration and in witness to it.

The new evangelization implies that Christian communities, together with their evangelization methods, revise their pastoral programme; the path of people reached with these new methods cannot but be linked to the path of other believers asking each of them for greater mutual attention in mutual enrichment. In this way the new evangelization would become the life of a Church capable of reawakening listless believers, re-launching the missionary commitment and thus resuming her journey. I would like to conclude by citing the words of an Italian priest, Fr Primo Mazzolari, who, in different times, goaded the Church by recalling that we 'risk dying of prudence in a world that cannot wait'. This citation speaks of the urgency of the choices that the Church has to make today; this is a time for courage, a time for choices that cannot be delayed. If our Church has enough faith to take this first step, it will then be this first step that reawakens the life of a renewed Church.

10

The Journey of the Young Churches:
An African Perspective

Richard K. Baawobr

The main concern of Pope John XXIII as he convened the Second Vatican Council was to seek, together with the council bishops and fathers, how to ensure that the Catholic Church would engage with the secularized and modern world of the time. This, in his mind, would be possible only through a renewal of the manner of proclaiming the gospel of Jesus Christ. For this to happen, he was convinced, it was not enough to make some cosmetic changes here and there. A profound renewal was called for.

The documents that we now have from the council are the fruit of 4 years of hard work (11 October 1962–8 December 1965) which were not without their ups and downs. Some documents have had a greater impact than others. This is to be expected. On the whole, today, many of us take the results of the council for granted and even ignore its history. It is like the story of the small fish in the ocean: The little fish had heard of the ocean and wanted to know what it looked like. One day as it swam along, it met a bigger fish and asked it: 'Excuse me, where is the ocean?' The bigger fish replied: 'My dear, you are already swimming in the ocean, this is the ocean.' To this the younger fish replied: 'But this is only water. I want to see the ocean.' And with this he swam away in search of another more enlightened fish who would show it the ocean. As you can guess, it did not find another fish to answer the question 'Where is the ocean?' Fifty years after the Second Vatican Council, I believe our reflections can awaken us to its treasures and enable us to see how to re-appropriate them for our world today.

As superior general of a missionary society founded in 1868 by Cardinal Charles Lavigerie for the evangelization of Africa,[1] our work comes directly under the responsibility of the Congregation for Evangelization of People, of which Fernando Cardinal Filoni is the prefect. In this volume, he opens up the subject from a much wider perspective than I will be able to do. I will limit my attention to the following: First, père impact of Vatican II on our missionary society and our practice of mission; second, the impact that we have seen at the grassroots in the local churches in Africa and third, some of the issues we see that need to be addressed in response to the call for new evangelization. All this will be from our perspective as a society working mainly in Africa and recently with Africans outside of Africa. I limit my references to one continent, Africa, and to one missionary family, the Missionaries of Africa (White Fathers) and Missionaries Sisters of Our Lady of Africa (White Sisters). However, my interaction with other missionary institutes and congregations (female and male), in Africa and elsewhere in the world, has made me realize that there are many more common features that have shaped and that are shaping us all since the celebration of the 'marvellous and generous gift' that the Second Vatican Council represents for humanity.[2]

The impact of Vatican II on our missionary society

One of the key moments when a religious institute like ours takes the pulse, looks at its past and plans for the future is at the time of the general chapter. Following the call for *aggiornamento*, like many other institutes, we held a general chapter in 1967. There were several Missionaries of Africa in the Council: 43 bishops, the superior general (Fr Leo Volker) and some experts and secretaries. This gave them a first-hand taste of the council. The rest of our members followed the events of the council with a lot of interest through the media and through the regular communications from the generalate in Rome (*Centrum Informationis Patrorum Alborum*) and the *Petit Echo*, our internal journal.

---

[1] For historical background, see François Renault, *Le Cardinal Lavigerie, 1825–1892. L'Elise, l'Afrique et la France* (Paris: Fayard, 1992); Aylward Shorter, *Cross and Flag in Africa: The White Fathers during the Colonial Scramble (1882–1914)* (Maryknoll, NY: Orbis Books, 2006); Jean-Claude Cellier, *Histoire des Missionnaires d'Afrique (Pères Blancs). De la fondation par Mgr Lavigerie à la mort du fondateur (1868–1892)* (Paris: Karthala, 2008); Francis Nolan, *White Fathers in Colonial Africa (1919–1939)* (Nairobi: Paulines Africa, 2012).

[2] James Kroeger, *Exploring the Treasures of Vatican II* (Quezon City: Claretian Publications and Jesuit Communications, 2011), p. 1.

Several stepping stones had already prepared our members to be open to Vatican II and thus enabled us to take the council on board in very explicit ways as a long awaited renewal. Among them, I note the following six major elements: First, the missionary vocation and living in international communities brought to many of our members the awareness that we stand in permanent need of updating (*aggiornamento*) to others because we live and work in contexts completely different from our own. From the pastoral perspective, it also became more and more obvious, for example, to many missionaries that they had to use a language that people would understand in the liturgy; that the preparation for baptism (the catechumentate, etc.) had to be taken seriously. Second, our initial formation had exposed many members before their priestly ordination or commitment by oath to new methods of exegesis, theology and morals because the professors did not limit themselves to the textbooks but incorporated already the new trends in biblical and theological studies through the polycopy texts that they distributed to the students. Third, the political context in many African countries at the time was that of independence. When the council was announced in 1959, there were some ten independent sovereign states in Africa.[3] In 1960, 17 others gained political independence and 16 more between 1960 and 1970.[4] Although the missionaries were not related to the colonial masters, some associations were unavoidable and the new state of affairs was shaking us up and obliging us to rethink the purpose of our presence and the urgency to be committed to human rights issues and the Social Teaching of the Church. The fourth factor was the growth of an African hierarchy. At the opening of the Council, there were 280 Bishops residing in Africa of whom 66 were Africans.[5] There was a gradual instauration of a local hierarchy in the different 'mission territories' which finally ended the *ius commissionis* system (on 24 February 1969) so that the missionary activity in specific territories was no longer confided to missionary institutes under the umbrella of Propaganda Fide. There was now more and more talk of a 'self-governing', 'self-ministering' and 'self-supporting' missionary Church. Fifth, ecumenism was something that many of our members felt as an urgency because of their direct experience of the scandal of division among Christians in the missions. Sixth, interreligious

---

[3] These were Egypt, Ethiopia, Ghana, Guinea (Conakry), Liberia, Libya, Morocco, South Africa, Sudan and Tunisia.
[4] See Alfred Guy Bwidi Kitambala, *Les Evêques d'Afrique et le Concile Vatican II. Participation, contribution et application du Synode des Evêques de 1994* (Paris: Karthala, 2010), pp. 18–9.
[5] According to Kitambala, *Les Evêques d'Afrique*, only 17 of the 53 countries (independent or still colonized) had native bishops in 1959 and these numbered 36 (27 of the Latin rite and 9 of the Oriental rite). Thirty eight others were ordained shortly afterwards.

encounter and dialogue have been important for us because of our foundation in Algeria, in a majority Muslim milieu.

The earlier factors coupled with the insights from Vatican II gave an impetus and insight for the preparation of the 1967 General Chapter which has also remained a point of reference for us.[6] Twelve of the sixteen documents of Vatican II were quoted in our 1967 General Chapter, as shown in the following table:

Constitutions	X	Decrees	X	Declarations	X
Sacrosanctum concilium	16	*Unitatis redintegratio*	1	*Presbyterorum ordinis*	40
Lumen gentium	63	*Christus dominus*	14	*Gravissimum educationis momentum*	1
Gaudium et spes	49	*Perfectae caritatis*	14	*Nostra aetate*	10
Ad gentes	205	*Optatam totius ecclesiae renavotionem*	9		
		Dignitatis humanae	4		

In all the quotations from Vatican II documents were twice as many as those from the Bible: 477 times as against 243 times, respectively. It shows the interest the delegates at the chapter had in the council and the desire to make it part and parcel of our identity as missionaries in the Catholic Church.

A look in our archives reveals the following major changes in our missionary society in the period after the council, which we now take for granted. From the juridical point of view, following the abrogation of the *ius commissionis*, like many other congregations and missionary societies, we were no longer responsible for some specific mission territories. The ordinaries (bishops) were the first ones responsible for the mission all over the world. Our role now became that of being at the service of the local churches to which we were sent. Our recent general chapters and different conventions with dioceses and our internal *Constitutions and Laws* (2006) in Africa underline this state of affairs. There have been chapters in which we have sought to redefine our identity in the light of this major change, as indicated by their themes, notably, 1967: 'At the service of the local church'; 1974: 'What is this service?' and 1980: 'Who are the Missionaries of Africa?' It was a difficult time also for us as some members, in the wake of

[6]   The results are contained in a 437-page document: Society of Missionaries of Africa (White Fathers), *XXth Chapter. Capitular Documents* (Roma: Società Tipografica Italia, 1968). This has been the reference document for a long time that spelt out the Society's identity and charism.

the council and in the time of searching for a new identity, left the priesthood or ended their commitment as brothers. This was a common phenomenon at the time in the whole Church.

Our conception of our missionary vocation also underwent a renewal in keeping with the renewal in the theology of mission based more on the Bible and on the history of salvation. Whereas earlier on missionaries would see themselves as planting the Church (*plantatio ecclesiae*), there was an awareness that the mission is of God (*missio Dei*) in his unconditional loving reaching out to humanity to which he invites us to participate in his name. The recent general chapters have come back in different ways to the trinitarian source of our mission and have stressed that we are sent by God who is love (Jn 3.16; 1 Jn 1.1–4) with Jesus's message of hope, reconciliation and forgiveness, justice, peace, encounter and compassion and healing, and that we are empowered by the Spirit.[7]

Our pastoral practice was another aspect influenced by Vatican II in areas such as liturgy, catechetics, the involvement of the laity, the different commissions at the parish level to promote a greater participation of the laity and so on. Vatican II's impact on our daily life could also be seen in the shift from obedience to the rules and to the superiors to a greater sense of responsibility of individual members and communities for the mission. Whereas previously the same rules were applied all over the missionary family, irrespective of the context, greater room was given to local initiatives. Just as the council promoted a collegial model of leadership, we also moved from a vertical and very hierarchical model of leadership to a horizontal and more communitarian one. Obedience was no more seen in terms of a submission but in the light of dialogue. In keeping with this, the literary style of our chapter texts has also changed. Just as Vatican II made a shift from the legal and canonical form of texts of the Council of Trent to more pastoral documents, our society has also moved in the post-Vatican II years from the directory style of text which tried to lay down rules for all aspects of life to more spiritually and pastorally inspiring texts.

Following the council, a lot of investment was made for updating confrères through different sessions. This was done through our internal publication in

---

[7] Cf. 'Our Mission Today and Tomorrow', in Society of Missionaries of Africa, *Chapter 1992*, Vol. I (Paris: Edition Voix d'Afrique, 1992), pp. 1–2; *Capitular Acts 1998* (Rome, 1998), pp. 37–42, 48–50, 57; *Capitular Acts: XXVth General Chapter*. Rome 10 May–16 June 2004 (Rome: Istituto Salesiano Pio XI, 2004), pp. 25–34; *Capitular Acts: XXVII General Chapter*. Rome 10 May–12 June 2010 (Rome: Istituto Salesiano Pio XI, 2010), pp. 20–6.

the *Petit Echo* and through theological conferences in the communities. Each year, all the communities received a programme of theological conferences as follows: 1963–4 *Mater et magistra*; 1964–5 *Pacem in terris*; 1965–6 *Lumen gentium*; 1966–7 *Ad gentes, Nostra aetate* and *Dignitatis humanae*. In addition to these, renewal programmes were organized in different places either by the society or in collaboration with other institutes. Part of the ongoing renewal was also done through setting up good libraries and encouraging people to use them and in addition to taking personal subscriptions to some theology journals. This renewal drive ensured that the fruits of the council were known by the members but it also had the effect of members reading less in our own traditional sources.

As is to be expected, not all were enthusiastic about the council and not all made the effort to enter into the spirit of Vatican II. But these were just a tiny minority who have not had a significant influence in the society and who have not been able to change the tide. Consequently, today, although our younger generations might not always be aware of it, like the little fish in the story earlier, they are in the ocean of the renewal brought about by the Second Vatican Council.

Vatican II's impact at the grassroots in some African local churches

Among the documents of Vatican II that have been influential in many parts of Africa, I would like to mention the following: the Constitution on the Church (*Lumen gentium*; LG); the 'Decree on the Church's Missionary Activity' (*Ad gentes*); the 'Constitution on Divine Revelation' (*Dei verbum*); the 'Constitution on the Sacred Liturgy' (*Sacrosantum concilium*); the 'Constitution on the Church in the World' (*Gaudium et spes*) and the 'Declaration on the Relation of the Church to Non-Christian Religions' (*Nostra aetate*). These documents, like the other texts, enable us to return to the source of our faith and to see how to make it relevant to the people of today.

The promotion of the idea of the Church as communion (LG 32) and 'People of God' (LG 4) in *Lumen gentium* ('Dogmatic Constitution on the Church') has been an important moment for the universal Church. This has been felt in the local Churches in many parts of Africa. This biblical image was dear to St Cyprian of North Africa (martyred in 258). It promoted better the idea of community and co-responsibility. This is complemented by the other image of the Church as body of Christ with its many parts but all of which build up the one body (1 Cor. 12.12–27). The council underlined that what unites the disciples of Christ is the common baptism through which all participate in the prophetic, priestly and royal vocation of Christ. The attitudes that will help sustain the communion within the people of God are the sense and respect of equality, reciprocity in the service, co-responsibility and dialogue.

In the wake of Vatican II, several bishops' conferences in Africa took this image of the Church as people of God seriously and organized the pastoral life around Small Christian Communities (SCC).[8] This was the case in the AMECEA region[9] when they made the SCC the pastoral option in 1973 and invested a lot in conscientizing the faithful and the priests in this light.[10] In the RD Congo in the 1971–2 conflict between Mobutu and the Church, it became obvious that to survive and to have an impact in society, SCC had to be created, ministries found for lay people and structures provided for ongoing formation at all levels.

After the council, African Churches were no longer seen as out-centres of the Vatican or elsewhere but as fully fledged Churches that have something prophetic to say to their people.[11] Different episcopal conferences have sometimes taken courageous positions in the face of political and social injustices of their countries.[12] The participation of people at different levels in the life of the Church through the presbyteral council, different commissions, lay councils, parish councils and so on, has fostered this sense of Church and provoked some thought. In the case of the Church in Africa, it eventually gave rise to

---

[8] Also known as Basic Christian Communities. Cf. Richard K. Baawobr, 'L'apport des communautés chrétiennes de base', *Voix de l'Eglise africaine* (14 March 2011), at http://www.mafrome.org/communautes_Ecclesiales_de_base.pdf.

[9] AMECEA (Association of Member Episcopal Conferences in Eastern Africa) consists of the Episcopal Conferences of Kenya (1961), Malawi (1961), Tanzania (1961), Uganda (1961), Zambia (1961), Ethiopia (1979), Sudan (1979) and Eritrea (1993). There are two affiliated members: Seychelles (1979) and Somalia (1995).

[10] For some of the basic texts on the question, see Rodrigo Mejia, *The Church in the Neighborhood. Meetings for the Animation of Small Christian Communities* (Nairobi: St Paul Publications Africa, 1992); Joseph G. Healey and Jeanne Hinton, *Small Christian Communities Today. Capturing the New Moment* (Maryknoll, NY: Orbis Books, 2005); James O'Halloran, *Living Cells: Vision and Practicalities of Small Christian Communities and Groups* (Dublin: Columba Press, 2010) and Joseph G. Healey, 'Building the Church as Family of God: Evaluation of the Growth and Impact of Small Christian Communities in the AMECEA region as AMECEA Celebrates Its Golden Jubilee' (Paper given at the Thirteenth Interdisciplinary Theological Session on the theme 'The Faculty of Theology of CUEA Celebrates the Golden Jubilee of AMECEA' at the Catholic University of Eastern Africa (CUEA) in Nairobi, Kenya on 3 March 2011 – revised on 27 June 2011).

[11] Anne Béatrice, 'L'homme de Tékoa: un questionnement de la fonction prophétique de l'Eglise en Afrique', *SEDOS Bulletin* 42/1–2 (2010), pp. 19–25.

[12] In preparation for the First African Synod, there was an interesting collection and commentary on some major texts of the bishops conferences in Africa by Maurice Chez, Henri Derriotte and René Luneau, *Les évêques d'Afrique parlent, 1969-1991* (Paris: Centurion, 1992).

the image of the Church as 'Family of God' during the First Special Assembly of the Synod of Bishops for Africa (10 April–8 May 1994).[13] This was taken up by theologians[14] and the Second Special Assembly of the Synod of Bishops for Africa (4–25 October 2009)[15] and several dioceses make it the leitmotiv of their deliberations.[16]

The 'Decree on the Church's Missionary Activity' (*Ad gentes*)[17] that stressed the missionary nature of the Church was important for all missionary societies and ours was no exception. The trinitarian origin of the mission is recognized. The mission belongs to God (*missio Dei*) and we participate in it in order to share the good news of salvation in Christ with others. This idea is part and parcel of the change in the concept and practice of mission today.[18] It has been taken on board in our different general chapters and in our formation programmes, thus bringing home the point that we are not the ones saving people, but rather that we are collaborating with God.

As the young Churches in different parts of Africa acquired their own structures and hierarchy, the presence of missionaries reminded them of the missionary nature of the Church. The catechists, alongside bishops, priests and deacons, continue to play an important role in ensuring that the Church reaches out to corners that it would not otherwise have reached out to. Today, there are many from the younger Churches in the global South who are participating in the mission elsewhere. The missionary movement is no longer bi-directional (north to south or west to east) but is multi-directional.[19] Even local Churches that do not have enough priests or religious in Mali and Burkina Faso, for

[13] Commonly referred to as 'the African Synod'. The results were published by Pope John Paul II in the post-synodal exhortation, *Ecclesia in Africa* (1995).

[14] See Edward B. Tengan, *House of God. Church-As-Family from an African Perspective* (Leuven: Acco, 1997); Augustin Ramazani Bishwende, *Eglise-famille de Dieu dans la mondialisation. Theologie d'une nouvelle voie africaine d'évangélisation* (Paris, L'Harmattan, 2006); Francis Appiah-Kubi, *Eglise famille de Dieu. Un chemin pour les Eglises d'Afrique* (Paris: Karthala, 2008).

[15] The results were published by Pope Benedict XVI as *Africae Munus* (2011). For a study of the document, see Richard K. Baawobr, '*Africae Munus* et les enjeux de la mission pour l'église-famille de Dieu en Afrique', at http://mafrome.org/ (original); Richard, K. Baawobr, '*Africae Munus* and What Is at Stake For Mission in the Church-Family Of God in Africa' (Donald MacLeod (trans.)) (2012), www.africamission-mafr.org/.

[16] Cf. Archevêché de Lubumbashi, Commission Centrale Préparatoire du Synode, *II\`ème Synode diocésaine. L'Eglise – Famille de Dieu de Lubumbashi: Bilan et perspectives. Lineamenta* (30 July 2011); *Instrumentum Laboris* (2 February 2012).

[17] Promulgated on 2 December 1965 by Paul VI with 2,394 for and only 5 against.

[18] For some bibliography, see Richard K. Baawobr, 'Wind of Change and Its Effect on Mission and Church Relationship', paper presented at the World Council of Churches' Conference on World Mission and Evangelism, Manila, 21–28 March 2012, at http://mafrome.org/.

[19] See the reflection of Sr Janice McLaughin, 'Turned Upside-Down: Learning and Challenges. A Missioner's Journey in Southern Sudan', *SEDOS Bulletin* 43/9–10 (2011), pp. 256–67, especially pp. 265–7 on the implications of this new face of mission and for the ones who are sent and for the ones who receive.

example, share their pastoral agents with other local Churches in other parts of Africa and the world where there is a greater need. For them to be effective in their new milieu, a time of linguistic and cultural preparation is necessary.

The Constitution on Divine Revelation (*Dei verbum*)[20] has been important for many local Churches because of its insistence on making the word of God accessible to all. The Bible was no longer reserved for a few, but all disciples of Christ were encouraged to meet God who comes in a loving way to meet us. In order to make the word of God easily accessible to all in and through the biblical pastoral ministries, at diocesan and national levels, bible translations have been made, commentaries on biblical texts have been written for scholars and for simple people, bible study groups of different levels have been encouraged and formed.[21] At times this has been an ecumenical venture and at other times each denomination has done its own translation.

In the SCCs, the word of God has a central place as people gather to listen to it, to pray with it and to welcome the light it sheds on the different situations of their life and guidance how to act accordingly. Different synods like the First African Synod (1994); the Word of God in the Life and Mission of the Church (2008) and the Second African Synod (2009) and documents like that on the *Interpretation of the Bible in the Church* (1995) of the Pontifical Biblical Commission have further emphasized the primary role of the word of God in the life of God's people. There is an evolution in the way catechism is conceived and taught. The manuals have moved from the doctrinal question and answer approach to a more biblical and historical one.

The rise of New Religious Movements (or sects) in many African countries and of fundamentalist interpretations of the Bible that often accompany some of them have shown the importance of studying the word of God in a serious way. Our local Churches owe it to Vatican II's insistence on the knowledge of the word of God as word of Life. One of the most impressive things I have seen as a missionary was the determination with which the illiterate mother of a priest in Kinshasa (Democratic Republic of Congo) followed the evening classes in order to learn how to read and write. When I asked her why she bothered at her age, her answer was: 'I want to be able to read the New Testament myself!' We were glad to offer her a complete Bible when she completed her course!

---

[20] Promulgated on 18 November 1965 by Paul VI after having been approved by 2,344 for and 6 against.

[21] For example, Richard K. Baawobr has published a series of Bible studies on the gospels and on the secondary readings for each year in English and in Swahili published by Paulines, Nairobi between 2000 and 2010.

The Constitution on the Liturgy (*Sacrosanctum concilium*)[22] has probably been the most implemented across the universal Church.[23] The use of the local languages, songs, symbols and suchlike have fostered a greater participation of the laity in the liturgical action and a better understanding of what is happening. There has probably been more enthusiasm and effort to inculturate the liturgies than there have been in other areas (like commitment to changing unjust social structures, dialogue with other religions and so on), even though these are just as important. All over sub-Saharan Africa, the cultural centres and liturgical commissions, diocesan or national, have done a remarkable job in making the liturgy speak to the people. This still has to be continued in order to ensure that there is a proper theological understanding behind some efforts and proposals of inculturation; that gospel values are promoted in the culture and that the culture itself is evangelized. Some missiologists in the past have spoken about the culture as carrying seeds of the Gospel. This is still very true.

The Constitution on the Church in the Modern World (*Gaudium et spes*)[24] has had, and still has, a challenging effect on the local Churches in Africa. With its resolute invitation to enter into dialogue with the world of today, recognizing the joys and pains of humanity, it brings home the point that the Church lives in the world and has a mission to and in the world. In some places, like RD Congo, there have been ongoing formation sessions organized by the Better World Movement for the pastoral agents, lay, religious and ordained alike which stressed the importance of the Church to be committed to the world.

Justice and Peace commissions in different dioceses (e.g. in Zambia and South Africa) have shown the importance for the Church to be committed to charity and development but especially to unmasking and fighting against unjust structures, structures of sin. In view of this, it is important to give the example in the Church itself. This was emphasized again by Pope Benedict XVI in the post-synodal apostolic exhortation *Africae munus* (2011).[25] A lot of development projects run by the Church have improved the lives of people in many places. The commitment of the Church, in some cases, has been instrumental in

---

[22] Promulgated by Paul VI on 4 December 1963 with 2,147 for and only 4 against.

[23] The Extraordinary Synod of Bishops on in December 1985 declared the liturgical renewal to be the most apparent fruit of the entire Council! Cf. Cardinal Paul Poupard, *Le Concile Vatican II* (Paris: Salvator, 2012), p. 61.

[24] Promulgated in the last public session of the Council on 7 December 1965 by Pope Paul VI after it had received 2,309 votes for, 75 against and 7 nullified votes.

[25] *Africae Munus* 102–5 calls to care for their priests, to financial accountable and transparent and to avoid tribalism. A powerful message.

preparing people for peaceful transition to other forms of government or in preparing and holding democratic elections. This work is often ecumenical and at the grassroots.[26]

The 'Decree on Ecumenism'[27] and the 'Declaration on the Relation of the Church to Non-Christian Religions'[28] have been helpful in revisiting the approach of many missionaries to other Christian churches and to African Traditional Religion. Proclamation of and witness to the person, message and lifestyle of Jesus Christ remain important and central to missionary activity. However, that is not seen in opposition to dialogue and encounter. The ecumenical contact with other Christian churches in the mission territories, the awareness of the harm that division is causing in the witness and the realization of the good work that is also done elsewhere, outside of the Catholic Church, prepared our members to engage ecumenically with other Christian churches. In some places there are ecumenical translations of the Bible into local languages and in others it is more through social action together.

On the matter of interreligious dialogue, our members working in North Africa, for example, are fully missionaries even though they live their missionary vocation in a way that is very different from those in sub-Saharan Africa where there are large Christian communities to pastor to. We have learnt a lot in our encounter and dialogue with Muslims and we try to approach African Traditional Religion with the same respect as we do with our Muslim brothers and sisters.[29] This dialogue takes different forms: the dialogue of life – people sharing the same realities of life as persons; dialogue of (social) action – people collaborate in order to improve social justice and create a better world for all and dialogue of theological exchange – people share the richness of their spirituality and thus allow the others to appreciate their spiritual and human values. They also discover the similarities and differences between their religions and this, sometimes, leads to soul-searching questions. Finally, dialogue of spiritual or religious experience – people rooted in their faith reflect and pray together (not the same prayer though) for a particular intention; for example, the Assisi experience of

---

[26] Such was the case in the 1990s with the national conferences in many countries where Church leaders assumed the roles of moderators (Benin, Zaïre [now RD Congo]) and in the transition from apartheid to today's South Africa. In the preparation for the creation of the new state of South Sudan, the Church played an important role also in education and the joint efforts of several congregations – the Solidarity with South Sudan – is contributing in the formation of teachers and nurses and priests and religious in rebuilding the country.

[27] Promulgated by Paul VI on 21 November 1964 after having been adopted by 2,137 votes to 11.

[28] It was approved on 28 October 1965 with 2,221 for, 88 against, 2 abstentions and 1 nullified vote.

[29] See Society of Missionaries of Africa, *Capitular Acts*, XXVII General Chapter, pp. 30–2.

1986, 2000 and 2011.[30] The growing interest of some people in North Africa to know about Christianity, with a few, in some cases, becoming Christians,[31] is a new phenomenon for our members and challenges them to be open also to journeying with those who are searching but without proselytizing.

New evangelization

As is to be expected 50 years on, some of the enthusiasm is probably going down in terms of our engagement in the world, and in mission and in inculturating the message of the gospel, but this is not a rejection of Vatican II. It is a challenge to look at it from a new perspective and this, I hope, will be a main preoccupation in answer to the call for a new evangelization. A lot of things have changed in the world at large: The end of the Cold War, the end of Communism, the electronic age, globalization and so on. In Africa, political independence, the growth of strong local churches with local leaders, the various conflicts and the urgency of inter-religious dialogue. It has become imperative to re-examine how the gospel message is announced in Africa also.

Pope Benedict XVI surprised most of us when, in the final part of the Post-Synodal Apostolic Exhortation *Africae munus*, he talked about the 'new evangelization' (159–71), although to my knowledge, this had not been part of the agenda of the Second African Synod, which focused on the role of the Church in Africa at the service of reconciliation, justice and peace.[32] Consequently, the question of the new evangelization was neither in the 57 *Propositions* submitted to Pope Benedict nor in the *Final Message* of the Synod Fathers to the people of God. However, it was mentioned by the Pope as he reminded the Church-Family of God in Africa that she is part of a bigger picture and that what is happening in one part of the family concerns her also. The interconnectedness

---

[30] Cf. Pontifical Council for Interreligious Dialogue and the Congregation for the Evangelisation of Peoples, *Dialogue and Proclamation* (1991). Cf. also Stephen B. Bevans and Roger P. Schroeder, *Constants in Context. A Theology of Mission for Today* (Maryknoll, NY: Orbis Books, 2004), pp. 383–4; *Prophetic Dialogue. Reflections on Christian Mission Today* (Maryknoll, NY: Orbis Books, 2011), pp. 68–9; Michael L. Fitzgerald and John Borelli, *Interfaith Dialogue A Catholic View* (London: SPCK, 2006), pp. 28–35. For a recent collection of articles on dialogue with Muslims, see Catarina Belo and Jean-Jacques Pérennès, *Mission in Dialogue: Essays in Honour of Michael L. Fitzgerald* (Louvain and Paris: Editions Peeters, 2012).

[31] Cf. Salah Guemriche, *Le Christ s'est arrêté à Tizi-Ouzou. Enquête sur les conversions en terre d'Islam* (Paris: Editions Denoël, 2011).

[32] In August 2008, there was a Continental Conference in Dar es Salaam, the proceedings of which are entitled *Towards a New Evangelization of African Society*. However, the focus of the conference was on the *Compendium of the Social Doctrine of the Church*.

in the world takes us beyond our regional, national and continental boundaries for better or for worse. We need each other as human family and all the more so as brothers and sisters sharing a common faith. We are all affected by the globalization of injustice that pushes people out of their homeland in search of better opportunities of life; so are we also of the fate of those who are victims of human trafficking, of the widening of the gap between rich and poor, of the disappearance of some values in society. However, there are also signs of hope like a greater awareness of our responsibility for each other, of the desire for human and political freedom and so on. These signs of hope should not blind us to the challenges of today's society. It is up to us to transform the challenges into opportunities for a new evangelization – 'new in its ardour, methods and expression' in our encounter with the person of Jesus, and in the witness we bear to his resurrection (*Africae munus* 160, 163, 165).

Conclusion

In experience of many young churches, where primary evangelization is still happening, Vatican II holds a lot of treasures that have still to be exploited. At the conclusion of his book on Vatican II, Jacques Vermeylen had the following to say:

> Vatican II has already produced sweet fruits in different areas, but there is still a lot to do, at the local level as at the level as well as of the Universal Church. If its programme were better implemented according to the letter and to the spirit, the face of Catholicism would be different! In this sense, at least, the Council is still in front of us. Let us it not consider it as the point of arrival, but rather as a promise![33]

Fifty years later on, the Second Vatican Council is still current and opens up areas for us to consider seriously in relation to the new evangelization. This new evangelization has to begin first of all with a personal conversion to the Gospel of Jesus by each one of us. May the Spirit of Jesus guide us in this endeavour!

The words of Pope Benedict XVI at the beginning of his pontificate speak volumes of the opportunities and challenges. On 20 April 2005, addressing the Cardinals, the faithful and men and women of good will, he said the following

---

[33] Jacques Vermeylen, *Vatican II* (Namur: Fidélité, 2011), p. 126 (my translation).

concerning Pope John Paul II and the importance of the Second Vatican Council for the pontificate which he was beginning:

> Pope John Paul II rightly pointed out the Council as a 'compass' by which to take our bearings in the vast ocean of the third millennium . . . Also, in his spiritual Testament he noted, 'I am convinced that it will long be granted to the new generations to draw from the treasures that this twentieth century Council has lavished upon us . . .' . . . I also wish to confirm my determination to continue to put the Second Vatican Council into practice, following in the footsteps of my Predecessors and in faithful continuity with the 2000-year tradition of the Church . . . As the years have passed, the Conciliar documents have lost none of their timeliness; indeed, their teachings are proving particularly relevant to the new situation of the Church and the current globalized society.[34]

---

[34] Kroeger, *Exploring the Treasures*, p. vii.

11

The New Evangelization and Other Religions: Facing Three Objections to Evangelization in Regard to the World Religions

Gavin D'Costa

What's 'new' about evangelization in regard to the world religions?

The answer is 'quite a lot'. In fact, there is a genuine crisis in the Catholic Church about the nature and necessity of evangelization in regard to the world religions. Some theologians argue that mission to the other religions is patronizing and demeaning as those from other religions, especially the theistic religions, are already in relationship with God. Those in need of mission are the 'gentiles', those who are religion-less. There are complex differences among the theologians on this issue but I simply state the most radical position. At the other end of the spectrum is the position that mission should be conducted to each and every person who does not know Christ and that God is trinity. This tension is to be expected because we have entered a new cultural period and that is precisely what the 'new' evangelization recognizes and attempts to address. It is worth stepping back to get a broader picture to understand the contemporary situation.

Father Reniero Cantalamessa's Advent Sermons to the Papal Household on this matter in 2011 are most helpful in identifying the key Vatican documents, sketching out four periods of evangelization in the Church and noting various problems to be addressed. His periodization of the history of evangelization is as follows:

1. The spread of Christianity in the first three centuries, until the eve of Constantine's edict, which is led by, first, the itinerant prophets, and then the bishops;

2. The sixth to ninth centuries in which we witness the re-evangelization of
   Europe after the Barbarian invasions – evangelization led by the work above
   all of monks;
3. The sixteenth century, with the discovery and conversion to Christianity of
   the peoples of the 'New World' – the work above all of friars;
4. The present age, which sees the Church committed to a re-evangelization of
   the secularized West, with the decisive participation of the laity.[1]

Here, I want to build on Father Reniero Cantalamessa's contribution and a vast
literature developing on this matter. The key point is two-fold: the secularized
West now also includes many people from the world religions; and the role
of the laity is very central to this new moment in history. With these factors
in mind, I want to discuss three objections to evangelization in regard to the
world religions that arise from Roman Catholic theologians as well as other
Christians and non-Christians. The objections all arise from our new cultural
context as well as from various interpretations (and misinterpretations) of
Vatican II.[2] I will indicate key sources in my notes and keep the arguments to
the fore of my presentation so that issues are central. My attention is primarily
on an intra-Church discussion, but only so that the extra-Church activity of
evangelization can be developed. I realize that my response to the objections is
very limited – and clearly a wider ranging discussion is required. But one has
to begin somewhere.

Objection 1

Vatican II marked a change of epoch, from a time when non-Christians were
seen to be outside the pale of salvation (*extra ecclesiam nulla salus* – no salvation
outside the Church) to a new period when: (a) it is acknowledged that non-
Christians can be saved while they are not part of the visible church and (b) the
Council teaches that the world religions can be the means by which truth and
grace might be found by sincere seekers within the religions. The two Vatican

---

[1] See Reniero Cantalamessa, 'The First Wave of Evangelization', at http://www.zenit.org/en/articles/
    father-cantalamessa-s-1st-advent-sermon--4. See also the helpful literature assembled by Scott
    Hahn on this matter, both official documents and more popular and specialist articles: http://www.
    scotthahn.com/newevangelization.html. And see, Cardinal Avery Dulles SJ, *John Paul II and the
    New Evangelization* (The Laurence J. McGinley Lectures; New York: Fordham University Press,
    2008), pp. 87–102.
[2] See *Vatican II: Catholic Doctrines on Jews and Muslims* (Oxford: Oxford University Press, 2014).

documents related to non-Christian religions: *Lumen gentium* ('Dogmatic Constitution on the Church') and *Nostra aetate* ('Declaration on the Relation of the Church to Non-Christian Religions') are the key documents that have shifted the Church into a new life where listening, learning and cooperation with the world religions should be at the forefront of the Catholic agenda. Furthermore, Pope John Paul II developed a clear doctrine that the Holy Spirit is at work in the non-Christian religions, both in hearts, minds and most importantly, religious cultures (i.e. in the religions).[3] In the light of these teachings at Vatican II, evangelization to the world religions is no longer appropriate. The secularized non-religious person is the object of true evangelization for they do not yet know God.

Responses to objection 1

(A) The two key themes noted earlier in *Lumen gentium* 14–6 and *Nostra aetate* 1–4 are indeed cause for celebration and do indicate a new development in the Catholic Church's approach to other religions. There can be no question about these two matters: first salvation is possible outside the Catholic Church and second 'seeds of the word', 'rays of that truth that enlightens all women and men' and holiness and goodness are to be found in the world religions. These two teachings consolidate a new epoch in the Church's life. However, I would contest that they undermine evangelization in any way at all. Rather, they require a different form of evangelization that takes notice of these points.

The first matter, salvation outside the church, was formally clarified in 1948 in the famous Fr Leonard Feeney SJ case, where the zealous and faithful Fr Feeney refused to retract his interpretation of *extra ecclesiam nulla salus*. He had argued that it meant that Protestants and Hindus were both excluded from salvation. They were not members of the Roman Catholic Church. The Holy Office outlawed his interpretation and when Feeney would not retract this false interpretation, he was excommunicated, deemed *extra ecclesiam*. Fortunately, Fr Feeney was reconciled to the Church before his death.

Fr Feeney was a forerunner to the equally zealous and pious Archbishop Marcel Lefebvre who agreed in substance with Feeney's position. Augustine, the extreme rigorist on this matter, was interestingly quite relaxed about accepting

---

[3] I discuss some Catholic theologians in detail in 'Pluralist Arguments: Prominent Tendencies and Methods', in Karl Josef Becker and Ilaria Morali (eds), *Catholic Engagement with World Religions* (Maryknoll, NY: Orbis Books, 2010), pp. 329–44.

that there were many *before* Christ who were part of the invisible Church and thus included in salvation. He, like so many major theologians after him, assumed that *after* the time of Christ those who were not Christians had either: (a) intentionally rejected the gospel; (b) were heretics or (c) were schismatics. The *extra ecclesiam* teaching was actually formulated with these three groups in mind and not what we would today call 'non-Christians'. Indeed, the two major 'non-Christian' groups in the Church's predominantly Western history, the Jews and Muslims, were for the main part viewed as heretics and schismatics. They were not seen as what *Lumen gentium* and *Nostra aetate* recognize as 'non-Christians'.

As regards the second matter, the sixteenth century was a decisive turning point in the discovery of the so-called new world and it was in this context that two distinctive 'discoveries' happened. I admittedly overplay this point and the historical story is far more complex.[4] First, what happened was that there was an important recognition of millions of non-Christians who had never known the gospel through no fault of their own. This faultless situation came to be characterized as those who are in a state of 'invincible ignorance'. Second, among sensitive missionaries, there was recognition that these people had profoundly spiritual and important elements within their own cultures which saved them from being degenerate; and precisely these elements helped them to follow the moral law. These sensitive missionaries never for a moment felt this insight absolved them from the task of evangelization and conversion. Nevertheless, we can see the teachings of the Council consolidating these positive insights in two particular ways: first, the emergence of the idea of genuinely non-Christian women and men who were in 'good faith' or technically in a state of invincible ignorance, and secondly, that non-Christian religions and cultures were not simply demonic. They had elements of truth, goodness and holiness within them.

To reiterate: salvation is possible outside the Church for the non-culpable non-Christians who follow their conscience; and non-Christian religions may not only contain 'seeds of the word' but also testify to the promptings of the Holy Spirit. Pope John Paul II developed doctrine from the Council teachings in this latter area. If Christians do not listen and learn from these religions, they are guilty of possibly being inattentive to the Holy Spirit. It is as radical as that, and in this sense, it marks a really new epoch or context of evangelization. The traffic

---

[4] See Francis A. Sullivan, *Salvation Outside the Church? Tracing the History of the Catholic Response* (London: Geoffrey Chapman, 1992).

of insight is not one way. But this does not diminish the necessity of preaching Christ and the good news.

(B) None of the above should occlude other themes present and taught in the Council which have been underplayed in contrast to the two positive themes I have highlighted. I will mention only two contrasting themes that bring a fuller balance to the issue and present the new evangelization in its proper and broader context.

First, in all instances of positive references to other religions in *Lumen gentium*, *Nostra aetate* and *Ad gentes* (AG), the council fathers made clear that, at their best, the non-Christian religions are *praeparatio evangelica*, that is, a preparation for the gospel.[5] Through the tradition, this term has a positive and negative sense. Positively, it has meant that such preparatory truths help form a bridge to the fullness of truth to be found in the gospel. Negatively, it has meant that such partial truth can also form barriers to receiving the gospel, for by holding on to a part, rather than the whole, people may not see the fullness of Christ. For example, it may well be that Muslims tend to reject the incarnation but often because they think that the incarnation means that there is a mixing of the divine and the human and is thus *shirk*, the identification of the human with the divine. I am not suggesting that Muslims are ignorant or ill-informed, but giving a speculative example (with some reasonable historical grounding) of how a truth (that the divine and human cannot be mixed) can become a stumbling block as the incarnation is rejected wrongly (in so much as this is not taught by orthodox Christians), but for right reasons.

It has also been understood negatively, because such preparatory religions can contain error and the works of Satan. This means that while not denying natural and supernatural truths within these religions, they are not given legitimation *per se*. They are seen as containing points of contact both in similarities of doctrine and practice, but they may also contain errors and even have Satanic elements. The Council is clear in pointing out concrete instances of positive elements in both *Lumen gentium* and *Nostra aetate* and rightly refrains from pointing to negative elements in such a public document. But it does not mean that Catholics should blind themselves to the complex positive and negative reality of the non-Christian religions. As a whole, they are not adequate and in need of Christ. Christianity and Christians, likewise, are always in need of conversion to Christ so that a deepening of faith and growing into the fullness of truth may take place.

---

[5] See Joseph Carola, 'Appendix: Vatican II's Use of Patristic Themes Regarding Non-Christians', in Karl Josef Becker and Ilaria Morali (eds), *Catholic Engagement with World Religions*, pp. 143–53.

The Council did not formally attend to this point about the exact theological status of other religions, but it inevitably became a disputed question after the Council.[6] It is precisely because of these disputes that *Dominus Iesus* was published in 2000. It teaches (4) that other religions could be understood as providential in a *de facto* manner, not in a *de iure* manner. That is, they could provide the means of grace, but not in the sacramental sense of means, as when used of the Church as a means of salvation. In this reading, other religions provide grace of many types, but justifying grace can only finally be conferred through faith in Christ. The important point about *Dominus Iesus* here is that other religions are not *de iure* willed by God. They are a stepping stone to the fullness of truth to that religion *de iure* willed by God, the Catholic Church. This is the teaching of *Lumen gentium* 14.

Before proceeding, let me illustrate the *de iure* and *de facto* point for it carries important implications which have not always been taken up in the literature on *Dominus Iesus*. For example, in Islam there is a profound and lofty monotheism which is true and awe inspiring, as well as erroneous, although possibly non-culpable, in its rejection of the truth of the incarnation. The latter means that objectively speaking there is error in Islam. This does not mean that Muslims knowingly and culpably embrace error in their being good Muslims. So in their subjective life they may seek the good and true God while denying the incarnation on the basis of their following the teachings of their religions. But these very teachings are in an objective sense wrong. I hope this help makes the point a little more clear. In this sense Islam could not be willed *de iure* by God, although clearly God may well operate graciously through elements within Islam.

The issue about error and Satan being present is not exclusively applicable to non-Christian religions. It can be applied to the Christian churches as well, but not in the sense of the *de iure* elements, such as the gift of the sacraments and the promises made by Christ to remain with his Church in the Spirit through the teaching authority of the magisterium (in a carefully defined sense). *Lumen gentium* addresses these questions consolidating and developing Catholic teachings here, but it is not possible to look at those teachings further. Hence, the Catholic Church, despite its many failings, can be said to be the means to salvation in its sacramental visible signification. This cannot be said *per se* or *de iure* about any other non-Christian religion.

---

[6]   See the debate in Miikka Ruokanen, *The Catholic Doctrine on Non-Christian Religions According to the Second Vatican Council* (Leiden: Brill, 1992), pp. 133–56.

Second, in the Council, the necessity of mission is central to the very nature of the Church.[7] *Lumen gentium*'s opening paragraph insists on the universal mission of the Church for the gospel is good news for everyone. Nevertheless, the early Christians became martyrs for this truth and many women and men throughout the ages have suffered, loved and worked endlessly in providing this witness to each and every person. Likewise, abuses, contempt, racism and financial exploitation have also been present in some missionary activity and this should be acknowledged and properly criticized. This is precisely what was done so movingly by Pope John Paul II in his millennium prayers of repentance for the church. None of this undermines the importance of an evangelizing mission that has the single goal of bringing friendship with Christ and thus forming a new community that invites others to enjoy this new life and to be united with the universal community of Catholic Christians.

Let me provide a simple personalist analogy to illustrate this point. Aquinas asks what should we desire for a person that we love? Think of someone you really care about. His answer is that we should always seek that person's good, which is not necessarily what they demand or what they think is their good. Of course, one can never trespass upon the freedom of the person in attempting to provide for their good. This respect of a person's freedom has not always been emphasized in past Christian history when punishment and even torture were sometimes justified for the 'good of the person'. But again, Vatican II emphasizes this respect of the person as non-negotiable and brings to the fore this particular concern: in 'spreading religious faith and introducing religious practices, everyone should refrain at all times from any kind of action which might seem to suggest coercion or dishonest or improper persuasion, especially when dealing with poor or uneducated people' (*Dignitatis humanae* 5). Of course, there are qualifications to this analogy. We do not know the good of the person in any respect other than in friendship with Christ and sacramental growth in his community. Suggesting we know the good for others can lead to a terrible type of imperialism, but in this particular case, it is pointing to Christ's teachings and promises and good news, not to ourselves. The cultural paternalism of some missionaries from the past is no longer appropriate or adequate, but unless we see Christ as one cultural option among others, this is not part of paternalism.

---

[7] See Ralph Martin, *Will Many Be Saved? What Vatican II Actually Teaches and Its Implications for the New Evangelization* (Grand Rapids, MI: William B. Eerdmans, 2012) who makes this case most carefully.

(C) Combining these two points certainly rebuts the claims that Vatican II as a whole does not support mission to all religions. Clearly, when the Council speaks positively about religions, this does not undermine the necessity for mission. That would be to bring in a simplistic either–or: either mission is only appropriate to totally demonic religions or it is inappropriate. Life is far more complex and rich.

So the real challenge that faces the new evangelization is how to be missionary in a changed context, whereby the culture of the non-Christian religions is one where we learn from, listen to and are challenged – *while* also preaching the good news. The first three characteristics, while always being present in different measures to various heroic missionaries, have never been emphasized so boldly and officially as they are now in official Catholic teaching. And this positive and right regard is to be celebrated. But it has, sadly and inevitably, caused some of the faithful to question mission. I hope to have begun to show that the council was able to balance a number of themes together with integrity and depth: mission and dialogue are not incompatible; respect and reverence for other religious traditions are not incompatible with preaching the truth of Christ, the trinitarian nature of God's love and forgiveness and the sacramental strengths imparted upon Christ's body, his Church.

I suspect historians may look back to our times and see the move towards relativism as inevitable once the Church made the bold and necessary step of showing reverence, due regard and respect to other religions. But it is a move that is neither inevitable nor necessary. Vatican II was able to see that with clarity. The Catholic Church is yet to fully appropriate that complex balance of teachings. I would like to cite some of Pope Francis's letter, *Evangelii gaudium*, 'The Joy of the Gospel' which was not published when this paper was first written. The quotations might indicate that the lines developed in this paper are in keeping with the current magisterium's perception of the task of the new evangelization. In *Evangelii gaudium* 251, Pope Francis captures the complex but necessary balance between dialogue and proclamation and a concern that these are never compromised:

> In this dialogue, ever friendly and sincere, attention must always be paid to the essential bond between dialogue and proclamation, which leads the Church to maintain and intensify her relationship with non-Christians. A facile syncretism would ultimately be a totalitarian gesture on the part of those who would ignore greater values of which they are not the masters. True openness involves remaining steadfast in one's deepest convictions, clear and joyful in one's own

identity, while at the same time being 'open to understanding those of the other party' and 'knowing that dialogue can enrich each side'. What is not helpful is a diplomatic openness which says 'yes' to everything in order to avoid problems, for this would be a way of deceiving others and denying them the good which we have been given to share generously with others. Evangelization and interreligious dialogue, far from being opposed, mutually support and nourish one another.

Let me move to objection 2.

Objection 2

Your argument earlier is accepted, but there is a horrible cultural arrogance involved in the claims you are making which mimic the worse aspects of colonialism: we Westerners know best, and when we speak about conversion and evangelization are we not simply exporting and affirming Western forms of Christianity over non-Western peoples? Christian mission is still Western European dominance over other cultures. Thus mission lacks credibility in a post-colonial age.

Response to objection 2

This criticism is not necessarily based on an interpretation of Vatican II, but has tended to arise in the new cultural context in which we live. But I will again draw on Vatican II in giving a response to defend and explicate the new evangelization.

   (A) I think one has to concede a truth in this charge and not equivocate: Christian mission has sometimes been allied to Western supremacism, cultural arrogance, and has been too closely entangled with political imperialism. While we should be careful in condemning the past with the benefit of hindsight and sometimes from an all too smug present, none of these particular traits are acceptable and they should not be condoned in any new situation of evangelization. But, and this is all important, these objections do not *per se* scuttle the new evangelization which is cognizant of these factors. I want to develop this in two ways drawing on Vatican II.

   (B) Vatican II in *Ad gentes* (16, 18, 19, 22) and *Gaudium et spes* (especially 22) was unambiguous about the importance of inculturation, as have been successive magisterial teachings including the synodal preparation for the meetings on the new evangelization.

I would argue there are four stages in inculturation in regard to our question. First, when the missionary is engaging with another culture or religion they should joyfully and gladly affirm that which is good, true and beautiful and in one sense seek to integrate this wisdom into their own Christian practice if appropriate, regardless of whether a person from that culture converts to Christianity. Vatican II envisages the missionary as one who is actually from this culture and also envisages a missionary who is not – which is precisely the situation on the ground in the 1960s. Each person has different tasks demanded of them. What is unambiguously clear is that inculturation is required from the very nature of the incarnation, taking on flesh and form, and is not an added option for trying to make mission more effective. It just is part of being an Asian, English, Colombian, Japanese or Chinese Catholic Christian. Second, as *Gaudium et spes* 22 emphasizes, all these inculturated elements must be Christologically integrated and undergo a Christian baptism so that their incorporation into Christian thinking and practice renders them both continuous and discontinuous with their past. One only has to look at Cardinal Newman's history of the development of Christianity to see that this process takes place in regard to the development of the Western Church, namely, inculturation from Roman and Greek culture.[8]

There is of course always a danger of uncritical assimilation and one might plausibly argue that the history of the Western church and its various heresies are a narration of forms of inculturation that have become one-sided or over-emphasized. Ebionitism is a result of remaining too inculturated within Judaism just as current forms of 'degree Christology' are sometimes a result of secular humanism and scientisms' refusal of the possibility of God's intervention in history. Once miracles go, then incarnation cannot survive. The point I am making is that bad inculturation has happened and happens endlessly in regard to Western culture. When it comes to criticisms of some forms of inculturation which come from Eastern religions or other cultural forms, we should not simply cry out racism or imperialism, without careful discrimination. Some of the reactions to the Congregation for the Doctrine of the Faith's reflections on Eastern forms of meditation evoked some critically uncritical responses.[9]

Regarding this matter, one also has to be aware of what the African Yale theologian, Lamin Sanneh, calls the 'Western guilt complex'. He uses this term

---

[8] See John Henry Newman, *An Essay on the Development of Christian Doctrine* (London: James Toovey, 1846).

[9] Congregation for the Doctrine of the Faith, Letter 'On Some Aspects of Christian Meditation' (1989).

to denote the post-colonial guilt that surrounds the history of imperialism which is then confused and conflated with mission. He also uses this to indicate when Westerners romanticize the exotic and the foreign and sometimes 'go native'.[10] For example, they may end up extolling an Eastern religious tradition in a form which bears more resemblance to the European Romanticization of that tradition rather than the actual practice of that religion. This has certainly happened with Hinduism and Buddhism which was initially filtered through to a secularized Europe that was seeking spiritual alternatives and, through the influence of Schopenhauer, began to see the alternative as the 'East'.[11] Getting away from Western imperialism is difficult, even in its reverse imperialism form! I have expressed this over-forcefully, but there are elements of this critique that might be applied to such saintly figures as Swami Abishiktananda and Bede Griffiths in India, both Catholic European monks who went native. Abishiktananda was French and Bede was quintessentially English! Their inculturations have been subject to devastating critiques by actual Hindus who have converted to Christianity and who have identified these monastic forms of inculturations as endorsing Brahmanical elitism that has been the cause of native Indian subjugations. They left Hinduism and converted to Christianity precisely because of the features that are being praised by their Western progressive Christian brothers: the rituals of Brahmanical Hinduism. This same drama has a parallel with secularism and in both cases the right balance will require time, experimentation and also the courage to see failure. The cost of real inculturation requires a long period of history with careful discernment and involvement by the universal church so that parochialism does not have the last word.

Third, to return to my main argument, when inculturation happens slowly and organically and accountably it represents the true pulse of Catholicism. It celebrates all of human culture and draws it into the praise and glorification of the living God. The liturgy and cultural life of local Churches must be fully inculturated if evangelization is to be focused and specific and effective. However, on the doctrinal front, this inculturation must be related to the universal church and be accountable to it as well as maintaining doctrinal concurrence. I take it that doctrinal plurality in faith and morals is not permissible, but every other form of plurality should be celebrated and carefully fostered. At the present time, because various forms of inculturations related to both Eastern religions

---

[10] Lamin Sanneh, 'Christian Mmission and the Western Guilt Complex', *Christian Century* 8 (April 1987), pp. 330–4.

[11] See the European idealization of the East in Wilhelm Halbfass, *India and Europe: An Essay in Understanding* (New York: State University of New York, 1988 [1981]).

and Western non-religions have gone too far, there is a certain timidity about exploring inculturation with rigour and openness. Pope Francis, as we shall see, is opening the door again to these steps, but not without a self-critical eye for the necessity of deep discernment. These differences in emphasis among individual popes are inevitable. And patience is a virtue given the complex organism of a global church.

This tension between the past and the future is nicely expressed in John Paul II's comment in *Faith and Reason* (73) regarding inculturation in India. Some Indian Catholic theologians have argued that the allegiance to Catholicism should not involve allegiance to a long history of Western-based formulations and teachings. John Paul writes that:

> in engaging great cultures for the first time, the Church cannot abandon what she has gained from her inculturation in the world of Greco-Latin thought. To reject this heritage would be to deny the providential plan of God who guides his Church down the paths of time and history. This criterion is valid for the Church in every age, even for the Church of the future, who will judge herself enriched by all that comes from today's engagement with Eastern cultures and will find in this inheritance fresh cues for fruitful dialogue with the cultures which will emerge as humanity moves into the future. Thirdly, care will need to be taken lest, contrary to the very nature of the human spirit, the legitimate defence of the uniqueness and originality of Indian thought be confused with the idea that a particular cultural tradition should remain closed in its difference and affirm itself by opposing other traditions. . . . What has been said here of India is no less true for the heritage of the great cultures of China, Japan and the other countries of Asia, as also for the riches of the traditional cultures of Africa, which are for the most part orally transmitted.

The fourth and final point about inculturation is this: the great dialogue and evangelization process that must take place in the new evangelization means that the shape of the Church will change and develop, as new challenges arise and new responses are required. Inculturation should make us realize how much more we have to learn about our own faith when it is engaged by the new and the Other. I know from my own experience the questions about animals and ecology posed by Hinduism and forms of neo-Buddhism which made me search hard in my Catholic tradition for responses to the issues of animal suffering and the demands of ecological balance. I know from the sacramental forms of temple worship in Hinduism that I found my way back to the liturgy when I had lapsed from my Catholic faith as a university student. Inculturation means confident pilgrims, the church, sojourning in a strange new world, discovering real areas of growth and development in its engagement with the world while continuing with the single task of evangelization. This pilgrimage will generate both a settled and unsettling deepening relationship with Christ and his mother, the Church.

(C) I conclude that the objection has some truth which is very important, but alone it does not suffice as an objection against culturally sensitive evangelization whose blueprint is to be found in *Ad gentes* – and in certain earlier practices of various missionaries. Such evangelization will be both intra- and extra-: a preaching of the good news to the world; and a transformation of the Church through the process of inculturation which is required in any act of preaching. But evangelization need not be complicit in imperialism. And that is central to my defence.

As with the previous section, I would like to cite some of Pope Francis's exhortation, 'The Joy of the Gospel' (*Evangelii gaudium*). The quotations might indicate that the lines developed in this paper are in keeping with the current magisterium's perception of the task of the new evangelization. In *Evangelii gaudium* 69, Pope Francis captures the different dynamics of inculturation and its necessity as well as its shortcomings:

> It is imperative to evangelize cultures in order to inculturate the Gospel. In countries of Catholic tradition, this means encouraging, fostering and reinforcing a richness which already exists. In countries of other religious traditions, or profoundly secularized countries, it will mean sparking new processes for evangelizing culture, even though these will demand long-term planning. We must keep in mind, however, that we are constantly being called to grow. Each culture and social group needs purification and growth. In the case of the popular cultures of Catholic peoples, we can see deficiencies which need to be healed by the Gospel: machismo, alcoholism, domestic violence, low Mass attendance, fatalistic or superstitious notions which lead to sorcery, and the like. Popular piety itself can be the starting point for healing and liberation from these deficiencies.

Pope Francis is also a stern critic, no less than his predecessors, of the dangerous elements of secular culture that are too often uncritically inculturated into Catholic practices. In *Evangelii gaudium* 62, he pulls no punches and draws on the bishops conferences from around the world to make his critique be part of the local communities' voice:

> In the prevailing culture, priority is given to the outward, the immediate, the visible, the quick, the superficial and the provisional. What is real gives way to

appearances. In many countries globalization has meant a hastened deterioration of their own cultural roots and the invasion of ways of thinking and acting proper to other cultures which are economically advanced but ethically debilitated. This fact has been brought up by bishops from various continents in different Synods. The African bishops, for example, taking up the Encyclical *Sollicitudo Rei Socialis*, pointed out years ago that there have been frequent attempts to make the African countries 'parts of a machine, cogs on a gigantic wheel. This is often true also in the field of social communications which, being run by centres mostly in the northern hemisphere, do not always give due consideration to the priorities and problems of such countries or respect their cultural make-up'. By the same token, the bishops of Asia 'underlined the external influences being brought to bear on Asian cultures. New patterns of behaviour are emerging as a result of over-exposure to the mass media . . . As a result, the negative aspects of the media and entertainment industries are threatening traditional values, and in particular the sacredness of marriage and the stability of the family'.

Objection 3

You have made a provisionally convincing case in general, but in particular there are real problems applying your position to the Jewish people for three theological reasons and one psychological reason. The theological reasons: First, Vatican II affirmed the validity of the Jewish covenant in both *Lumen gentium* and *Nostra aetate* and John Paul II has continued this teaching and affirmed the validity of Israel's covenant today. Second, the word revelation is applied exclusively to Jewish scripture and to no other religion in the council documents which means that mission is *ad gentes* to the gentiles, and no longer to the Jews. Third, Pope Benedict said that the return of the Jewish people is an eschatological event in God's hands and not a goal of contemporary Church activity. The psychological reason: mission to Jews is synonymous with the eradication of their identity and thus synonymous with the Holocaust. Conclusion: the new evangelization must exclude the Jewish people.

Responses to objection 3

I cannot possibly respond to this in adequate detail, so even more than above, this is a skeleton of an answer. I will take the points in the order presented but also because the psychological point only needs addressing if the others fail.

(A) While a large amount of literature suggests Vatican II affirmed the contemporary validity of the Jewish 'covenant', in the council's teachings in *Nostra aetate*, the jury is still out on this matter. Recently Cardinal Koch, who is head of the Secretariat for the Jewish People, argued that this was not the teaching of the council but an issue only raised by John Paul II during his pontificate.[12] While it is a highly contested issue, I want to side step it and argue that *even if* the Jewish covenant is still valid and thus, so is contemporary Judaism, does that *per se* invalidate the necessity of evangelization?

I think not for three reasons. First, Jesus assumed the validity of the Jewish covenant as did his disciples, but like many Jewish sectarian groups at the time Jesus and the first Christians believed that their interpretation of the covenant was the right and constituted faithful adherence to God. In this sense the fact that Jesus's mission was almost exclusively to Jews suggests that if we fail to keep faithful to our Lord's impulse to preach and teach among the Jews by now keeping his message away from these, his chosen people, we are failing in our discipleship to him. Second, throughout the Church's tradition there has not been any formal teaching indicating that the Jews should be excluded from the good news. Indeed, there is room to argue that this might be a new form of anti-Jewishness to exclude just these people from evangelization. While negative anti-Semitism needs purging from the church's traditions, we should not allow a new form enter through the back door. Third, one might argue that if we can carefully distinguish between fulfilment, supersessionism and abrogation it may be possible to justify evangelization on fulfilment grounds. Terminologically, supersessionism and abrogation have implied the invalidity of Judaism and a negative view of all Jewish spirituality. Fulfilment on the other hand affirms the positive elements within Judaism and its profound spirituality, but seeks to find the completion and fulfilment of these positive elements. Too often fulfilment is confused or conflated with supersessionism and abrogation.

(B) The second point regards the fact that the Old Testament is the Hebrew Bible and is considered as revelation in the Council documents (*Dei verbum* 14–6). This however does not lead to the conclusion that Judaism is a religion of revelation and thus there should be no mission to the Jewish people. It is

---

[12] See his speech on Jewish–Catholic dialogue since Vatican II, *Vatican News*, 17 May 2012, at http://www.news.va/en/news/cardinal-koch-on-jewish-catholic-dialogue-since-va. He said: 'That the covenant that God made with his people Israel persists and is never invalidated – although this confession is true – cannot be read into "*Nostra aetate*". This statement was instead first made with full clarity by Pope John Paul II when he said during a meeting with Jewish representatives in Mainz on 17 November 1980 that 'the Old Covenant had never been revoked by God.'

simply part of the same point as earlier: the Old Testament is fulfilled in the revelation of Christ and is a pre-condition of that revelation. In itself, it cannot be considered adequate or else Christ need not have come.

(C) What of Benedict's now often quoted statement from his second volume of *Jesus of Nazareth*? Here, two points are in order. First, the book has no status at all other than a glimpse into the private thoughts of a Catholic theologian who happened to be the pope. In the preface to the first volume, Joseph Ratzinger made clear that the book was a 'personal search' and not an exercise of the magisterium.[13] Second, while the final 'coming in' of Israel is up to God and will happen in His end times as Paul writes in Romans, does this actually mean there should be no evangelization towards the Jewish people? Paul, the author of Romans, does not think it means that evangelization should not be carried out. Rather, Paul explains the theological significance of Israel's historical no, as it was a deeply embarrassing no.

This and the earlier two points are a clear acknowledgement that in the new evangelization Jews cannot be considered as just another non-Christian religion, because the roots and shoot of Christianity lie in the Jewish covenant. Judaism has a special status and is nearest to Christianity in the objective order. But this recognition in *Lumen gentium* and *Nostra aetate* does not lead to the conclusion that evangelization to the Jews is inappropriate. But it may well be inappropriate in psychological terms, which leads to the final part of this objection.

(D) The psychological issue is profound and one cannot easily bypass it. One might recall Rabbi Abraham Heschel famous remark: 'I am ready to go to Auschwitz any time, if faced with the alternative of conversion or death.'[14] If *Ad gentes* 5 required evangelization to avoid 'all forms of coercion or dishonest or improper persuasion', one must ask whether evangelization is simply perceived as a terrifying threat to Jews, given the recent horrific history of the Jewish people under the Nazi's tyranny. The answer to such a question is complex, because there is evidence that some Jews would answer yes and some would answer no and others would answer, it depends. Here it is worth citing two strands of evidence that suggest the picture is deeply complicated. First, there are Jews who become Catholics and rejoice in this and they are committed to evangelization of their brothers and sisters. Second, there are Jewish groups who are unchurched in the gentile sense of church, such as Jews for Jesus, Hebrew

---

[13] Joseph Ratzinger, *Jesus of Nazareth. From the Baptism in the Jordan to the Transfiguration* (London: Bloomsbury, 2007), p. xxiii.
[14] *Herald Tribune*, 3 September 1964.

Christians and Messianic Jews. They likewise feel the need to evangelize to their fellow Jews. Both groups are a reminder that gentile mission to Jews is fraught in the light of recent history, but Jewish mission to Jews can be classified either as self-hating Jews (as these disciples are sometimes characterized by both Jews and Christians) or as a real witness to the truth of the gospel. I go for the latter choice and think it defensible.

As with the previous sections I will cite Pope Francis to indicate that these thoughts, written before *Evangelii gaudium*, may indeed be in line with the mind of the magisterium. In *Evangelii gaudium* 249, after reiterating the positive teachings of the council towards the Jewish people, the Pope unequivocally states the differences between the two communities and the importance of giving witness of Jesus as 'Messiah', the Jewish term indicating the hope of Israel:

> God continues to work among the people of the Old Covenant and to bring forth treasures of wisdom which flow from their encounter with his word. For this reason, the Church also is enriched when she receives the values of Judaism. While it is true that certain Christian beliefs are unacceptable to Judaism, and that the Church cannot refrain from proclaiming Jesus as Lord and Messiah, there exists as well a rich complementarity which allows us to read the texts of the Hebrew Scriptures together and to help one another to mine the riches of God's word. We can also share many ethical convictions and a common concern for justice and the development of peoples.

Conclusion

The new evangelization has sometimes incorrectly been associated with a mission to secularized Europe, but within Europe religious diversity is alive and healthy as it is across the globe. The new evangelization is faced with 'new' objections to mission, which is just one facet of what makes it 'new'. It is purely this facet that I have been focusing on in this chapter. I have tried to argue that the three objections I have looked at, while all containing serious elements of truth, are in the final analysis not decisive. We are still faced with the question: how, in this new climate, should mission be carried out; and how is the form of that mission appropriate for the laity who have a special calling in this age? But to get to those questions, it has been necessary to clear the ground so that the real questions are in place.

12

The New Evangelization and Other Religions: Proclamation and Dialogue

Annemarie Mayer

This contribution draws a line from the Second Vatican Council to the Synod of Bishops on the New Evangelization in October 2012. After comparing evangelization and new evangelization, it takes a quick look at the situation today, outlines the perspective of the Second Vatican Council regarding other religions and highlights the continuation of the Council in the document *Dialogue and Proclamation*.[1] It ends with some reflections on new evangelization in a multi-religious context.

Evangelization and new evangelization: two different kettles of fish?

In December 2007, the Congregation for the Doctrine of the Faith (CDF) provided a clear definition of the terms 'evangelization' and 'new evangelization' in comparison to 'mission'. 'The mission of the Church is universal and is not restricted to specific regions of the earth.'[2] In contrast to this,

> [e]vangelization [. . .] is undertaken differently according to the different situations in which it occurs. In its precise sense, *evangelization* is the *missio ad gentes* directed to those who do not know Christ. In a wider sense, it is used to

---

[1] Pontifical Council for Interreligious Dialogue and the Congregation for the Evangelization of Peoples, *Dialogue and Proclamation. Reflection and Orientations on Interreligious Dialogue and the Proclamation of the Gospel of Jesus Christ* (19 May 1991).

[2] Congregation for the Doctrine of the Faith (CDF), Doctrinal Note 'On Some Aspects of Evangelization' (3 December 2007).

describe ordinary pastoral work, while the phrase 'new evangelization' designates pastoral outreach to those who no longer practice the Christian faith.[3]

In view of this definition, we have to put the question more sharply: What have new evangelization and non-Christian religions to do with each other? Do these two terms not belong to two opposing concepts? Are 'other religions' not unequivocally to be assigned to the area of first evangelization, whereas 'new evangelization' deals with the 'abandonment of the faith – a phenomenon progressively more manifest in societies and cultures which for centuries seemed to be permeated by the Gospel'?[4] With exactly these words, Pope Benedict summed up the intention of new evangelization on the occasion of the founding of the Pontifical Council for Promoting the New Evangelization.[5] So, we have two different concepts, first evangelization, on the one hand, and new evangelization, on the other. But already Pope John Paul II linked the two and stated in his encyclical *Redemptoris missio* (1990; 34):

> the boundaries between *pastoral care of the faithful, new evangelization and specific missionary activity* are not clearly definable, and it is unthinkable to create barriers between them or to put them into watertight compartments. [. . .] The Churches in traditionally Christian countries, for example, involved as they are in the challenging task of new evangelization, are coming to understand more clearly that they cannot be missionaries to non-Christians in other countries and continents, unless they are seriously concerned about the non-Christians at home. Hence missionary activity *ad intra* is a credible sign and a stimulus for missionary activity *ad extra*, and vice versa.

In addition to this, both first evangelization and new evangelization are facing similar problems and challenges today.

The situation today

Pluralism is one of the most striking features of our time. Plurality is a phenomenon that always has existed. What is new is not the plurality as such, but the fact that it is now rated so positively. Plurality is a value in itself, while

---

[3] CDF, Doctrinal Note.
[4] Benedict XVI, *Ubicumque et Semper*, Apostolic Letter issued Motu Proprio 'Establishing the Pontifical Council for Promoting the New Evangelization' (21 September 2010).
[5] Cf. the already detailed description in John Paul II, *Christifideles Laici*, Apostolic Exhortation 'On the Vocation and the Mission of the Lay Faithful in the Church and in the World' (1988), p. 34.

unity by now requires justification. This is what marks the step from plurality to pluralism, which today is pervasive in most sectors of modern society. Besides, everything is close within the global village. Also other religions are right next door and need to face together with Christianity common problems such as the marketing of religion or the charge that religion automatically leads to fanaticism and violence. Moreover, other than recent forecasts of secularism would have it, religion has not lost its influence. On the contrary, on a worldwide scale religious phenomena are rapidly gaining strength. Yet this happens mostly outside the boundaries of the traditional churches, and sometimes the combination of bits and pieces from different religious or ecclesial traditions can lead to rather weird personal beliefs when people are searching for answers and a meaning to their life. Rather than secularism, this patchwork-religiosity is one of the hallmarks of post-secular post-modern society on its way to post-post-modernism.

What does all this mean for a church that aims at being shaped by evangelization and new evangelization? Almost 50 years ago, the Second Vatican Council set the course for our answer to this question:

> The joys and the hopes, the griefs and the anguish of the people of our time, especially of those who are poor or afflicted, are the joys and hopes, the griefs and anguish of the followers of Christ as well. Nothing that is genuinely human fails to find an echo in their hearts. For theirs is a community of people united in Christ and guided by the Holy Spirit in their pilgrimage towards the Father's kingdom, bearers of a message of salvation for all of humanity. That is why they cherish a feeling of deep solidarity with the human race and its history (*Gaudium et spes* 1).[6]

It is remarkable that *Gaudium et spes*, the 'Pastoral Constitution on the Church in the Modern World', does not lapse into lamenting, but views the contemporary context and situation of society as a positive opportunity for the Church to develop a gospel-oriented relationship towards the world. The same positive attitude marks the introductory paragraph of *Nostra aetate*, the 'Declaration on the Relation of the Church to Non-Christian Religions' (NA) which reflects on what people have in common and states a fundamental unity of humankind: 'One is the community of all peoples, one their origin, for God made the whole human race to live over the face of the earth. One also is their final goal, God' (NA 1). Is this naïve? No, I would rather say it is honest. Certainly there are differences among human beings, but a basic unity of all

---

[6] If not indicated otherwise, the quotes of Vatican II documents are taken from the Vatican website: http://www.vatican.va/archive/hist_councils/iI_vatican_council/index.htm.

humankind springs from the very nature of the human person. All human beings are faced with the same questions – about the meaning of life, about suffering and death, about genuine happiness. *Nostra aetate* does not say that all religions are in a position to answer these questions in a satisfactory way, but it says that human beings turn 'to their different religions for an answer to the unsolved riddles of human existence' (NA 1). These questions are still posed today. Neither has scientific progress nor an increase in wealth or in what human beings can achieve been able to eliminate them. Rather today even new dimensions should be added to them.

But, are people nowadays really still turning to religion to look for answers? This is the crucial question given the basic conditions of the Christian witness in a de-Christianized society.[7] It also is the crucial question linking 'new evangelization' and 'other religions'. Do people (still) turn to religions for the answers to their existential questions? I would venture to say: Yes, more often than not. And the fact that they do make it necessary for the Catholic Church to deal with these religions also in the context of the new evangelization, especially concerning the question of their redemptive or salvific relevance.

Vatican II on other religions

The Second Vatican Council states its perspective on the other religions in a number of documents focused on religious matters like *Nostra aetate* and *Dignitatis humanae*, 'on the Right of the Person and of the Communities to Social and Civil Freedom in Matters Religious', but also in *Lumen gentium*, the 'Constitution on the Church' (LG) and *Gaudium et spes* (GS). The Council emphasizes not so much the dividing but the uniting elements among the religions and cultures, although it does not ignore the differences. The question of salvation, however, is not answered by the traditional apologetic approach. Rather, *Gaudium et spes* states that by his incarnation the Son of God has united himself with each human being: 'For, since Christ died for all men (cf. Rom. 8:32), and since the ultimate vocation of man is in fact one, and divine, we ought to believe that the Holy Spirit in a manner known only to God offers to every man the possibility of being associated with this paschal mystery' (GS 22). This

---

[7] Cf., for example, Gert Kelter, 'Christliche Mission in einer postmodernen Gesellschaft: Überlegungen zu den Rahmenbedingungen des christlichen Zeugnisses in einer entchristlichten Gesellschaft unter besonderer Berücksichtigung Ostdeutschlands', *Lutherische Beiträge* 16 (2011), pp. 41–50.

mystical dimension forms the basis for the unity of all humankind. Moreover, the core sentence of the Catholic soteriological approach to other religions reads: 'The Catholic Church rejects nothing that is true and holy in these religions' (NA 2). Does the term 'holy' already imply that these religions contain elements of grace which allow their followers to attain to salvation? No. Neither does the Council explicitly qualify these other religions as legitimate ways of salvation of their own right nor does it explicitly deny this possibility. Its formulations are left to be interpreted and continued afterwards.

Continuing Vatican II in *Dialogue and Proclamation*

The continuation of the council's teaching concentrates on *Nostra aetate* 2 in which it is stated that it is Christ 'in whom men may find the fullness of religious life, in whom God has reconciled all things to Himself'. Regarding this fullness, one line of concretion refers to the council's assertion that the Church is necessary for salvation, since 'it is only through Christ's Catholic Church, which is "the all embracing means of salvation" that they can benefit fully from the means of salvation' (*Unitatis redintegratio* 3). This line of concretion leads to the CDF document *Dominus Iesus* where the teaching authority of the Catholic Church has stated clearly that other religions are not recognized as alternative ways of salvation of their own right. There is only one salvation, and only one way to salvation, the way of the paschal mystery. God offers the possibility of entering into this 'paschal mystery' (GS 22). How this can come about is for instance explained in *Lumen gentium* ('Dogmatic Constitution on the Church') 14–6.

On the other hand, there are ecclesiologically rather cautious formulations by the council which are taken up by the second line of concretion: 'truth and grace are to be found among the nations, as a sort of secret presence of God' (*Ad gentes* 9). God's saving action through Jesus Christ in the Holy Spirit mysteriously works in other religions which thus become indirectly ways of 'being associated with the paschal mystery' (GS 22). Both lines of concretion converge in asserting that Christ remains the one and only Saviour, be it explicitly by emphasizing the role of the Church or implicitly by referring to the action of the Holy Spirit.

If we want to pin this second line of concretion down in terms of a document, an example might be the Instruction *Dialogue and Proclamation. Reflection and Orientation of Inter-religious Dialogue and the Proclamation of the Gospel of*

Jesus Christ (DP), published on 19 May 1991 by the Pontifical Council for Inter-religious Dialogue and the Congregation for the Evangelization of Peoples. On the basis of the council's teaching, this document underlines the fact that in other religions there are the 'seeds of the Word' (AG 11; 15) and the 'truth which enlightens all men' (NA 2) and that the Holy Spirit is operating universally in other religions (DP 26–7). Yet *Dialogue and Proclamation* goes even further than the Council itself by saying:

> From this mystery of unity it follows that all men and women who are saved share, though differently, in the same mystery of salvation in Jesus Christ through his Spirit. Christians know this through their faith, while others remain unaware that Jesus Christ is the source of their salvation. The mystery of salvation reaches out to them, in a way known to God, through the invisible action of the Spirit of Christ. Concretely, it will be in the sincere practice of what is good in their own religious traditions and by following the dictates of their conscience that the members of other religions respond positively to God's invitation and receive salvation in Jesus Christ, even while they do not recognize or acknowledge him as their saviour. (cf. AG 3, 9, 11) (DP 29)

This does not mean that Christians should see the aim of engaging with other religions in the fact 'that a Hindu becomes a better Hindu, a Buddhist a better Buddhist, and a Muslim a better Muslim' as some postulated.[8] Nor does this mean a sort of 'blanket canonization' of other religions, for it is still possible, legitimate and even necessary to point out that some aspects in these religions are incompatible with the Christian understanding, that they are deficient, have shortcomings and so on. The decisive-specific Christian difference, however, lies in the clarity of the way of salvation, and not in the fact that salvation happens in Jesus Christ through the Spirit. This is the case with any salvation.

Dialogue thus gains a new quality, or as Pope John Paul II put it, 'dialogue is a means of seeking after truth and of sharing it with others.'[9] Already in *Nostra aetate*, the simultaneous presence of a call to both dialogue and proclamation has necessarily led to reflecting on the compatibility of these two elements of the Church's mission. Thus John Paul II's encyclical *Redemptoris missio*

---

[8]   Hubert Halbfas, *Fundamentalkatechetik. Sprache und Erfahrung im Religionsunterricht* (Düsseldorf: Patmos, 1968), p. 241.
[9]   John Paul II, Address to representatives of different religions in Madras, India (5 February 1986), p. 4.

concludes: 'Inter-religious dialogue is a part of the Church's evangelizing mission [. . .] In the light of the economy of salvation, the Church sees no conflict between proclaiming Christ and engaging in inter-religious dialogue [. . .] These two elements must maintain both their intimate connection and their distinctiveness' (RM 55).

New evangelization in a multi-religious context

In the face of other religions and cultures, new evangelization is a challenge to be a 'mission-shaped' church. In a society shaped by religious plurality and freedom of conscience, a fundamental problem arises when transmitting and proclaiming the gospel: The faith convictions of the Church no more find *general* agreement but also encounter indifference, rejection or even contradiction. The Church's own internal communication may no longer be identical to the external communication; for what may be understandable and plausible to the interior may be rather incomprehensible and more or less controversial for the exterior. If church and society are no longer identical, the elementary acts of witnessing and confessing need to be more clearly distinguished. Confessing is the form of communication *ad intra*.[10] It articulates the common belief of the faithful and therefore presupposes an initiation into the faith community and a personal consent.[11] Witnessing is the form of communication to the outside.[12] It fundamentally aims at convincing.[13] The contents of the message of the kingdom of God should be exemplified in a *convincing* manner as an important truth for life and be made cognitively plausible to the outsider. Hence 'evangelization can be understood as a twofold dialogue about God's truth: as witnessing in a dialogue with the world – and as confessing in the dialogue of the Church's *communio* with God; these two forms of dialogue need to be linked perichoretically to each other.'[14]

---

[10] Cf. Edmund Arens, *Christopraxis. Grundzüge theologischer Handlungstheorie* (Quaestiones disputatae 139; Freiburg i.Br./Basel/Wien: Herder, 1992), pp. 138–47.

[11] Paul VI explains this in his apostolic exhortation *Evangelii Nuntiandi* (1975), 23. Cf. also Arens, *Christopraxis*, p. 108.

[12] Cf. Arens, *Christopraxis*, p. 107.

[13] Cf. Arens, *Christopraxis*, pp. 131–3; and Edmund Arens, *Bezeugen und Bekennen. Elementare Handlungen des Glaubens* (Düsseldorf: Patmos, 1989).

[14] Karl Bopp, '"Missionarisch Kirche sein" angesichts fremder Religionen und Kulturen. Praktisch-theologische Überlegungen zum Missionsauftrag der Kirche heute', *Trierer Theologische Zeitschrift* 120 (2011), pp. 357–69 (p. 363).

Although church and society are no longer identical, new evangelization cannot be conceived as a collective re-Christianization of society.[15] It was part of the great genius of Pope John Paul II that he kept admonishing the Church to continually renew herself in order to live her mission of service:

> The new evangelization is therefore the order of the day. This does not mean the 'restoration' of a past age. Rather it is necessary to risk taking new steps. Together we must again proclaim the joyful and liberating message of the Gospel [. . .] in order to create a civilization in which the true human values transmitted by the Christian faith have a permanent place.[16]

The missionary witnessing to the Christian faith is primarily aimed at announcing to all people the liberating and healing proximity of God's kingdom and to let them experience, at least in fragments, the promised salvation. The ultimate truth of the evangelizing mandate is *Deus caritas est* – God is love and from there *caritas Christi urget nos* – the love of Christ impels us. The Christian relationship to the world is based on love. And evangelizing requires taking the risk of a loving open and dialogical encounter. Here the concept which the bishops of France already proposed in 1996 still seems to be ground-breaking for first and new evangelization: 'Proposer la foi dans la société actuelle' – to offer the faith in today's society.[17] The main goal of the pastoral and evangelizing work is 'service to the salvation of the world'.[18]

The central content of evangelization, however, is not the Church but Jesus's promise of the kingdom of God. Ecclesio-monism would therefore not be appropriate. Already the apostolic exhortation *Evangelii nuntiandi* by Pope Paul VI states: 'Evangelizing is in fact the *grace* and vocation proper to the Church, her deepest identity. She exists in order to evangelize' (14 – my italics). A church forgetting that God's grace precedes her evangelizing task runs the risk of forgetting that there still is an eschatological proviso. In the theological tradition, therefore, the claim to 'absoluteness' – or as Christian theologians today prefer to say – to the 'uniqueness' of Christianity is argued from four

---

[15] There is a risk that, if the goal is to re-Christianize Europe, claims of political and cultural hegemony might supersede the missionary concepts of the Church in a subtle way. Cf. Andreas Wollbold, 'Mission vor der eigenen Tür? Eine Synopse missiontheologischer Modelle', in Matthias Sellmann (ed.), *Deutschland – Missionsland. Zur Überwindung eines pastoralen Tabus* (Freiburg i.Br.: Herder, 2004), pp. 69–91 (mainly pp. 81–91).

[16] John Paul II, 'Apostolic Visit to Germany, June 21–23, 1996', *L'Osservatore Romano*. Weekly English Edition 27/5 (3 July 1996), p. 3.

[17] Conférence des évêques de France, 'Proposer la foi dans la société actuelle', Lettre aux Catholiques de France' (9 November 1996) at http://www.eglise.catholique.fr/.

[18] Paul M. Zulehner, *Pastoraltheologie, Vol. 1: Fundamentalpastoral* (Düsseldorf: Patmos, 1989), p. 54 calls this 'Dienst am Heil der Welt'.

different angles: (1) from Christology: Jesus Christ is the ultimate revelation of God (*Dei verbum* 4); (2) from pneumatology and the doctrine of grace: God's universal salvific will extends to all people and includes them all into the healing ministry of Jesus Christ, wherever and however they attain salvation (LG 1; GS 22); (3) from eschatology: the salvation in Christ is 'once' and 'for all' ultimately valid and lasts in an unparalleled way (Heb. 9.25–28) and (4) from ecclesiology: according to her self-understanding, the Church is the universal sacrament of salvation (LG 1, 48).

This last point is also highlighted in *Dialogue and Proclamation* 33:

> The Church has been willed by God and instituted by Christ to be, in the fullness of time, the sign and instrument of the divine plan of salvation (cf. LG 1), the centre of which is the mystery of Christ. She is the 'universal sacrament of salvation' (LG 48), and is 'necessary for salvation' (LG 14). The Lord Jesus himself inaugurated her mission 'by preaching the good news, that is, the coming of God's Kingdom'. (LG 5)

The Church is conscious of the necessity of proclaiming Jesus Christ to the world. '[T]o proclaim the name of Jesus and to invite people to become his disciples in the Church is a sacred and major duty which the Church cannot neglect' (DP 76). Proclamation has priority over every other form of the Church's activity, while dialogue is one of the integrating elements (DP 9). Evangelization is derived from *evangelium*. The gospel is the message which God sent to humankind by Jesus Christ and today by the Church. Since the Gospel is an appeal addressed to all human beings, the Church is talking to everyone. This is a requirement of catholicity. This process of dialogue does not lead to waiving evangelization.[19] Rather dialogue and encounter lead to a deeper commitment and conversion to God (DP 36).

In this, *Dialogue and Proclamation* 36 and the *Instrumentum laboris* for the Bishops' Synod in 2012 converge. The *Instrumentum* rehearses a variety of scenarios of new evangelization. It speaks first of all in connection with the political scenario of the 'new economic, political and religious actors' (57) and then specifically mentions as an example the 'Islamic world'. This only superficially sketched picture, however, quickly becomes concrete in the subtitle 'The changes in the religious scenario' (before 63). Number 67 indicates that the encounter and dialogue with other religions has opened the possibility to get to

---

[19] Cf., for example, Jean-Luc Brunin, 'Quand des chrétiens dialoguent avec d'autres croyants doivent-ils renoncer à évangéliser?' *Pro Dialogo* 119 (2005), pp. 197–205 (p. 205).

know the complexity of forms and modes of expression of human religiosity by other religions and thus also to be able to better place and appreciate the specific form of one's own Catholic religiosity and spirituality. Thus, for the Church worldwide in the context of a pluralistic society with many different cultures and religions a learning task is inextricably linked with evangelization: The Church can use the dialogue with religions and cultures unfamiliar to her to understand her own truth more deeply.

Numbers 73–5 of the *Instrumentum* are dedicated to Christians in a multi-religious setting. A distinction is made between countries in which Christianity is in a majority position, and countries where it forms a minority. In the former case, the presence of other world religions, especially the spread of Islam, encourages the local churches to develop new forms of visibility and presentation of the Christian faith. The questions by people of other faiths induce Christians to better understand their own faith and thus to engage in it more intensively.

In a minority situation, however, the picture looks different, especially if Christians have no chance of practising their religion freely. In the context of persecution the experience of evangelization merges with the experience of Jesus, namely an experience of obedience and loyalty up to the Cross. *Martyria* and being a martyr are not just etymologically connected. These churches make us bear in mind that it is not enough to measure evangelization just according to quantifying performance criteria and parameters.

Whether in new or first evangelization, the Church has the obligation to proclaim the gospel everywhere and at all times and to enter into dialogue with other religious traditions. For, even though in Europe we may be living in a de-Christianized society, but that does not necessarily mean that it also is a secularized society. Other religions may well be present and even flourishing. Yet, God wills the good news of salvation to be proclaimed to all humankind and, thus, we are all companions on the path leading to God.

Part Four

Practising the New Evangelization

13

The *Catechism of the Catholic Church* and the New Evangelization

Petroc Willey

This chapter seeks to appreciate some of the reasons why the *Catechism of the Catholic Church* (CCC), published in its definitive form in 1997,[1] is seen by the magisterium of the Church to be an irreplaceable point of reference for the work of the new evangelization, capturing and setting forth an understanding of the new evangelization in its essential contours and emphases and providing an indispensable tool for its promotion. Following recent documents of the pontifical magisterium, we can identify three elements which are intrinsic to the achievement of a new evangelization in the Church and for which the publication of the CCC is particularly important.

Transmission of the faith

The first element is the recovery of a *traditio Evangelii*,[2] a faithful transmission of the good news, of the gospel. To support an appreciation of this need, the Church in her magisterial documents has been putting forward the understanding of evangelization as a broad concept involving the lifelong apprenticeship of persons and communities in all dimensions of the Christian life. This understanding of evangelization is presented in a range of successive documents of the pontifical magisterium, including *Evangelii nuntiandi* (1975), *Redemptoris missio* (1990) and *Novo millennio ineunte* (2001) as well as the two great catechetical directories, published in 1971 and 1997.

---

[1] The *editio typica* of the *Catholicus Catholicae Ecclesiae* (hereafter *CCC*) was published on 15 August 1997 (English revised edition; London: Burns & Oates, 1999).

[2] A phrase used in paragraph 26 of the *Instrumentum Laboris* (IL) for the XIII Ordinary General Assembly of the Synod of Bishops, dedicated to 'The New Evangelisation for the Transmission of the Christian Faith' (Vatican City: Libreria Editrice Vaticana, 2012).

In the seminal magisterial work on evangelization, *Evangelii nuntiandi* (1975), Paul VI emphasizes that 'evangelization' is a term indicating the entire process of conversion:

> For the Church, evangelizing means bringing the Good News into all the strata of humanity, and through its influence transforming humanity from within and making it new: 'Now I am making the whole of creation new' (Rev. 21.5; cf. 2 Cor. 5.17; Gal. 6.15).[3]

He continues, 'But there is no new humanity if there are not first of all new persons renewed by Baptism (cf. Rom. 6.4) and by lives lived according to the Gospel (cf. Eph. 4.24–25; Col. 3.9–10)' (EN 18). As used by Paul VI, then, 'evangelization' includes within its scope not only a turning to God expressed through a profession of faith and a life of prayer but also the sacramental activity and the lived commitment of the Church's members. A new humanity requires new persons, and persons are renewed through baptism and they express their union in Christ through renewed lives.

These multi-faceted dimensions of evangelization are presented in a comprehensive way in the four parts of the *Catechism*, which treat of the faith received and affirmed, the liturgy celebrated, the new life in Christ embraced and the life of Christian prayer – it is the whole of this that is referred to by the term 'evangelization'. The Church evangelizes culture when she transmits the whole of this from generation to generation.[4]

This making of new persons follows a process which may be analysed according to a range of models and shortly before the turn of the millennium, in 1997, the *General Directory for Catechesis*[5] conceptualized this 'transforming [of] humanity from within' in terms of three 'moments' of evangelization: first, initial witness and the proclamation of the kerygma,[6] bringing about a fundamental

---

[3] Paul VI, Apostolic Exhortation *Evangelii Nuntiandi* 18 (1975). The theme of the Gospel as a new creation is highlighted by Paul VI through his choice of the date of publication, 8 December 1975, the Feast of the Immaculate Conception, celebrating the beginning of the redemptive work of Christ, the restoration of the purity of a new origin for creation and for the Second Adam, in his mother Mary.

[4] See CCC no. 3, 13–7. The *Catechism of the Catholic Church* grounds its structure not only on the great catechisms from the tradition, but also from that first synopsis of the life of Church in Jerusalem presented in Acts 2.42. See further on this, Pierre de Cointet, Barbara Morgan and Petroc Willey, *The Catechism of the Catholic Church and the Craft of Catechesis* (San Francisco: Ignatius Press, 2008), pp. 15–22.

[5] *General Directory for Catechesis* (Vatican City: Libreria Editrice Vaticana, 1997).

[6] The kerygma, the basic proclamation of the good news, has been variously identified and described, but it necessarily focuses upon the coming among us of the Son of God made incarnate by the Holy Spirit for our redemption, whose work of redemption is made present by the Holy Spirit in the sacramental life of the Church, together with an understanding of the immense dignity of each

conversion to Christ; then a significant period of catechesis, deepening this conversion and fostering faith and finally, on the completion of this systematic and comprehensive schooling in the faith, an ongoing educative process related to the specific vocational situation and life experiences of each particular person.[7] 'Evangelization' is the overarching umbrella term for the whole of this process.

While it might appear that the *Catechism* focuses exclusively on the second 'moment' in this process, assisting in the development of the 'school of faith' of the baptised, in fact all three 'moments' of the progressive deepening of conversion that together express the scope of evangelization are present in the *Catechism*. In the situation which has called for a 'new evangelization', where many who would describe themselves as Catholics have moved away from the practice of their faith, unclear as to its very heart and centre, the *Catechism* provides an account of the faith which is structured so that the kerygma is announced in and through each aspect of the faith. The school of faith is kerygmatic in character.[8] This means that when catechesis is given it can at the same time be providing the basic proclamation of the faith for all who need to receive the call to a foundational conversion to Christ.

The *Catechism* also supports the third 'moment', that of an ongoing education and formation in the faith. It does so principally in two ways. First, through its commitment to an 'organic' presentation of the faith, whereby the adult reader is continually challenged to reflect upon how faith, working through hope, fosters love so that a virtuous circle supporting the integration of the whole person is created.[9] Secondly, the *Catechism* fosters continuing Christian development through its attentiveness towards making visible and accessible a broad and rich range of sources from Scripture and Tradition so that readers can be renewed from these, 'at the living sources of the faith'.[10]

For an understanding of what is involved in this recovery of a *traditio Evangelii*, the work of the recent Synod on *The New Evangelization for the Transmission of the Christian Faith* is also particularly important, as well as

---

person, made in the image and likeness of God, and our call to respond in faith, hope and love to the unfailing mercy of the Father who reaches out to bring each of us to himself. These truths, taken together, form what has been called the 'kerygmatic' centre of the Church's faith.

[7] See *General Directory for Catechesis*, pp. 51–71. The *General Directory for Catechesis* bases these moments on what it calls the model and paradigm for catechetical activity, the baptismal catechumenate, a model drawn from the patristic period (p. 90).

[8] For a brief account of how the kerygma is present in the *Catechism* and its parts, sections and articles, see de Cointet et al., *The Catechism of the Catholic Church*, pp. 105–7.

[9] For the *Catechism*'s own statement of its purpose in this regard see, for example, *CCC* no. 11, 18, 89–90.

[10] This phrase is found in the opening section of John Paul II's Apostolic Constitution, *Fidei Depositum* (1992) introducing the newly published *Catechism*.

Benedict XVI's founding document for the Pontifical Council for Promoting the New Evangelization, *Ubicumque et semper* (2010) and the apostolic letter *Fides per doctrinum* (2013) which transferred the competence for catechesis to this newly erected Council. The latter document opens with the significant statement that 'Faith needs to be strengthened *through teaching*, so that it can enlighten the minds and hearts of believers' (italics original). The document is a reminder that *doctrina*, 'teaching', is a verb: faith is transmitted through the activity of *doctrina*, of teaching.[11] As long as the phrase 'the teaching of the Church' is viewed as referring to an object to be studied and understood only, rather than as also referring to the activity of the Church making present the *traditio Evangelii*, the desired transmission will not take place. The pontifical magisterium has therefore been re-emphasizing the understanding of 'doctrine' both as that which is learned and also that which is passed on. We should note the importance, in this light, of the opening sentence of John Paul II's *Fidei depositum* (1992) indicating the purpose of the newly published *Catechism* through its uniting of the concepts of guarding the deposit of faith and engaging in mission: 'Guarding the Deposit of Faith is the mission which the Lord entrusted to his Church and which she fulfils in every age.' And again, this time referring to the work of the Second Vatican Council: 'to guard and to present better the precious deposit of Christian doctrine . . .'. A true guarding of doctrine includes the ability to transmit it, to make 'the truth of the Gospel shine forth' (1).[12]

One of the reasons why the *Catechism* has such a significant place in the task of new evangelization is that it provides a definitive account of *doctrina* in both of its aspects. The *Catechism* was published for this dual purpose: to provide definitive guidance concerning the content of the faith and also to enshrine for the Church the pedagogy of the faith.[13] This latter dimension of the *Catechism*

---

[11] In classical Latin, *doctrina* originally covered not only the content of what was taught, but also the process of teaching and handing on this content. Kevane demonstrates, in writers such as Cicero and Quintilian, that *doctrina* is used as the direct translation for the Greek concept of *paideia* and that when Augustine came to title his classic work on the content and the transmission of the faith, *De Doctrina Christiana*, he was consciously building on this more ancient Greek heritage also. See Eugene Kevane, '*Translatio imperii*: Augustine's *De Doctrina Christiana* and the Classical *Paideia*', *Studia Patristica* XIV (1976), pp. 446–60 (p. 458). For some of the ways in which this concept is being retrieved by the Church in her contemporary catechetical documentation, see Caroline E. Farey, Waltraud Linnig and M. Johanna Paruch FSGM (eds), *The Pedagogy of God: Its Centrality in Catechesis and Catechist Formation* (Steubenville: Emmaus Road Publishing, 2011), pp. 15–79.

[12] The choice of the date of publication of *Fidei Depositum*, 11 October 1992, is significant as the thirtieth anniversary of the opening of the Second Vatican Council. At the time of the Second Vatican Council, when the Church was following the old calendar, this was the Feast of the Maternity of the Blessed Virgin Mary, a Feast that celebrates Mary's title of Theotokos, 'God-bearer'. Mary's traditional role as the defender against heresies derives from this title in particular and it is a significant choice of patronage for the Council, as well as accentuating the Council's Christocentric nature.

[13] See the *Instrumentum Laboris* for the Synod of Bishops, 2012, p. 101.

tends to be neglected, in part because 'pedagogy' is thought to be synonymous with 'methodology' and methods of teaching and transmission are clearly not the concern of the *Catechism*. But 'pedagogy' refers to overarching and universally valid principles governing the transmission of the faith whereas 'methodology' is reserved for concrete applications of these principles for specific groups, ages, contexts and situations.[14] The period of catechetical activity since the Second Vatican Council is judged by the *General Directory for Catechesis* to have been one in which there has been 'excessive insistence on the value of method and techniques' at the expense of attention given to the 'demands and to the originality of that pedagogy which is proper to the faith'.[15] Methods always need to be judged according to their capacity to transmit faithfully the content of the faith and this means that they need to be measured against the perennial pedagogy of the faith. This dual character of the *Catechism*, then, where the doctrines of the Church are enshrined in a pedagogy that can faithfully support its transmission, means that the *Catechism* can provide the bridge that has been needed in the area of the transmission of the faith, between content and method, supporting the *traditio Evangelii*.

The *Communio* of the Churches

If the first key to the recovery of the *traditio Evangelii* is the embracing of this understanding and practice of *doctrina*, in the aspects both of a faithful understanding and faithful transmission, the second concerns our understanding of both the particular and universal dimensions in which this *traditio* is carried out.

A careful reading of *Ubicumque et semper* and of the preparatory documentation for the 2012 Synod enables one to see that the complexity of the situation within which this *traditio Evangelii* is to be supported and fostered across the universal Church is well-appreciated.[16] Crucially, it depends upon the theology and practice of communion between the particular Churches, with

---

[14] For a discussion of the relationship between pedagogy and methodology, see C. E. Farey et al., *The Pedagogy of God*, passim.
[15] *General Directory for Catechesis*, p. 30.
[16] So, for example, in the Synod itself there were three contexts within which the sense of communion could be shared and expressed: general sessions in which all of the bishops were gathered with the successor of St Peter and each spoke and listened out of the context of his particular Church; language groupings and continental and regional groupings (the Synod here was continuing the work of the continental meetings of bishops in local synods in order to explore the question of the new evangelization – see *Instrumentum laboris* 45, note 35). There was also an emphasis laid upon the development of ecumenical relationships.

each other and with the Successor of Saint Peter in Rome.[17] In a situation of growing globalization, the Churches of the 'old world', many of them Churches founded in the first millennium, are now embedded in cultural contexts in which the Christian faith has been severely compromised or partially overwhelmed by other intellectual currents and social practices, in which the purity of the *traditio* is both difficult to discern and hard to maintain. The rapidly growing media of social communication are largely secularist in character expressing, at the very least, a practical atheism, or indifference towards the Christian faith, if not hostility.

In this situation, the maintenance of an understanding of the faith that is 'catholic' (i.e. universal, not bound by the specifics of any particular culture) is one key task. The other is to develop the avenues of communion between the Churches for a rich sharing of the faith so that the older Churches may be reinvigorated by the newer and the newer supported by the resources and historical experience of the older. 'Above all', says Benedict XVI in *Ubicumque et semper*, this challenge 'pertains to Churches of ancient origin', those Churches in which the *traditio Evangelii* took its first roots and where the contours and shape of much of the *doctrina* emerged and this requires a 'thorough examination and understanding of the root causes of the situation in the Christian West'.[18] Yet the challenge to participate fully in the *communio* of the Churches and achieve a transmission of the Gospel in one's own particular culture is common to all Christians, not only in the West, but also in America, Asia and Oceania.

Within this situation, the ability to identify the voice of the universal magisterium, the united teaching of all of the bishops in communion with the successor of Peter, and at the same time to appreciate the universal communion of the Church, is held and expressed in a unique way by the *Catechism*, which is important in the first place because it has challenged the ideology of cultural relativism which makes genuine communion impossible.[19] It also means that, in the transmission of the faith, authority is vested, not in the teacher nor in the learner, but beyond both of them.[20] The *Catechism* is also important because it represents the gathering of the *traditio* across time as well as across space,

---

[17] Important here is the document of the Congregation for the Doctrine of the Faith, Letter 'On Some Aspects of The Church Understood as Communion' (28 May 1992).

[18] *Instrumentum Laboris* 87, and see also 85–9 for the broader consideration of the application of the concept of new evangelization to all of the Churches.

[19] See Avery Dulles, 'The Challenge of the Catechism', *First Things* (January 1995), pp. 46–53.

[20] Alasdair MacIntyre points out that it was this conviction of an authority beyond both the teacher and the student that led to the style of disputation which characterized the universities of the medieval period: 'it was because both audience and lecturer accepted standards of truth and rationality independent of either that each could summon the other to test any particular thesis in the forum of disputation'. *Three Rival Theories of Moral Enquiry* (London: Duckworth, 1990), p. 33.

encapsulating in its pages the gathering of the energies of the Church through the communion of all of the particular Churches and through the voices of each age of the Church in tradition.[21] In this way, the project of developing a universal *Catechism* responded to the desire for a gathering of energies for evangelization that had been variously expressed by both Paul VI and John Paul II. In *Evangelii nuntiandi*, Paul VI noted that the Synod of 1974 called for a new 'period of evangelization',[22] a renewal of energy in the Church for the work of mission. John Paul II was to take up this desire of the Synod and of Paul VI by dedicating the 1980s as a 'Decade of Evangelization'. And in his own encyclical letter on evangelization, John Paul II reiterated this desire for a drawing together of the resources and commitments of the universal Church to focus on the task of evangelization.[23]

In *Fidei depositum* (1) then, John Paul II wrote of his 'deep feeling of joy' at the 'harmony of so many voices' present in the *Catechism*. Every bishop in the world was involved in commenting, over a period of 6 years, on the text of the *Catechism*, as were 'numerous theologians, exegetes and catechists'. A study of the index of citations in the *Catechism* reveals the extraordinary scope and richness of the retrieval and presentation of Christian sources. And since new evangelization is a challenge particularly facing the Churches of the first millennium, there is a focus in the *Catechism* upon the heritage from these Churches, from the Fathers and the Councils of the early centuries and from this initial period of Christian history, from both Eastern and Western traditions.[24]

The ardour of a renewed spirituality

The third key for the recovery of a *traditio Evangelii*, and for which the *Catechism* is especially important, can be called, variously, the restoration of 'ardour',[25] or the grounding of the transmission of the faith within spirituality.

[21] As John Paul II expressed it in the Apostolic Constitution *Fidei Depositum* (2), the *Catechism* contains 'both the new and the old'.
[22] '. . . feliciora evangelizationis tempora valeret afferre' (EN 2). This paragraph follows Paul VI's Address for the Closing of the Third General Assembly of the Synod of Bishops (26 October 1974).
[23] See *Redemptoris Missio* 3: 'I sense that the moment has come to commit all of the Church's energies to a new evangelization and to the mission *ad gentes*'. The importance of drawing together the energies of the whole Church is emphasized again in *Instrumentum Laboris* 4, which speaks of the need to avoid 'any danger of a dispersion of energy or fragmented efforts'.
[24] See the appreciation by David McLoughlin, 'The New Catechism and the Christian East', *The Sower* (September 1992), pp. 29–30.
[25] On a new 'ardour' see the well-known statement made by John Paul II, Speech to the XIX Assembly of CELAM, Port au Prince (9 March 1983), p. 3.

One of the points that most surprises readers of the *Catechism* is its profoundly spiritual character. Far from being a mere dictionary of terms or a series of mini-articles on aspects of the faith, it is a holistic presentation of the new way of life made possible in Christ, rooted in a dogmatic spirituality. It sets out to present an account of the Christian faith that is intrinsically attractive and compelling, rooted in a life of prayer, 'the habit of being in the presence of the thrice-holy God and in communion with him',[26] grounded in a strong sense of the central dogmatic truths of the faith and expressed in the dual commandment of love, in a new life made possible through the abundance of sacramental grace.[27] Its central thrust is to provide a convincing account of how a fruitful Christian life derives from the organic bonds forged between the dogmas and the spiritual life.

One major focus of magisterial teaching on the new evangelization, then, concerns its spiritual nature. The analysis presented in the 2012 *Instrumentum laboris* is both searching and realistic in this regard:

> ... we cannot forget that the proclamation of the Gospel is primarily a spiritual matter. The need to transmit the faith, which is essentially an ecclesial, communal event and not singly or done alone, should not result from seeking effective communication strategies or in choosing a certain group of recipients ... but must look to who is entrusted with this spiritual work. The Church must question herself in this matter. This allows the problem to be approached from within, involving the entire life and being of the Church.[28]

While an interest in new methods and means of presenting the faith is certainly an aspect of the new evangelization,[29] an over-attentiveness towards this is seen here as a distraction from the core questions and challenges. In *Evangelii nuntiandi* (15) Paul VI had called for the Church to continue to examine her 'constant need of being evangelized, if she wishes to retain freshness, vigour and strength in order to proclaim the Gospel', and this call became more insistent during the pontificates of John Paul II and Benedict XVI.

In order to carry out the work of evangelization, the Church is being called to be ever more attentive to God's work of healing grace in her midst and to the ongoing conversion of her members. From thinking of herself primarily as the agent of evangelization, the Church is being called to recognize herself as the

---

[26] CCC 2565.
[27] See, for example, CCC 1692–5 and 2558 for short summaries of this overall characterization of the *Catechism*'s purpose.
[28] IL 39.
[29] See John Paul II, Speech to the XIX Assembly of CELAM, Port au Prince (9 March 1983), p. 3.

object of God's evangelizing love. In his apostolic exhortation *Christifideles laici* (1988; 34), John Paul II wrote, 'Without doubt a mending of the Christian fabric of society is urgently needed in all parts of the world. But for this to come about what is needed is to *first remake the Christian fabric of the ecclesial community* itself present in these countries and nations' (italics original). The outward movement of evangelization is not being denied, but the emphasis of the new evangelization lies in this mending of the ecclesial fabric. The *Instrumentum laboris* (38) reminded Synod members that from the beginning of her history, as illustrated by the story of the disciples on the road to Emmaus, the Church has needed to remember that she can 'be the bearer of a message that does not give life, but stops short in the death of the Christ who is proclaimed, in the announcers themselves, and, consequently, in the recipients of the announcement also'. The *traditio Evangelii* can radically falter. The response of the Church called for in the new evangelization is not to begin a project of self-help, but to become aware that this is not her own work: 'Conversion is first of all a work of the grace of God who makes our hearts return to him: "Restore us to thyself, O Lord, that we may be restored!" God gives us the strength to begin anew.'[30]

The *Catechism*, with its emphasis on the primacy of God's grace, assists the members of the Church in gaining this perspective.[31] The authors of the *Catechism* restored the section on grace to the third part of the work, 'Life in Christ', the treatment on morality, where it was placed by St Thomas in his *Summa Theologica*, so that its grounding of the whole of the Christian life might be clearly seen. And the life of grace is not presented as a new set of inner resources so much as the capacity for a new *relationship* to the Blessed Trinity: the Spirit of the Son attuning us to the will of the Father, to make us more and more receptive to his immeasurable love for us. The life of grace, life in Christ, enables the restoration of our spiritual lives.

In this seeking of a fundamental spiritual renewal, an appreciation of the significance of the word 'new' in 'new evangelization' can also assist us. In his introduction to an *Enchiridion* of texts concerned with the new evangelization, Rino Fisichella, the president of the Pontifical Council for Promoting New Evangelization, points us first of all to the Scriptures, to the numerous passages in the 'New' Testament in which Christ and the apostles highlight the newness of the Gospel. A *new* covenant has been made, a *new* commandment given and a *new* way of life uncovered. Those who follow this way receive a *new* name

---

[30] CCC 1432.
[31] See Christoph Schönborn and Joseph Ratzinger, *Introduction to the Catechism of the Catholic Church* (San Francisco: Ignatius Press, 1994), pp. 48–9.

and are sharers in the *new* Jerusalem – and indeed in the *new* heavens and *new* earth.[32]

The primary reference point of the 'newness' of the call to evangelization, therefore, is always the person and gospel of Christ himself, pointing us to rediscover in a fresh way all that the Lord came to bestow, which means discovering Christ himself as the Father's gift (Cf 1 Jn 1.1–4). It is a new 'ardour' that the Church begs for herself, a recovery of that instinct towards the complete gift of self in a movement of spousal love in response to this gift 'from above' (see Jn 3.31).[33] For this reason, 'new' evangelization is always in the first place a *ressourcement*, a return, a restoration. Over and again, it is emphasized that the Church is not looking for a new project, a new message to be proclaimed or a new revelation to amend or correct which was delivered once and for all to the saints. Jesus Christ is 'the same yesterday, today and for ever' and his revelation will never be surpassed (Heb. 13.8).[34] The *newness* of the new evangelization has its first reference point in Christ himself who is discovered as the one who is 'ever-ancient, ever-new'.[35]

Importantly, this point helps us to avoid any misunderstandings in the mending of the *traditio Evangelii* that might lead us to adopt a theology of revelation as ongoing – of the kind that has, for example, been influential through the catechetical writings of Gabriel Moran, for whom all experience is revelational.[36] Revelation, on this view, is seen not as that which is perfectly

---

[32] See, for example, among the many passages in the New Testament, Lk. 22.20; 1 Cor. 11.25; Jn 13.34; Rom. 7.6; Rev. 2.17; 3.12; 21.2; 2 Pet. 3.13. Pontifical Council for Promoting New Evangelisation, *Enchiridion della Nuova Evangelizzazione: testi del Magistero pontificio e conciliare 1939-2012* (Vatican City: Libreria Editrice Vaticana, 2012). For the introduction by Rino Fisichella, see pp. v–xi.

[33] The loss of this love is the complaint against the Church at Ephesus, of course, in the Book of Revelation (Rev. 2.4–5).

[34] John Paul II makes the point powerfully in *Novo Millennio Ineunte* 29.It is not therefore a matter of inventing a "new programme". The programme already exists: it is the plan found in the Gospel and in the living Tradition, it is the same as ever. Ultimately, it has its centre in Christ himself, who is to be known, loved and imitated, so that in him we may live the life of the Trinity, and with him transform history until its fulfilment in the heavenly Jerusalem. This is a programme which does not change with shifts of times and cultures, even though it takes account of time and culture for the sake of true dialogue and effective communication. This programme for all times is our programme for the Third Millennium.

[35] See Augustine's famous cry of discovery of God as eternal Beauty in the *Confessions* 10:27.

[36] Moran's position regarding the theology of revelation developed from his early *Catechesis of Revelation* (New York: Herder & Herder, 1966), in which his main task was to develop the more Christocentric and personalist foundations of the understanding of revelation contained in *Dei Verbum*, 'Dogmatic Constitution on Divine Revelation'. A significant work following this, which saw the evolution of his thinking in a more existentialist direction was *The Present Revelation* (New York: Herder & Herder, 1972). For a much briefer and representative account of his position, one can see his 'Revelation as Teaching-Learning', *Religious Education* 95/3 (Summer 2000), pp. 269–84. Moran is proposing a fundamental shift in this understanding of continuing revelation and Berard L. Marthalar is therefore disingenuous when he suggests that resistance to notions of continuing

present in the Person of Christ and which is guarded and transmitted in the definitive deposit of faith, but is rather 'God contacting man in every moment in experience.'[37]

The 'newness' of the new evangelization, then, is not to be seen in terms of a new content, of 'a different gospel' (Gal. 1.6).[38] New evangelization does not entail moving beyond that definitive revelation made present in the historical Christ, but is rather a rediscovery of the wonder of this original encounter. The Trinitarian-Christo-centricity of the *Catechism*, together with its clear presentation of the doctrinal heritage of the faith, and its *nova et vetera* approach,[39] ensure that the way is opened for a receptivity to that original revelation in Christ, in whom the Father 'has said everything.'[40]

That original revelation is made available through the media of Scripture and Tradition. Augustine enables us to appreciate the importance of this commitment that the *Catechism* makes in assisting the members of the Church to access the living sources for themselves by distinguishing, in *De Doctrina Christiana*, between two ways of transmission. The first way, in which a teacher informs his students of what he knows, Augustine describes as 'reading'. While this way has its obvious value, it is a form of transmission akin to a person reading aloud to another person: 'He who teaches how the Scriptures are to be understood is like a teacher who advises how the words are to be read.' The second way, Augustine asserts, is a genuine 'teaching'; it is *doctrina* in the authentic sense. This is where the student is provided with the tools to access the inspired sources for himself. Augustine distinguishes between the two ways as follows: 'He who reads to others pronounces the words he recognizes; he who teaches reading does so that others may also read.' In this second way, the student has been taught to read and no longer needs another to read to him. Through the sources, God can guide the person directly.[41]

---

revelation is simply 'nostalgia for the simple world of the Baltimore Catechism'. *The Catechism Yesterday and Today: The Evolution of a Genre* (Collegeville, PA: The Liturgical Press, 1995), p. 137. For an account of the significant change involved, see M. Johanna Paruch's doctoral work, *A Study of the Direct Ramifications of Vatican Council II on Catechetics* (Birmingham: Maryvale Institute, 2007), especially pp. 182–205.

[37] See James Michael Lee, another exponent of a theology of ongoing revelation, in his *The Shape of Religious Education: A Social Science Approach* (Mishawaka, IN: Religious Education Press, 1971), p. 16. Lee sets in opposition falsely static notions of the deposit of faith and of the doctrinal heritage with the idea of a continuing revelation, in which God meets people in the events of their everyday lives.

[38] As Paul continues, 'If anyone is preaching to you a gospel contrary to that which you received, let him be accursed' (Gal. 1.9b).

[39] Cf. Aidan Nichols, *The Splendour of Doctrine* (Edinburgh: T&T Clark, 1995), p. 5.

[40] CCC 65.

[41] *De Doctrina Christiana* (D. W. Robertson Jr (trans.); Indianapolis, IN: Bobbs-Merrill Educational Publishing, 1958), Prologue, 9.

The stones will cry out

One of the striking aspects of magisterial writing on the new evangelization is the strong sense of hope. In his introductory letter in *Youcat*, Benedict XVI reflected on the time when 'Israel was at the lowest point in her history', the time of the Exile.[42] This was, of course, the period when Israel witnessed the collapse of the kingdom of Judah, the taking of the people into slavery and the destruction of the temple. This period of apparent rejection was really one of purification and from it emerged the great prophets who learned how to speak to God's people in an alien land. One of the great themes of the prophets of the exilic and post-exilic period, of course, was that the barren landscape will become fruitful once more, and this note of hope was struck in Benedict XVI's teaching on the new evangelization from the beginning of his pontificate. 'The Church as a whole and all her Pastors, like Christ, must set out to lead people out of the desert, towards the place of life, towards friendship with the Son of God, towards the One who gives us life, and life in abundance.'[43] The waste places will be fruitful; Newman's 'second spring'[44] will indeed come. Powerful reminders lie around us, in the old world of the Churches of the first millennium, the ruins of bygone glory and beauty. And shall these ruins be able to speak? Can Elizabeth conceive in her old age?

If the Church chooses an authentic response to this call for a new evangelization, the seeds for the new spring need to be sown precisely in this period of apparent barrenness. Trees are planted in winter because it is then that their roots must strike deep into the ground to seek the nourishment and water they need. Their capacity for growth in the spring depends upon this period of winter. Like working in hard ground, the *Catechism* does not offer an easy access to the faith. It makes considerable demands upon us. The *Catechism* is offered to the Church in this inhospitable season so that Christ's faithful can strike deep roots to draw from the living sources of the faith, to find there the living water welling up to eternal life.

---

[42] Benedict XVI, 'Foreword', in *Youcat* (San Francisco: Ignatius Press, 2011), pp. 6–11.
[43] Homily 'For the Beginning of his Petrine Ministry as the Bishop of Rome' (24 April 2005).
[44] See John Henry Newman, *The Second Spring: A Sermon by John Henry Newman* (with introduction, notes and exercises by F. P. Donnelly S. J.; London: Longmans, 1934).

14

John Henry Newman and the New Evangelization

Stephen Morgan

The real claim of faith illustrated in the life of John Henry Newman provides important indicators for the new evangelization. Newman's vocation was primarily that of a pastor and, aside from a very few short interludes, he was engaged in pastoral ministry for over 65 years. His intellectual work was at the service of his pastoral work and was ordered primarily to the care and salvation of souls. This was the imperative that drove his controversial writing, his poetry, his philosophical and his theological work. These were all put at the service of a heart speaking to hearts.

Newman's example is indispensable for a theology at the service of an evangelization new in its ardour, new in its methods, new in its expressions, aimed at making disciples of Jesus Christ in his body, the Church. *Cor ad cor loquitur* is the paradigm of the new evangelization of those places where the struggle between the conviction of the heart and the scepticism of the mind that characterized Newman's life of faith, both as an Anglican and as a Catholic, is a common experience. It was this that lay behind Newman's lifelong battle against 'liberalism' in religion. It was driven by a real assent to dogmatic truths of faith that provided the impulse for his extraordinary pastoral and intellectual energy and suggests a model that can usefully inspire the Church today.

Newman's choice of '*Cor ad cor loquitur*'

When an individual is invited to choose a motto or a distinguishing phrase to sum up a life or a mission, a number of factors come into play. In the present day, especially for those who have the privilege of working with families in planning the funerals of deceased family members, wit or at least attempts at occasionally inappropriate humour are often upper most in people's minds. Corporate mottos seem veer between the narcissistic (e.g. L'Oreal's 'Because you're worth it'), the pretentious (Lloyds Bank's 'For the journey') and the clichéd (Nike's 'Find your greatness') and a review of a selection of heraldic mottos chosen by the newly armigerous over the last 10 years reveals some serious choices, not a few flippant ones and some plainly crass. It has not always been so and, on his being made a cardinal in 1879, Blessed John Henry Newman gave serious thought to the choice of his motto. The expression he chose, *cor ad cor loquitur* – 'heart speaks unto heart' – captured in four short words the whole of his approach to faith and offers a paradigm for the new evangelization. It is one that, if properly understood, can speak very effectively to people in those places where the struggle between the conviction of the heart and the scepticism of the mind is a common experience. Furthermore, Newman's motto describes a theological methodology that enables the proclamation of the Good News about Jesus Christ while charting a safe course between the Scylla of the religion of 'feelings' and the Charybdis of arid, positivist, propositional legalism – or what Pope Francis has called 'self-absorbed, promethean neo-pelagianism' (*Evangelii gaudium* 94).

In choosing *cor ad cor loquitur*, Newman had thought that he was quoting a phrase from Sacred Scripture or, perhaps, from Thomas à Kempis.[1] In fact the expression, or something very like it, comes from St Francis de Sales, *Treatise on the Love of God*, where the sixteenth-century saint was writing of the relationship between theology and prayer. He wrote:

> Truly the chief exercise in mystical theology is to speak to God and to hear God speak in the bottom of the heart; and because this discourse passes in most secret aspirations and inspirations, we term it a silent conversing. Eyes speak to eyes, and heart to heart, and none understand what passes save the sacred lovers who speak.[2]

Cor ad cor loquitur as deep friendship

Newman had encountered this passage long before he chose the motto, which might excuse his vagueness about its provenance when he selected it. He had come across it at least as early as 1855 when, during his attempts to establish a

---

[1] Charles Stephen Dessain (ed.), *The Letters and Diaries of John Henry Newman*, Vol. XXIX (in 32 vols; London and Oxford: Oxford University Press, 1961–2008), p. 108.

[2] St Francis de Sales, *Treatise on the Love of God* (Henry Benedict Mackey (trans.); Rockford, IL: Tan Books, 1997).

Catholic university in Dublin, he quoted it in a public letter to the Coadjutor Bishop of Kerry, David Moriarty. There he suggested that it expressed the proper character of preaching within a Catholic university.[3] His point then, and his point nearly 25 years later, was that the communication of the Christian Faith is primarily an act of love modelled on God's love, as his self-communication to humanity in Jesus Christ. As such, it is an expression of the desire of the lover to give of self, entirely and fully, to the beloved. For St Francis de Sales the expression, in the form he used it, *cor cordi loquitu* the word *cor* – heart – is used in its classical sense, as the seat of both the intellect and affections. It is neither primarily an intellectual nor an affective act: it is an act *of* the whole person *to* the whole person, and it is ordered towards precisely the encounter with the person of Christ that Pope Benedict put right at the heart of the new evangelization when he announced the Year of Faith 2012–3:

> Ever since the start of my ministry as Successor of Peter, I have spoken of the need to rediscover the journey of faith so as to shed ever clearer light on the joy and renewed enthusiasm of the encounter with Christ. During the homily at the Mass marking the inauguration of my pontificate I said: 'The Church as a whole and all her Pastors, like Christ, must set out to lead people out of the desert, towards the place of life, towards friendship with the Son of God, towards the One who gives us life, and life in abundance.' It often happens that Christians are more concerned for the social, cultural and political consequences of their commitment, continuing to think of the faith as a self-evident presupposition for life in society. In reality, not only can this presupposition no longer be taken for granted, but it is often openly denied . . . '*Caritas Christi urget nos*' (2 Cor 5:14): it is the love of Christ that fills our hearts and impels us to evangelize. Today as in the past, he sends us through the highways of the world to proclaim his Gospel to all the peoples of the earth (cf. Mt 28:19). Through his love, Jesus Christ attracts to himself the people of every generation. . . .[4]

Cor ad cor loquitur as recognition of the truth of the church's dogmatic teaching

It is scarcely possible to read Newman's great poem, *The Dream of Gerontius* or to sing his hymns, such as *Praise to the Holiest in the Height* or *Lead Kindly Light,*

---

[3] John Henry Newman, *Catholic University Gazette* (Dublin, 1855), revised and reproduced in *The Idea of a University* (uniform edition; London: Longman & Green, 1878), p. 410.

[4] Benedict XVI, *Porta Fidei*, Apostolic Letter issued Motu Proprio 'For the Indiction of the Year of Faith' (11 October 2011).

without recognizing this same intense and personal Christological imperative. Nor can that be done without coming to know something of the depth of feeling with which his Christian faith imbued Newman. These are works of profound emotion, deep personal insight and undeniable affective maturity. They point unerringly and unremittingly towards the person of Christ and yet they are also profoundly dogmatic, deeply theological and are marked by an undeniable doctrinal richness of astonishing complexity. They speak of a religion where head and heart, reason and faith, are not opposed one to another but complementary, each strengthening the other. They are expressions of Christianity that manifest that truth which St John Paul II named at the beginning of his 1998 encyclical *Fides et ratio* (1998) when he wrote: 'Faith and reason are like two wings on which the human spirit rises to the contemplation of truth.' If the Church is to engage in the evangelization of those societies and cultures which were formerly predominantly Christian, it must propose such a vision of the Christian faith, one where faith and reason are in a complementary harmony that point to the one proper, necessary and sufficient subject of both: 'Jesus Christ, and him crucified' (1 Cor. 2.2).

Writing in 1864, Newman recalled his first recollections of faith. He sketched a childhood religious practice grounded firmly in the reading of the Bible, of perfect knowledge of the catechism, but it was a religion devoid of serious affective conviction. At the age of 15, he was overcome by that 'great change of thought'[5] that he later accounted his conversion to Evangelicalism. The particular character of that conversion, at least as he recalled it 48 years later,[6] was one where 'I fell under the influences of a definite creed, and received into my intellect impressions of dogma, which, through God's mercy, have never been effaced or obscured.'[7]

Newman's conversion was, then, a conversion to an explicitly dogmatic conception of the Christian faith: a faith whose creeds, he believed, 'were facts,

[5] John Henry Newman, *Apologia Pro Vita Sua: Being a Reply to a Pamphlet Entitled 'What Then Does Mr Newman Mean?'* (1st edition; London: Longman, Roberts & Green, 1864) (hereafter *Apologia*), p. 58.
[6] Newman's account of his own religious history in the *Apologia* has been called into question ever since it was first published. His sincerity was questioned by Charles Kingsley in his own lifetime and Lytton Strachey's waspish *Eminent Victorians* (London: Chatto & Windus, 1918), did nothing to redress the balance. In more recent years, there have been several attempts at perpetuating the argument that Newman's own account was unreliable and deliberately dissembling. Nonetheless, the account given in the *Apologia* is consistent with the documentary evidence from Newman's own letters and diaries contemporaneous with the events described. He is, contrary to the claims of his detractors, a remarkably accurate, candid and reliable autobiographer: see my 'The Search for Continuity in the Face of Change in the Anglican Writings of John Henry Newman' (unpublished doctoral dissertation; Oxford: University of Oxford, 2013).
[7] Newman, *Apologia*, p. 58.

not opinions'.[8] Furthermore, although it had immediate profound affective and existential consequences for him, the conversion Newman remembered was one that was primarily about the apprehension of the reality of religious truths expressed in propositional form. It would be a mistake, however, to read this as being a purely intellectual conversion. It was, rather, a religious experience of the whole man: it was knowing with the whole person. He recalled its effect on him as an event that he remembered as 'making me rest in the thought of two and two only absolute and luminously self-evident beings, myself and my Creator'.[9] This is a description of religious feeling that has more of the intimacy and intensity of the profound knowing of one another by the lover and the beloved, than it is of mere sentiment or belief in doctrinal proposition. It is a profoundly affective statement and yet it is expressed in the language of faith and reason. What he described was a conversion of *cor ad cor loquitur*.

It is one of the theological tragedies of our time – and there are more than a few of those – that Newman is often misappropriated to this or that party to religious controversy. He is read, or quoted, as the morning star of the ecumenical movement[10] or as the man who finally saw the folly of his Anglican ways and became a Catholic;[11] he is the model of manipulative insincerity, a traitor to the Church of England seduced by *Roma iniquita et speciosa*[12] or he is the Vatican II progressive *avant la lettre*.[13] Most egregiously, his carefully nuanced and perfectly loyal theology of conscience is marshalled in a half-understood and wilfully misquoted manner to justify dissent from the teaching

---

[8] John Henry Newman, *Arians of the Fourth Century: Their Temper, Doctrine and Conduct Chiefly as Exhibited in the Councils of the Church between A.D. 325, and A.D. 381* (1st edition; London: J. G. and F. Rivington, 1833), p. 148.

[9] Newman, *Apologia*, p. 59.

[10] For example, Heinrich Fries, 'John Henry Newman, Ein Wegbereiter der Christenlich Einheit', *Catholica*, 15 (1961), pp. 60–70; or John Coulson, Arthur M. Allchin and Meriol Trevor, *John Henry Newman: A Portrait Restored. An Ecumenical Revaluation* (London: Sheed & Ward, 1965).

[11] The classic example of this genre being Wilfrid Ward's, *The Life of John Henry Cardinal Newman Based on his Private Journals and Correspondence* (in 2 vols; London: Longmans, Green & Co., 1912).

[12] An approach taken by Newman's own brother Frank Newman in *Contributions Chiefly to the Early History of Cardinal Newman* (London: Kegan Paul, Trench, Trübner & Co., 1891), most famously by Lytton Strachey in the already cited *Eminent Victorians*, and by Geoffrey Faber in his *Oxford Apostles: A Character Study of the Oxford Movement* (London: Faber & Faber, 1933). More recently, it is how Diarmaid MacCulloch has chosen to present Newman both on television and in the press. In an interview with the *Church Times* in September 2009, to promote the launch of his magisterial *A History of Christianity: The First Three Thousand Years* (London: Allen Lane, 2009) – a book which, without any apparent hint of self-reflection, ascribes to Newman a 'not uncharacteristic feline sarcasm' – he claimed that Newman was both '[t]he most overrated theologian of the 19th century' and 'devious, slippery and manipulative'.

[13] This claim is made by so many that it is difficult to cite a representative example; however, Edward Ondrako's *Progressive Illumination: A Journey with John Henry Cardinal Newman 1980–2005* (Binghamton, NY: Global Academic Publishing, 2006) is a recent publication in this vein.

of the Church's magisterium.[14] In truth, he was none of these caricatures and believed in none of those positions. If there was an over-arching meta-narrative to Newman's religious trajectory, it was the one he recounted in the 'Biglietto Speech'. What he describes there accords entirely with that conception of religion as he understood it as a newly converted 15-year-old Evangelical. The tale he told on being made a cardinal was one of his battle to identify, cleave to and defend those early 'impressions of dogma'. He wrote:

> [A]ll through what I have written, is this . . . I rejoice to say, to one great mischief I have from the first opposed myself. For thirty, forty, fifty years I have resisted to the best of my powers the spirit of liberalism in religion. Never did Holy Church need champions against it more sorely than now, when, alas! it is an error overspreading, as a snare, the whole earth; and on this great occasion, when it is natural for one who is in my place to look out upon the world, and upon Holy Church as in it, and upon her future, it will not, I hope, be considered out of place, if I renew the protest against it which I have made so often . . . Liberalism in religion is the doctrine that there is no positive truth in religion, but that one creed is as good as another . . . It is the anti-dogmatic principle to which I have ever been opposed.[15]

If that was true in 1879, it is all the more true 135 years later. In 2010, Newman's motto was adopted as the theme of the papal visit to Great Britain, a visit that the Pope Benedict explicitly set within his call for a new evangelization:

> In addressing the citizens of that country, a crossroads of culture and of the world economy, I kept in mind the entire West, conversing with the intellect of this civilization and communicating the unfading newness of the Gospel in which it is steeped. This Apostolic Journey strengthened a deep conviction within me: the ancient nations of Europe have a *Christian soul*, which is one with the 'genius' and history of the respective peoples, and the Church never stops working to keep this spiritual and cultural tradition ceaselessly alive.[16]

Sadly it was the more obvious aspects, the superficial meanings, the mere sentiment, that those asked to comment on the motto in the Catholic press and the broadcast media focused on, reducing *cor ad cor loquitur* to little more than the

---

14 In, for example, the autobiographies of Charles Curran, *Loyal Dissent: Memoir of a Catholic Theologian* (Washington DC: Georgetown University Press, 2006) and Hans Küng, *My Struggle for Freedom* (John Bowden (trans.); Grand Rapids, MI: Wm B. Eerdmans, 2003).
15 John Henry Newman, 'Biglietto Speech', in William P. Neville (ed.), *Addresses to Cardinal Newman and His Replies* (London: Longmans, Green & Co., 1905), pp. 63–5.
16 Benedict XVI, General Audience, St Peter's Square, Rome (22 September 2010).

communication of warm, feel-good emotions. Pope Benedict's words were much more in tune with Newman's meaning. It was this more authentic conception of Newman's understanding of his own motto which, perhaps surprisingly, became current in the days immediately after the visit. It became commonplace for commentators to remark on the sincerity and gentleness of the Pope, in the same breath as engaging with the ideas about which he was speaking: ideas that were anything but superficial or 'feel-good'. The presumed dichotomy between the 'good' religion of sentiment and the 'bad' religion of dogma appeared, briefly, to breakdown in the minds of the commentariat. Benedict's words and actions were a vindication of the young Anglican cleric Newman's remark, in the fifth University Sermon, that the truth of the gospel: 'has ever been upheld in the world not as a system, not by books, not by argument, nor by temporal power, but by the personal influence of such men . . ., who are at once the teachers and patterns of it'.[17]

Later in the same sermon, entitled 'Personal Influence, the Means of Propagating the Truth', he talked of: 'ardent Christians . . . [who] become bearers of light, bright torches in a world of darkness and gloom. Illuminated by the light of Christ, they have an overwhelming influence on others, enkindling the fire of Christ in their hearts . . . A few highly-endowed men will rescue the world for centuries to come'.[18] What Newman here described, and to what his history of relationships and his correspondence bear witness, is a method of evangelization that is, in effect, a theology of evangelization by friendship. Indeed, the Opus Dei priest and Newman scholar, Fr Juan Vélez has suggested that so strong is this theme in Newman's work that, should he be ever declared a Doctor of the Church, it should be under the title *doctor amictiae* – doctor of friendship.[19]

This evangelization through friendship depends, not merely on personal magnetism, nor is it simply about one infecting the other with a particular taste or passion. Placed alongside Newman's explicitly dogmatic faith it points to the need to integrate the propositional with the affective, such that the 'overwhelming influence' exerted by the Christian witness Newman identified is one which points to what Vincent Cardinal Nicholls has recently called the 'the faith in its entirety, in its symphonic wholeness'.[20] That notion of 'symphonic

---

[17] John Henry Newman, 'Personal Influence, the Means of Propagating Truth', a sermon preached at St Mary the Virgin, Oxford on 22 January 1832, in John Henry Newman, *Fifteen Sermons Preached Before the University of Oxford Between AD 1826 and 1843* (London: Longmans, 1871), sermon V, pp. 91–2.

[18] Newman, 'Personal Influence', p. 97.

[19] Juan Vélez, 'Heart Speaks to Heart', in *MercatorNet* (10 September 2010).

[20] Vatican Radio, 'Archbishop Nichols on Youth Evangelisation' (8 May 2012).

wholeness' neatly captures the notion of personal integrity that lies behind Newman's theology of evangelization through friendship and the motto *cor ad cor loquitur*. It is about as far from the notion of glib sentiment as it is possible to envisage, and it is a concept which is related to a further aspect of Newman's thought to which *cor ad cor loquitur* alludes and which provides a further key to the new evangelization.

Cor ad cor loquitur as real assent to the dogmatic truths

Writing his *An Essay in Aid of a Grammar of Assent* in 1870, Newman described and contrasted two distinct ways in which we give our agreement to propositions: notional assent and real assent. The former 'tend to be mere assertions without any personal hold on them on the part of those who make them,'[21] whereas the latter 'representing as they do the concrete, have the power of the concrete upon the affections and passions, and by means of these indirectly become operative.'[22] 'Real assent' is that assent which, when we give it to a proposition, changes the way we behave, the way we believe. It is the latter, 'real assent', which is, for Newman, the character of 'belief', and this is, he argued, a precondition for the communication of faith.

Jean Giraudoux is reputed to have said that 'The secret of success is *sincerity*. Once you can fake that you've got it made.'[23] While emblematic of much of the world-weariness that characterized the France of the *fin-de-siècle* within which he wrote, Giraudoux's epigram is the polar opposite of Newman's conception of 'real assent' and its relation to *cor ad cor loquitur*. The cynicism, which Giradoux's remark exemplifies, hints at a particular difficulty facing those engaged in the new evangelization. Exposure to such insincerity in major figures in society has left individuals in the Western world, and particularly in those societies making up, what Aidan Nicholls has helpfully described as, 'North Atlantic civilization',[24] particularly sensitive to hypocrisy. Such widely perceived hypocrisy on the part

---

[21] John Henry Newman, *An Essay in Aid of a Grammar of Assent* (uniform edition; London: Longman, Green & Co., 1870), p. 40.

[22] Ibid., p. 89.

[23] Arthur Bloch (ed.), *Murphy's Law Book Two: More Reasons Why Things Go Wrong* (London: Magnum, 1981).

[24] Aidan Nicholls, 'A Revelation to Transmit: The Magisterial Project', in John Redford (ed.), *Hear, O Islands: Theology and Catechesis in the New Millennium* (Dublin: Veritas Publications, 2002), p. 152. This appears to be a more helpful and a more accurate expression for those countries and the values prevalent in them than what is often called simply 'the West'. Not only it is more geographically precise, but also it locates properly the axis of thought, and its attendant developmental dynamic, in the transatlantic exchange between the *bien pensantistes* of Western Europe and North America.

of those in the Catholic hierarchy, whose actions in response to the sexual and physical abuse of children and other vulnerable people ranged from the woefully inadequate to the demonstrably criminal, is arguably more damaging to the project of the new evangelization than the abuse itself – dreadful though that has been. The personal integrity, genuine conviction and much-needed courage that derive from real assent to the dogmatic truths of the Catholic faith will be indispensable if the voice of the Christ speaking through his Church is to be heard again in those societies.

Newman wrote scores of letters from the time of his own conversion onwards in which he described the necessary preconditions for taking the step he had himself taken in becoming a Catholic.[25] In all of these letters he counselled that no action should be taken, no change of allegiance attempted, until the individual contemplating it was so convinced of the truths of the Catholic Church's claims for itself – its oneness, its holiness, its catholicity, its apostolicity and the attendant infallible authority that it possesses by virtue of those notes – that the individual was compelled to act. What he described in these letters is a process by which an individual comes to real assent to the dogmas 'impressed upon his intellect', not as theoretical notions or platonic ideas, but as the concrete with the power of the concrete upon the affections and passions. It is then, and only then, that the moment of conversion has truly arrived, that it must be acted upon and its consequences faced, often – as with Newman himself – at a high personal price.

It seems appropriate to say a few words here about Newman's much misrepresented idea of conscience. The *Letter to the Duke of Norfolk* is often cited because of a remark that Newman made towards the end of it, in which he said: '. . . if I am obliged to bring religion into after-dinner toasts (which indeed does not seem quite the thing), I shall drink, to the Pope, if you please – still, to conscience first and to the Pope afterwards.'[26] This flippant quip has been used as justification for dissent from the Church's teaching ever since, but those who use it to do that misunderstand and misrepresent Newman and they do so by taking his own words and using them completely out of context. Those who did it during his own life appalled him and he reserved some of the sternest criticism in the 'Biglietto Speech' for them. What he was not prepared to pardon, because

---

[25] For example, the correspondence between Newman and Catherine Ward beginning in September 1848 and ending with her reception into the Catholic Church in June of the following year. See *The Letters and Diaries of John Henry Newman*, Vol. XII, pp. 265–8; 289–94; 332–7; 354–6; 377–9; and Vol. XIII, p. 75.

[26] John Henry Newman, *Letter to the Duke of Norfolk* (uniform edition; London: Longmans & Green, 1881), p. 261.

of the damage he thought it did, both to the soul of the individual and to the life of the Church, we should be no more ready to tolerate.

Newman certainly had a very high conception of conscience: it was matter that is treated of time and again in his letters and diaries and he preached on it frequently. Early in the *Letter to the Duke of Norfolk*, written to defend Catholic teaching in the period of foment immediately after the First Vatican Council and the definition of papal infallibility, he wrote of conscience in the following terms: it was 'the Law of God apprehended in the minds of individual men'; it is 'the voice of God'; it is 'the Aboriginal Vicar of Christ'. We are bound to obey it. But for Newman, conscience was that faculty which classical Catholic teaching had always presented it to be: it was, as he noted in the words of St Thomas Aquinas, 'practical judgment or dictate of reason, by which we judge what *hic et nunc* is to be done as being good, or to be avoided as evil'. Newman wrote that 'conscience is not a judgement on any speculative truth, on any abstract doctrine but bears immediately on something . . . to be done or not done.' He continued: 'It [i.e. conscience] cannot come into conflict with the Church's or the Pope's infallibility, since these are engaged on general propositions.'[27]

So for Newman, our consciences are not about whether we can accept this teaching or that of the Church: he thought the question a nonsense – he called such things 'counterfeit' and 'mere self-will'[28] – and he did so because, as he wrote: 'I say there is only one Oracle of God, the Holy Catholic Church and the Pope as her head. To her teaching I have ever desired all my thought, all my words to be conformed.'[29] Even when it came to acting contrary to a Papal instruction – not an infallible dogma, nor even a solemn teaching but a mere instruction or injunction – Newman set the bar for dissent very high. He asserted that: 'Unless a man is able to say to himself, as in the Presence of God, that he must not, and dare not, act upon the Papal injunction, he is bound to obey it.'[30] It is clear, therefore, that attempting to use Newman to justify so-called loyal dissent is, to say the least, thoroughly to misrepresent him.

---

[27] Ibid., p. 256. Cf. Thomas Aquinas, Summa Theologiae: *A Guide and Commentary* (Brian Davies (ed. and trans.); Oxford: Oxford University Press, 2014), *Pars Prima Secundae*, q. 79, a. 13.

[28] Newman, *Letter to the Duke of Norfolk*, p. 257.

[29] Ibid., p. 346.

[30] Ibid., p. 258.

Conclusion

In conclusion, it is the three characteristics of Newman's approach to faith that constitute his understanding of *cor ad cor loquitur*, the heart speaking to heart: the necessity of personal influence, sincerity and integrity, that is of deep friendship, as the medium of communication; the recognition of the truth of the Church's dogmatic teaching; and real assent to those dogmatic truths as the foundation of that influence, sincerity and integrity. This is the *cor ad cor loquitur*. It is these three that provide a paradigm for the new evangelization: one new in its ardour, new in its methods and new in its expressions, aimed at making disciples of Jesus Christ in His body, the Church. This poses a serious obstacle to a Church where – if the opinion pollsters are to be believed – the vast majority of not only Mass-going Catholics, but also those in religious communities and ordained ministry, conform closely to secular societal norms and beliefs regarding sexual conduct, bio-ethics and social justice. The widespread ignorance of the Church's dogmatic teaching about, for example, the person of Christ, and the indifference, even opposition, to her sacramental teaching and discipline, merely compounds the problem. The widely reported results of the responses to the consultation ahead of the Extraordinary Synod on the Family demonstrate a yawning chasm between the teaching of the Church on marriage and family life, on the one hand, and the views of Catholics, clergy, religious and the laity, in those formerly Christian cultures of the North Atlantic Civilization, on the other.

The legacy of dissent from the constant teaching of the Church as expressed in, among other documents of the Magisterium, the *Catechism of the Catholic Church*, *Humanae vitae*, *Evangelium vitae* and *Ordinatio sacerdotalis*, of the predictable and now plainly apparent failure of the pedagogical methods and approaches to doctrine of much catechetical practice and the distortion of the notion and liberties of conscience, means that there is much work to be done. It will only be possible with the gracious assistance of the Holy Spirit, but grace builds on nature, and therefore, we should not rely entirely on hoped-for extraordinary and extrinsic interventions, where the ordinary and intrinsic operation of grace can achieve so much. The key to such ordinary and intrinsic grace is to be found in the new ardour, methods and expressions that are necessary for the new evangelization to succeed. They, in turn, are to be found powerfully expressed in the recognition of the objective truth of Christian doctrine, the exercise of personal influence and in lives lived in real assent to the claims of Christian faith. They are to be found in Newman's paradigm: in *cor ad cor loquitur*.

15

Conversion to Christ: Teaching, Theology and Practice Since Vatican II

Andrew Brookes

In my experience many, and very probably most, practising Catholics in the United Kingdom do not feel competent to proclaim the gospel of Jesus Christ and call people to conversion to Christ. Thinking it to be an evangelical Protestant enterprise, Catholics often distance themselves from it. A lack of adequate information and training as well as scepticism and fear are other significant factors. As a result, the work of evangelization is seriously hampered.

My aim is to address this lack of competence, as far as space allows. I begin by establishing that proclamation of the gospel and/or conversion to Christ is a significant focus of Church teaching and, as such, authentically Catholic. I then establish the extent of the need for it in contemporary Britain. Next a properly Catholic understanding of faith and conversion are outlined since this is what is aimed at, and also since this influences the content and methods of proclamation. Since actual proclamation is, I think, a particularly weak area among Catholics this is then focused on, reviewing some problems and then offering a new proposal about the structure and content of proclamation. I conclude by briefly outlining some aspects of practical application.

So as to address non-academic Catholics, and other Christians, that is practitioners and would-be practitioners, and due to limits of space, I shall not overburden this chapter with references. Some suggestions are given for those who wish to follow up ideas.

The relevance of Vatican II and magisterial teaching

Ad gentes, 'Decree on the Missionary Activity of the Church' (especially 13–4) taught what was involved in conversion to Christ. Vatican II frequently called all Catholics both to ongoing conversion and to share in the work of proclaiming Christ. Magisterial documents since then have consistently and repeatedly stressed the same points. While they teach that conversion is a complex long process, lifelong in some respects, they stress that there is a need for a radical and definitive 'initial conversion' in response to a proclamation of the life and paschal mystery of Jesus Christ. That faith is described in terms of a deep personal relationship with Jesus and a conversion of life. Throughout these documents, the language is very biblical, and, one could say, evangelical. However, this focus on an evangelical and personal faith in Jesus is integrated with a stress on an ecclesial and sacramental faith, which again is presented as an encounter with Jesus.

By way of example on the gospel to be proclaimed, Pope Paul VI's exhortation *Evangelii nuntiandi* (EN) 22 says: 'There is no true evangelization if the name, the teaching, the life, the promises, the kingdom and the mystery of Jesus of Nazareth, the Son of God are not proclaimed.' John Paul II wrote beautifully on conversion in the encyclical *Redemptoris missio* (1990):

> The proclamation of the Word of God has *Christian conversion* as its aim: a complete and sincere adherence to Christ and his Gospel through faith. Conversion is a gift of God, a work of the Blessed Trinity. (. . .) From the outset, conversion is expressed in faith which is total and radical, and which neither limits nor hinders God's gift. At the same time, it gives rise to a dynamic and lifelong process which demands a continual turning away from 'life according to the flesh' to 'life according to the Spirit' (cf. Rom 8:3–13). Conversion means accepting, by a personal decision, the saving sovereignty of Christ and becoming his disciple (46).

The need for such conversion to happen before catechesis can be most effectively undertaken is frequently stressed.[1] Such primary proclamation is to be addressed to those who have never known Christ – that is as part of permanent evangelization – but also to those who have become religiously indifferent or whose faith formation was very inadequate – that is, it is part of new evangelization.[2]

This stress on the need to proclaim Christ in magisterial documents is supported strongly by various cultural studies undertaken on the UK population.

---

[1] Among other examples are the following. International Commission on English in the Liturgy (ICEL), *Rite of Christian Initiation of Adults* (RCIA; ICEL, 1985), especially pp. 36 and 42. Congregation for the Clergy, *General Directory of Catechesis* (London: CTS, 1997), pp. 55–7, 61–2.

[2] For examples of this distinction, see *Evangelii Nuntiandi* 52, *Redemptoris Missio* 33–4, *General Directory of Catechesis* 58–9.

About 18 per cent of UK Catholics (1 million) go to Mass weekly, so the other Catholics are potential recipients of new evangelization. Total numbers of Catholics make up around 9 per cent of the population.

The 2011 National Census results indicate that the number of people identifying as Christian is 59 per cent (down from 72 per cent 10 years earlier). Those claiming no religion rose to 25 per cent from 15 per cent.[3] A research institute conducted a large survey of those who said they were Christian to find out in more detail what church activities they engaged in and what their beliefs really were.[4] Of these, only 17 per cent go to Church at least weekly and a further 12 per cent each month . Their beliefs about Jesus, selected from a list, are helpful to this study:

'Jesus is the son of God, Saviour of the world' – 44 per cent

'Jesus was a man who gave us a good example' – 32 per cent

'Jesus was just a man' – 13 per cent

'I do not believe Jesus really existed' – 4 per cent

On the resurrection of Jesus, selections were as follows:

'Jesus came back to life physically after being dead' – 32 per cent

'Jesus came back spiritually but not physically after being dead' – 39 per cent

'I do not believe in the resurrection' – 18 per cent

(Nearly all the rest indicated regarding these questions that 'they do not know' or 'preferred not to say'.) These figures are for just over half the total population, but they indicate the scope of the need for new evangelization in the country as a whole, grouping all Christians, practising or non-practising, together.[5]

A survey of recent research published by the think-tank Theos gives a helpful profile of the non-religious people (that is, who never attend services).[6] Making up about 25 per cent of the population, they are not uniformly secular

---

[3] Office for National Statistics, *Religion in England and Wales 2011.* http://www.ons.gov.uk/ons/dcp171776_290510.pdf.

[4] Richard Dawkins Foundation for Reason and Science (UK), 'Religious and Social Attitudes of UK Christians in 2011' (Ipsos MORI Research, 2011).

[5] It seems to me that the division of people into those needing pastoral care, those needing new evangelization and those needing evangelization proper, as often articulated by the Vatican, does not give adequate consideration to countries in which the majority of non-practising Christians are not Catholic and, specifically, to an analysis of residual Christian, but non-Catholic culture, any hostility or openness to Catholicism and so the suitability of Catholic evangelization. This merits attention and is the situation in the United Kingdom.

[6] Nick Spencer and Holly Weldin, *Post-Religious Britain: The Faith of the Faithless* (London: Theos Publications, 2012).

materialist atheists. A variety of recent studies have shown these make up about 9 per cent of the population. The rest have some spiritual beliefs, values or practices. Approximately 35 per cent of them believe in some sort of God; 28 per cent definitely believe in life after death (25 per cent being unsure) and 44 per cent in the human soul (24 per cent being unsure). Forty-one per cent regard the Bible as inspired (7 per cent) or useful as a guide (34 per cent). This figure probably indicates the approximate numbers that think Jesus was a good man and moral guide. However, 13 per cent believed in the resurrection of Jesus, a further 24 per cent being not sure.[7] Eighteen per cent of non-attenders pray at least once a year, 5 per cent at least weekly. Although more regard themselves as spiritual to some degree, 66 per cent of non-attenders do not regard themselves as spiritual at all. The 2011 Census indicated 4.5 million who claim to belong to other major religions, these holding a variety of views about Jesus.

To sum up, these statistics give some indication of the scale of evangelization that is needed if also some potential points of interest in Catholicism. Only 25 per cent of the population believe that Jesus is the Son of God and Saviour of the world, and only 9 per cent attend Church each week. At least 75 per cent of the population, and probably a lot more, could potentially benefit from an effective proclamation of the Gospel, although in many cases many other approaches will be needed as well.

Faith and conversion: theological and pastoral foundations

Effective proclamation requires us to be clear about a number of aspects of the Catholic theology of faith and conversion. These, in turn, give rise to some important pastoral principles. I have gathered these into seven 'foundations' below. At the outset it is important to realize that faith is multi-faceted, and being converted (even initial conversion) is part of a journey, sometimes of almost imperceptible shifts, if at times also marked by clear decisions and sometimes by key experiences. Thus conversion and faith involve many components and their interaction is complex and varied. A good grasp and application of these will help people proclaim the gospel, and pastorally and prayerfully facilitate conversions in an authentic and confidently Catholic manner.

---

[7] I think it likely that most 'non-religious materialist atheists' regard Jesus as a real man, but not as a moral guide.

First, faith includes the use of reason. The Catholic Church rejects complete dependence on human reason to the exclusion of the supernatural action and revelation of God for us (rationalism), a dependence that prevents faith. It also rejects a complete repudiation of reason (fideism) which results in so-called blind faith.[8] Therefore, an important activity in evangelization is to build up, by persuasion and discussion, the meaning and credibility of religious and specifically Christian ideas, and to present the historical evidence for Jesus and his ministry and resurrection. Discussion of church history and also of moral and philosophical issues may also matter. All this is the basis of apologetics and may need to precede and even accompany proclamation. A single line of argument can be compelling, but more typically strands will accumulate, as multiple issues are dealt with, enabling a strong rope to be built up, one strong and convincing enough to rely on (to use an illustration of John Henry Newman).[9] Faith has intellectual content and support. At the same time, it is important to help people realize that God is 'bigger' than our words. Also reason may lead people to faith, and support faith, but faith is not the conclusion of an argument.[10]

Second, faith makes use of the imagination. The imagination is powerful and aids rational thinking, memory, moral reasoning and emotional responses. It also helps integrate these. Building up an image of Jesus is very helpful. I do not particularly mean what he looked like – though some version of that will come into play. I mean a sense of the shape of Jesus's life, of his outlook and values, his teachings, of his language about God. Jesus is the visible image of God: who Jesus is and what he does uniquely express God. Newman held that it was the image of Christianity (principally a vivid sense of the incarnation held in the imagination) that sustained and animated the early Church.[11] It is still important. It is permeated with reason and also affect, yielding dogmas, and also sustaining devotion, but is not reducible to cold rationalist philosophy or dogmatism, or to emotional subjectivism. A

---

[8] This was authoritatively taught in Vatican I's *Dei Filius*, Dogmatic Constitution on the Catholic Faith (1870), chapters 2–4, in Josef Neuner and Jacques Dupuis (eds), *The Christian Faith* (revised edition; London: Collins, 1982), pp. 40–8.

[9] This is classically developed in John Henry Newman, *An Essay in Aid of a Grammar of Assent* (uniform edition; London: Longman, Green & Co, 1870). An excellent critical edition is John Henry Newman, *An Essay in Aid of a Grammar of Assent* (Ian T. Ker (ed.); Oxford: Clarendon Press, 1985).

[10] A very helpful essay on this and other aspects of conversion is Avery Dulles, 'Fundamental Theology and the Dynamics of Conversion', *The Thomist* 45 (1981), pp. 175–93.

[11] For an excellent complex analysis of the role of imagination in faith according to Newman, see Terrence Merrigan, *Clear Heads and Holy Hearts – The Religious and Theological Ideal of John Henry Newman* (Louvain: Peeters Press, 1991).

narratively structured presentation and proclamation of Jesus (perhaps along the lines I give) may help nurture this sense of Jesus within us through our imagination.

Third, faith involves moral conversion. Conversion involves turning from sin and to God. Humans are inevitably concerned with what makes them happy and fulfilled. They also have to address issues of how to be just, how to treat others kindly and how to deal with their own moral weaknesses and failures. Moving towards and into faith involves seeing Jesus and the God he proclaimed as the source of that fulfilment and happiness and as goodness itself. Jesus taught and modelled a moral code, a way of love that is merciful and just. He also empowers us to live it, offering a life of moral goodness to us. If one accepts Jesus as telling the truth about God, then one will have to make an attempt to live in the light of his teachings, and they cover the gamut of human activities, applied in more detail by the Church. Such moral conversion can follow recognition of the truth about Jesus being God, but aspects of it may also be needed before faith can be properly accepted. Jesus talked often of sin blinding people to the truth of his words and the correct interpretation of his actions. In other cases, the desire for forgiveness and/or moral improvement and empowerment can be the starting point for conversion.

Fourth, faith is about experience, including our emotional and bodily life. Proclamation and faith both interpret experience anew, and lead to new and changed experience. Committed faith integrates all our faculties and our range of experience and orientates them towards God known in Jesus. As human, he experienced the human condition and so is a powerful focus for this orientation to the divine. That is why our relationship with God can be experienced and expressed in deeply human terms.[12]

It is very helpful for Christians to share their own experiences of Christian life and conversion. These need not be dramatic though they may be. Such personal testimonies can, by their humanity, resonate and build connections with potential converts, and also help them imagine or see what lived faith is like, and, contrasting it with their present situation, arouse a desire for faith.

Fifth, faith is communal. Faith is personal but we are made for relationships and society. We are made to belong. Jesus restores, heals and blesses all these

---

[12] For a helpful introduction to human experience and its religious dimension, see Gerald O'Collins, *Fundamental Theology* (London: DLT, 1982), chapter 2. Chapter 5 provides a good overall treatment of how we, including our cognitive, volitional and imaginative faculties respond to divine revelation in faith.

aspects of who we are. That is why faith takes us into the Church, into the faith of the Church. Building up good relationships matters and really helps sustain faith.

Sixth, faith requires grace. Grace is absolutely essential. Evangelization involves the various human activities of preaching, teaching, explaining, witnessing, loving, listening – all of which need grace. Proclamation proper is fundamentally a declaration in faith of the core content of the gospel, or kerygma. It needs a response that is informed, well-motivated and freely chosen, but this response too is grounded in the action of God in the person.

This graced activity is entirely co-operative with our reason, meaning that at some point we simply 'know' or 'see' Jesus to be God come in the flesh, and simply accept on divine authority the words he spoke to us and the actions he did for us, trusting them as efficacious. Grace works co-operatively with our freedom and will: it increases our capacity to see truth and walk in goodness. We decide for God, for Jesus, but with God's help, given in the action of the Holy Spirit, and in response to what Jesus has done. For these reasons, it is essential that the preacher trusts God, seeks to discern the action of God in the other and also helps them to discern it accurately.

Prayer is essential, and expectant faith is useful. Introducing people to Christian prayer is also important. Helping them frame and express conversion, belief and commitment in prayer can be a huge blessing. God can and does act both in gentle and in unusual dramatic ways. We should be open to accept both. Opposition of a spiritual nature is very likely indeed.

Seventh, faith is linked to hope and love, and involves trust, worship and perseverance. Conversion means putting God as revealed in Jesus at the centre of their lives. It is a grateful response to what God has done and offers. A person believes what God has said and, repenting, puts their trust in God's saving action. A life of Christian worship and obedience begins. This is the core of initial conversion, one that has a definite content and a decisive stance. But such a decision and conversion need to become ongoing conversion, so that a person becomes like Christ. That process takes time. It expresses and nurtures love of God. Faith informs Catholics that they *have been saved* by what God did historically in Jesus; *are being saved* by the ongoing action of God in them as they walk in the obediently loving faith of relationship with God in Christ and that they *hope to be fully saved*, looking especially to the life of heaven and the return of Jesus and our bodily resurrection and full transformation into Christ. Human choice persists so Christians can fall, and are called to have a vigilant, humble and persevering faith, but, because of what he has done for them, they can have a joyful, peaceful and hopeful faith, trusting confidently in the ongoing goodness and gracious mercy of Jesus Christ, and growing in God's love.

Exegetical and dogmatic issues in determining the content of primary proclamation

Evangelization, and especially proclamation, aims at bringing people into a saving relationship with Jesus Christ. At its centre, it needs to present the truth about Jesus. In the twentieth century, there were difficulties with this. Some presentations were considered too abstract and technical, if dogmatically correct, while others, though rich in biblical incident and language, were seen as sometimes lacking truth. In short, a major problem in presenting, and especially proclaiming, Jesus Christ has been, I suggest, that of synthesizing biblical criticism with the Church's dogmatic understanding of Jesus. A resolution of this would produce a presentation that is at once evangelical and Catholic.[13]

The dogmas and doctrines of the Church have been formulated, under the guidance of the Holy Spirit, to help us understand the true meaning of Scripture. Dogmatic and New Testament theology ought to be in agreement about Jesus (though scholarship may require some creative tension at times). Dogmatic theology holds that Jesus's mission was to implement God's plan to save us by taking us up into the life of God, in the process revealing in a uniquely clear way who God is. It states that Jesus is the human-God, fully divine and fully human, but such that his self-articulated identity flows from his awareness of being the eternal Son of God. Put slightly more technically, he is the Second Person of the Trinity incarnate.

Vatican II called for the use of a more biblically rich understanding and presentation of Jesus. It encouraged a proper use of historical and literary methods of research as part of this. The heart of such critical methods involves deciding to what extent the early Church teachers who produced the New Testament documents were faithful to Jesus, and to what extent they were inventive in what

---

[13] The literature in this area is vast. I have found the following helpful and sympathetic to the critique I develop: John McDade, 'Jesus in Recent Research', *The Month* 31 (1998), pp. 495–505; John Redford (ed.), 'Scripture and Catechesis', in *Hear, O Islands – Theology and Catechesis in the New Millennium* (Dublin: Veritas, 2002), pp. 209–16; Robert Barron, *The Priority of Christ: Towards a Post-Liberal Catholicism* (Grand Rapids, MI: Brazos Press, 2007), especially Parts I and II. A newer approach to biblical studies is articulated in more detail in N. Thomas Wright, *The New Testament and the People of God* (London: SPCK, 1992), Parts I and II. For an accessible and cogent of somewhat simplified version of this material, see John Redmond, *Bad, Mad or God? Proving the Divinity of Christ from St John's Gospel* (London: St Paul's Publishing, 2004).

they passed on. Clearly the apostles would have continued to reflect on what Jesus said and did and they had some scope to determine what was presented. However, fundamentally were they faithful to him? Who is the source of the claim that Jesus is God come in the flesh? Did Jesus really act consciously as a special divine instrument, as though he was God, or was that written back into the Gospel accounts? In short, who is the originating and creative source and 'genius' behind the gospels (and all New Testament documents and the historical fact of the Church)? Is it Jesus, or one or more of the apostles and their colleagues, or perhaps a combination? If it is a combination, we still have to determine if infidelity to the historic memory of Jesus is possible in the timeframe during which the New Testament was written, and also what would have been their motivation, and if there is any evidence for such a supposed motive, given that they all consistently indicate that Jesus is the source.

The problem has been with determining what proper historical method is, what its limits are and what one does with religious claims within historical study. Much of the non-Catholic historical research about Jesus, while often accepting that Jesus had some sort of healing and exorcism ministry, simply would not countenance the possibility of linking the historical Jesus with prophecy, nature miracles, resurrection and, less still, incarnation or trinity. Most, or all, of these features (and most especially the divinity of Jesus) were explained as the 'invention' of the Church as it moved from a Jewish environment, which it claimed would not seriously countenance such thought, to Greek and other pagan cultures that had a multitude of gods, and stories of semi-divine heroes. Some versions allowed Jesus in his lifetime, besides being an extraordinary healer and wise teacher, perhaps to have been a prophet and possibly someone who claimed to be a human messiah of some sort, but they very rarely considered that he claimed more than that.

After Vatican II, Catholic scholarship was influenced by the presuppositions, methods and findings of already existing scholarship, taking it up, or dialoguing with it. At risk of generalization, this has often resulted in presentations of Jesus as a preacher and healer of profound goodness, but who did not communicate that he was divine in clear terms before his death. It was argued that the resurrection appearances then gave the apostles significant faith in him as a heavenly messiah and over time, under the guidance of the Holy Spirit, they came to understand him to be God – something that Jesus always was but was unable to say to them clearly during his lifetime. It is generally considered that this view can be squared with later dogmatic teaching about Jesus. It is not without problems though. It seems to me to raise the question whether Jesus actually knew he was divine. It also compromises a confident and effective Gospel-based proclamation of Jesus as God actually revealing God. Proclaiming or narrating a merely human Jesus, however noble a figure, does not offer us a share in the divine life through the action of God on our behalf.

However, more recently, since the 1990s approximately, there has been recognition of the inherent limits of certainty in any historical inquiry. The methodological exclusion of supernatural intervention could also now be pointed out and questioned more easily. At the same time, all the historical work has allowed a detailed picture to be built up of the Palestinian world of Jesus, and its cultural and religious mentality. This combination of shifts in the academic world means that more holistic constructions of the life and ministry of Jesus are being put forward, ones that may not be absolutely provable (in the old sense) but which fit the evidence and are coherent. The criterion of plausibility (and the degree of it) and overall fit with as much data as possible are seen as adequate to assess these accounts of Jesus.

In my view, historically plausible versions of the biblical Jesus which are compatible with the dogmatic teaching of the Church and suitable for use in evangelization can now be constructed. These would claim and narrate that Jesus was conscious of being God, of enjoying communion with God the Father and the Holy Spirit, and of having a mission to save us in a uniquely divine way as God's definitive instrument, thereby fulfilling the promises made by God to the Jews. Sitting alongside all this is the claim that the apostles grasped the essentials of this by Pentecost, even if their understanding of the implications grew later. First Jesus, and then his disciples, expressed all this by taking up, and creatively using, the Jewish religious culture of his day.

The structure, shape and content of gospel proclamation

Primary proclamation is not any sort of account of the life of Jesus and what it achieved. It consists in outlining, in the required amount of detail, the life of Jesus, including his death and resurrection, communicating that in it God is offering us salvation (which needs some explanation) and calling people to convert and receive it (explaining what this involves).[14]

The nuanced richness and often technical sophistication of Catholic theology and the intricacy of biblical scholarship tends, I think, to overwhelm many

---

[14] This appears to be the pattern of the early Church. See Acts 3.12–26; 10.36–43; 13.17–41.

Catholics. Some are rendered mute by its bulk. Others deliver a presentation that is not clear or sharp enough to convey the key information or to invite the response of conversion and faith. An alternative approach used by some Catholics that is concise and sharp is to take over, and sometimes adapt, evangelical Protestant versions of proclamation, especially those based on the so-called Four Spiritual Laws: (1) God made us for him; (2) we sinned; (3) Jesus died for us; (4) repent, believe and be saved.[15] Catholics often add, or include in the fourth law, the need be baptised and join the Church. Apart from the risks (which with care can be avoided) of taking over Protestant theologies of sin, atonement and justification, a problem with this approach is that it excludes wider consideration of the life of Jesus. When evangelizing people and cultures ignorant of a proper knowledge of Jesus (such as most of the United Kingdom), this is highly pertinent.

With this in mind, I have personally constructed and now outline a structured approach to the ministry, death and resurrection of Jesus, shaped with a view to inviting conversion and faith. It draws on the biblical and historical research outlined earlier.[16] I consider the presentation of Jesus to be very 'plausible', and it is in line with the dogmatic teaching of the Church, and with the pastoral suggestions and guidelines found in the *General Directory of Catechesis* (97–117).

Jesus brought in the 'day of the Lord' and the 'kingdom of God'

This 'day', that is event, would establish the kingdom and reign of God. In Jewish thought, it is to be a day or event in which God overcomes evil and establishes justice and peace, and this victory and its justice and peace shall last forever. It is a reckoning before what is most real, most truthful, that is to say before God who has the integrity and the capability to bring such justice and peace into existence. It is to be a day of judgement, which means a revelation of the true worth of things, and people and their actions, with consequent rewards and punishments, and ultimately heaven and hell. It respects and takes seriously human freedom and responsibility. It includes abundant mercy but not at the cost of justice. Rather, mercy builds up justice, giving forgiveness and help where pardon and purpose of amendment (which is a commitment to justice) are expressed. The

---

[15] For example, see Michelle Moran, *Pass It On! Practical Hints on Sharing your Faith* (London: DLT, 1990; amended and reprinted privately in 2001), pp. 29–39.

[16] I recommend that in the first place readers unfamiliar with the scriptural themes follow consult appropriate entries in Xavier Leon-Dufour (ed.), *Dictionary of Biblical Theology* (revised 2nd edition; London: Geoffrey Chapman, 1988).

Day of the Lord's goodness is such that the imagery of marriage between God and his people is also used of it, and that of a huge celebratory banquet, marked by joy. Bodily resurrection of the dead is included in the day of the Lord – such is its scope and power. All of this is included in what is meant by salvation.

Jesus made clear that in his ministry and in himself this Day of the Lord was being ushered in. God was visiting his people, making known his truth, dealing with his enemies (sin and Satan, and those actively and freely taking their side, and death) and establishing his Kingdom of righteousness.[17]

Jesus taught about God: of himself as unique Son of the Father, and bearer of the Spirit

He taught about God, the God to whom we have to give an account of our lives and with whom we are called into relationship. Grasping the truth about who God is and what he is like really matters. He pointed to God but also to himself. He talked about himself in relation to God in ways that linked himself with God in a unique way, a divine way.

Chief among the ways he expressed his divine consciousness was his description of himself as Son, and God as Father, making clear he understood this sonship in a unique way. He also spoke of himself as possessing and bearing the Holy Spirit of God in a unique way, such that he could give the Spirit to others. Such Father–Son and also Spirit language is found in the synoptic gospels, including some of the parables, even if it is perhaps more obvious in John. At the same time he affirmed the oneness of God, as held in Judaism, citing it in the greatest command (Mk 12.28–30, and parallels). The three-ness of God understood within the oneness of God is what was later articulated as the doctrine of the Trinity. It is a reflection on what Jesus had already said and revealed. He identified himself with the temple. God dwelt with his people in a special way in the temple and he claimed to be that temple, that divine presence, in his own person. He undertook actions only considered performable by God, such as the forgiveness of sins. In all these cases, the significance was not lost on his hearers: they knew he was making claims to a unique link with God and suspected or accused him of blasphemy on a number of occasions, culminating in his trial before the Sanhedrin, when he was formally condemned for it.

---

[17] This came to be seen as Jesus's three-fold ministry of prophet, priest and king, which I shall tease out and develop as distinct strands though it is all interwoven in his life.

He established, formed, led, ruled and provided for a people (i.e. the Church)

God himself was to be the great shepherd, king, teacher and ruler of his people. Jesus took on all these roles, and claimed many of them quite explicitly. He formed a new Israel (which is the Church) based on the 12 apostles. He taught about it, interpreted and applied law for it with authority, gathered members into it, including the broken members of Israel (sinful or not) and healed them, showing further divine power, authority and protection over his people by his exorcisms.[18]

He dealt with sin and its consequences, becoming both priest and sacrifice

He ministered to the outcasts, and to sinners. He forgave sin and healed people. He was a man of prayer and he predicted his death, offering it as a ransom for many. Knowing the hostile opposition he faced, his last visit to Jerusalem was at the feast of Passover, adding much depth to the sense of his death being a sacrifice that would be liberation from sin for the people. In his last hours, he was identified as a sinner, condemned by the religious authorities, made ritually unclean in many ways, brutally treated and hung on a tree, which was seen as a sign of being cursed by God (Gal. 3.13–14). He may have let his psyche experience unusually deeply some of the effects of sin. But all the time he acted as an innocent, and prayed, offering all to God his Father in union with his will.[19] Made into sin, he offered himself and it to God, while not actually being a sinner, and so in him God reconciled the world to himself.

He was declared Son of God with power by the Holy Spirit in his resurrection

If Jesus had lied or been mistaken or was mad, or possessed, his death would be the end. The gospel records indicate that all these suspicions or accusations

---

[18] One of the consequences of this is that when one converts to Jesus, one enters relationship with his people, not just with him.

[19] One must be careful in how one presents the relationship of Father and Son during the passion. One must not pit one against the other, for instance presenting Jesus mopping up the anger of a vengeful God in an unjust way, having Jesus, as a mild merciful God (or man), save us from a just or angry God. Jesus reveals the Father's justice *and* mercy. The Father and Son work co-operatively in a united way. All the gospels testify to this, John very strongly indeed. Nor does sin destroy their divine relationship or the unity of Father and Son, not for a moment. The opposite happens. The words 'My God, my God, why have you forsaken me?' expressive of immense anguish of soul are part of a psalm (22) addressed to God and culminating in the vindication of the speaker who then praises God in the divine assembly.

were raised against him during his public ministry. But if Jesus was truly aware of a divine identity and mission, and had truly manifested it in word and action, then his death could not be the end. Jesus had gone so far as to declare that his heavenly Father, and indeed he himself, would act to raise him from the dead. It seems the Jewish leaders knew of this and, fearing a fabrication by the theft of his body by the apostles, requested guards for the tomb.

Jesus did rise. The tomb was empty, something everyone seemed to accept. He appeared in a glorified form to his followers. His powerful resurrection, an action of the Holy Spirit, meant for anyone who could accept it that, within this very human workman from Nazareth, dwelt the fullness of the presence and power of God. The divine significance of Jesus's claim to be the Son of God and the extent of his power to save were declared by his Resurrection (cf. Rom. 1.3–4). The implications began to sink in. The disciples really believed in him, kept believing, and preached Christ to others, calling for conversion to him.

Raised to new life Jesus Christ is head of a new humanity and a new creation

His paschal mystery still more fully brought in the day of the Lord. His life, his teaching and especially his death and resurrection are an act of judgement, showing evil for what it is, exposing its weakness, but, at the same time, being an offer of mercy. On the cross, he effectively showed what a truly good human life is like, obedient unto death and not seeking the privilege or honour befitting to God (unlike Adam). In this way, he laid naked the extent of our sinfulness, and demonstrated the virtue in which we should aspire to be clothed. In his resurrection, he overcame death and any need to fear it. His death and resurrection together showed that the powers of this earth, be they religious, political or spiritual, cannot overcome him. Indeed, they end up serving his purposes (cf. Jn 16.8–11). The new life of resurrection expresses aspects of judgement: the reward of goodness, the fruits of victory.

The resurrection also brought in new life, a new humanity and the beginning of a new creation. His ascension in his glorified flesh to the right hand of the Father, above all the heavens, showed his power over all material and spiritual realms. Humanity on earth is now called to enter into this new spiritual realm, enter this new humanity in Christ, accessing it even while on earth. Jesus forgave those who abandoned him and offers the same forgiveness to all who turn to him. He also gave the gift of the Holy Spirit, which brought inner renewal, empowerment, and as they reflected on it, a sense that they were now caught up into the very life of God, made manifest in Jesus.

Repent and believe! Confess that Jesus is Lord and follow him in the power of the Holy Spirit!

How did, how does, one enter this new creation, and receive the Spirit? In the first place, by responding to the message brought by Jesus. The kingdom of God is at hand: repent and believe in Jesus Christ, for he is the Good News! Confess that Jesus is Lord, God who has come in the flesh. Begin the process of being conformed to his teaching, that is put on the mind of Christ and follow him. Be open to and co-operative with the action of the Holy Spirit within oneself. And be baptized.

He gives us life in the Spirit which is also life in the Church which is his body

Baptism matters since Christ came to reconcile us to each other as well as to God, and to form a people. Among other things, baptism requires the involvement of the Church and makes the recipient part of the Church. It is part of the work of Christ. One encounters Christ and his blessings there. Christ's teachings are given and expounded there. He gave a double command of love, of God and of neighbour. The saving action of God in Christ shows God is love: God gave us himself to save us from our sins, enabling us to receive the life of God, and so be formed in divine love, able to give ourselves to God and others in a pure and generous loving way.

This new kingdom, this new creation, this new humanity, which one has entered, is spiritual at heart, but also physical as we are physical. God works in it through flesh and through matter as he did in the life and actions of Jesus on earth. The Spirit comes in lots of ways but a guarantee of his ongoing presence is given in confirmation and the laying on of hands. The riches of his saving death and resurrection are made available to us in the Eucharist in which we encounter Christ. Those who are in Christ receive Christ, so as to be ever more fully converted into him to whom they have been converted.

Persevere until he comes! Go out and proclaim the good news that Jesus has come, is here and is coming!

Jesus, and the apostles after him, taught that what God was doing in him was decisive for all of humanity: Jesus will draw all people to himself – he is the centre of history. But Jesus also taught that not all the fruit would be given at once. There would be a gap before his full power, glory and judgement of all are made known publicly. This gap is the time of the Church. It is not an ordinary time: they are the last days, or if you prefer, the early hours of the day of the Lord, and not yet its full midday brightness. We live in hope, hope informed by knowledge of, and faith in, what Jesus has done and promised, mindful of his gracious mercy. We seek to co-operate with grace, being ever more fully transformed into the likeness of Christ. What he has done for us, he also intends to do in us: we are to die to sinfulness and rise to godliness.

That is not all Jesus planned for, even while on earth. He gave the apostles and many other disciples training and experience as missionaries, sending them out ahead of him, to say he was coming and to call people to conversion in preparation. He repeated this command after his resurrection, giving them the Holy Spirit specifically for this purpose. The Church exists to evangelize. As part of a new creation already breaking in, Christians are to build signs of it now in society, in works of merciful justice, which will help others, but also point to the kingdom to come. They are to share their testimony and, in expectant faith, preach and call people to faith. As heralds go ahead of a victorious king, to announce his coming and tell people to prepare, so Christians are to go out joyfully as heralds and preach the day of the Lord because Jesus Christ has come, is present and will come: 'Repent and believe the good news of Jesus Christ!'

Concluding practical remarks

The content earlier has a clear and organic link with the four gospels and their wider New Testament interpretation. It allows a full Catholic proclamation in a unified way, and comprehensive catechesis can be built upon it. It is also explicitly Christocentric and invites a conversion focused on Christ and through him on the Trinity into whose life we are introduced. Its narrative form may well appeal to contemporary sensibilities and it allows doctrinal, apologetic or other issues to be introduced in support of the narrative. As such, it allows proclamation to be integrated into a wider and longer journey towards and into conversion. It may still seem like a lot of material to come to grips with but I think it is manageable, something made easier by its division into sections. These allow for both contraction and expansion of the material. This is useful since flexibility in quantity and pacing of content is important in proclamation. According to need, the material could be contracted to the sub-headings, and some of these fused for even shorter summaries.[20]

---

[20] The gospel can be reduced to that most pithy and useful of summaries, beloved of the Church Fathers: In Jesus Christ, God took on human nature so that we could share in the divine nature. Jn 3.16 is another excellent summary.

The structure earlier could be used as the basis of the pre-catechetical (i.e. kerygmatic section) of the Rite of Christian Initiation of Adults (RCIA) – an area that tends to be poorly resourced and often superficially implemented (or even omitted) in this country.[21] A similar course could be run as part of new evangelization. In both these contexts, and perhaps others, it would be possible to adopt a format that integrates communal meals with a talk and then open discussion, a method that has been used in many evangelistic settings, including adult initiation. These accept that belonging, believing and behaving, all part of conversion, develop together.[22] Presentations can be more intellectual, testimonial or practical in tone, or a mixture, depending on speaker and audience. The style may likewise range from persuasion, to invitation to challenge. All these considerations point us back to the need to consider the nature of faith and conversion and thus to an earlier section. As such, this is a good place to end.

I hope I have managed to lay out useful foundations to help Catholics be more informed about the work of calling people to conversion to Christ. I also hope I have shown that being evangelical can make us more Catholic, not less: we do not need to fear proclamation as a threat to our identity.[23] Indeed we have far more to fear from not engaging in this crucial work, so needed in our secularized culture. Scepticism is best refuted by the joyful realization that in Jesus Christ, who is alive, God is in our midst to save us: we are not alone or the main protagonist in this work. It will be further refuted by actually trying to undertake this work, and persisting in it with faith and courage. So, however, we see fit to proclaim Christ, to make his presence known, and however we call people to conversion, let us take to heart the words of Blessed John Paul II and 'launch out into the deep'.[24]

---

[21] Official RCIA documentation (see Note 3), no. 36, 37 and 42, gives sparse but useful guidelines for the pre-catechumenate (evangelistic) phase.

[22] For those who wish to undertake such work, the following may offer useful support. The *General Dictionary of Catechesis* provides wise principles. Extensive explanation of principles and practical application are provided in Barbara A. Morgan and William J. Keimig (eds), *The RCIA Leaders' Manual* (2nd edition; Clinton, MA: The Association of Catechetical Ministry, 2007). The Maryvale Institute in Birmingham, UK has developed a number of courses, drawing in part on ACM resources.

[23] For a more focused discussion of the Evangelical–Catholic interface, see Andrew Brookes, 'Evangelical Catholics?' in Philip Knights (ed.), *Changing Evangelisation* (London: Churches Together in Britain and Ireland, 2007), pp. 37–46.

[24] John Paul II, *Novo Millenio Ineunte*, Apostolic Letter 'At the Close of the Great Jubilee of the Year 2000' (6 January 2001), p. 58. The whole document is a manifesto for evangelization as we entered the new millennium, organized around a presentation of Christ and a call to focus on him.

16

Meeting God in Friend and Stranger: Making the Theology of *Nostra Aetate* Relevant for Teaching and Practice in England and Wales

Katharina Smith-Müller

The one central question that this chapter aims to answer is a simple and, at the same time, complex one: 'why?' Why choose to get involved in another area of work, interreligious dialogue, in an already busy parish, when both priests and lay people are already pushed for time, and feel pulled many ways by the vast number of initiatives and expectations on them?

Meeting God in friend and stranger

One document that has been trying to answer that question for the Catholic community of England and Wales for the last 2 years is *Meeting God in Friend and Stranger: Fostering Mutual Respect and Understanding between the Religions*, a teaching document by the bishops of England and Wales that is widely available in both print and online.[1] One of the document's main achievements is its successful attempt to lay out the reasons why Catholics should view interreligious dialogue as something that is intrinsic to the work of the Church. It does this in clear and accessible language, on less than 100 A5 pages. The use of the document is further facilitated by study materials that provide summaries of each of the chapters, questions for discussion and ideas for action.[2]

---

[1] Catholic Bishops' Conference of England and Wales, *Meeting God in Friend and Stranger: Fostering Mutual Respect and Understanding between the Religions* (London: Catholic Bishops' Conference of England and Wales, 2010).

[2] These can be accessed at the website of the Catholic Bishops' Conference of England and Wales alongside the electronic copy of the document.

Why, then, does interreligious dialogue hold such importance? In its central chapter, 'Dialogue in the Teaching of the Catholic Church', a number of points are made that demonstrate just how closely dialogue is linked to the Church's mission. One central belief of the Church is that all human beings are linked by the same Creator, and by the same good plan that he has for all his creatures. In *Nostra aetate* (NA), the central Vatican II document on interreligious dialogue, this is put as follows: 'All nations are one community and have one origin, because God caused the whole human race to dwell on the face of the earth. They also have one final end, God, whose providence, manifestation of goodness and plans for salvation are extended to all' (NA 1). In his Christmas address to the Roman Curia in 1986, following the meeting of Christians from different denominations and non-Christian religions to pray for peace, Pope John Paul II evoked these words and called the unity of the human race 'radical, fundamental and decisive', stressing that 'differences are a less important element'.[3] From this, it follows that each human being has the same rights but also the same expectations placed on them: namely that they will respond to the calling of the God who created them by seeking his truth in their lives. The Church's defence of religious freedom springs exactly from this conviction, which also forms the basis for the promotion of dialogue that sees all partners involved as equals, and respects their right to seek the truth that all humans are seeking in the way they have discerned to be the right one.

The reasons for promoting the importance of interreligious dialogue, however, go deeper than this, and more to the core of the Church's self-understanding. The Church teaches that Jesus, 'rising from the dead, sent his life-giving Spirit upon his disciples and through this Spirit has established his body, the Church, as the universal sacrament of salvation' (*Lumen gentium* 48) meaning that the Church is, and should strive to be, an outward sign of the salvation that Christ brings. This also means that the Church has, in its interactions with others, to symbolize the real unity between all people that, as I discussed earlier, springs from the one God's good plan for all mankind, and from the universal brother- and sisterhood of being God's creatures. Similarly, the Church cannot afford to be the point at which dialogue ends. It has come into being, and continues to exist, only through the dialogue into which God enters with his Church.

In his encyclical *Ecclesiam suam* (6 August 1964), Pope Paul VI called this the 'dialogue of salvation' – God calling to his Church through his Son and

---

[3] John Paul II, Christmas Address to the Roman Curia (22 December 1986), p. 7.

through the Holy Spirit, a gift to the Church that is too valuable to limit to only one group of people (73). When Catholics go out, then, to seek out the other in interreligious dialogue, they continue that dialogue in which God continually engages his Church. It is, as the bishops of England and Wales put it, 'a continuation, knowingly or unknowingly by those involved, of that divine dialogue'.[4] It is this very connectedness by the One Spirit that also naturally leads on to a number of different, yet no less important, reasons for interreligious dialogue: the first one being the fact that the Holy Spirit is at work not only in the visible Church of Christ, but also beyond and outside it. Pope John Paul II affirms this in his encyclical letter *Redemptoris missio* (1990) saying that 'The Spirit's presence and activity affect not only individuals but also society and history, peoples, cultures and religions' (17). Realizing this not only leads, by necessity, to a degree of humbleness, and openness to the other in dialogue, but also opens the mind to the fact that the Church and other religions are deeply connected, and that, in dialogue, it is possible to find 'nuggets' of the same Truth, inspired by the same Holy Spirit, in the practice and in the faith of others. Not to pursue this avenue of uncovering what is true and holy would then mean that Christians neglect one of the ways in which they can come closer to their God and his revelation to humankind.

The belief that the same Spirit is at work in the whole world, and throughout history, brings another motivation for Christians. They can rely on the fact that God guides his Church and his people, and live in the certainty that God is calling his Church into dialogue by guiding the circumstances in which the Church finds itself. This is noticeable in a number of developments that bring to the forefront the need for Christians to engage with people of other religions. It has not been for all that long that Christians have lived side by side with Muslim and Hindu neighbours in England and Wales, and that events worldwide, now learned of and followed by a global community, have started to shape the fate, and the perception, of large groups within British society. Reading these signs of the times is a duty, and a great opportunity, for the Catholic community in England and Wales.

Dialogue and proclamation

The fact that all the reasons that motivate and, in fact, obligate the Church to seek dialogue with other religions are intimately tied into the beliefs and self-

---

[4] Catholic Bishops' Conference of England and Wales, *Meeting God in Friend and Stranger*, p. 43.

image of the Church also means that dialogue, when done properly, should not remain shallow. Merely by laying out why they are interested in interreligious dialogue, Catholics can get to the very heart of their faith, and, in this way, make sure that dialogue does not miss its greatest opportunity, namely the frank and honest witnessing to their faith by all parties involved. *Dialogue and Proclamation*, a document issued by the Pontifical Council for Inter-religious Dialogue on the anniversary of NA (1991), states this as follows: dialogue 'reaches a much deeper level, that of the spirit, where exchange and sharing consist in a mutual witness to one's beliefs and a common exploration of one's respective religious convictions' (40).[5] Beyond that, however, there is another opportunity to deepen the Christian faith in the encounter with the other. Inevitably, interreligious dialogue arrives at a point where it becomes obvious that, beyond all differences, and even commonalities, there is a point at which the other religion is exactly that – other, beyond our grasp, our understanding and outside the categories that we use to define the world. It is here that, once again, the encounter with the stranger can lead us straight back to an encounter with God: his ways are mysterious, and can never be fully understood by us, however close a relationship we may have with him. In this way, the prayer life of a Christian should and can be a training ground for the ability to engage with the other without wanting to reduce its strangeness, or to make it fit preconceptions, and strengthening both: our relationship with God, and our relationship with our fellow human beings.

The attempt to move interreligious dialogue to the centre of the work of the Church, where it rightly belongs, is sometimes met with scepticism by people who care deeply about sharing the message of Christ, who can feel that an orientation towards other religions is inappropriate when the Church should be making every effort to invest in the formation of its people, and in making the Christian message known to all. There can also be fear that interreligious dialogue might be confusing to Christians who are not as firmly rooted in their faith as is desirable, and that it will send out the incorrect message that all religions are essentially the same, with some small cultural differences, or variations in worship. However, this is a misunderstanding. While of course interreligious dialogue as it is intended by the Church does not aim to convert the dialogue partner, it is still witnessing to the joy that Christians take in the Gospel. Here, *Meeting God in Friend and Stranger* mirrors the helpful distinction made by John

[5] Pontifical Council for Inter-Religious Dialogue, *Dialogue and Proclamation. Reflection and Orientations on Interreligious Dialogue and the Proclamation of the Gospel of Jesus Christ* (19 May 1991).

Paul II in *Redemptoris missio* between proclamation and dialogue, both of which he defines as a subgroup of the same legitimate drive to spread the good news of Jesus Christ, for which he uses the term evangelization.[6] In *Redemptoris missio*, John Paul II puts this into very clear words: 'the Church sees no conflict between proclaiming Christ and engaging in interreligious dialogue' (55).

Proclamation and dialogue share in common that they both involve witnessing to and sharing of own beliefs, albeit with different intentions. In fact, dialogue that respects the other and the other's cultural and personal situation, making her aware of the good news without forcing it on her, reflects exactly the ministry of Christ. It is thus, as the bishops of England and Wales put it, 'profoundly Christ-like work', which is an opportunity and a training ground for realizing Christian values such as love of neighbour and openness to the other and the contexts of their lives, as well as the background for their actions.[7]

Interestingly enough, it is precisely when people are very honest about their convictions and beliefs, and also about what they feel is non-negotiable in them, that interreligious dialogue is at its best. For any Christian, these non-negotiable items of faith include that Jesus Christ is the Son of God, true God and true man. Ironically, this deep conviction, and the sharing of it, is sometimes avoided as there is a fear that it will cause offence to those belonging to other religions. But this undermines the effort to make dialogue, when it focuses on the sharing of faith, about the very things that are at the heart of each of the religions involved. Deep dialogue occurs when participants articulate their own faith, and react to the questions that are posed by others. Often enough, these are challenging not because they are outlandish, but because they go to the very core of beliefs, due to the freshness of the outsider's perspective. This perspective will not allow Christians to hide behind received wisdom or pious phrases. This in turn leads, in the experience of almost every practitioner, to a renewed desire, and in fact a renewed need, to learn about and to reflect on his or her own, Christian, faith.

In fact, it is often through interreligious dialogue that it is learned that religions are not all the same, and that taking them seriously goes beyond a vague talk of spiritual needs that are common to all people. By engaging with other religions in a respectful manner, this message is broadcast loud and clear: precisely because religions are not 'all the same', it is so important that they cooperate, and know about each other; that they are also aware of where commonalities end, and can

---

[6] Catholic Bishops' Conference of England and Wales, *Meeting God in Friend and Stranger*, pp. 85–6.
[7] Ibid., p. 8.

state this without fear of causing offence to anyone. In this way, interreligious dialogue is not a one-way street that leads to the other, but a round trip that leads ever deeper into the original faith of the people involved.

Another important part that interreligious dialogue can play in the deepening of faith is the inspiration that is taken from the practice of others. In fact, Benedict XVI, during his 2010 visit to the United Kingdom, encouraged Catholics to 'shar[e] their spiritual riches' stressing that all people of faith make a unique and deeply important contribution to society.[8] Practically, the deep connection that is made by praying for each other, and in the presence of each other, also means that people who get involved in interreligious dialogue often have a new-found appreciation of prayer. Prayer is also a means of engagement that can be carried on where other avenues are blocked, and that is appropriate in even the tensest or most complicated situations. In my practical experience, it is the people of faith who actually appreciate the assurance of prayer, and appreciate the prayerfulness of a dialogue partner as an inspiration to them.

Choosing this expression – 'spiritual riches' – Benedict XVI indirectly picked up the wide definition of dialogue that the Church is promoting, opening up the notion of dialogue to a wide range of people who might feel that they are not in an ideal position to enter into dialogue. This also promotes the special role that lay people, who have everyday contact with people of other religions, play in this endeavour of the Church. The four different types of dialogue that come from *Dialogue and Proclamation* are the dialogue of life; the dialogue of action; the dialogue of theological exchange and the dialogue of religious experience (42). Interestingly enough, it is this last type of dialogue, the one which, in my experience, more conservative Catholics are most wary about, that, since NA, has had a long history of popes engaging in it – most notably, perhaps, Pope John Paul II's silent moment of prayer and contemplation at the Central Synagogue in Rome, on the same occasion at which he called the Jews our 'beloved older brothers'.[9] More recently, the conferral of the Papal Knighthood on a Sikh leader (alongside the Catholic coordinator for the Birmingham Archdiocese) has given a moving and colourful example of the dialogue of religious experience, especially when the service closed with a Sikh hymn that was performed inside the Cathedral.

---

[8] Benedict XVI, Meeting with clerical and lay representatives of other religions, St Mary's University College, London (17 September 2010).
[9] John Paul II, Allocution in the Great Roman Synagogue (13 April 1986). English translation at http://www.sacredheart.edu/faithservice/centerforchristianandjewishunderstanding/ documentsandstatements/johnpauliiallocutioninthegreatromansynagogueapril131986/ (Accessed on 27 February 2014).

Making the theology of NA relevant in England and Wales

So what shape does the interreligious work of Catholics in England and Wales take practically, in parishes, on the diocesan level, and nationally? First, it is important to say that this is work that rests largely on the shoulders of volunteers, unpaid people of good will, who need and deserve the support of the wider community. It is easy for them to see themselves as 'lone callers in the desert'. This is why there is a national network of diocesan interreligious advisers who, in turn, form teams in their dioceses to take forward the work which is so necessary in our time. They meet twice a year to share good practice and important experiences. The exact role of these coordinators does, of course, vary from diocese to diocese, but many organize central events such as the shared pilgrimage of Muslim and Catholic women to the shrine of Our Lady in Jesmond, Newcastle-upon-Tyne in 2012, which was the third year running in which women came together to pray. This event uses the fact that Mary is an important figure to both Muslims and Christians, having a whole sura (chapter) dedicated to herself in the Qur'an.

In other areas, contact with other religions is hard to come by, and the main task of the Diocesan commission can be to prepare young people for an eventual encounter, for example when leaving home for university, by educating them on other religions and giving them the chance to visit places of worship on longer trips. Often, it also falls to these teams to organize events to mark special days and occasions, such as Holocaust Memorial Day, which benefit from a whole community standing together, or lighter events that give people of different religions a chance to engage – interfaith cricket matches are just one such example. A large part of their mission is also the work inside the Catholic community, making other Catholics aware of the need for, and the benefits of, interreligious dialogue, and training them in spotting opportunities for dialogue where they arise.

It is, however, also important to note that very good work is done too by people who do not have a special appointment for interreligious work. In fact, interreligious dialogue is so intrinsically linked with the areas of work that the Church rightly considers central to her mission that they can be appropriate avenues for interreligious dialogue. On a parish level, this means that events do not need to be specifically interreligious. Parish festivals, toddler groups, fundraising to help the poor and youth work – all areas of work covered by parishes already – can be easily transformed into interreligious events by inviting along representatives of local congregations of other religions, and by organizing them in an open, welcoming way that reflects the unprejudiced love and openness of Jesus's ministry. On a less local level, it can mean that the person best placed to promote interreligious dialogue on the diocesan level is a lay person who is engaged in one of the many areas that, in its normal course, brings about contact with other religions. This might be the charitable work of a diocese, or the care for migrants and travellers that is, rightly and thankfully, taken very seriously in many areas of England and Wales. Care for Catholics in education, be it at schools, sixth form colleges or universities, also brings rich and diverse opportunities for encounters with people of other religions. Often, this is not an encounter that is intended, or branded in any way as interreligious dialogue, but an almost inevitable coming together of people of faith in situations where this faith becomes particularly important to them. These are valuable and valued occasions, and demonstrate the very spirit of meeting on the road, and walking together, that is so very present in Christ's ministry.

This principle is also reflected on a national level, where social action and development work are becoming increasingly ecumenical and interreligious, in a recognition that there is an abundance of concerns and values that are shared by all people of faith, be they the dignity of the dying, the centrality of family life or a concern for vulnerable people who have difficulties in making themselves heard in society. It also recognizes the fact that only speaking with one voice will ensure that the priorities that people of faith share are not seen as a minority pursuit, but as central to the way most people in society want to live their lives. It is true, after all, that over two-thirds of people in England and Wales declared a belonging to a religion in the recent census.[10] Interreligious work often means recognizing that this is the case, and acting as a connection point between those people who have knowledge about and confidence in engaging with people of other faiths, and between those who work in areas where interreligious dialogue happens almost as a by-product of work that is already going on. Equally important, it consists of encouragement given to good work, and generous openness to encounters that would otherwise go unnoticed and, due to this, perhaps unappreciated. In that sense, interreligious work is concerned with spotting the sacramental signs of the kingdom of God in this world – a brief that could not be more central to the mission of the Church.

Lay Catholics are also widely engaged in existing interreligious organizations, such as faith forums, and are encouraged to be so by their bishops. Without a

[10] Office for National Statistics, *Religion in England and Wales 2011.* http://www.ons.gov.uk/ons/dcp171776_290510.pdf.

special mandate, they succeed in contributing a uniquely Catholic perspective simply by witnessing to their faith and the life of their community within existing frameworks. Many Catholic parishes and individuals do, for example, take part in peace walks that are organized all over the country, and gain special relevance in 2012 with the Olympic Games and its associated peaceful togetherness of athletes of all origins and beliefs. Initiatives on a national level and beyond can provide resources and encouragement for this work, but is often secondary when a local need has been identified, and can never replace the engagement at the grassroots that is so valuable in the peace and community-building function that interreligious dialogue can also fulfil. The work interlinks ideally where central initiatives are fruitful for the local work, as is, for example, widely experienced in the case of the greeting messages that the Holy See offers on the festivals of other religions. Local Catholics take these as opportunities to expressly acknowledge the people of other religions, and their places of worship, in their neighbourhood, and to bring good wishes on the celebration of their festivals.

Conclusion

Overall, then, many Catholics in England and Wales have received, and acted on, the wisdom of the Second Vatican Council, and, particularly in this context, the call to dialogue which is expressed in NA. The bishops of England and Wales have provided a focus, and a justification, for the engagement in interreligious dialogue, which has in turn strengthened the important local work that is carried out by many Catholics. As with many teachings of the Second Vatican Council, however, their reception on the ground could still be wider, and more comprehensive, and there is some work to do still to make sure that every Catholic sees interreligious dialogue as an intrinsic part of the work they are called to do by their baptism. This should, however, be seen as a motivational rather than a negative development: the very fact that the task ahead is large should lead back, once again, to the rich faith present in the Catholic community, and the trust it rightly has in God leading his Church to do what is right, and what furthers his Kingdom, or, as the bishops of England and Wales put it: 'to turn away from even the attempt to dialogue is to despair of the power of God and of his risen Son to advance his own Kingdom of peace and love.'[11]

---

[11] *Meeting God in Friend and Stranger*, p. 88.

17

Conclusion

Paul Grogan

The conference which was the foundational event for this book provided those of us who participated in it with an opportunity to 'reframe' our experience of life within the Church.[1] An abiding temptation, I have found, is to focus unduly upon factors such as declining congregations out of a desire to confront reality head on. However, this leads us, paradoxically, into unreality: we perceive ourselves merely in terms of being besieged and marginalized; the result is paralysis. In this context, the new evangelization is profoundly liberating. The Church dismantles her defences, not because she is defeated, but because only so can she engage in her primary task, namely the service of all (*Gaudium et spes* 3). Moreover, the Church which has in many places been definitively excluded from the public square is now striding purposefully with St Paul to speak to the Council of the Areopagus (Acts 17.19–34).

The chapters in this volume show how the new evangelization is a natural progression of the Second Vatican Council, which was essentially missionary.[2] When Pope John XXIII called the Council, he was well aware of the profound crisis of secularism which had already begun to affect the Church and which has simply become more marked in subsequent decades.[3] This crisis is so massive that it has been compared with the fall of the Roman Empire in terms of its historical

---

[1] See Austen Ivereigh, *How to Defend the Faith Without Raising Your Voice: Civil Responses to Catholic Hot-button Issues* (Huntington, IN: Our Sunday Visitor, 2012).

[2] John Paul II, *Redemptoris missio* (1990), p. 1.

[3] Mathijs Lamberigts, Chapter 2, this volume. Also, Walter Kasper, 'Neue Evangelisierung – eine pastorale, theologische und geistliche Herausforderung', in Augustin George and Klaus Kramer (eds), *Mission als Herausforderung: Impulse zur Neuevangelisierung* (Freiburg: Herder, 2011), pp. 23–41 (p. 26).

impact.[4] The new evangelization does not constitute an emergency strategy: it is a renewed engagement of the Church in her perennial task of drawing people to Christ, albeit within cultures which have become particularly hostile to the truth claims of Catholicism. Moreover, it is aimed not just at revivifying the 'tired faith' of people in the West[5]: it is global, adapting itself to overcome whatever social circumstances in a given region impede inhabitants' capacity to assent to the gospel which has already been proclaimed there in an earlier period of evangelization.[6]

Conversion is the leitmotif of the new evangelization

One of the remarkable aspects of the current life of the Church is that those who are engaged in new evangelization projects are frequently irrepressibly joyful, regardless of the limited success of their work. On the other hand, many Catholics find it profoundly unsettling to be in a Church which is in a state of transition. Indeed, it often feels that the Church we once knew is dying. In these circumstances, our ability to engage in evangelization is to a large extent governed by how much we have processed the negative feelings associated with loss. Here new explorations by psychologists of the dynamics of institutional change, based on Elizabeth Kübler Ross's description of the stages of coping with terminal illness, can be very helpful.[7] Most of us have moved beyond a first stage of denial but many are still caught somewhere in a second stage of resistance – hence, for example, the frequently passionate opposition to parish closures – or in a third stage of exploration, where activity is rather unfocused. Only a few have reached a fourth stage of integration which is marked by a new vision and by more purposeful activity.[8]

What is happening on the psychological level is also a spiritual reality. We are participating in the Paschal Mystery. The dying is necessary if the new life is

---

[4] Rino Fisichella, *La nuova evangelizzazione: une sfida per uscire dall'indifferenza* (Milano: Mondadori, 2011), p. 6. See also Frédéric Manns, *Qu'est-ce que la nouvelle évangélisation?* (Montrouge Cedex: Bayard, 2012), pp. 18–26.
[5] Benedict XVI, *Homily for Maundy Thursday* (21 April 2011).
[6] Fernando Filoni (Chapter 9) and John F. Gorski (Chapter 3), this volume.
[7] See, for example, Esther Cameron and Mike Green, *Making Sense of Change Management: A Complete Guide to the Models, Tools and Techniques of Organizational Change* (3rd edition; London: Kogan Page, 2012).
[8] The Dioceses of Québec and Washington seem to be moving in this direction. See Gérald LaCroix, *La nouvelle évangélisation: urgence de réfléchir; urgence d'agir* (Forum; Montréal: Université de Montréal, 2012); Donald Wuerl, *New Evangelization: Passing on the Catholic Faith Today* (Huntington, IN: Our Sunday Visitor, 2013).

to be experienced. If we saw things with the eyes of faith, we would not want to retain the same Church infrastructure which is now in crisis. We cannot cling to the beauty of any particular moment in the unfolding of the life of the Church, just as Peter was foolish in seeking to prolong the moment of the Transfiguration so as to avoid Jesus's 'passing' which it proclaimed (Lk. 19.28–36). Like Peter, we are being called to conversion. The new evangelization is nothing other than individual Catholics living their faith more intensely,[9] which is why it is both so exhilarating and so deeply challenging.

The intrinsic connection between conversion and evangelization was expressed very beautifully by Pope Paul VI: '[the Church] has a constant need of being evangelized if she wishes to retain freshness, vigour and strength in proclaiming the gospel.' The way in which this evangelization takes place is through the Church 'listen[ing] unceasingly to what she must believe.'[10] An important part of this 'listening' is the process by which the Church receives what the Holy Spirit is saying to her precisely through the teachings of the Council.[11] Our conference demonstrated how this process is multifaceted, takes time and requires diligence and planning – and is fruitful.[12]

The process of receptivity is often considered from an intra-ecclesial perspective: post-conciliar debates have focused upon the issue of adherence to magisterial teaching. However, in the frame of reference provided by the new evangelization, receptivity is shown to have a profound extra-ecclesial significance. If, as the Council teaches, all the members of the Church are co-responsible for evangelization (*Ad gentes* 11) all are called upon personally to appropriate that which the Church teaches and to be transformed by it in order that they may transmit it to others, not least through the witness of their lives.[13]

The evangelization of the Church

How then is the Church to be evangelized by her own Council in this privileged moment of ecclesial and personal conversion? I suggest that a simple way of responding to this question would be to allow Jesus to exhort us as he did those whom he addressed in his very first public utterance: 'The time is fulfilled, and

---

[9] Benedict XVI, *Porta fidei* (2011), p. 13.
[10] Paul VI, *Evangelii nuntiandi* (1975), p. 15.
[11] John Paul II, *Redemptoris missio*, p. 1.
[12] Richard K. Baawobr, Chapter 10, this volume.
[13] Paul VI, *Evangelii nuntiandi*, p. 21.

the kingdom of God has come near; repent, and believe in the good news' (Mk 1.15). I will look briefly at three realities emerging from this exhortation: the urgency of the moment; the centrality of Christ and the Church as the sacrament of Christ.

The new evangelization is characterized by a double urgency. First, it constitutes a call to members of the Church to emerge from a collective amnesia about the beauty of the apostolic tradition which has been entrusted to them.[14] Fundamental to this is a revivification of the sacramental imagination so that the immediacy of Christ's intervention in our lives in the power of the Holy Spirit may be more fully apprehended. Secondly, there is the urgency of responding to unbelief. Many of us have underestimated how dark life can be without faith in Christ and how needful people are for us to intervene in their lives in his name and draw them into community with us.[15]

Christ, and this is the second point, is actually all we have to offer people (see Acts 3.6). The kingdom which he proclaimed is revealed principally in his Person (*Lumen gentium* 6). A good question to ask therefore is whether the profound Christocentrism of the Council[16] has penetrated into Catholic culture in the West? I think that in fact there are indications of a drift towards a general theism, and this for two reasons: the latter is perceived to be less in conflict with other faith groups' understanding of God in our increasingly religiously pluralistic society; also, it is mistakenly perceived to be a more defensible position in the face of the aggressive atheism which is such a feature of our times.

Yet this new atheism is merely a rejection of an Enlightenment God which bears no resemblance to the God of Jesus Christ. It might be said that it is precisely through Christians' timidity about speaking of the Blessed Trinity that atheism has for the moment gained such a purchase in the collective psyche.[17] The Council texts are a profound encouragement to us to embrace once more the 'scandal of particularity' which the doctrine of the Incarnation requires. Jesus is the sole saviour of the world (Acts 4.12) and the sole mediator between God and humankind (1 Tim. 2.5). The Christian God is not a remote being whose existence, or lack of, can be coolly assessed according to the criteria of the positive sciences as if he belonged to the created order; rather, as St Paul noted in Athens, 'in him we live and move and have our being' (Acts 17.28) – he is the

[14] Benedict XVI, *Message for the 26th World Youth Day*, 2011; also, Andrew Brookes, Chapter 15, this volume.
[15] Francis, *Evangelii gaudium* (2013), p. 49.
[16] Tracey Rowland, Chapter 4, this volume.
[17] I am indebted for this insight to John McDade, Trinity Lecture, Leeds Trinity University, 2011.

ground of all truth, in other words – and he has revealed himself to us in his Son (Jn 14.9). This Son in turn reveals us to ourselves: as the Council so evocatively noted, it is 'only in the mystery of the incarnate Word' that 'the mystery of man takes on light' (*Gaudium et spes* 22).

From this, much follows. For a start, the purpose of human life becomes, as recent Popes have startlingly noted, entering into friendship with Jesus Christ.[18] Christian life is irreducibly relational[19] and it cannot be lived as a thin observance of 'kingdom values'. An indicator of this Christocentrism within the new evangelization is the increased usage of the terms 'discipleship' and 'vocation' to describe the Christian life: a disciple is one who follows the Master who has called him or her.[20] Discipleship requires us to 'go out of ourselves'[21] and to serve others unstintingly, following his example (Jn 13.12–15), and while this may initially seem daunting and unattractive, in fact experience shows us that a life lived according to the dictates of generosity corresponds with our deepest needs. In this, we detect our likeness to God (Gen. 1.27) who in Christ is revealed as a unity of Persons bound together in an eternal movement of reciprocal self-donation.[22] Lastly, reflection on the Incarnation allows the Church to help each person to perceive his or her incomparable dignity. In a culture which rightly champions the concept of human rights, the Church is in a position to explain the provenance of those rights and thus to promote justice and peace in a more coherent fashion than any other body.

Through focusing anew upon Christ, we gain a fresh understanding of the Church, which is the 'seed' of the kingdom which he proclaimed and which 'shone' out in him (*Lumen gentium* 5). Often evangelization projects are evaluated in terms of whether they contribute to the growth of the Church as a 'visible society' but this is to operate from an outdated ecclesiology. Once we have accepted that the Church is a sign or sacrament drawing all people into unity with God and with one another (*Lumen gentium* 1), or in other words that its essential nature is 'communion' understood in both its horizontal and vertical dimensions, the process of reaching out to people in Christ's name assumes a new, rich and mysterious quality. It remains true that the purpose of proclaiming

---

[18] See, for example, Benedict XVI, Homily 'For the Beginning of his Petrine Ministry as the Bishop of Rome' (24 April 2005).
[19] See, for example, Sherry A. Weddell, *Forming Intentional Disciples: The Path to Knowing and Following Jesus* (Huntington, IN: Our Sunday Visitor, 2012).
[20] Francis, *Evangelii gaudium*, p. 119.
[21] Ibid., p. 20.
[22] Petroc Willey, Chapter 13, this volume.

Christ is ultimately to incorporate people into his Church,[23] but the very act of fostering unity becomes an integral part of the salvific process, not a prelude to it.[24] Besides, the emphasis upon personal conversion which lies at the heart of the new evangelization is a reminder that ecclesial unity is not something which is simply possessed by the affiliates and lacking in those still searching: rather it is that which the Holy Spirit is incessantly cultivating both within and without the visible corporate communion.

Once we embrace the fact that Christ is drawing us all into that unity of which the Church is a sacrament, some striking truths emerge which were treated in-depth at our Conference. First, relationships within the Church assume a new importance. In this regard, and perhaps surprisingly, the importance of papal and episcopal authority is underscored precisely because if the communion were not hierarchical it would dissolve (*Lumen gentium* 18). Secondly, the principle of radical equality of all members of the Church by virtue of baptism becomes apparent. The hierarchy is raised up so that it may serve those whom it governs and some of those whom the bishops govern also need to exercise leadership within the Church according to the charisms which they have received.[25] Thirdly, relational dysfunctionality within the Church, as manifested for example in clericalism, misogyny or homophobia, is seen to be a major issue precisely because it corrodes the Church's core identity, that is a communion of persons: addressing such social sins thus becomes a priority. Fourthly, the ecclesiology of communion points the way to 'world Catholicism', or in other words a truly 'networked Church'[26] which allows for a mutual enrichment of local churches. In Cardinal George's phrase: 'everyone gives, everyone receives';[27] and as Cardinal Filoni tellingly notes, the newer churches are 'open to a fuller meaning of life' than in the West.[28] In this context, the unreflective assumption of superiority on the part of churches in the developed world is turned on its head. The qualities of African Catholic culture, for example, as described in *Africae munus*,[29] constitute that which most Catholics in the developed world are yearning for: for example, strong family life, respect for elders, a generosity of spirit manifested in working for the common good. Fifthly, ecumenical and inter-religious dialogue become

---

[23] John F. Gorski, Chapter 3, this volume.
[24] Susan K. Wood, Chapter 5, this volume. One can think here of ecclesial movements such as the Focolare Movement, which seeks to foster unity, and the Sant'Egidio Community, which seeks to resolve conflicts.
[25] *Catechism of the Catholic Church*, p. 799.
[26] Ian Linden, Chapter 8, this volume.
[27] Francis George, Chapter 6, this volume.
[28] Fernando Filani, Chapter 9, this volume.
[29] Benedict XVI, *Africae munus* (2011).

in their several ways occasions for ongoing personal conversion for Catholics who find that God calls to them through the witness of faith of those whom they encounter.[30]

The evangelizing Church

As the Church becomes more evangelized by her Council, what principles might guide her in fulfilling her role as being, in him, a herald of his good news? A few points occur to me, reflecting on the chapters in this volume. First, given that faith in Jesus Christ is the normative way of attaining to that fullness of humanity which God desires all people should enjoy, we cannot be indifferent to the fact that so many people have no relationship at all with Jesus Christ. The 'easy universalism' with regard to salvation[31] which seemed so ground-breaking in the immediate post-conciliar years is now being critiqued.[32] In our time the terminology of 'saving souls' no longer seems archaic, albeit that salvation is seen in terms of inclusion within the communion rather than as a hyper-individualistic escape from death.

Secondly, evangelization is not in the first instance our job: it is the work of the Holy Spirit; as Fr Richard Baawobr notes pithily, 'God saves, we don't.'[33] The role of members of the Church is to cooperate with the Spirit in his mission. This truth is powerfully enunciated in *Nostra aetate*'s vision of Christians receiving and then handing on the Father's communication to humanity in the Son (*Nostra aetate* 2). Evangelization, seen thus, is nothing less than a participation in the life of the Blessed Trinity. It is, on our part, perhaps the fullest expression of charity of which we are capable (2 Cor. 5.14): we are sharing with others that which is most precious to us. The power of our 'personal influence' in Christ on others is incalculable.[34] Seen in this light, evangelization acquires the character of self-offering on the part of the evangelizer modelled on and drawing strength from Christ's self-offering in the Eucharist.

Thirdly, the fact that we have had only limited success to date in engaging in the new evangelization makes possible a new sharing in Christ's passion and

---

[30] Gavin D'Costa (Chapter 11), Annemarie Mayer (Chapter 12), Katharina Smith-Müller (Chapter 16), Paul D. Murray (Chapter 7), this volume.
[31] Francis George, Chapter 6, this volume.
[32] See, for example, Ralph Martin, *Will Many Be Saved? What Vatican II Actually Teaches and Its Implications for the New Evangelization* (Grand Rapids, MI: William B. Eerdmans, 2012).
[33] Richard K. Baawobr, Chapter 10, this volume.
[34] Stephen Morgan, Chapter 14, this volume.

hence becomes a new moment of fruitfulness for us. That which we most fear, insignificance (at least in the eyes of many), we are being called upon to embrace. No guarantee is offered to us concerning when the Church's mission might prove more successful. In the midst of this uncertainty and with our human resources, in many nations, severely depleted, we are instructed to persevere. It has been noted by many that beauty constitutes an essential part of the new evangelization. I know of few things more beautiful (nor more suggestive of the power of the Holy Spirit) than the fidelity of a small and dwindling group of septuagenarians continuing the charitable activities of a parish St Vincent de Paul Society or the steeliness of a young woman resolutely continuing to go to Sunday Mass at university when so many of her peers have given up.

Bibliography

Conciliar documents

Vatican I

Dei Filius: Dogmatic Constitution on the Catholic Faith, in Josef Neuner and Jacques Dupuis (eds), *The Christian Faith* (revised edition; London: Collins, 1982).
Pastor Aeternus, in Josef Neuner and Jacques Dupuis (eds), *The Christian Faith* (revised edition; London: Collins, 1982).

Vatican II

English translations are available on the website of the Holy See at http://www.vatican.va/archive/hist_councils/iI_vatican_council/index.htm.

Constitutions

Sacrosanctum concilium (SC), 'Constitution on the Sacred Liturgy' (4 December 1963).
Lumen gentium (LG), 'Dogmatic Constitution on the Church' (21 November 1964).
Dei verbum (DV), 'Dogmatic Constitution on Divine Revelation' (18 November 1965).
Gaudium et spes (GS), 'Pastoral Constitution on the Church in the Modern World' (7 December 1965).

Declarations

Nostra aetate (NA), 'Declaration on the Relation of the Church to Non-Christian Religions' (28 October 1965).
Dignitatis humanae (DH), 'Declaration on Religious Freedom' (7 December 1965).

Decrees

Ad gentes (AG), 'Decree on the Missionary Activity of the Church' (2 December 1965).
Unitatis redintegratio (UR), 'Decree on Ecumenism' (21 November 1964).
Apostolicam actuositatem, 'Decree on the Apostolate of the Laity' (18 November 1965).
Presbyterorum ordinis, 'Decree on the Ministry and Life of Priests' (7 December 1965).
Christus dominus, 'Decree Concerning the Pastoral Office of Bishops in the Church' (28 October 1965).

Papal documents

Unless otherwise stated, English translations are available on the website of the Holy
    See at www.vatican.va.
Pius XI, *Mortalium animos*, 'Encyclical Letter on Fostering Religious Union' (6 January
    1928).
Pius XII, *Mystici corporis christi*, 'On the Mystical Body of Christ' (29 June 1943).
— *Humani generis*, 'Concerning Some False Opinions Threatening to Undermine the
    Foundations of Catholic Doctrine' (12 August 1950).

Paul VI

Pope Paul VI, *Ecclesiam suam*, Encyclical on the Church (6 August 1964).
— Address for the Closing of the Third General Assembly of the Synod of Bishops
    (26 October 1974).
— *Evangelii nuntiandi*, Apostolic Exhortation 'On Evangelization in the Modern World'
    (8 December 1975).

John Paul II

John Paul II, *Redemptor hominis*, Encyclical 'At the Beginning of His Papal Ministry'
    (4 March 1979).
— Homily at the Shrine of the Holy Cross, Mogila, Poland (9 June 1979).
— Meeting with Visiting Jewish representatives, Mainz (17 November 1980).
— *Dives in misericordia*, Encyclical 'On Divine Mercy' (30 November 1980).
— Speech to the XIX Assembly of CELAM, Port au Prince (9 March 1983).
— Address to the Roman Curia (21 December 1984).
— Address to Representatives of Different Religions in Madras, India (5 February
    1986).
— Allocution in the Great Roman Synagogue (13 April 1986).
— *Dominum et vivificantem*, Encyclical 'On the Holy Spirit in the Life of the Church
    and the World' (18 May 1986).
— Address to the Aborigines and Torres Strait Islanders in Blatherskite Park, Alice
    Springs (29 November 1986).
— Christmas Address to the Roman Curia (22 December 1986).
— *Christifideles laici*, Apostolic Exhortation 'On the Vocation and the Mission of the
    Lay Faithful in the Church and in the World' (30 December 1988).
— *Redemptoris missio*, Encyclical 'On the Permanent Validity of the Church's
    Missionary Mandate' (7 December 1990).
— *Fidei depositum*, Apostolic Constitution 'On the Publication of the Catechism of the
    Catholic Church' (11 October 1992).

— Inaugural Address, The Fourth General Conference of the Latin American Bishops, Santo Domingo (12 October 1992).

— *Ut unum sint*, Encyclical 'On Commitment to Ecumenism' (25 May 1995).

— *Ecclesia in Africa*, Apostolic Exhortation (14 September 1995).

— 'Apostolic Visit to Germany, June 21–23, 1996', *L'Osservatore Romano*, Weekly English Edition 27/5 (3 July 1996).

— *Fides et ratio*, Encyclical 'On the Relationship Between Faith and Reason' (14 September 1998).

— *Ecclesia in America*, Apostolic Exhortation (22 January 1999).

— *Ecclesia in Asia*, Apostolic Exhortation (6 November 1999).

— *Novo millenio ineunte*, Apostolic Letter 'At the Close of the Great Jubilee of the Year 2000' (6 January 2001).

Benedict XVI

Benedict XVI, Homily 'For the Beginning of his Petrine Ministry as the Bishop of Rome' (24 April 2005).

— 'A Proper Hermeneutic for the Second Vatican Council', in Matthew L. Lamb and Matthew Levering (eds), *Vatican II: Renewal within Tradition* (New York: Oxford University Press, 2008), pp. ix–xv.

— *Caritas in veritate*, Encyclical 'On Integral Human Development in Charity and Truth' (29 June 2009).

— Message for the 26th World Youth Day, 2011 (6 August 2010).

— Meeting with Clerical and Lay Representatives of Other Religions, St Mary's University College, London (17 September 2010).

— *Ubicumque et semper*, Apostolic Letter issued Motu Proprio 'Establishing the Pontifical Council for Promoting the New Evangelization' (21 September 2010).

— General Audience, St Peter's Square, Rome (22 September 2010).

— 'Foreword', in *Youcat* (San Francisco: Ignatius Press, 2011), pp. 6–11.

— Homily for Maundy Thursday (21 April 2011).

— Address to the *Bundestag* (22 September 2011).

— *Porta fidei*, Apostolic Letter issued Motu Proprio 'For the Indiction of the Year of Faith' (11 October 2011).

— *Africae munus*, Post-Synodal Apostolic Exhortation 'On the Church in Africa in Service to Reconciliation, Justice and Peace' (19 November 2011).

— *Fides per doctrinum*, Apostolic Letter issued Motu Proprio (16 January 2013).

Francis I

Francis, *Evangelii gaudium*, Post-Synodal Apostolic Exortation 'On the Proclamation of the Gospel in Today's World' (24 November 2013).

— General Audience (22 January 2014).

Other documents

Archevêché de Lubumbashi, Commission Centrale Préparatoire du Synode, *IIième Synode diocésaine. L'Eglise – Famille de Dieu de Lubumbashi: Bilan et perspectives. Lineamenta* (30 July 2011); *Instrumentum laboris* (2 February 2012).

Catechism of the Catholic Church (English revised edition; London: Burns & Oates, 1999).

Catholic Bishops' Conference of England and Wales, *Meeting God in Friend and Stranger. Fostering Mutual Respect and Understanding between the Religions* (London: Catholic Bishops' Conference of England and Wales, 2010).

CELAM, Report of the Second Latin American Bishops' Conference (CELAM) in Medellín, Colombia, 1968, at http://www.celam.org/conferencia_medellin.php.

— Report of the Third Latin American Bishops' Conference (CELAM) in Puebla, Mexico in 1979, at http://www.celam.org/conferencia_puebla.php.

Conférence des évêques de France, 'Proposer la foi dans la société actuelle', Lettre aux Catholiques de France' (9 November 1996), at http://www.eglise.catholique.fr/.

Congregation for the Clergy, *General Directory of Catechesis* (London: CTS/Vatican City: Libreria Editrice Vaticana, 1997).

Congregation for the Doctrine of the Faith, Letter 'On Some Aspects of Christian Meditation' (1989).

— Letter 'On Some Aspects of The Church Understood as Communion' (28 May 1992).

— *Dominus Iesus*, 'On the Unicity and Salvific Universality of Jesus Christ and the Church' (6 August 2000).

— Doctrinal Note 'On Some Aspects of Evangelization' (3 December 2007).

International Commission on English in the Liturgy (ICEL), *Rite of Christian Initiation of Adults* (ICEL, 1985), at www.liturgyoffice.org.uk.

International Theological Commission, 'Faith and Inculturation', *Origins* 18/47 (1989), pp. 800–7.

Pontifical Council for Promoting New Evangelization, *Enchiridion della Nuova Evangelizzazione: testi del Magistero pontificio e conciliare 1939–2012* (Vatican City: Libreria Editrice Vaticana, 2012).

Pontifical Council for Interreligious Dialogue and the Congregation for the Evangelization of Peoples, *Dialogue and Proclamation. Reflection and Orientations on Interreligious Dialogue and the Proclamation of the Gospel of Jesus Christ* (19 May 1991).

Pontifical Council for Interreligious Dialogue, World Council of Churches and World Evangelical Alliance, *Christian Witness in a Multi-Religious World: Recommendations for Conduct* (2011), at www.vatican.va.

Society of Missionaries of Africa (White Fathers), *XXth Chapter. Capitular Documents* (Roma: Società Tipografica Italia, 1968).

Society of Missionaries of Africa, 'Our Mission Today and Tomorrow', in Society of Missionaries of Africa, *Chapter 1992*, Vol. I (Paris: Edition Voix d'Afrique, 1992).

— *Capitular Acts 1998* (Rome, 1998).

— *Capitular Acts: XXVth General Chapter*. Rome 10 May–16 June 2004 (Rome: Istituto Salesiano Pio XI, 2004).

— *Capitular Acts: XXVII General Chapter*. Rome 10 May–12 June 2010 (Rome: Istituto Salesiano Pio XI, 2010).

Synod of Bishops, *The Church, in the Word of God Celebrates the Mysteries of Christ for the Salvation of the World. The Final Report of the 1985 Extraordinary Synod* I.5, at www.ewtn.com.

— *Lineamenta*, 'The New Evangelization for the Transmission of the Christian Faith' (2011) in preparation for the XIII Ordinary General Assembly of the Synod of Bishops from 7 to 28 October 2012 (2 February 2011).

— *Instrumentum laboris* for the XIII Ordinary General Assembly of the Synod of Bishops, dedicated to 'The New Evangelization for the Transmission of the Christian Faith' (19 June 2012).

— 'Message to the People of God' (26 October 2012).

— Final List of Propositions (27 October 2012).

United States Conference of Catholic Bishops, *To the Ends of the Earth: A Pastoral Statement on World Mission* (Washington, DC: USCCB, 1986).

Other sources

Alberigo, Giuseppe and Joseph A. Komonchak (eds), *History of Vatican II*, Vols 1–5 (Leuven: Peeters/Maryknoll, NY: Orbis Books, 1995–2006).

Allen, Roland, *Missionary Methods: St. Paul's or Ours?* (Cambridge: Lutterworth Press, 2006 [1912]).

Amaladoss, Michael, *Making All Things New: Mission in Dialogue* (Maryknoll, NY: Orbis Books, 1990).

Appiah-Kubi, Francis, *Eglise famille de Dieu. Un chemin pour les Eglises d'Afrique* (Paris: Karthala, 2008).

Arens, Edmund, *Bezeugen und Bekennen. Elementare Handlungen des Glaubens* (Düsseldorf: Patmos, 1989).

— *Christopraxis. Grundzüge theologischer Handlungstheorie* (Quaestiones disputatae 139; Freiburg i.Br./Basel/Wien: Herder, 1992).

Augustine, *De Doctrina Christiana* (D. W. Robertson Jr (trans.); Indianapolis, IN: Bobbs-Merrill Educational Publishing, 1958).

— *Confessions* (Carolyn J.-B. Hammond (ed. and trans.); Cambridge, MA: Harvard University Press, 2014).

Baawobr, Richard K., '*Africae Munus* et les enjeux de la mission pour l'église-famille de Dieu en Afrique', at http://mafrome.org/ (original); Richard K. Baawobr, '*Africae Munus* and What Is at Stake For Mission in the Church-Family Of God in Africa' (Donald MacLeod (trans.)), 2012, at www.africamission-mafr.org/.

— 'L'apport des communautés chrétiennes de base', *Voix de l'Eglise africaine* (14 March 2011), at http://www.mafrome.org/.

— 'Wind of Change and Its Effect on Mission and Church Relationship', paper presented at the World Council of Churches' Conference on World Mission and Evangelism, Manila, 21–28 March 2012, at http://mafrome.org/.

Balthasar, Hans Urs von, *Bernanos: An Ecclesial Existence* (San Francisco: Ignatius, 1996).

Barron, Robert, *The Priority of Christ: Toward a Post-Liberal Catholicism* (Grand Rapids, MI: Brazos Press, 2007).

Barth, Karl, *Ad Limina Apostolorum* (Edinburgh: St. Andrews Press, 1969).

Béatrice, Anne, 'L'homme de Tékoa: un questionnement de la fonction prophétique de l'Eglise en Afrique', *SEDOS Bulletin* 42/1–2 (2010), pp. 19–25.

Belo, Catarina and Jean-Jacques Pérennès, *Mission in Dialogue: Essays in Honour of Michael L. Fitzgerald* (Louvain and Paris: Editions Peeters, 2012).

Beozzo, José Oscar, 'The External Climate', in Giuseppe Alberigo and Joseph A. Komonchak (eds), *History of Vatican II, Vol. I. Announcing and Preparing Vatican Council II: Toward a New Era in Catholicism* (Maryknoll, NY: Orbis Books, 1995), pp. 355–404 (pp. 388–92).

— 'Die brasilianische Kirche nach dem Konzil. Zeichen der Zeit und aktuelle Herausforderung', in Peter Hünermann (ed.), *Das Zweite Vatikanische Konzil und die Zeichen der Zeit heute* (Freiburg-Basel-Vienna: Herder, 2006), pp. 451–73.

Bevans, Stephen B. (ed.), *A Century of Catholic Mission*. Regnum Edinburgh Centenary Series 15 (Oxford: Regnum, 2013).

Bevans, Stephen B. and Roger P. Schroeder, *Constants in Context: A Theology of Mission for Today* (Maryknoll, NY: Orbis Books, 2004).

— *Prophetic Dialogue. Reflections on Christian Mission Today* (Maryknoll, NY: Orbis Books, 2011).

Bishwende, Augustin Ramazani, *Eglise-famille de Dieu dans la mondialisation. Theologie d'une nouvelle voie africaine d'évangélisation* (Paris: L'Harmattan, 2006).

Bloch, Arthur (ed.), *Murphy's Law Book Two: More Reasons Why Things Go Wrong* (London: Magnum, 1981).

Boeve, Lieven and Ben Vedder, 'In Memoriam Edward Schillebeeckx, OP (1914–2009)', in Lieven Boeve, Frederiek Depoortere and Stephan van Erp (eds), *Edward Schillebeeckx and Contemporary Theology* (London: T&T Clark, 2010).

Boff, Leonardo, *Church: Charism and Power. Liberation Theology and the Institutional Church* (John W. Diercksmeier (trans.); New York and London: Crossroad & SCM Press, 1985 [1981]).

Bopp, Karl, '"Missionarisch Kirche sein" angesichts fremder Religionen und Kulturen. Praktisch-theologische Überlegungen zum Missionsauftrag der Kirche heute', *Trierer Theologische Zeitschrift* 120 (2011), pp. 357–69.

Bredeck, M., *Das Zweite Vatikanum als Konzil des Aggiornamento: zur hermeneutischen Grundlegung einer theologischen Konzilsinterpretation* (Paderborner theologische Studien 48; Paderborn: Schöningh, 2007).

Brookes, Andrew, 'Evangelical Catholics?' in Philip Knights (ed.), *Changing Evangelisation* (London: Churches Together in Britain and Ireland, 2007), pp. 37–46.

Brunin, Jean-Luc, 'Quand des chrétiens dialoguent avec d'autres croyants doivent-ils renoncer à évangéliser?' *Pro Dialogo* 119 (2005), pp. 197–205.

Burkhardt, Frederick H., Fredson Bowers and Ignas K. Skrupskelis (eds), *The Works of William James, Vol. I. Pragmatism* (Cambridge, MA: Harvard University Press, 1975).

Cameron, Esther and Mike Green, *Making Sense of Change Management: A Complete Guide to the Models, Tools and Techniques of Organizational Change* (3rd edition; London: Kogan Page, 2012).

Cantalamessa, Reniero, 'The First Wave of Evangelization', at http://www.zenit.org/en/articles/father-cantalamessa-s-1st-advent-sermon – 4.

Caprile, Giovanni, *Il Sinodo dei Vescovi, III Asamblea Generale (1974)* (Roma: Edizioni Civiltà Cattólica, 1975).

Carola, Joseph, 'Appendix: Vatican II's Use of Patristic Themes Regarding Non-Christians', in Karl Josef Becker and Ilaria Morali (eds), *Catholic Engagement with World Religions* (Maryknoll, NY: Orbis Books, 2010), pp. 143–53.

Castells, Manuel, *The Rise of the Network Society* (2nd edition; Malden, MA: Blackwell, 2000).

Cavalletti, Sofia, *The Religious Potential of the Child: Experiencing Scripture and Liturgy with Young Children* (Chicago: Liturgy Training Publications, 1992).

— *History's Golden Thread: The History of Salvation* (Chicago: Liturgy Training Publications, 1999).

Cavalletti, Sofia and Patricia Coulter, *Ways to Nurture the Relationship with God* (Chicago: Liturgy Training Publications, 2010).

Cellier, Jean-Claude, *Histoire des Missionnaires d'Afrique (Pères Blancs). De la fondation par Mgr Lavigerie à la mort du fondateur (1868–1892)* (Paris: Karthala, 2008).

Chauvet, Louis-Marie, *Symbol and Sacrament* (Collegeville, MN: Liturgical Press, 1995).

Chenaux, Philippe (ed.), *L'Eredità del Magistero di Pio XII* (Dibattito per il millennio 13; Rome: Lateran University Press, 2010).

Cheza, Maurice, Henri Derriotte and René Luneau, *Les évêques d'Afrique parlent, 1969–1991* (Paris: Centurion, 1992).

Congar, Yves, *Mon Journal du Concile* (presented and annotated by E. Mahieu; Paris: Cerf, 2002).

Cornwell, John, *The Pope in Winter* (New York: Viking, 2004).

Coulson, John, Arthur M. Allchin and Meriol Trevor, *John Henry Newman: A Portrait Restored. An Ecumenical Revaluation* (London: Sheed & Ward, 1965).

Creary, Nicholas M., *Domesticating a Religious Import: The Jesuits and the Inculturation of the Catholic Church in Zimbabwe, 1879–1980* (New York: Fordham University Press, 2011).

Curran, Charles, *Loyal Dissent: Memoir of a Catholic Theologian* (Washington, DC: Georgetown University Press, 2006).

D'Costa, Gavin, 'Pluralist Arguments: Prominent Tendencies and Methods', in Karl
     Josef Becker and Ilaria Morali (eds), *Catholic Engagement with World Religions*
     (Maryknoll, NY: Orbis Books, 2010), pp. 329–44.
— *Vatican II: Catholic Doctrines on Jews and Muslims* (Oxford: Oxford University
     Press, 2014).
D'Sa, Francis X., *Dio l'Uno e Trino e l'Uno-Tutto. Introduzione all'incontro tra
     cristianesimo e induismo* (Brescia: Queriniana, 1996 [1987]).
Daniélou, Jean, '*Les orientations présentes de la pensée religieuse*', *Études* 249 (1946),
     pp. 5–21.
Davie, Grace, *Europe – The Exceptional Case: Parameters of Faith in the Modern World*
     (London: Darton Longman & Todd, 2002).
de Cointet, Pierre, Barbara Morgan and Petroc Willey, *The Catechism of the Catholic
     Church and the Craft of Catechesis* (San Francisco: Ignatius Press, 2008).
De Lubac, Henri, *Carnets du Concile*, Vol. I (introduced and annotated by Loïc
     Figoureux; Paris: Cerf, 2007).
Doran, Robert, *What is Systematic Theology?* (Toronto: University of Toronto Press, 2005).
Dulles, Avery, 'Fundamental Theology and the Dynamics of Conversion', *The Thomist*
     45 (1981), pp. 175–93.
— 'The Challenge of the Catechism', *First Things* (January 1995), pp. 46–53.
— *John Paul II and the New Evangelization* (The Laurence J. McGinley Lectures;
     New York: Fordham University Press, 2008).
— 'Nature, Mission, and Structure of the Church', in Matthew L. Lamb and Matthew
     Levering (eds), *Vatican II: Renewal within Tradition* (New York: Oxford University
     Press, 2008), pp. 25–36.
Dupuis, Jacques, *Toward a Christian Theology of Religious Pluralism* (Maryknoll, NY:
     Orbis Books, 1997).
Faber, Geoffrey, *Oxford Apostles: A Character Study of the Oxford Movement* (London:
     Faber & Faber, 1933).
Faggioli, Massimo, *Vatican II: The Battle for Meaning* (Mahwah, NJ: Paulist Press, 2012).
Farey, Caroline E., Waltraud Linnig and Johanna M. Paruch FSGM (eds), *The Pedagogy
     of God: Its Centrality in Catechesis and Catechist Formation* (Steubenville: Emmaus
     Road Publishing 2011).
Feingold, Lawrence, *The Natural Desire to See God According to St. Thomas Aquinas and
     His Interpreters* (Ave Maria, FL: Sapientia Press of Ave Maria University, 2010).
Fisichella, Rino, *La nuova evangelizzazione: une sfida per uscire dall'indifferenza*
     (Milano: Mondadori, 2011).
Fitzgerald, Michael L. and John Borelli, *Interfaith Dialogue A Catholic View* (London:
     SPCK, 2006).
Flannery, Austin (ed.), *The Basic Sixteen Documents: Vatican Council II* (Dublin:
     Dominican Publications/Costello Publishing Co., 1996).
Fogarty, Gerald P., 'Vereinigte Staaten von Amerika', in Edwin Gatz (ed.), *Die britischen
     Inseln und Nordamerika* (Kirche und Katholizismus seit 1945, 4; Paderborn-
     Munich-Vienna-Zürich: Schöningh, 2002), pp. 89–143.

Fouilloux, Étienne, 'Mouvements' théologico-spirituels et concile (1959–1962)', in Mathijs Lamberigts and Claude Soetens (eds), *A la veille du Concile Vatican II. Vota et réactions en Europe et dans le catholicisme oriental* (Instrumenta Theologica 9; Leuven: Peeters, 1992), pp. 185–99.

— 'The Antepreparatory Phase: The Slow Emergence from Inertia (January, 1959–October 1962)', in Giuseppe Alberigo and Joseph A. Komonchak (eds), *History of Vatican II, Vol. I. Announcing and Preparing Vatican Council II: Toward a New Era in Catholicism* (Maryknoll, NY: Orbis Books, 1995), pp. 55–166.

Francis de Sales, *Treatise on the Love of God* (Henry Benedict Mackey (trans.); Rockford, IL: Tan Books, 1997).

Fries, Heinrich, 'John Henry Newman, Ein Wegbereiter der Christenlich Einheit', *Catholica* 15 (1961), pp. 60–70.

Gabriel Moran, *Catechesis of Revelation* (New York: Herder & Herder, 1966).

— *The Present Revelation* (New York: Herder & Herder, 1972).

— 'Revelation as Teaching-Learning', *Religious Education* 95/3 (Summer 2000), pp. 269–84.

Gerald O'Collins, *Fundamental Theology* (London: DLT, 1982).

Godin, Henri and Yvan Daniel, *La France, pays de mission?* (Lyon: Cerf, 1943).

Gollwitzer, Helmut, 'Why Black Theology', in Gayraud S. Wilmore and James H. Cone (eds), *Black Theology: A Documentary History, 1966–1979* (Maryknoll, NY: Orbis Books, 1979), pp. 152–73.

Gonnet, Dominique, *La liberté religieuse à Vatican II. La contribution de John Courtney Murray* (Cogitatio Fidei) (Paris: Cerf, 1994).

Grand'Maison, Jacques, *La seconde évangelisation. I: Les témoins. II: Outils d'apport. II/1: Outils majeurs. II/2: Les témoins* (Montréal: Fides, 1973).

Grasso, Domenico, 'Il kerygma e la predicazione', *Gregorianum* 41 (1960), pp. 424–50.

— 'Evangelizzazione, Catechesi, Omelia', *Gregorianum* 42 (1961), pp. 242–67.

— *L'annuncio della salvezza. Teologia della predicazione* (Napoli: M. D'Auria, 1966).

— 'La predicazione missionaria', in Johannes Schütte (ed.), *Il destino delle missioni. Il successo o il fallimento delle missioni dipende dal loro radicale ripensamento* (Roma and Brescia: Herder & Morcelliana, 1969), pp. 215–30.

— 'Evangelizzazione. Senso di un termine', in Mariasusai Dhavamony (ed.), *Evangelisation* (Roma: Università Gregoriana Editrice, 1975), pp. 21–47.

Gregory, Brad S., *The Unintended Reformation. How Religious Revolutions Secularized Society* (Cambridge, MA: Harvard University Press, 2012).

Gremillion, Joseph (ed.), *The Gospel of Justice and Peace: Catholic Social Teaching since Pope John* (Maryknoll, NY: Orbis Books, 1976).

Guemriche, Salah, *Le Christ s'est arrêté à Tizi-Ouzou. Enquête sur les conversions en terre d'Islam* (Paris: Editions Denoël, 2011).

Gutiérrez, Gustavo, *We Drink from Our Own Wells* (Maryknoll, NY: Orbis Books, 1984).

Habermas, Jürgen, 'Ein Bewusstsein von dem, was fehlt. Über Glauben und Wissen und den Defaitismus der modernen Vernunft', *Neue Zürcher Zeitung*, 10 February 2007.

Habermas, Jürgen and Joseph Ratzinger, *The Dialectics of Secularization. On Reason and Religion* (Brian McNeil, C. R. V. (trans.); San Francisco: Ignatius Press, 2006).

Hahn, Scott, 'New Evangelization' (Fall 2012), at http://www.scotthahn.com/newevangelization.html.

Halbfas, Hubert, *Fundamentalkatechetik. Sprache und Erfahrung im Religionsunterricht* (Düsseldorf: Patmos, 1968).

Halbfass, Wilhelm, *India and Europe: An Essay in Understanding* (New York: State University of New York, 1988 [1981]).

Harris, Robert, *The Fear Index* (London: Hutchinson, 2011).

Hart, David Bentley, 'God or Nothingness', in Carl E. Braaten and Christopher R. Seitz (eds), *I Am the Lord Your God: Christian Reflections on the Ten Commandments* (Grand Rapids, MI: Eerdmans, 2005), pp. 55–77.

Hauerwas, Stanley, 'The Christian Difference or Surviving Postmodernism', in Graham Ward (ed.), *The Blackwell Companion to Postmodern Theology* (Oxford: Blackwell, 2007), pp. 144–62.

Healey, Joseph G., 'Building the Church as Family of God: Evaluation of the Growth and Impact of Small Christian Communities in the AMECEA region as AMECEA Celebrates Its Golden Jubilee'. Paper given at the Thirteenth Interdisciplinary Theological Session on the theme 'The Faculty of Theology of CUEA Celebrates the Golden Jubilee of AMECEA' at the Catholic University of Eastern Africa (CUEA) in Nairobi, Kenya on 3 March 2011 – revised on 27 June 2011.

Healey, Joseph G. and Jeanne Hinton, *Small Christian Communities Today. Capturing the New Moment* (Maryknoll, NY: Orbis Books, 2005).

Hollenbach, David, 'Human Rights and Interreligious Dialogue: The Challenge to Mission in a Pluralistic World', *International Bulletin of Missionary Research* 6/3 (July 1982), pp. 98–101.

Ivereigh, Austen, *How to Defend the Faith Without Raising Your Voice: Civil Responses to Catholic Hot-button Issues* (Huntington, IN: Our Sunday Visitor, 2012).

Kasper, Walter, *Il futuro dalla forza dello Spirito. Sinodo straordinario dei vescovi 1985 – Documenti e commento* (Brescia: Queriniana, 1986 [1985]).

— 'Neue Evangelisierung – eine pastorale, theologische und geistliche Herausforderung', in Augustin George and Klaus Kramer (eds), *Mission als Herausforderung: Impulse zur Neuevangelisierung* (Freiburg: Herder, 2011), pp. 23–41.

— *The God of Jesus Christ* (new edition; New York: T&T Clark International – Continuum, 2012), pp. 65–115.

Kelter, Gert, 'Christliche Mission in einer postmodernen Gesellschaft: Überlegungen zu den Rahmenbedingungen des christlichen Zeugnisses in einer entchristlichten Gesellschaft unter besonderer Berücksichtigung Ostdeutschlands', *Lutherische Beiträge* 16 (2011), pp. 41–50.

Ker, Ian, 'Newman, the Councils and Vatican II', *Communio: International Catholic Review* 28 (Winter 2001), pp. 708–28.

Kevane, Eugene, '*Translatio imperii*: Augustine's *De Doctrina Christiana* and the Classical *Paideia*', *Studia Patristica* XIV (1976), pp. 446–60.

Kitambala, Alfred Guy Bwidi, *Les Evêques d'Afrique et le Concile Vatican II. Participation, contribution et application du Synode des Evêques de 1994* (Paris: Karthala, 2010).

Koch, Kurt, 'Cardinal Koch on Jewish-Catholic dialogue since Vatican II', Vatican News, 17 May 2012, at http://www.news.va/en/news/cardinal-koch-on-jewish-catholic-dialogue-since-va.

Komonchak, Joseph A., 'The Struggle for the Council during the Preparation of Vatican II (1960–1962)', in Giuseppe Alberigo and Joseph A. Komonchak, *History of Vatican II, Vol. I. Announcing and Preparing Vatican Council II: Toward a New Era in Catholicism* (Maryknoll, NY: Orbis Books, 1995), pp. 167–356.

— 'Novelty in Continuity', *The Tablet* (31 January 2009), pp. 5–6.

Krieg, Robert A., *Catholic Theologians in Nazi Germany* (London: Continuum, 2004).

Kroeger, James, *Exploring the Treasures of Vatican II* (Quezon City: Claretian Publications and Jesuit Communications, 2011).

Küng, Hans, *My Struggle for Freedom* (John Bowden (trans.); Grand Rapids, MI: Wm B. Eerdmans, 2003).

LaCroix, Gérald C., *La nouvelle évangélisation: urgence de réfléchir; urgence d'agir* (Forum; Montréal: Université de Montréal, 2012).

Lamberigts, Mathijs and Leo Declerck, 'Mgr E. J. De Smedt et le texte conciliaire sur la religion juive (*Nostra aetate*, n 4)', *Ephemerides Theologicae Lovanienses* 85 (2009), pp. 341–84.

— 'Vatican II on the Jews: A Historical Survey', in Marianne Moyaert and Didier Pollefeyt (eds), *Never Revoked*: Nostra Aetate *as Ongoing Challenge for Jewish–Christian Dialogue* (Leuven/Grand Rapids, MI/Cambridge: Peeters, 2010), pp. 13–56.

Lash, Nicholas, *Theology for Pilgrims* (Notre Dame, IN: University of Notre Dame Press, 2008), pp. 253–84.

— 'What Happened at Vatican II', in *Theology for Pilgrims* (London: Darton, Longman & Todd, 2008), pp. 240–8.

Lee, James Michael, *The Shape of Religious Education: A Social Science Approach* (Mishawaka: Religious Education Press, 1971).

Leon-Dufour, Xavier (ed.), *Dictionary of Biblical Theology* (revised 2nd edition; London: Geoffrey Chapman, 1988).

Liégé, Pierre-André, 'Évangélisation', in *Catholicisme* IV (Paris: Letouzey & Ané, 1956), pp. 756–64.

Linden, Ian, *A New Map of the World* (London: Darton, Longman & Todd, 2004).

— *Global Catholicism: Diversity and Change since Vatican II* (2nd edition; New York: Columbia University Press, 2009).

Long, Steven A., *Natura Pura: On the Recovery of Nature in the Doctrine of Grace* (New York: Fordham University Press, 2010).

Lord Halifax (ed.), *The Conversations at Malines, 1921–1925: Original Documents* (London: Philip Allan, 1930).

Lossky, Nicholas, José Miguez Bonino, John Pobee, Tom F. Stransky, Geoffrey Wainwright and Pauline Webb (eds), *Dictionary of the Ecumenical Movement* (2nd edition; Geneva: World Council of Churches Publications, 2002).

Lytton Strachey, *Eminent Victorians* (London: Chatto & Windus, 1918).

MacClaren, Duncan, 'Reining in Caritas', *The Tablet* (12 May 2012), pp. 8–9.

MacCulloch, Diarmaid, *A History of Christianity: The First Three Thousand Years* (London: Allen Lane, 2009).

MacIntyre, Alasdair, *Three Rival Theories of Moral Enquiry* (London: Duckworth 1990).

Maffettone, Sebastiano, 'Global Justice: Between Leviathan and Cosmopolis', *Global Policy* 3/4 (November 2012), pp. 443–54.

Manns, Frédéric, *Qu'est-ce que la nouvelle évangélisation?* (Montrouge Cedex: Bayard, 2012).

Marchetto, Agostino, *The Second Vatican Ecumenical Council: A Counterpoint for the History of the Council* (Kenneth D. Whitehead (trans.); Scranton: University of Scranton Press, 2010 [2005]).

Marthalar, Berard L., *The Catechism Yesterday and Today: The Evolution of a Genre* (Collegeville, MN: Liturgical Press, 1995).

Martin, Ralph, *Will Many Be Saved? What Vatican II Actually Teaches and Its Implications for the New Evangelization* (Grand Rapids, MI: William B. Eerdmans, 2012).

McDade, John, 'Jesus in Recent Research', *The Month* 31 (1998), pp. 495–505.

McLaughlin, Janice, 'Turned Upside-Down: Learning and Challenges. A Missioner's Journey in Southern Sudan', *SEDOS Bulletin* 43/9–10 (2011), pp. 256–67.

McLoughlin, David, 'The New Catechism and the Christian East', *The Sower* (September 1992), pp. 29–30.

McNeil, Louis, 'Evangelization', in *The New Dictionary of Theology* (Wilmington, DE: Michael Glazier, 1987), pp. 357–60.

Mejia, Rodrigo, *The Church in the Neighborhood. Meetings for the Animation of Small Christian Communities* (Nairobi: St Paul Publications Africa, 1992).

Merrigan, Terrence, *Clear Heads and Holy Hearts – The Religious and Theological Ideal of John Henry Newman* (Louvain: Peeters Press, 1991).

Minnerath, Roland, 'La déclaration Dignitatis Humanae à la fin du Concile Vatican II', *Revue des sciences religieuses* 74 (2000), pp. 226–42.

Moran, Michelle, *Pass It On! Practical Hints on Sharing Your Faith* (London: DLT, 1990; amended and reprinted privately in 2001).

Morgan, Barbara A. and William J. Keimig (eds), *The RCIA Leaders' Manual* (2nd edition; Clinton, MA: The Association of Catechetical Ministry, 2007).

Morgan, Stephen, 'The Search for Continuity in the Face of Change in the Anglican Writings of John Henry Newman' (unpublished doctoral dissertation; Oxford: University of Oxford, 2013).

Murray, John Courtney, 'The Church and Totalitarian Democracy', *Theological Studies* 14 (December 1952), pp. 525–63.

— 'Leo XIII on Church and State: The General Structure of the Controversy', *Theological Studies* 14 (March 1953), pp. 1–30.

— 'Leo XIII: Separation of Church and State', *Theological Studies* 14 (June 1953), pp. 145–314.

— 'Leo XIII: Two Concepts of Government', *Theological Studies* 14 (December 1953), pp. 551–67.

— 'Leo XIII: Two Concepts of Government: Government and the Order of Culture', *Theological Studies* 15 (March 1954), pp. 1–33.

Murray, Paul D. (ed.), 'Receptive Ecumenism and Catholic Learning: Establishing the Agenda', in *Receptive Ecumenism and the Call to Catholic Learning: Exploring a Way for Contemporary Ecumenism* (Oxford: Oxford University Press, 2008), pp. 5–25.

— 'Expanding Catholicity through Ecumenicity in the Work of Yves Congar: *Ressourcement*, Receptive Ecumenism, and Catholic Reform', in Gabriel Flynn and Paul D. Murray (eds), *Ressourcement: A Movement for Renewal in Twentieth-Century Catholic Theology* (Oxford: Oxford University Press, 2012), pp. 457–81.

— 'Roman Catholicism and Ecumenism', in Lewis Ayres and Medi-Ann Volpe (eds), *The Oxford Companion to Catholicism* (Oxford: Oxford University Press, forthcoming in 2015).

Newman, Frank, *Contributions Chiefly to the Early History of Cardinal Newman* (London: Kegan Paul, Trench, Trübner & Co., 1891).

Newman, John Henry, *Arians of the Fourth Century: Their Temper, Doctrine and Conduct Chiefly as Exhibited in the Councils of the Church between A.D. 325, and A.D. 381* (1st edition; London: J. G. and F. Rivington, 1833).

— *An Essay on the Development of Christian Doctrine* (London: James Toovey, 1846).

— *Apologia Pro Vita Sua: Being a Reply to a Pamphlet Entitled "What Then Does Mr Newman Mean?* (1st edition; London: Longman, Roberts & Green, 1864).

— *An Essay in Aid of a Grammar of Assent* (uniform edition; London: Longman, Green & Co., 1870).

— 'Personal Influence, the Means of Propagating Truth', a sermon preached at St Mary the Virgin, Oxford on 22 January 1832, in *Fifteen Sermons Preached Before the University of Oxford Between AD 1826 and 1843* (London: Longmans, 1871), pp. 91–2.

— *The Idea of a University* (uniform edition; London: Longman & Green, 1878).

— *Letter to the Duke of Norfolk* (uniform edition; London: Longmans & Green, 1881).

— 'Biglietto Speech', in William P. Neville (ed.), *Addresses to Cardinal Newman and His Replies* (London: Longmans, Green & Co., 1905), pp. 63–5.

— *The Second Spring: A Sermon by John Henry Newman* (with introduction, notes and exercises by F. P. Donnelly S. J.; London: Longmans, 1934).

— *An Essay in Aid of a Grammar of Assent* (Ian T. Ker (ed.); Oxford: Clarendon Press, 1985).

— *The Letters and Diaries of John Henry Newman* (in 32 Vols; Charles Stephen Dessain (ed.); London and Oxford: Oxford University Press, 1961–2008).

Nichols, Aidan, *The Splendour of Doctrine* (Edinburgh: T&T Clark, 1995).

— 'A Revelation to Transmit: The Magisterial Project', in John Redford (ed.), *Hear, O Islands: Theology and Catechesis in the New Millennium* (Dublin: Veritas Publications, 2002).

Nolan, Albert, *Jesus before Christianity* (3rd edition; Maryknoll, NY: Orbis Books, 2001).

Nolan, Francis, *White Fathers in Colonial Africa (1919–1939)* (Nairobi: Paulines Africa, 2012).

O'Donovan, Oliver, *The Desire of the Nations: Rediscovering the Roots of Political Theology* (Cambridge: Cambridge University Press, 1996).

O'Halloran, James, *Living Cells: Vision and Practicalities of Small Christian Communities and Groups* (Dublin: Columba Press, 2010)

O'Malley, John, *Tradition and Transition: Historical Perspectives on Vatican II* (Wilmington, DE: M. Glazier, 1989).

Oakes, Edward T., 'The *Surnaturel* Controversy: A Survey and a Response', *Nova et Vetera*, English Edition 9/3 (2011), pp. 625–56.

Office for National Statistics, *Religion in England and Wales 2011*, at http://www.ons.gov.uk/ons/dcp171776_290510.pdf.

Ondrako, Edward, *Progressive Illumination: A Journey with John Henry Cardinal Newman 1980–2005* (Binghamton, NY: Global Academic Publishing, 2006).

Ouellet, Marc, *Divine Likeness: Toward a Trinitarian Anthropology of the Family* (Grand Rapids, MI: Wm B. Eerdmans, 2006).

Paruch, Johanna M., *A Study of the Direct Ramifications of Vatican Council II on Catechetics* (Birmingham: Maryvale Institute, 2007).

Perreau-Saussine, Émile, 'French Catholic Political Thought from the Deconfessionalism of the State to the Recognition of Religious Freedom', in Ira Katznelson and Gareth Stedman Jones (eds), *Religion and the Political Imagination* (Cambridge: Cambridge University Press, 2010), pp. 150–70.

Peter, Henriot, 'Africa's Women Deserve Better', *The Tablet* (3 December 2011), p. 2.

Peters, Edward N., *The 1917 Pio-Benedictine Code of Canon Law* (San Francisco, CA: Ignatius Press, 2001).

Pieris, Aloysius, 'The Place of Non-Christian Religious and Cultures in the Evolution of Third World Theology', in Virginia Fabella and Sergio Torres (eds), *Irruption of the Third World: Challenges to Theology* (Maryknoll, NY: Orbis Books, 1983), pp. 113–39.

— *An Asian Theology of Liberation* (Maryknoll, NY: Orbis Books, 1988).

Poulat, Émile, *Les prêtres ouvriers: naissance et fin* (Paris: Cerf, 1999).

Poupard, Paul, *Le Concile Vatican II* (Paris: Salvator, 2012).

Ratzinger, Joseph, *Theological Highlights of Vatican II* (New York: Paulist Press, 1966).

— *Principles of Catholic Theology* (San Francisco: Ignatius, 1987).

— (ed.), 'The Progress of Ecumenism', in *Church, Ecumenism and Politics: New Essays in Ecclesiology* (Slough and New York: St Paul & Crossroad, 1988 [1987]), pp. 135–42.

— *Introduction to Christianity* (San Francisco: Ignatius, 1990).

— 'On the Ecumenical Situation', in Stephan Otto Horn and Vinzenz Pfnür (eds), *Pilgrim Fellowship of Faith: The Church as Communion* (Henry Taylor (trans.); San Francisco: Ignatius, 2005 [2002]), pp. 253–69 (p. 253). Originally printed in Jean-Louis Leuba (ed.), *Perspectives actuelles sur l'œcuménisme* (Louvain-le-Neuve: Artel, 1995), pp. 231–44.

— *Salt of the Earth: The Church at the End of the Millennium* (San Francisco: Ignatius, 1996).

— 'Guardini on Christ in our Century', *Crisis Magazine* (June 1996), pp. 11–5.

— Sorbonne Address, '2000 Years after What?' address at the Sorbonne, Paris, 27 November 1999.

— *Truth and Tolerance: Christian Belief and World Religions* (San Francisco: Ignatius, 2003).

— *The End of Time* (Mahwah, NJ: Paulist Press, 2004).

— 'The Ecclesiology of the Constitution *Lumen Gentium*', in Stephan Otto Horn and Vinzenz Pfnür (eds), *Pilgrim Fellowship of Faith: The Church as Communion* (Henry Taylor (trans.); San Francisco: Ignatius, 2005 [2002]), pp. 123–52.

— 'Europe in the Crisis of Cultures', *Communio: International Catholic Review* 32 (2005), pp. 345–56.

— *Images of Hope* (San Francisco: Ignatius, 2006).

— *Jesus of Nazareth. From the Baptism in the Jordan to the Transfiguration* (London: Bloomsbury, 2007).

Ratzinger, Joseph with Vittorio Messori, *The Ratzinger Report: An Exclusive Interview on the State of the Church* (Salvator Attanasio and Graham Harrison (trans.); San Francisco: Ignatius Press, 1985).

Rawls, John, *Political Liberalism* (New York: Columbia University Press, 1993).

Redford, John (ed.), 'Scripture and Catechesis', in *Hear, O Islands – Theology and Catechesis in the New Millennium* (Dublin: Veritas, 2002), pp. 209–16.

Redmond, John, *Bad, Mad or God? Proving the Divinity of Christ from St John's Gospel* (London: St Paul's Publishing, 2004).

Renault, François, *Le Cardinal Lavigerie, 1825–1892. L'Elise, l'Afrique et la France* (Paris: Fayard, 1992).

Richard Dawkins Foundation for Reason and Science (UK), 'Religious and Social Attitudes of UK Christians in 2011' (Ipsos MORI Research, 2011).

Rico, Hermínio, *John Paul II and the Legacy of* Dignitatis Humanae (Washington, DC: Georgetown University Press, 2002).

Rigal, Jean, *L'ecclesiologie de communion. Son evolution historique et ses fondements* (Paris: Cerf, 1997).

Routhier, Gilles, 'The Hermeneutic of Reform as a Task for Theology', *Irish Theological Quarterly* 77/3 (2012), pp. 219–43.

Routhier, Gilles, Philippe Roy and Karim Schelkens, *La théologie catholique entre intransigeance et renouveau. La réception des mouvements préconciliaires à Vatican II* (Bibliothèque de la Revue d'histoire ecclésiastique 95; Louvain-la-Neuve: Leuven, 2011).

Roy, Philippe J., *Le Coetus internationalis patrum, un groupe d'opposants au sein du Concile Vatican II* (unpublished dissertation; Québec: Université Laval, 2011).

Ruddy, Christopher, '*Ressourcement* and the *Enduring* Legacy of Post-Tridentine Theology', in Gabriel Flynn and Paul D. Murray (eds), *Ressourcement: A Movement for Renewal in Twentieth-Century Catholic Theology* (Oxford: Oxford University Press, 2012), pp. 185–201.

Ruokanen, Miikka, *The Catholic Doctrine on Non-Christian Religions According to the Second Vatican Council* (Leiden: Brill, 1992), pp. 133–56.

Sanneh, Lamin, 'Christian Mission and the Western Guilt Complex', *Christian Century* 8 (April 1987), pp. 330–4.

Sarto, Pablo Blanco, 'Logos and Dia-Logos: Faith, Reason (and Love) According to Joseph Ratzinger', *Anglican Theological Review* 92/3 (2010), pp. 499–509.

Saward, John, 'Chesterton and Balthasar: The Likeness is Greater', *Chesterton Review* XXII/3 (August 1996), pp. 301–25.

Scatena, Silvia, *La fatica della libertà. L'elaborazione della dichiarazione «Dignitatis Humanae» sulla libertà religiosa del Vaticano II* (Testi e ricerche di scienze religiose. Nuova serie, 31; Bologna: Il Mulino, 2003).

Schatz, Klaus, 'Die Missionen auf dem I Vatikanum', *Theologie und Philosophie* 63 (1988), pp. 342–69.

Schenk, Richard, '*Officium Signa Temporum Perscrutandi*: New Encounters of Gospel and Culture in the Context of the New Evangelization', in Steven Boguslawski and Robert Fastiggi (eds), *Called to Holiness and Communion: Vatican II on the Church* (Scranton, PA: University of Scranton Press, 2009), pp. 69–105.

Schindler, David C., 'Towards a Non-Possessive Concept of Knowledge: On the Relation between Reason and Love in Aquinas and Balthasar', *Modern Theology* 22/4 (October 2006), pp. 577–607.

Schmitz, Kenneth L., 'Postmodernism and the Catholic Tradition', *American Catholic Philosophical Quarterly* LXXIII/2 (1999), pp. 223–53.

Schönborn, Christoph and Joseph Ratzinger, *Introduction to the Catechism of the Catholic Church* (San Francisco: Ignatius Press, 1994).

Scola, Angelo, '"Claim" of Christ, "Claim" of the World: On the Trinitarian Encyclicals of John Paul II', *Communio* 18 (Fall 1991), pp. 322–31.

— 'El Peligro de una Falsa "Autonomia"', *Humanitas: Revista de Antropologica y Cultura Christianas* 66 (Fall 2012), pp. 296–301.

Scruton, Roger, *The Philosopher on Dover Beach* (Manchester: Carcanet, 1990).

Shorter, Aylward, *Cross and Flag in Africa: The White Fathers during the Colonial Scramble (1882–1914)* (Maryknoll, NY: Orbis Books, 2006).

Siebenrock, Roman A., 'Theologischer Kommentar zur Erklärung über die
Haltung der Kirche zu den nichtchristlichen Religionen Nostra aetate', in Peter
Hünermann and Bernd Jochen Hilberath (eds), *Herders Theologischer Kommentar
zum Zweiten Vatikanischen Konzil*, Vol. III (Freiburg-Basel-Vienna: Herder,
2005), pp. 657–8.

Siviero, Guiseppe M., 'La libertà religiosa dalla Dignitatis Humanae ai nostri giorni',
Quaderni di Diritto Ecclesiale 11 (1998), pp. 244–66.

Spencer, Nick and Holly Weldin, *Post-Religious Britain: The Faith of the Faithless*
(London: Theos Publications, 2012).

Stephen Morgan, 'The Search for Continuity in the Face of Change in the Anglican
Writings of John Henry Newman' (unpublished doctoral dissertation; Oxford:
University of Oxford, 2013).

Sullivan, Francis A., *Salvation Outside the Church? Tracing the History of the Catholic
Response* (London: Geoffrey Chapman, 1992).

— 'A Response to Karl Becker, S. J., on the Meaning of *Subsistit In*', *Theological Studies*
67 (2006), pp. 395–409.

— 'The Meaning of *Subsistit In* as Explained by the Congregation for the Doctrine of
the Faith', *Theological Studies* 69 (2008), pp. 116–24.

Tanner, Kathryn, *The Economy of Grace* (Minneapolis, MN: Fortress Press, 2005).

Taylor, Charles, 'Conditions of an Unforced Consensus on Human Rights', in Joanne
R. Bauer and Daniel A. Bell (eds), *The East Asian Challenge for Human Rights*
(Cambridge: Cambridge University Press, 1999), pp. 124–44.

Tengan, Edward B., *House of God. Church-As-Family from an African Perspective*
(Leuven: Acco, 1997).

Teuffenbach, Alexandra von, *Die Bedeutung des subsistit in (LG 8): Zum
Selbstverständnis der katholischen Kirche* (Munich: Herbert Utz, 2002).

Thomas Aquinas, Summa Theologiae: *A Guide and Commentary* (Brian Davies (ed. and
trans.); Oxford: Oxford University Press, 2014).

Trower, Philip, *Turmoil and Truth: The Historical Roots of the Modern Crisis in the
Catholic Church* (San Francisco: Ignatius, 2003).

Vanzan, Piersandro (ed.), *Enchiridion. Documenti della Chiesa Latinoamericana*
(Bologna: EMI, 1995).

Vatican Radio, 'Archbishop Nichols on Youth Evangelisation' (8 May 2012), at
www.news.va.

Vélez, Juan, 'Heart Speaks to Heart', in *MercatorNet*, 10 September 2010, at
www.mercatornet.com.

Vermeylen, Jacques, *Vatican II* (Namur: Fidélité, 2011).

Ward, Wilfrid, *The Life of John Henry Cardinal Newman Based on his Private Journals
and Correspondence* (in 2 Vols; London: Longmans, Green & Co., 1912).

Weddell, Sherry A., *Forming Intentional Disciples: The Path to Knowing and Following
Jesus* (Huntington, IN: Our Sunday Visitor, 2012).

Welch, Lawrence J. and Guy Mansini, OSB, '*Lumen Gentium* No. 8, and *Subsistit in*, Again', *New Blackfriars* 90/1029 (2009), pp. 602–17.

Wojtyła, Karol, *Person and Community: Selected Essays* (Theresa Sandok (trans.); New York: Peter Lang, 1993).

Wollbold, Andreas, 'Mission vor der eigenen Tür? Eine Synopse missiontheologischer Modelle', in Matthias Sellmann (ed.), *Deutschland – Missionsland. Zur Überwindung eines pastoralen Tabus* (Freiburg i.Br.: Herder, 2004), pp. 69–91.

Wood, Susan K. (ed.), 'Presbyteral Identity within Parish Identity', in *Ordering the Baptismal Priesthood* (Collegeville, MN: Liturgical Press, 2003), pp. 175–94.

Wright, Thomas N., *The New Testament and the People of God* (London: SPCK, 1992).

Wuerl, Donald, 'Relatio ante disceptationem' (Synod of Bishops; 8 October 2012), at http://www.vatican.va/roman_curia//synod/index.htm.

— 'Relatio post disceptationem' (Synod of Bishops; 17 October 2012), at http://www.vatican.va/roman_curia//synod/index.htm.

— *New Evangelization: Passing on the Catholic Faith Today* (Huntington, IN: Our Sunday Visitor, 2013).

Zenit, '6.1 Million Pilgrims Visit Guadalupe Shrine' (14 December 2009), at www.zenit.org.

Zulehner, Paul M., *Pastoraltheologie, Vol. 1: Fundamentalpastoral* (Düsseldorf: Patmos, 1989), p. 54 calls this 'Dienst am Heil der Welt'.

Index